C0-AJW-294

GROVER CLEVELAND

Also by Alyn Brodsky

THE KINGS DEPART

MADAME LYNCH & FRIEND

IMPERIAL CHARADE

ALYN BRODSKY

GROVER CLEVELAND

A Study in Character

TRUMAN TALLEY BOOKS
ST. MARTIN'S PRESS
NEW YORK

www.stmartins.com

Design by Kathryn Parise

LIBRARY OF CONGRESS CATALOGING-IN-PUBLICATION DATA

Brodsky, Alyn.

Grover Cleveland : a study in character / Alyn Brodsky.—1st ed.

p. cm.

"Truman Talley books."

Includes bibliographical references and index.

ISBN 0-312-26883-1

1. Cleveland, Grover, 1837–1908. 2. Presidents—United States—Biography. I. Title.

E697 .B84 2000

973.8'5'092—dc21

[B] 00–040258

First Edition: September 2000

10 9 8 7 6 5 4 3 2 1

To the late Edward Levien

Loyal friend and fellow admirer
of Grover Cleveland

CONTENTS

PART III
1884

PART IV
1885–1888

PART V
1888–1889

PART VI
1889–1893

PART VII
1893–1896

PART VIII
1897–1907

He made the reform of abuses in public life a business: not a profession. He loved humanity in all its various forms: and sympathized with its joys and sorrows; he hated hypocrisies, shams, Pharisees, pretenders, and liars; he despised none but incompetents and toadies. The outstanding points in his character were: sturdy manliness, unyielding, inherent honesty of life and opinions, and the virility found only in real men. While the need for these qualities remains, his memory ought to furnish both example and inspiration.

—George F. Parker

What is exceptional and peculiar in Cleveland's career is the way in which political situations formed about him without any contrivance on his part, and as it were projected him from office to office until he arrived in the White House.

—Henry J. Ford

GROVER CLEVELAND

INTRODUCTION

Grover Cleveland, our twenty-second and twenty-fourth President, was the only Democrat to be elected between our fifteenth, Buchanan, and our twenty-eighth, Wilson. That is to say, between the run-up to the Civil War and the run-up to the First World War. This phenomenon—and a phenomenon it was—is not easy to understand. It would be easier to explain why he should *not* have won the office than why he did.

Though only in existence as a party four years when Lincoln was elected, the Republicans emerged from the war as saviors of the nation. They had abolished slavery and preserved the union. It seemed not to concern the electorate that Lincoln's five successors (Johnson, Grant, Hayes, Garfield, and Arthur) left as much to be desired as the four prewar Whigs (William Henry Harrison, Tyler, Taylor, and Fillmore) from whose party the Republicans evolved.

This despite the fact that under those five the nation had become divided—and mutually antipathetic—along sectional lines; divisions as deep as an abyss and seemingly immune to equitable resolution. The sectionalism ("states' rights") that was in truth the underlying cause of the Civil War was as alive and well when Cleveland first took office as when Lincoln first took office.

Two decades after the war, North and South still had not achieved reconciliation. Such a reconciliation would not succeed unless it was achieved by the generation which fought the war. Should that generation die unreconciled, its hatreds would become the next generation's legacy, and conceivably would be perpetuated. And it is a melancholy historical truism that inheriting hatreds is a near-inevitability, eradicating them a near-impossibility. That the reconciliation was effected within the life of that Civil War generation was a spectacular achievement to which Grover Cleveland, the self-proclaimed Tribune of the People who "turned himself into a plausible national sheriff of public law and order"[1] made an incalculable contribution.

Not only did the North and South stand in opposition philosophically, a new rivalry was added: East vs. West. That rivalry was essentially an economic one: western farmers and silver miners vs. the eastern moneyed interests.

The Industrial Revolution, which had begun decades earlier in England, did not take hold in the United States until the postwar era. When it did, it led to westward expansion. Those areas of the Louisiana Purchase—all the land between the Mississippi and the Rocky Mountains—which had not yet achieved statehood had achieved territorial status, with integration into the Union just beyond the horizon.

In the post–Civil War period the United States not only expanded industrially beyond all projections, its population multiplied more rapidly than that of any other country in history. When Cleveland entered the White House for the first time, in 1885, the total had passed the 50 million mark. Eight years later, as he prepared to take office for the second time, it was 63 million and growing at a rate of 25 percent a year. The increase was attributable mainly to the concomitant decline in infant mortality and rise in life expectancy, complemented by mass immigration, mostly from northwestern Europe. Agriculture was the main source of employment and wealth, with close to half the population working in this area. The center of gravity of this labor force, which would take a precipitate downward curve as the country industrialized, had moved from near Baltimore, where it stood in 1790, to Ohio and was even now crossing Indiana. Some 15 million acres were added yearly for farming purposes, mostly in the trans-Mississippi West. Meanwhile, the American frontier had "closed," a fact which came perilously close to an obsession among those calling for extension of the nation beyond its natural border, the Pacific Ocean.

As the Republican-dominated nation expanded westward it turned to the right philosophically. That the five immediate postwar Presidents were a dismal lot was not deemed worthy of serious concern. They were as eager to effect that turn to the right as were those who put them in office.

Faced with a myriad of major, potentially insurmountable problems—notably superfluous high tariffs (protectionism), silver vs. gold as currency (bimetallism), illegal seizure of the vast western lands by rapacious railroads and avaricious land speculators, hideous abuse of the autochthonous Native Americans, a corrupt civil service, and an equally corrupt Veterans Bureau—the nation pursued Manifest Destiny: the belief that we were destined, as if by God, to expand the nation to its westernmost geographical limit, the Pacific Ocean. Having reached the Pacific (and, along the way, made illegal war on Mexico and enriched ourselves territorially), that limit would be extended across the Pacific, to embrace the independent Hawaiian Islands and the Philippines.

Logic would dictate that Cleveland, whose meteorlike rise to eminence has few parallels in our nation's political history, should never have won the presidency. Why? Quite simply, because he opposed just about everything that was finding favor with the majority of the American people: governmental corruption, bimetallism, protectionism, a ghastly Indian policy, what is referred to euphemistically as "the taming of the West" but was in truth its spoliation, and, above all, the ideology of Manifest Destiny.

Moreover, Cleveland refused to do what was politically expedient. He insisted on doing what was morally expedient, even if by doing so, as on more than one occasion, it meant placing his political career in jeopardy. The man was more than a political outsider in every sense of the word. He was, in essence, a political freak.

Which brings us to the obvious question: How, then, did he win the presidency?

This book will answer that question. Furthermore, it will reevaluate our generation's perception of the man and evaluate him in the context of his deplorable successors we have known.

That perception is rooted in what is tantamount to presidential trivia: the only man to be elected mayor of a major city, governor of a major state, and President of the United States all within a four-year period; the only President born in New Jersey and the only one to serve two nonconsecutive terms; the first to marry in the White House, and the first to have a child born in the White House; and the heaviest President prior to William Howard Taft.

Lost in this litany of trivia is the fact that here was a man prepared, if need be, to incur the wrath (and finally lose the support) of his own party because of stands on certain major issues he refused to abandon or alter, out of the conviction—justified, as events proved—that his positions best served the American people. Here, indeed, was that rarest of political animals: one who believed his ultimate allegiance was to the nation, not to the party.

To Allan Nevins, his greatest biographer, Cleveland was a paradigm of honesty, integrity, and resolution who achieved greatness through strength of character; a man who, though flawed, exemplified "courage that never yields an inch in the cause of truth, and that never surrenders an iota of principle to expediency." To Rexford Tugwell, his greatest critic, he was a "narrow conservative . . . nothing could cause him to lift his eyes to a larger future for the nation."[2]

Cleveland's chroniclers were not the only ones unable to achieve a consensus. Neither could the historians. In 1948, Arthur Schlesinger, Sr., of Harvard asked fifty-five "experts," most of them professional historians, to rate all the Presidents through Franklin D. Roosevelt from "Great" down to "Failure." (Excluded were Truman, for the obvious reason that his presidency was ongoing at the time, and William Henry Harrison and Garfield, because the brevity of their presidencies precluded cogent evaluation.) Cleveland was ranked eighth-greatest, below Lincoln, Washington, Roosevelt, Wilson, Jefferson, Jackson, and Theodore Roosevelt. (The first six were ranked as "Great"; Theodore Roosevelt and Cleveland, followed by John Adams and Polk, were ranked as "Near Great.")[3] In a follow-up poll fourteen years later by Professor Schlesinger, this time of seventy-five respondents (including most of those polled earlier, along with journalists and political scientists), Cleveland fell to eleventh place, below Polk, Truman, and John Adams.

In a 1982 poll conducted by historians Robert K. Murray and Tim H. Blessing, 846 respondents demoted Cleveland to seventeenth place. A year later, in yet another poll, this one by the *Chicago Tribune*, Cleveland bounced back to thirteenth place.[4] It would seem that older historians valued Cleveland's accomplishments more than younger ones did. Presumably, as the older historians die off, Cleveland will not rise much above his current ranking, and may well sink even lower.

To compare Grover Cleveland with our four most deplorable post-Harding Presidents—Nixon, Reagan, Bush, and Clinton—is to contrast a paradigm of virtue with the quintessence of duplicity. The fact that these men lied blatantly to the public about their historically demonstrable roles in a multiplicity of scandals is doubtless the least reprehensible aspect of their appalling behavior as men and as Presidents.

No: What is most reprehensible is that they willingly involved themselves in the conduct that led to their exposure as men of less than sterling moral fiber. Admittedly, there always have been, and always will be, scandals in high places. The fact that Grover Cleveland was never touched by any—a few did involve members of his own official family, and he sought to resolve them to the nation's satisfaction—both affirms his estimable integrity and enables us to conjecture that he might not only have damned the actions of these successors (plus, of course, those of Harding), he would have damned them as well. Cleveland had absolutely nothing in common with these men, who had so much in common with each other.

If there was one successor to whom Grover Cleveland can be analogized, it is Harry S. Truman, inarguably our most principled post–World War II President. Like Truman, Cleveland was compassionate, courageous, scrupulous, ever prepared to follow his conscience and moral responsibility no matter the impediments that so often cluttered his path. His contempt for deceit was complemented by an absolute abhorrence of self-aggrandizement.

Cleveland was in no sense an intellectual in the Jeffersonian and Wilsonian mode; it was his character rather than his mind that informed his presidencies. As the *New York Times* editorialized on March 5, 1893, following his second inauguration, Cleveland

> may not be a learned expositor of institutions or a brilliant defender of principles, but he has an absolutely sound conception of the functions of the Government of these United States and of the principles upon which its administration must be conducted if its popular character is to be maintained. He has the unerring instinct of a clear common sense as to the policy that

must be maintained to guard our great heritage of popular institutions from the insidious influences that tend to undermine it.

Cleveland's concerns were always with the majority, never with the favored few—but only so long as the majority position was the legally and morally correct one. He staffed the highest tier of government with men who qualified on the basis of what they might contribute to their office, and not what they contributed to his election.

Unlike Truman, Cleveland was not a political animal in the demotic sense of the word. And here the adverbial qualifier "unfortunately" would not be out of place. Had he been more Trumanesque in that regard—had he sought avenues of compatibility with the more fractious elements of his own party—Cleveland would have spared himself much of the grief that made his second presidency and especially his last months in office so discomfiting. Not even Carter left office so rejected by his own party.

For the powerful dissident factions within his own party, notably the pro-silver western Democrats and the eastern high-tariff projectionists, Cleveland not only refused to effect a *modus vivendi* that might have redounded to his advantage politically; he made it known that they should expect precious little more from him than the metaphorical back of his hand.

Here one can offer in Cleveland's behalf if not exculpation then surely justification. He operated on the theory that every elected official has a constituency whose needs must be served: a mayor his city, a governor his state, a legislator his district—whereas a President's constituency encompasses all the people.

Given the immense and complex problems that challenge the United States today, we demand in our Presidents not only brains but brains of a quality capable of confronting these problems. (That we do not always get them is another matter.) In 1885, when the social factors stirred up by the Civil War and rapid national growth were jelling, we needed a leader who typified reform. Cleveland fit the bill. Eight years later, we needed a man capable of holding the line against fiscal chaos and the antagonisms of class and sectionalism. He again fit the bill. Thus was Grover Cleveland, in the classic sense, the right man for his times.

"Mr. Cleveland," wrote one contemporary observer, "always insisted upon this, that if right political policies were simply and clearly put before the American people, they would generally make a wise and honest decision. He was sometimes discouraged; but I do not think he was ever fundamentally shaken in his belief. He realized that there might be long periods of indecision or mistake, but he looked forward to a final satisfactory outcome."[5]

Cleveland venerated the Constitution, and in particular, Madison's wisdom and foresight in the conception, division, and separation of federal powers. He believed that the agglomeration of deleterious laws and regulations which had accreted since the founding of the Republic to benefit the few at the expense of the many must be corrected, so as to bring the nation back into harmony with Madison's original design. Insisting that the office of the President "represents the sovereignty" of every American, he urged the voters of all generations:

> Watch well, then, this . . . most precious possession of American citizenship. Demand for it the most complete devotion on the part of him to whose custody it may be intrusted, and protect it not less vigilantly against unworthy assaults from without. Thus will you perform a sacred duty to yourselves and to those who may follow you in the enjoyment of the freest institutions which heaven has ever vouchsafed to man.[6]

PART I

1837–1881

1

Stephen

The name Cleveland is of Saxon origin, from a district near the Suffolk town of Whitby, seventy miles northeast of London, that was celebrated for its abundance of "clefts" or "cleves"—indentations in the rock formations. In those long-ago days when one was indulged the conceit of spelling his surname (or anyone else's) as fancy dictated, the name was variously rendered Cliveland, Clyveland, Clievland, Cleivland, Cleaveland, Cleviland, and Cliffland—even, on occasion, Cleveland. Moses, the president's first American antecedent, preferred Cleaveland; it was son Aaron who fixed the spelling as we know it. English genealogists have traced the family back to the Norman Conquest. We need go back no farther than the seventeenth century, when Moses arrived at Massachusetts from the Suffolk, England, market town of Ipswich as an indentured servant. On gaining his independence in 1648, Moses married a Massachusetts girl named Ann Winn, by whom he begat the line which flourishes to this day.

Every Cleveland generation gave at least one son to the Protestant ministry, either Congregational or Presbyterian. Of those from whom the future President descended lineally, two deserve mention: Moses's great-grandson Aaron, and Aaron's son and namesake. (The name Aaron was borne by the eldest son in five generations.) The senior Reverend Aaron, Harvard-educated son of a Cambridge, Massachusetts, tavern keeper, contractor, and land speculator, dedicated his life to the ministry, starting out as a Puritan, later switching to Anglicanism. After marrying into the Boston aristocracy, he occupied pulpits in Massachusetts and Connecticut for fifteen years before switching to Episcopalianism. His few remaining years (he died at forty-two) were spent overseeing two parishes in the Delaware colony, where he became renowned for his wit, scholarship, and leadership. A hint of the distinction Aaron enjoyed throughout the colonies may be inferred from the fact that when he was sought out by the Grim Reaper, he was run to ground in the Philadelphia home of Benjamin Franklin. Franklin eulogized his friend in print as "a gentleman of humane and pious disposition, indefatigable in his ministry, easy and affable in his conversation, open and sincere in his friendship, and above every species of meanness and dissimilation."[1]

Aaron's son and namesake—for clarity's sake, let us call him the junior Reverend Aaron—did not feel the call to preach until his fifty-third year, which brings us to 1797, by which time he was a prosperous Connecticut hat manufacturer and ardent abolitionist. During a single term in the colonial legislature he introduced the Connecticut colony's first bill to "exterminate slavery." Here was a man who fought for manumission long before it became a fashionable cause.

A penchant for committing admirable deeds was by now endemic in the Cleveland clan. Aaron's brother Stephen, of Salem, Massachusetts, won the admiration of New England abolitionists after successfully prosecuting two Salem shipowners for their participation in the African slave trade.[2] A Congregational minister who preached in New York, Connecticut, and Vermont, Aaron was also an essayist and poet of some renown. But it was as patriot, abolitionist, and man of the cloth that he was best remembered.

Aaron's son William, declining to follow his father and grandfather into the ministry, pursued a more secular (and more remunerative) career as silversmith, watchmaker, and jeweler, first in Westfield, Massachusetts, later in Norwich, Connecticut, where he settled down with his wife, Margaret Falley, to raise a family. Though he felt no call to the pulpit, William did feel called to a life of piety; he served as a deacon in the Norwich Congregational church and dedicated his firstborn son to the ministry. This son, named Richard Falley for his maternal grandfather, was born on June 19, 1804, and was to sire the subject of this biography.

By the time Richard came along, what material wealth his father had amassed was dissipated. He had to devote his after-school hours to clerking in a Norwich dry goods store owned by a cousin, William Dodge, later one of New York's most affluent and public-spirited merchants. After graduating from Yale with honors and a determination to serve in the Presbyterian ministry, Richard began his theological studies in Baltimore. Two factors dictated his choice of cities: the opportunity to study theology with an esteemed older Yale alumnus, and the opportunity to earn money for advanced study at the Princeton Theological Seminary (later Princeton University), which he did as tutor in a private academy.

Richard's abolitionist kinfolk wished he had not selected Baltimore, given its proslavery sentiment. Still, it proved to be a fortuitous choice. There he met and fell in love with Ann Neal, of whom we know little other than that she was two years his junior, her father was a fairly successful publisher of law books who was driven from his native Ireland for embracing the Protestant faith, and her mother was a Pennsylvania-born German Quaker. Ann must have been a woman of character. A lesser woman would hardly have sacrificed a life of ease through marriage into one of Baltimore's better families in order to wed a poor divinity student who had chosen for his life's calling a vocation never known in early America to allow for much in the way of upward fiscal mobility. But Ann loved the handsome Richard. When he had saved enough money for further study at Princeton and hoped that she'd wait for him, she swore she would. And she did. They were wed in 1828, after Richard's ordination, and left immediately for Windham, Connecticut, where he accepted a call by the First Congregational Church.

When Richard brought his bride to Windham, a prototypically puritanical New England village, his congregants were appalled at what Ann brought to Windham: a lavish wardrobe of bright gowns and jewelry, considered proscriptive by the locals for a minister's wife; and the black slave woman who had cared for her since infancy, considered prohibitive by the locals for any man's wife. Richard had to agree that a woman bringing a slave into Connecticut, especially a woman who liked bright colors and low décolletage, would incur suspicion if not animosity. Ann obediently sent the slave back to Baltimore, became an abolitionist, packed away her bright gowns and jewelry, and had herself measured for the somber apparel decorous for the spouse of an indigent village cleric. She no more regretted doing so than would she ever regret the station in life into which she had married down. The young couple were poor only in goods. They had culture, congeniality, and spiritual wealth—resources enough to encourage hope for a happy future.

The couple remained at Windham till the autumn of 1832, when a decline in Richard's health took them to Portsmouth, Virginia, where the climate was more salubrious. Two years later, his health improved, Richard accepted a call from the Caldwell, New Jersey, Presbyterian church. He and Ann were by then the parents of Anna and William Neal, born at Windham, and Mary Allen, born at Portsmouth; Richard Cecil was born shortly after their arrival at Caldwell around Christmas of 1834. There Richard endeared himself for the "awakening" he co-staged with a local evangelist, which added seventy-five new members to the congregation, and for raising the then staggering sum of $22,000 to remodel and repair the fifty-year-old church. Shortly before Richard's "awakening," Ann gave birth in the Caldwell parsonage on March 18, 1837, to the third of their four sons and fifth of their nine children. He was named to honor the memory of Richard's predecessor, who had founded the church in 1787: Stephen Grover. ("Stephen" would be truncated to "S" and later abandoned altogether by Grover in his teen years, though it did survive in "Big Steve," as he was known among close friends in his pre-political period.)

2

"My mind revels in retrospection"

An isolated New Jersey village whose inhabitants numbered in the hundreds, Caldwell was connected to the state's northeastern hub city of Newark by a series of ill-kept roads; travelling them was an adventure most people were prepared to forgo, given the option. Though it would ever after pride itself as the birthplace of the only

President from the Garden State, Caldwell held no memories for Cleveland. The first town that would was Fayetteville, New York, where the family relocated in Grover's fourth year, when his father accepted the pulpit of the town's Presbyterian church.

Richard's yearly stipend of $600 was hardly extravagant, even when augmented with a small legacy left Ann by her publisher father. Being by nature frugal, and adept at living off the land, the Clevelands, now with three children of each gender, managed to cover not only the necessities but even a few indulgences. The family, completed over the next few years with the arrivals of Lewis Frederick, Susan, and Rose, though hardscrabble poor never knew poverty.

Founded fifty years earlier, Fayetteville—twelve hundred inhabitants, four churches, an "educational academy," and a medley of stores, mills, and "mechanical establishments"—was a satellite of the contiguous town of Manlius. Eight miles from Syracuse, four miles from the western railroad, and a mile from the Erie Canal, Manlius, with five thousand inhabitants, contained a lime factory, tannery, and barley mill which offered employment for wage earners not committed to farming or the professions. Fayetteville and Manlius typified the upper and western New York region of the period, which was now welcoming settlers in ever increasing numbers as the nation slowly emerged from the Panic of 1837. Among the area's communities then beginning their evolution into major cities was the port city Buffalo, which in later years could boast it was there that Grover Cleveland began the spectacular political career that led to the White House.

Richard believed it was never too early to commence a child's education; the Cleveland children learned while still toddlers the Puritanical obedience in which the family was steeped. "Often as a boy," young Grover recalled in later years, "I was compelled to get out of my warm bed at night, to hang up a hat or other garment which I had left on the floor."[3] He was also obliged to comply with the biblical commandments, commit to memory the Westminster Catechism, and comport himself in a manner consonant with Puritan conviction.

Grover would wait until he was out on his own before viewing life in other than puritanical terms. A Deist in the Jeffersonian sense, he believed in God, but not in all the man-crafted accretions to that belief. He would revert to the enforced conventions of childhood when he returned home for family visits, but this was less out of ingrained habit than out of respect for his adored mother. The future President's home life and training "tended to produce a keen sense of personal responsibility, to make trustworthy character; for its ethical basis was absolute. It taught that there is a right which is eternally right, and a wrong which must remain forever wrong." Such training accounted for Cleveland's tendency to view all matters, great and small, in absolute terms—just or unjust, right or wrong, black or white—as well as for the duality in his nature. This duality caused contemporaries to see in him two antipathetic personalities. "To his last days, his intimates never ceased to be amazed by the gulf which separated the exuberant, jovial, sociable Grover and the stern, unbending, socially responsible Grover."[4]

Cleveland's duality manifested itself differently at various stages of his adult life. During his early years in Buffalo, the man who had matured into a proper, rather rigid, one might say inflexible attorney, known to pore over briefs through the night into early morning, was also known to divide his recreational hours between Level's Livery Stable, where he enjoyed the bawdy jokes and smutty tales that were contrapuntal to the often lively euchre or poker games, and such favorite German beer gardens as Diebold's, Schwabl's, and Louis "the Dutchman" Goetz's, where, in the company of good friends who shared his bachelor status and bachelor tastes, he surrendered for a few hours to the Circe lure of good lager, good music, good food, and not-necessarily-good women. On rare occasion the characteristically nonconfrontational Grover was not above partaking in a street brawl if he considered such behavior justified, as when he heaved one Mike Falvey into a Seneca Street gutter after a heated colloquy on politics culminated in an irreconcilable divergence of opinion.[5]

By the time Cleveland assumed the responsibilities of marriage and fatherhood, though, the roistering, which had abated in his early political years, was a distant memory. His duality then assumed a different form: the lighthearted, effervescent Grover could be transformed abruptly into strict, uncompromising Mr. Cleveland. Too much should not be made of this, though. Duality is, after all, a quality found in many people, from all walks of life. The purpose in discussing it apropos of Grover Cleveland is not to set him apart from other men; he was, really, in so many respects—perhaps even most—an ordinary man. Rather, the purpose is to retire, if possible for all time, the erroneous conclusion arrived at by contemporaries and etched in stone by commentators who came later that Grover Cleveland was a one-dimensional borderline nonentity verging on ineptitude who stumbled into the presidency. Twice.

Discipline in the Cleveland home was strict. But this was to be expected in a family dominated by an austere ecclesiastic. There was family worship nightly, and only the babies were excused from two obligatory Sunday church services plus prayer meeting. The Sabbath regimen would begin Saturday at sundown, when all the children's toys were put away and an early supper was followed by the weekly bath. Sunday's heavy dose of religious activity was broken at noon with a sumptuous dinner, followed by the day's only permissible activity of a recreational nature: a stroll in the formal garden, Fayetteville's first, which Richard and Ann laid out.

Young Grover's childhood had its lighter moments: candy pulls and popcorn parties in the Cleveland kitchen; evening games in the parlor; fun-filled hours in the nut groves and hills surrounding the town, and in the swimming holes along Limestone Creek and the Chittenango; and fishing in Green Lake, where he cultivated a love of the sport that evolved into a lifelong passion. Villagers later recalled fondly Grover's proclivity for such pranks as attaching a long rope to the academy bell and ringing it to awaken the town in the dead of night. His partner in these larks was invariably his eldest and favorite brother, William.

As he approached his teen years, Grover assumed the chores incumbent on all the Cleveland boys: cutting wood, carrying water, hoeing the garden. At times he earned money helping move the rock lime that was Fayetteville's principal export. To market a shipment, the local processors had to hail empty lime barges as they floated along the Erie Canal and turn them into the feeder channel a mile from the village. A dime went to any boy who thus snagged a boat on demand. Learning that a shipment was being readied for the morrow, Grover would rise long before dawn to beat out the other youngsters for that dime. Being large and muscular for his age, he succeeded in breaking up a monopoly in barge-hailing organized by some of the older village boys. (When, during his years as a public figure, his weight passed the three-hundred-pound mark, Cleveland was often referred to among his inner circle—but never addressed directly—as

"Big Steve" or "the Big One." To his nieces and nephews, he was always "Uncle Jumbo.")

Grover's memory of his ten years at Fayetteville were among life's happiest. Decades later, on a flying visit while President, he gave a brief speech, one of the few autobiographical pieces found among his papers, which concluded on this nostalgic note:

> If some of the old householders were here I could tell them who it was that used to take off their front gates. I mention this because I have been accused of so many worse crimes since I have been in Washington that I consider taking off gates something of a virtue. I would be sadly at fault if I failed to recall the many inestimable benefits I received at your hands—my early education, the training of the Sunday school, the religious advantages, the advantages of your social life. And so, when in short intervals of freedom from the cares and duties of my office, my mind revels in retrospection, these early recollections are the truest, pleasantest, and brightest spots on which my memory lights. [6]

Grover's formal studies were begun in the district school, a little red frame affair no less rudimentary than the quality of education it offered. Shortly thereafter, he was transferred to Fayetteville Academy, where the quality of study was little better than that found in any rural area of the times, but no worse. Father Cleveland valued education and insisted all his children, the girls included, be exposed to it. He supplemented their studies with home courses that included, besides religion, Latin and mathematics, two areas in which Grover would maintain a lifelong interest (though not a proficiency).

3

Plans for college ended

When Grover was fourteen, his father's health, never robust, began to fail; Richard's condition was exacerbated by the need to sustain so large a family—it now included the last four of his and Ann's nine children—on so meager a salary. To relieve the strain, he accepted the post of district secretary of the Central New York Agency of the American Home Missionary, at $1,000 per annum. This brought the family to Clinton, a small town on the Oriskany River, not far from Buffalo, that boasted, among other amenities, access to some of the best educational facilities in the region. For the younger children, there was the so-called Clinton Academy (more properly, the Clinton Liberal Institute); for the older boys, Hamilton College (where William was preparing for the ministry); for the older girls, nearby Houghton Seminary.

Grover's scholastic progress was marked more by determination than academic brilliance. According to his sister Margaret (known in the family as Louise), he was "resourceful—but as a student Grover did not shine. The wonderful powers of application and concentration which afterwards distinguished his mental efforts were not conspicuous in his boyhood."[7]

A year after the move to Clinton, it was decided that Grover should contribute to the financially hard-pressed family. He returned to Fayetteville to work in Deacon John McVicar's general store for $50 yearly plus board and lodging. Concurrently, he resumed his secondary education at the Clinton Academy, where just before his sixteenth birthday he organized a debating society ("gymnasium"). As Vice-Archon it was his responsibility to arrange what were not so much formal debates as lectures and discussions. One dealt with the question of whether an attorney is justified in defending a client whom he knows to be guilty. Cleveland argued that he is not. He always maintained that view.

When Grover returned to Clinton a year later to prepare to enter Hamilton College in the fall, his father's health was again in decline, mainly because of the frequent travel his missionary duties demanded, usually over inferior roads in nasty weather. This led him to accept the less arduous pulpit at Holland Patent, a quiet village a dozen miles above Utica on the Black River, in the same region of the state. A few days after the family's arrival in early September, Richard delivered his first sermon. It was also the last of his life. Suffering from a gastric ulcer, he was too weak to get out of bed. Two weeks later he died suddenly from acute peritonitis.

Richard had been the primary influence during Grover's formative years, and son emulated father in just about every aspect but the latter's politics, which leaned to extreme conservatism, and personality, which leaned to congenital self-abnegation. In the son we see the father's generous height and portly figure, blue eyes, balding brow, and, their most distinguishing shared trait, the prominent Roman nose. These, in addition to the senior Cleveland's charming manner and a studiousness that stopped short of brilliance, composed Reverend Richard's legacy to his middle, most famous offspring. In November 1907, when Grover Cleveland fell victim to the illness that would carry him off seven months later, he recalled his father's struggle as a country minister, "a hard-working country clergyman, bringing up acceptably a family of nine children, educating each member so that, in later life, none suffered any deprivation in this respect, and that, too, upon a salary which at no time exceeded a thousand dollars a year. It would be impossible to exaggerate the strength of character this revealed. It emphasizes the qualities of pluck and endurance which have made [the American] people what they are."[8]

His father's sudden death ended Grover's plans for college. Like his two older brothers, he had to contribute to the maintenance of their mother and four younger siblings. (Anna and Mary, the two eldest, were by then married. Ann's widow's mite was negligible, and the meager bequest from her late father's estate had been drastically reduced by a dishonest trustee. Pride would not allow her to accept help from neighbors and parishioners or the proposal advanced by Richard's superiors for a public subscription to educate her four youngest children. But she did accept when Richard's congregants insisted she stay on in the parsonage rent-free.)

To finance further study for the ministry, William was principal male teacher in the New York Institution for the Blind. He persuaded the school to hire Grover as bookkeeper and assistant to the superintendent, with the understanding that he help teach some of the basic subjects to the younger children. This state-financed institute, founded in 1831 and occupying the entire New York City block between Eighth and Ninth Avenues and Thirty-third and Thirty-fourth Streets, was in fact a public asylum, its student population drawn from poverty-stricken homes throughout the state. The 116 inmates were evenly divided between the sexes, ranging in age from eight to twenty-five. The halls were cold and dank, the meals practically inedible, the pay minimal; adding to the misery of all concerned, the superintendent was a martinet who seemed to take a perverse delight in convincing students and faculty alike that it was their lot in life to dwell and labor in a charitable vineyard of tribulation. The Cleveland brothers would always look back on the time they put in there as the bleakest in their lives.

Besides discharging his clerical responsibilities, Grover taught the younger students basic reading, writing, arithmetic, and geography; William taught the older students "intellectual philosophy," logic, introductory chemistry and physics, and history. That neither was trained to perform such duties mattered not. Those were the years when few demands were made on a pedagogue beyond mastering the art of staying one step ahead of the students and caning the more obstreperous among them. In addition to their responsibilities, William and Grover were in charge of the boys' dormitory. By the time they paid their expenses and sent money home to Holland Patent, the brothers were too destitute to take part in any of the city's numerous cultural activities. Their sole recreations were an occasional faculty tea and one or two "musical soirées." For the occasional decent meal there were invitations to the home of their wealthy Dodge kin.

Also on the faculty was Fanny Crosby, blind from infancy, who started at the institute as a pupil and went on to become one of the nation's most popular writers of hymns. Miss Crosby prepared a series of recollections of Cleveland from his institute days for the Democratic Campaign Committee during his first run for the White House. Its main interest lies in the fact that so much that became evident in the man was already apparent in the boy. His mind "unusually well developed for his years," he seemed to possess even then "the manner of a mature man." Every spare moment was devoted to self-improvement. A persistent reader who had developed even in those days "something of a bent for the law, which he was finally to make his calling," he had developed "the faculty of hard work, which has so distinguished his later career." What particularly impressed Miss Crosby was that young Grover "was always kindly and sympathetic," and "resented occasional cruelties" on the superintendent's part. "He could not, of course, in his position, take steps to resent it by a physical demonstration, but he showed in every word and action that he would like to punish its perpetrator in the most effective way."[9]

The Cleveland boys left the New York Institution for the Blind after a year, William to enter the Union Theological Seminary, where he was ordained in 1856, Grover to return to Holland Patent, having decided on the law as his life's vocation. Before he could consider resuming his schooling, though, he was obliged to consider some form of employment. He sought as far away as Utica and Syracuse, but without success. Among Holland Patent's leading citizens was Ingham Townsend, a wealthy Presbyterian elder. Impressed by what he had observed and heard about the young man, Townsend offered to finance his college studies, conditional on a promise that he enter the ministry. To emulate his father career-wise was an option young Grover never considered. Nor would he consider making a promise he had no intention to keep. He refused Townsend's offer, and asked, instead, for a loan of $25, to finance a journey he and a friend were about to undertake. He was given the money and told he needn't repay it. Twelve years later, when in a position to do so, he returned the loan—with interest.

The two boys' reason for undertaking that journey was to find not only employment but their destiny. Grover decided they would head for Cleveland, Ohio, for no other reason than that it was named for a distant relative. But before doing so, he wished to visit with his uncle Lewis Allen's family in the Buffalo suburb of Black Rock. He had spent a pleasant holiday there with his cousins a few years before, and wished to say goodbye, perhaps forever, before heading west into an uncertain future.

Situated at the eastern end of Lake Erie and the upper end of the Niagara River, Buffalo was second only to New York City, some four hundred miles to the southeast, as the state's major metropolis, seaport, and financial center. It was not incorporated as a city in 1832, five years after the New England–born Lewis Allen settled there, drawn by the city's growth to economic eminence precipitated by the recent completion of the Erie Canal. Allen would in time become one of western New York State's most prominent citizens. Having made a fortune organizing a string of successful insurance companies and real estate ventures, and having served in the state legislature, Allen turned to his first love, cattle breeding, going on to develop the nation's leading center for the breeding of Shorthorn and Devon cattle and Southdown sheep.

Allen suggested that Grover stay on for a few months to help edit the American Shorthorn Herd Book, which he began in 1846 and took through twenty-four volumes, thereby establishing his reputation as one of America's most respected stockmen. Should things work out, Allen promised, he would use his considerable influence to apprentice the lad to one of the city's major law firms. Grover agreed, and bade farewell to his friend, who continued on west with no hard feelings. Though he could not have known it at the time, in Buffalo Grover Cleveland had found his destiny.

For a year or so, he lived in the comfortable Allen home overlooking the Niagara River two miles from downtown Buffalo, spending his free time fishing and hunting regularly with his cousins, enjoying periodic visits from his siblings, and letting Aunt Margaret (his father's sister) mother him as if he were one of her own. Though hardly the political activist he was to become over time, Grover identified as a Democrat and looked with modified disdain both on the Frémont candidacy of 1856 (the election in which he cast his first vote—for Buchanan, of course) and his uncle's Whig sympathies.

Upon completing his first year's work on the herd book, for which he was paid $60, Grover decided it was time he take the first step toward that hoped-for career at the bar. Allen arranged an introduction with Rogers, Bowen & Rogers, one of Buffalo's top law firms; the interview went well, and Grover was taken on as student clerk and copyist. As was customary for the time, he was paid nothing for the first two months. After convincing the three partners he was worth the expenditure, he was given a weekly salary of $4. This covered Grover's expenses at the boardinghouse he now called home. Weekends he returned to Black Rock, where his relationship with the Allens remained close, particularly with Aunt Margaret; this despite a religiosity which at times led Grover to fear that if he gritted his teeth with much more intensity when subjected to yet another of her chronic fits of piety, they would crumble in his mouth like soft chalk. From time to time he visited his mother at Holland Point and left what coins he could spare.

Cleveland started with Rogers, Bowen & Rogers a few days before Christmas of 1855 ("handed Blackstone's *Commentaries* and turned loose to browse in the library of a law office" was how he put it). Years later he recalled being so ignored by the partners and clerks that first day that when they went out for lunch they forgot he was seated in a corner poring through his Blackstone. ("Some day," he vowed to himself, "I will be better remembered.")[10]

The firm's practice, primarily corporate, was limited to a handful of substantial clients: manufacturers, shippers, and banks. Of the three partners it was thirty-five-year-old Dennis Bowen who most influenced the new clerk. Bowen, who had trained in former President Fillmore's office, was the firm's inside man. Unlike his father-and-son partners, whose strength lay in trial law, Bowen furnished good advice along with the well-researched briefs they argued. Honest and pragmatic, he viewed every question in terms of whether it was just or unjust, not solely from a legal advantage; and he had a great reputation for settling disputes without going to trial in a way that invariably left all litigants satisfied. These traits, plus an obsessive need to subject a case's every facet to microscopic examination, Bowen's young clerk was to make his own.

Not long after commencing his apprenticeship, Grover was able, by sharing expenses with a newly arrived friend from Fayetteville, to take rooms in the loft of the old Southern Hotel, a residential establishment favored by farmers and drovers. The rooms were adequate. For all Grover cared, they could have been a hovel. Living arrangements ranked low among the priorities of this young man eager to make his mark in his chosen field who spent practically every evening at his office studying toward that end. Years later, writing of this period in the third person, Cleveland allowed as how he "had adversity in abundance [and] plenty of willingness to work, plenty of faith, and a fair stock of perseverance in reserve. He had no misgivings. He actually enjoyed his adversities. Even then he was called stubborn. After he had become president of the United States he was still called stubborn, and he is accused of stubbornness to this day."[11]

Soon after his twenty-second birthday, Cleveland was admitted to the New York bar. Instead of going into practice on his own, he stayed on with Rogers, Bowen & Rogers, where he was made senior clerk. This enabled him to gain incalculable experience preparing briefs and learning trial technique, and the yearly salary of $1,000 enabled him to send money to his mother on a regular basis. The successes he had as a trial lawyer owed less to oratorical or histrionic talent than to meticulousness in preparation and presentation. After researching a case painstakingly, he would commit his argument to memory, an approach necessitated by his admitted lack of eloquence and discomfort with spontaneity, and, of greater concern, his fear of compromising a client by overlooking an important point. Exhaustive research and flawless delivery became hallmarks of Cleveland's style, even as a political figure. He would harvest all necessary information on a given subject and deliver the end result, even a major gubernatorial or presidential address, sans text, sans notes, and sans faltering.

4

Why did Grover become a Democrat?

After four years with Rogers, Bowen & Rogers, Grover left to become assistant district attorney for Erie County, which office had recently become vacant. While this meant a 40 percent reduction in income, the position was political in character, and Cleveland saw politics as the most expeditious path to success in the legal profession. His colleagues of the Buffalo bar agreed he was the right man for the job, as did a few of the leading Buffalo newspapers. Editorializing on the appointment, the *Buffalo Courier* said: "Mr. Cleveland is one of the most promising of the younger members of the bar, is a thoroughly read lawyer, and possesses talent of a high order. He will soon have an opportunity of demonstrating this and 'more too,' and, our word for it, he will prove himself equal to the occasion."[12]

As assistant DA, Cleveland prepared indictments, personally prosecuting many of the cases. Success in the position enabled him to extend his circle of friends throughout politically powerful Erie County. His recognition factor soared when it became obvious that the health of his boss, Cyrenius C. Torrance, having failed, "Big Steve" was practically carrying the workload on his own by now quite broad shoulders. His balanced, painstaking mastery of the facts in all cases, no matter their insignificance, quickly won him the confidence of judges and juries alike. Daunting to the opposition counsel was his letter-perfect pleading of even the most lengthy or complicated briefs from memory.

Though this was Cleveland's first political appointment, it was not his introduction to politics. While still clerking with Rogers, Bowen & Rogers, he was often seen at Democratic city conclaves. In November 1862, after a term as delegate from the second ward (the ward was heavily German, a group with whom he was especially popular), Cleveland was elected ward supervisor. "I had no aspirations to be a [political] 'boss,' " he recalled years later, "but I only followed the custom of my time in taking my place at the polls and distributing ballots to all those who asked for them, using my influence to convince the wavering, or to confirm those who belonged to my household of faith."[13]

The question now obtrudes: Why did Grover Cleveland become a Democrat? With the nation rapidly approaching its greatest crisis, Cleveland, as a scion of New England Presbyterianism, might have been expected to stand in opposition to slavery. Like so many Whigs, Lewis Allen, young Cleveland's surrogate father, was outraged by the Fugitive Slave Act of 1850. When four years later the Kansas-Nebraska Act nullified the Missouri Compromise of 1820 and opened the territories north of Missouri that were part of the Louisiana Purchase to slavery (and, in the process, sounded the Whig party's death knell), Allen joined the recently emergent Republican party. Presiding over the first convention in Erie County, he helped orchestrate its evolution as the principal party in upper and western New York State (a status it holds to this day). If Allen tried to influence his nephew's political orientation, he tried in vain. Cleveland became a Democrat because the party "seemed to represent greater solidity and conservatism"; moreover, he was "repelled" by the Republicans' first presidential candidate, John Frémont, whom he considered "flamboyant and theatrical."[14]

Against this rationale must be weighed the following realities. Dennis Bowen, who encouraged Cleveland to go into politics, was active in Democrat circles (he had been alderman from the predominantly Democratic tenth ward). That the Democrats controlled Buffalo's municipal government was a factor Bowen would have urged Cleveland to bear in hand. He was by now anticipating a career in politics, though he did not foresee himself in city hall or the statehouse; certainly not in the White House. A Congressional seat seemed a more realistic goal, though his preference was for some judicial position. An eventual seat on the Supreme Court formed the basis of a recurring fantasy—a fantasy that, he suspected, he stood a better chance of realizing, were he to affiliate himself with the Democratic party.

5

A blessing in disguise

As he entered upon his first public office, Cleveland's attention was focused, like that of all contemporary politicians, on the Civil War. A so-called War Democrat and fervid Unionist, he supported Lincoln's suspending the writ of habeas corpus ("the government has a right in time of war to resort to every possible method in order to protect itself"). Such was Cleveland's admiration for Lincoln, whom he referred to in later years as "a supremely great and good man," he is believed to have crossed party lines and voted for the Republican candidate in 1864.[15]

No sooner had Cleveland assumed his duties with the district attorney's office than the prospect of enforced military service threatened to delay, possibly abort, his career. The Conscription Act of March 3, 1863, called for the drafting into the Union army of all able-bodied males between ages twenty-five and thirty-five (forty-five if unmarried). Any draftee who so wished could provide a substitute or pay a commutation of $300. Cleveland was among those called on the first day.

He had by now become the main financial support of his mother and two youngest sisters still at home, Susan, eighteen, and Rose, fifteen. Anna and Mary were already married; Louise had left home to become a governess with a Long Island family. When Susan and Rose went off on their own as adults, Louise returned to take care of their mother. Brothers Cecil and Frederick were already in the army and in no financial position to help out more than nominally; nor was William, who had begun his own family and was barely making do on his meager salary as acting minister of a Long Island church. Too, the cost of living had risen dramatically, and both Susan and Rose looked forward to a college education; and brother Grover would not deny their wish, though it involved a more burdensome financial responsibility than his own income could bear.

Taking advantage of his legal options, Cleveland hired a Polish seaman, George Benninsky, to take his place—to he his "300 Dollar Man," as such substitutes were popularly referred to (though few, if any, actually received that sum). Cleveland assumed the matter was over and done with. It was an erroneous assumption, as he was to learn when it all came back to haunt him during his first run for the White House.

His three years as Buffalo's assistant district attorney won Cleveland a reputation throughout Erie County as a man of legal talent and probity. He attended all thirty-six grand juries that met during his term of office, drawing up most of the indictments and trying almost half the cases personally. On one occasion he argued four major cases concurrently, winning favorable verdicts in all four.

For Cleveland it was more the rule than the exception to sit down at eight o'clock in the evening to prepare for the next day, and remain at his desk until three o'clock in the morning. Eight in the morning would find him back again at the office, fresh for a day's combat against some of the best legal minds in the state. He was known at times to have toiled over thirty-six hours without sleep. Only by maintaining a grueling schedule could he examine in minutest detail every aspect of the question at hand. It was a work habit Cleveland would carry throughout his political life and into the White House.

In late 1865, Cleveland received the Democratic nomination for district attorney, to which the Democrat press in Buffalo added its enthusiastic endorsement: his "close application, gentlemanly deportment, and conceded ability have given him a standing at the bar which has seldom been gained by one of his years," said the *Courier*. He had "discharged his duties with an ability and fidelity which have secured the commendation of men of all parties. He is a young man, who, by his unaided exertions, has gained a high position at the bar, and whose character is above reproach." Cleveland, the paper foretold, would have the support of even "hundreds of Republicans."[16]

But the office was not to be his. Though Cleveland carried seven of the thirteen wards in Buffalo, the county seat and most populous city, his opponent won not only those other six wards but the suburban vote as well. It is a measure of Cleveland that he remained close friends with the man who defeated him in this, his first try for elective office: Lyman K. Bass, with whom he once shared rooms in the old Southern Hotel.[17] Bass's victory had the effect of putting Cleveland's career as a public official on hold for six years. Neither of them could have known it would prove over time to have been for Grover a blessing in disguise.

Cleveland spent those six years in private practice, first in partnership with Isaac K. Vanderpoel, who was well connected politically throughout the state, and then, when Vanderpoel became a police magistrate, with Albert P. Laning and Oscar Folsom. One of the most influential, politically connected Democratic leaders in western New York, Laning belonged to a new breed that had arisen after the Civil War, the corporate attorney; his clients included a number of major railroads. Oscar Folsom's contributions to the firm, in addition to a somewhat erratic brilliance, was a talent for attracting people that won the firm many prominent clients. Cleveland respected Laning. It was Folsom, though, to whom he became closest, finding his brightness, honesty, and broader education especially agreeable. (Folsom liked to tell a story that illustrated Cleveland's conscientiousness when it came to study, a conscientiousness the more gregarious Folsom did not share. Asking Cleveland one day for a point of law, he was told: "Go look it up, and then you'll remember what you learn.")[18]

Cleveland was soon one of Buffalo's most eminent attorneys. Like his mentor, Dennis Bowen, he would not take on any client he believed to be less than scrupulously honest, and much preferred, where possible, an equitable resolution of a case to a dazzling victory on a technicality. Not even his friends saw in him a man of incisive intellect, catholicity of ideas, or arresting personality. Rather, they saw a conscientious man endowed with common sense and a propitious talent for capably exploiting what opportunities came his way. Some of his cases soon began to attract favorable notice and contribute to Cleveland's growing reputation outside Buffalo.

One involved a group of fifteen hundred Irish nationalists (Fenians) who mounted an "invasion" of Canada in the late spring of 1866 and managed to raise their emerald-green flag on the south side of the Niagara River before suffering a total rout. When they were brought back to Buffalo in chains and it was learned they had neither a lawyer nor the funds to retain one, Cleveland organized a *pro bono* defense. Even citizens not passionate about the Irish cause were impressed that after defending them successfully Cleveland refused to accept the purse his indigent clients' supporters collected for him. Cleveland's association with the Fenians did not end there. In 1871, other Buffalonians of their persuasion, still convinced, for some abstruse reason, that one way to get the English out of Ireland was to first get them out of Canada, again agitated across the Niagara. This time the prisoners were taken to Canandaigua for trial. Cleveland, confined to Buffalo on a major case, arranged with a friend in Ontario County to defend them without fee. When they were convicted, he joined in a successful petition to President Grant for commutation of their sentences, maintaining that they posed no danger to our neighbors to the north, only to themselves.

One civil case that attracted wide attention was Cleveland's successful defense of the *Buffalo Commercial Advertiser* in 1868 for libel. As part of an attempt to break up some shenanigans in certain Great Lakes ports that were common practice yet quite unlawful, the paper publicly accused a wealthy Buffalo grain dealer, David S. Bennett, of obtaining a bank loan on a fraudulent receipt for stored grain. Bennett sought, and seemed likely to get, large damages when Cleveland undertook the defense. Though obliged to prove the truth of his client's charges, no mean feat given Bennett's civic standing and the esteem in which he was held by the jurors, Cleveland defeated the suit.

6
Sheriff Cleveland

In 1870, the Democrats, convinced that they had a winner in "Big Steve" Cleveland, offered him the nomination for sheriff of Erie County. He rejected the idea at first ("it is not usual for lawyers to be sheriffs"), but it took little persuasion by the pols to change his mind. Cleveland's friends agreed on the idea of his interrupting a growing law practice, with its ever-expanding list of important corporate clients, to run for public office. District attorney, perhaps. Or Congress. But *sheriff?* Not only in Erie County but throughout the United

States, the office was, as it remains to this day, invariably reserved for political hacks. The consensus of opinion had Cleveland being conned into the race by all those raffish characters with whom he associated in the hotel lobbies and watering holes of Buffalo.

Whether this was true or not, he opted for seeking the office serendipitously. His not too convincing reason: as sheriff, he would have time to catch up on his studies and thus make up for lack of a formal education. Besides, he would still be involved with the courts in a professional capacity. His true reason: the yield from fees for services performed, legal perquisites of the office, would be twice what he was realizing in private practice. And an increased income would mean an increase in assistance to his dependents back at Holland Patent.

Cleveland won, but by a mere 303 votes. Doubtless he could have done better, but he limited his efforts to five rather lackluster speeches, three in Buffalo and two elsewhere in the county. (Severely limiting public appearances when campaigning was a hallmark of Cleveland's style. He never appeared more than twice on the stump in any of his three runs for the White House.) Except for a twenty-foot-long banner reading "Grover Cleveland for Sheriff" hung high over a major traffic intersection, and a few newspaper editorials warning of what must befall the county if the voters turned their collective back on him, his participation in the race might have been a well-kept secret.

Buffalo was an ideal sandbox (some said cesspool) for sheriff. The city, which to all intents and purpose *was* Erie County, was home to the highest concentration of lowlife east of the Ohio River. Its seemingly inexhaustible supply of sailors, canal hands, dock workers, and run-of-the-mill drifters, be they residents or transients, produced a volume of crime that ran the gamut from simple theft to murder. To satisfy the city's basic social needs there were 673 saloons, an extravagant number in terms of the total population, and enough brothels, in addition to the freelance sidewalk trulls, to dispense service to all comers, no matter the hour. (To comply with Sabbath laws, pubs and cathouses were allowed to operate as "Sunday sacred concerts"; each could always anticipate a capacity "audience" of the dregs of Buffalo's squalid society.)

Erie County's jails had the dubious distinction of hosting more prisoners per square foot per annum than any other county jail in

New York State. Given the magnitude of the floating criminal population and the civic obligation to keep main thoroughfares at least moderately uncluttered, the city fathers preferred imposing jail terms to fines. No less dubious was the jails' collective distinction of being the most corrupt in terms of management. The new sheriff's first priority was to reverse the disorder left by his predecessors. Typical of his thoroughness: to confirm that all contractors supplied the full amount of cordwood specified instead of charging for a full load and delivering half, Cleveland personally measured the deliveries. That many of the sleazy contractors happened to be fellow Democrats was of no concern. To him they were no better than the lowest caliber of ward heeler, a species he looked down upon with contempt (and which reciprocated in kind).

What particularly impressed the folk of Erie County about their reforming sheriff—it also impressed many people beyond the county's limits—was his role in dispatching two celebrated murderers. By law, the sheriff could employ a freelance hangman or do the job himself. Cleveland preferred the second option—not because he wished to save the county money but because he would not let another man perform an abhorrent task he believed to be his moral responsibility, even though he found it "grievously distasteful."[19]

Cleveland did not oppose capital punishment; he did, though, detest the circus atmosphere in which it was customarily carried out in Buffalo. On both occasions, all sensation-seekers were barred from the premises, which were sheathed with canvas to block the view of spectators who had been jockeying since dawn for position on the surrounding housetops. Cleveland had the prisoner brought to the scaffold, and positioning himself at a point where he could not see him, personally sprang the trap. The public was disappointed at being denied these macabre spectacles. The politicians were impressed.

It was around this time that Cleveland suffered the simultaneous loss of his brothers Richard and Lewis (known in the family respectively as Cecil and Fred). Like Grover, the two were bachelors. Fred, the younger and more successful, owned a summer resort in Fairfield, Connecticut; in winters, he and Cecil operated a popular Nassau hotel on lease from the Bahamian government. In 1872, while en route to Nassau from New York to open for the season, they were lost at sea in a ship fire. Though only thirty-one, Cecil left a substantial estate to his mother and favorite sister, Louise, including the Holland

Patent manse, which Fred had purchased for Ann years before. After a few years Cleveland sold the Fairfield property and its furnishings and gave the proceeds to Louise (their mother having by then passed on). He continued the more profitable Nassau operation until the lease ran out. As was his custom when discharging responsibility, Cleveland made himself familiar with every aspect of the hotel's management, the better to deal intelligently with the on-site managers and Bahamian colonial authorities.

When his three-year term as Erie County sheriff ended toward the close of 1873, Cleveland declined a second term. He had earned $40,000, a heady sum for the time and added to his reputation as a reform-minded law-and-order man. Given the many inferior associates and sordid tasks that came with the territory, he believed that another three years might prove to be politically disadvantageous. Besides, he wished to resume his law practice. With Lyman Bass and Wilson S. Bissell, he formed a new firm, with offices in the Weed Block, a prestigious professional office building at the busy intersection of Main and Swan Streets. Called Bass, Cleveland and Bissell, the firm became Cleveland & Bissell when Bass went to Congress, developed tuberculosis, and moved to Colorado. It was subsequently reorganized as Cleveland, Bissell & Sicard. George J. Sicard, a graduate of Hamilton College, was a man of refinement and scholarly tastes with whom Cleveland formed a close lifelong friendship. While he played an advisory role in Cleveland's subsequent political career, it was Bissell who would function as Cleveland's man-on-the-scene in Buffalo during his Albany and White House years.

"Shan" Bissell, who had known Cleveland since 1868 when he was taken on as clerk in what was then the firm of Laning, Cleveland & Folsom, became Cleveland's lifelong closest friend and confidant, the only Buffalo friend to serve in either Cleveland presidency, and the recipient of more letters from the epistolary-oriented Cleveland than anyone else in his extended network of correspondents. In 1892, responding to a request from George Parker, who was writing a campaign brochure on Cleveland's early years, Bissell recalled Cleveland's being "generally the first one in the office in the morning and the last one out at night, and all the hours of these long days were devoted with patience and zeal to the work he found before him." During a trial, he went on, Cleveland "would devote himself to the case absolutely and completely, whether it was large or small, whether with fee or without, and for a rich client or for a poor one." While he often received large fees for his professional services, when it came to indigent clients he "tried many a case without fee or the expectation of it, and often intervened to prevent the doing of injustice because of his hatred of injustice."

Around the Buffalo law courts, Cleveland was esteemed for his willingness to advise young lawyers, often assisting with complicated cases even if it meant minimal remuneration, or even none at all. Among the judges, his reputation for fairness and integrity was such that he was frequently called upon to serve as impartial third party when a complex or exceedingly difficult case was before the court.[20]

Still in his thirties, and pursuing successfully a career that he loved free from financial worry, Cleveland was now in a position to devote more time to the enjoyment of life, and few things gave him greater enjoyment than good beer, good food, and the avoidance of regular exercise. A preferred recreation of choice was to spend Sunday evenings at Schenkelberger's, his favorite saloon, overindulging himself on sausages and sauerkraut. Consequently he became fat to the point of obesity. Still, he enjoyed excellent health, and his large frame (he stood an inch over six feet) carried all that poundage without his appearing grotesque (though it was observed that when seated in a chair he lacked the freedom to effect a change of position). Except that his sandy brown hair was beginning to thin at the top, his physical traits were by now fixed: pale blue eyes beneath heavy lids, strong Roman nose above a drooping brown mustache, strong jaw with double chin, and large hands with sausagelike fingers, complemented by a tenor voice that was flat in tone and cadence yet penetrating, and a complexion that was surprisingly pallid for a man who enjoyed such outdoor pursuits as hunting and fishing.[21]

Cleveland was not known to court any woman; his preference was for the occasional dalliance. One object of his attentions—and the attentions of a number of his cronies—was Maria Halpin, a merry widow newly arrived in town. Let us defer the sordid tale of Maria's involvement in Cleveland's life until we come to his first presidential campaign—which she, albeit unintentionally, helped to make perhaps the dirtiest in America's political history.

Once asked within the family if he ever thought of marriage, Cleveland cracked: "A good many times; and the more I think of it, the more I think I'll not do it." A few years later his sister Susan asked the same question. This time he replied: "I'm only waiting for my wife to grow up." Susan thought he was being facetious. As we shall see, he wasn't.

Cleveland's ideas on social relaxation did not extend to the parlor or the theater. He much preferred the hotel lounge or the saloon, where he enjoyed favorite card games like pinochle, poker, and something called "sixty-six." If the mood was upon him, he'd engage in ribald conversation. Outdoors, he preferred fishing on the Niagara River, hunting, and horse races, especially in the company of close friends like Sicard, Bissell, and Folsom. Ever the workaholic, he rarely took what might pass for an extended vacation; the occasional ten days or two weeks of duck hunting or bass fishing was his limit. Ever the faithful son, he spent periodic weekends back at Holland Patent, dancing attendance upon his mother and gossiping with the villagers. Ever the provincial, he had as little curiosity about travel as he did about professions other than the law; it was not until his White House years that he first saw the Mississippi River. Ever the sartorial dandy, he never appeared in public unless his dress was exactingly correct—invariably black broadcloth, faultless linen, and top hat. (Buffalo legend has it that once he was actually seen fishing thus attired.)[22]

Cleveland limited his personal client list to a few local corporations. When his law partner Laning died in 1881, the New York Central, whose general counsel for western New York Laning had been, offered Cleveland the lucrative position. Though his income would increase substantially, and the added prestige would raise him to the first rank among corporation attorneys not only in the state but throughout the East, Cleveland turned the offer down. He could not abide the idea of running to catch trains, staying in strange hotels, and preparing cases under pressure for hurried presentation. His savings now totaled $75,000, a somewhat remarkable sum at the time for a self-made man, so money was of no consideration. He wanted to be his own man, free to decide which cases he cared to handle. He could not see himself at the beck and call of a large corporation, trying cases on terms other than his own. The decision would in time prove to have been a fateful one. Had he gone with the New York Central, Cleveland would never have agreed to run for mayor of Buffalo (he probably would never have been asked!) and his political career would have ended with his résumé showing he had held but one elective office: sheriff of Erie County.

As for participating in Buffalo's civic affairs, Cleveland was too busy—or perhaps too uncaring. Affiliations were limited to the bar association, the City Club (which he and a group of Buffalo's most prominent business and professional men founded in the mid-1870s), and, toward the end of the 1870s, the Beaver Island Club, a private sports club he helped found that bought an island in the Niagara River where the members built a clubhouse and facilities for boating, fishing, swimming, and duck-hunting. He continued as a Democrat in good standing, attending ward meetings and city conventions, serving on party committees, and giving advice on the composition of political tickets when asked, but he attended no local or state conventions.

To sum up: by the age of forty-four, Grover Cleveland had abandoned the active pursuit of a political future. He still entertained the idea of a judicial appointment. But such an appointment, he insisted, must be prompted by his record before the bar, not by his soliciting public office. He was eminently satisfied with his private life and his law career; he neither looked for nor anticipated anything else for the remainder of his days. No one, not even Cleveland himself, could have foreseen he stood now on the threshold of a remarkable career; that within three and a half years he would be elected mayor of Buffalo, governor of New York, and President of the United States.

PART II

1881—1884

7
The Veto Mayor

Its prewar population of eighty thousand now doubled, and now a principal manufacturing center and East Coast port, Buffalo was arguably the only major American city where civic corruption was a bipartisan enterprise. Dominating the council of aldermen was a "ring" made up of Democrats and Republicans alike, no matter the outcome of any given election. The various mayors were, by and large, morally tolerable men; certainly as moral as they could be, given the circumstances. Though willing to wink at the rampant graft that was not so much a political prerogative as a philosophical article of faith, they could not properly be called crooks. Rather, they could be called incompetents. Cleveland worked to elect Democrat Solomon Scheu, a Bavarian-born brewer whose strongest suit was incorruptibility, and whose weakest suit was a disinclination to meddle in the city council's machinations. Scheu's successor was a Republican brick manufacturer whose integrity was above reproach but whose disinterest in reform was beneath contempt.

Since Democratic and Republican traditionalists connived to run Buffalo as they saw fit, it was logical that reform elements in both parties collude to rectify matters. The demand for reform, long heard in the land like the canonical voice of the turtle, reached epidemic proportions when it was pointed out to the concerned citizenry that dispensing with complaisant brewers and brick makers and electing aggressively honest men and rooting out the malefactors was an idea whose time had finally come.

In 1881, Republican party regulars nominated a malleable hack named Milton C. Beebe. The reform element, whom they dismissed as "Ishmaelites," "scratchers," "mutineers," and "croakers," approached their Democratic analogues with the notion of starting a third party. The reform Democrats found the idea potentially suicidal, but soon gave in to the argument that the only hope for Buffalo—and for the party—lay in selecting an honest candidate the "Ishmaelites" could get behind. They selected "Big Steve" Cleveland.

Big Steve wasn't interested. He had a heavy caseload, in addition to a number of trusts he was personally handling; he was still thinking in terms of an eventual judgeship; and being mayor of so corrupt a metropolis was hardly the sum of his ambition. Hoping to buy time while friends changed his mind, the Democrats manipulated their convention to select its entire slate except head of the ticket. After an intense barrage that he reconsider, Cleveland sent word that he might—not definitely, just might—run if the devious and corrupt Democratic "boss" John C. Sheehan, who was seeking the second-spot office of comptroller, was bounced from the ticket. This posed a problem: Sheehan was boss of the voter-heavy first ward, a mostly working-class Irish constituency. Besides, he was ringmaster of that year's nominating circus.

A miracle was wanted. A miracle was what the reformers got—courtesy of, of all people, Boss Sheehan. He convinced the old-line regulars that going along with the reformers would not only counteract all the tumult for change they were raising among a sympathetic press and concerned citizenry, it would, presupposing Cleveland's defeat, reveal the whole reform movement as no more than a bizarre chimera best relegated to the realm of bad remembrance. Confident he was backing a dead horse, Sheehan bowed out and encouraged Cleveland's candidacy.

Cleveland was pleading a case before Justice Albert Haight when a committee arrived from Tivoli Hall, where the Democrats were convening, to ask officially if he would accept the nomination. According to Judge Haight, Cleveland conversed with the committee briefly, then approached the bench and told the judge, "Those men are a committee from the Democrat city convention. They want to nominate me for mayor, and they come to see if I'll accept. What shall I do about it?"

Replied Judge Haight, "I think you had better accept. The Republicans have gotten into a tangle. A good many are dissatisfied with the candidate nominated. Your chances may be pretty good."

"But," Cleveland objected, "I'm practicing law and don't want it interfered with."

"The mayoralty is an honorable position," Judge Haight said. "We are all interested in having a good city government. You're an old bachelor. You haven't any family to take care of. I'd advise you to accept."[1]

In the meantime the convention had adjourned to a pub beneath Tivoli Hall to wet their collective whistle while awaiting Cleveland's decision. Around four-thirty, a committeeman rushed in and shouted joyfully that he had accepted. The delegates toasted their success and then went back upstairs to hear Daniel Lockwood, a leading party elder, put Cleveland's name into nomination. (Lockwood became a footnote in history as the man who nominated Cleveland for the governorship and presidency as well.) Barely was the nomination carried by acclamation when Cleveland entered the hall to a standing ovation. After accepting the nomination he spoke extemporaneously:

He had hoped "for personal and private considerations" that their choice "might fall upon some other and worthier member" of the party. The question of his acceptance was "a difficult one." But as he was a Democrat, "and no one has a right, at this time of all others, to consult his own inclination as against the call of his party and fellow-citizens, and hoping that I may be of use," and, moreover, to support their "effort to inaugurate a better rule in municipal affairs," he was accepting the nomination. He declared that much could be done, adding that "when we consider that public officials are the trustees of the people, and hold their places and exercise their powers for the benefit of the people, there should be no higher inducement to a faithful and honest discharge of a public duty."[2]

Three years later, when seeking the presidency, Cleveland asked journalist William Hudson to write the official campaign brochure. Seeking an appropriate slogan, Hudson recalled that the party's 1876 national platform had contained the words "presidents, vice-presidents, judges, senators, representatives, cabinet officers—these and all others in authority are the people's servants. Their offices are not a private perquisite; they are a public trust." Hudson studied Cleveland's speeches and noticed he had echoed this idea on several occasions: when accepting the mayoral nomination; in his first annual message as mayor ("We are the trustees and agents of our fellow citizens, holding their funds in sacred trust"); and when accepting the nomination for governor ("Public officers are the servants and agents of the people, to execute laws which the people have made and within the limits of a constitution which they have established"). From these sentiments Hudson created the phrase "Public Office Is a Public Trust," and took it to Cleveland for his consideration. "Where the deuce did I say that?" asked the governor. "You've said it a dozen times publicly, but not in those few words." "That's so. That's what I believe. That's what I've said a little better because more fully." "But," said Hudson, "this has the merit of brevity, and that is what is required here. The question is, Will you stand for this form?" "Oh, yes," replied Cleveland eagerly. "That's what I believe. I'll stand for it and make it my own."[3]

Cleveland accepted the nomination conditional on a brace of irrevocable ground rules: there was to be no purchase of votes on his behalf, and he would not personally canvas any of the saloons. Though such procedures were customary, Cleveland stood firm. It made no difference. Of the 26,648 votes cast, he won with a 3,592 majority. It helped that many of the leading Republican newspapers either openly supported him or declined to oppose him. In so doing, they started, albeit unwittingly, a tradition of sorts:

Grover Cleveland's becoming governor of New York and President of the United States would owe more to reformers within the Republican party than to the hidebound element within his own Democratic party.

Incumbents could retain their private sources of income, as the office paid only $2,500 a year. Cleveland arranged with his partners to handle his law business, with the understanding that he was always available for consultation so long as no conflict of interest was involved, and then set about to effect a sweeping program of municipal reform. Any suspicions, and there were a plethora, that the new mayor would give lip service to reform and then tolerate business as usual were laid to rest when he announced he was dispensing with the usual inauguration festivities and would be at his desk early the next morning—and expected all other municipal employees to be at theirs. What's more, the tradition of municipal offices closing early was abrogated, as was the customary practice of a full day's pay for a half day's work.

Cleveland's planned approach to the office was apparent in his inaugural address, of which the most pertinent passage was his inalterable conviction that elected officials "hold the money of the people in our hands, to be used for their purposes and to further their interests as members of the municipality." Too, it was "quite apparent" that when monies gleaned from the taxpayers went, as they say, south, instead of toward programs for which they were intended, "or when, by design or neglect, we allow a greater sum to be applied to any municipal purpose than is necessary, we have, to that extent, violated our duty."[4]

Within weeks of taking office, Cleveland not only started to clean up city hall, he started to clean up the city as well, literally. High on his list of priorities was public health. Thirty-six percent of all deaths reported that year were from "diseases, dependent, in some degree at least, upon surrounding conditions . . . and preventable." The board of health cited insufficient sewerage as the chief cause. Cleveland proposed a simple remedy: seal off all communal wells, improve the sewer system, and bring water from the Niagara River into every house through an adequate underground aquaduct. Told that the city engineers were preoccupied with routine duties, he suggested entrusting the project to a blue ribbon citizens' commission to award contracts based on competitive bidding—a first for Buffalo—and oversee construction.

The aldermen were distressed. They had already passed a bill awarding a five-year, $422,500 contract to one George Talbot, the darling of Buffalo's unscrupulous politicians, despite considerably lower competitive bids. Even the town idiot knew that a $50,000 payoff had been earmarked by Talbot for those aldermen with the deepest pockets. Cleveland was having none of it. In what became celebrated as his "Plain Speech Veto," he said there was "a time for plain speech," and then "plainly stated" his objection to the proposed contract, which he defined as "the culmination of a most bare-faced, impudent, and shameless scheme to betray the interests of the people."[5]

"Rarely," the *Buffalo Courier* editorialized, "have we heard such a universal and unanimous round of applause as that which everywhere yesterday greeted Mayor Cleveland's message." That applause helped convince the aldermen they might have erred in ignoring the bid of one Thomas Maytham, which had come in at $109,000 under Talbot's. Maytham was awarded the contract, the mayor's blue ribbon commission was installed, and Buffalo's clean water and sewage problems were resolved. There was even a bonus of sorts: Cleveland backed up the board of health's call to remove filthy dairies in which cows were being fed on waste waters from a local distillery.

Cleveland not only saved the city hundreds of thousands of dollars by insisting upon competitive bidding on all projects, he scrutinized every aspect of municipal expenditure. Just as he once counted cords of wood for the country jails to ascertain honest compliance by honest vendors, so did he check all contractors' invoices to ascertain that the only goods paid for were the goods ordered, and that nothing was ordered that was not needed. Money that would have wound up in corrupt hands now wound up funding such legitimate needs as improving rundown residential districts, extra funds for the severely underpaid city clerks, and the like.

Child welfare was a particular concern to Mayor Cleveland. He strongly backed the request by the Society for the Prevention of Cruelty to Children for a protective ordinance. "No pretext should be permitted to excuse allowing young girls to be upon the streets at improper hours," he insisted, "since its result must almost necessarily be their destruction." As for young boys of indigent families, Cleveland believed they should be encouraged to help out at home by taking jobs, but not jobs that might necessitate their being "in the street at late hours, to [their] infinite damage morally, mentally and physically, and to the danger of society."[6]

Six months after taking office, the Veto Mayor, as Cleveland was now known (he was also called "His Obstinacy, Grover of Buffalo"), was attracting attention beyond the bounds of Erie County.

For years, the people of New York's western region had been seeking to elect a governor from their area; they deemed it insupportable that the prize kept going to the powerful downstate wings of both major political parties. They now began to see in Buffalo's incumbent mayor a strong possibility to be the second governor in the state's history to come from west of the Genesee. That view was catalyzed when one of Buffalo's leading papers ran an editorial endorsing the idea.[7] Written by the paper's editor, Charles McCune, it started touting Mayor Cleveland to the Democratic state committee, of which

McCune was also a member, as the best man for the job. Adding his voice to the mayor's praises was the incumbent governor of New York, Alonzo B. Cornell—a Republican. Their paths had never crossed until only weeks before, as a consequence of the Flanagan murder case.

In and of itself, the Flanagan case was of no greater significance than countless others to be found in the annals of New York State's criminal justice system. Its true significance lay in convincing Grover Cleveland that he just might be meant for a more exalted public office than that of mayor. Martin Flanagan, a Buffalo grain elevator scooper, had been sentenced to death for the murder of his foreman, one John Kairns; the verdict was upheld on appeal. As Flanagan's execution date drew near, he became the chief local topic of conversation. Suspecting that Flanagan had been denied a fair trial by an overly zealous district attorney, Cleveland secured a three-week stay of execution from Governor Cornell to permit scrutiny of the facts. After meticulously poring over the arrest record and trial transcript, he discovered that one of Flanagan's counsels, the one scheduled for summing up, was so intoxicated his co-counsel, who was inept at summations, had to do so without notice—and made a mess of it. Flanagan had done the deed with a short-bladed Barlow knife "no one would have thought to be a deadly weapon," Cleveland discovered. "Moreover, he stabbed the victim in the right side, ignorant of the fact that the latter had, remarkably, a displaced heart, which was thus pierced."

Cleveland decided he must go to Albany to plead for the life of the doomed man before the governor. Along with him went most of the jury that had convicted Flanagan (now persuaded they would not have done so, were all the facts known), a few eyewitnesses, lots of affidavits and ancillary documents, and the district attorney, who was determined to defend the conviction. Cornell, who rarely granted executive clemency, received them all coolly, especially the Democratic mayor.

The latter presented the facts of, and circumstances surrounding, the crime, a review of the trial, and reasons for questioning the verdict. Cornell was not impressed. Cleveland then presented affidavits, letters, and papers to support his case, followed by the jurors' recommendation that the conviction be set aside. Asked by Cornell to present the case for the prosecution, the district attorney insisted that the evidence justified the verdict and that subsequent appeals had revealed no factual errors or technical irregularities. Convinced that enough had been said, Cornell decided he needn't hear any rebuttal from Cleveland. Cleveland decided otherwise. Jumping to his feet, he told Cornell—shouted at him, actually—"We come to you as to a king, pleading for mercy! It is your duty to hear us to the end!" Cornell was so taken aback, he allowed Cleveland to present his argument along with those of the other petitioners.

Some months later, while chatting with a reform-minded friend, Governor Cornell mentioned "a remarkable man in Buffalo" and his appeal in Flanagan's behalf: "It was a cold, dispassionate presentation of the unfortunate circumstances under which the killing was done, the provocation, and the shadow of presumptive justification for the act. [I] was so impressed with the sincerity and the legal cocksureness of the man that I commuted the sentence."[8]

Cornell's remarks received wide play, reinforcing what many prominent state Democrats were now suspecting—that the man who had won the Buffalo mayoralty with the help of reform-minded Republicans just might possibly win the New York governorship with like assistance.

8

"Let me rise or fall"

It is one of the great ironies of American political history that the man ultimately responsible for Grover Cleveland's becoming first New York State's, then the United States' chief executive was his Republican presidential predecessor, Chester Alan Arthur.

Only twenty-two years after the Republicans established themselves as one of the nation's two major political parties by electing Abraham Lincoln, the New York branch was in disarray, because of an imprudent act of interference by the nation's fourth "accidental President." Hoping to foil the reelection of Alonzo Cornell, with whom he shared a mutual detestation, Arthur persuaded Charles J. Folger, his Treasury Secretary, to contest Cornell for the nomination. Arthur had taken Folger from the New York Court of Appeals only a few months earlier and put him at Treasury. This was seen as a move to strengthen Folger for the gubernatorial race, a win that would strengthen the Vermont-born Arthur's position in his adopted state when he sought election to the White House in his own right two years down the line. To guarantee Folger's nomination, delegates to the state convention were coerced, in some cases bought off. Where lawful, key public officials were replaced by Arthur's people.

This so infuriated the Independents and reform Republicans, who despised Arthur to begin with and resented Folger's letting Arthur manipulate him for his own devious purposes, that they hinted at a willingness to back any reform-minded Democratic candidate of proven probity. Trouble was, neither of the two announced Democratic aspirants qualified. Roswell P. Flower, choice of the upstate leaders, was a successful financier and ex-congressman whose wealth, and the promise of a whopping campaign donation, was what most commended him. General Henry W. Slocum, downstate Brooklyn's choice, was an older, more prosaic gentleman whose celebrated Civil War record was based on his having led one wing of Sherman's army in its fabled March to the Sea.

The Albany-based state Democratic organization threw its support to Slocum—less out of conviction than prejudice. Daniel Manning, rapidly emerging as the party's true power in succession to the ailing Samuel Tilden, detested Flower, partly for having opposed him on a number of state matters, but primarily for soliciting the support of Tammany Hall, the party's powerful downstate faction and the Albany faction's implacable enemy. The nearer the election drew, the less appealing the lackluster Slocum seemed as a candidate to the Albany group. When Tammany endorsed him, the Tilden-Manning faction, in collaboration with the powerful Erie County Democrats—who detested Slocum and thought even less of Flower—began to eye the reform-minded Buffalo mayor, of whom such good things were being heard of late, as the man all factions should unite behind.

Enter now Edgar K. Apgar, a brilliant young Albany orator and political organizer and one of the most brilliant of Tilden's acolytes. Apgar's many duties included ferreting out up-and-coming Democratic talent, mostly by reading newspapers from around the state. In the spring of 1882, turned off by Slocum and fearful the party might nominate Flower, Apgar concentrated on the Buffalo papers, then celebrating almost daily its mayor's accomplishments.

Adding his voice in support of a Cleveland candidacy was yet another powerful young Democratic leader, David B. Hill, former speaker of the assembly and now mayor of Elmira. The politically ambitious Hill, who had yet to meet Cleveland, was eager to be lieutenant governor, envisioning that office as a springboard for the governorship and then the presidency. As he saw it, Cleveland was the man to provide that springboard. (Asked one day by a fellow pol, "Who do you figure will be our candidate for governor?" Hill responded, "I've been looking the ground over, and it looks to me as if it would be this man Cleveland." "Cleveland?" asked the pol. "Who in hell is *Cleveland?*")[9]

Militating in Cleveland's favor, his reputation as a reformer was untainted by past political quarrels or factional loyalties. Moreover, as prominent partisans like Daniel Lockwood and ex-mayor Scheu argued, it was even possible that Governor Cornell might throw his considerable Republican weight against President Arthur's imposed choice to succeed him. Manning now charged Apgar with ascertaining how much strength there might be in a pro-Cleveland movement.

In July—we are now in the summer of 1882—Cleveland rushed to Holland Patent on learning that his mother was critically ill. During his absence a number of Buffalo friends quietly launched a drive to gain him the nomination. Though aware, Cleveland made no mention of it. According to a friend, "During those last sad days of waiting, no one would have supposed any political ambitions were in his mind. Never once, during the last two weeks of her illness, did he leave the home town; and when the many letters and telegrams arrived, he answered them with no apparent concern, so that even the family group were not aware of the possibilities that lay so definitely before him."[10] Ann Cleveland died on July 19. By the time her son returned to Buffalo the "boom" for his nomination, led by the *Buffalo Courier*, was under way.

Cleveland was no Cincinnatus awaiting a call to arms he would accept only with reluctance. Neither was he prepared at this time to take an active part in the efforts of his supporters. But he did not discourage them. He was the party's candidate for a judgeship in his district, and believed that being prominently mentioned in connection with the state race would redound to his advantage in that contest. This might come across as either terribly naive or terribly cynical. But Cleveland honestly believed his chances for winning the nomination were minimal, especially against the popular General Slocum, yet was somewhat confident of winning the judicial post.

Apgar wrote Cleveland on August 23 suggesting he meet with Manning. In truth, it was not so much a suggestion as a royal summons. With Tilden in retirement, Manning was now the all-powerful chairman of the New York State Democracy (as the Democratic Party was commonly known). And without a face-to-face meeting, there was just so much he could learn about the man so many people were touting as the party's best—perhaps only—hope to win the statehouse. Apgar began by assuring Cleveland—whom he too had yet to meet—that the feeling in Albany among the party hierarchs was that he was their man (an opinion "confirmed and strengthened by time and thought"). While he "understood" Cleveland was not actively seeking the gubernatorial nomination, he was "sure that a conference with Mr. Manning would simplify the situation and enable everybody interested to reach the proper conclusion."

Apgar then appealed to Cleveland's moral obligation to the cause of democracy: "The Democratic party has so often, in recent years, abandoned its principles and made dishonest alliances for the sake of temporary success, which even in most cases it has failed to secure, that it has, naturally, largely lost the confidence of the people." Apgar concluded: "The weakness of our present position, in which we seem to depend more upon Republican dissensions and decay than upon any strength of our own, is, I think, much more due to our failures in the directions I have indicated than it is to any personal or factional quarrels which have existed among us."[11]

After pondering the letter and discussing the situation with a number of close friends, Cleveland replied that neither his "acquaintance in political circles" nor his "standing in the State Democracy, would for a moment suggest my name as a proper one to head the ticket." Were it not for his "abiding faith in the success of an honest effort to perform public duty," even *he* would "at times distrust my ability to properly bear the responsibilities . . . in case of election."

Having thus dispensed with the proper protestations of modesty, Cleveland felt "entirely certain" that total freedom "from the influence of all and any kind of factional disturbances, might make me an available candidate." Too, he felt that if nominated he "could be the instrument of bringing about the united action of the party at the polls," and thus be "of great value to the people and to the party." As for calling on Manning, however, he had to "admit" that his "impulse was at once to find my way to him by way of showing my respect for his position in the party, and the regard I have learned to entertain for him as a gentleman."

But, should they meet at this time it would "surely be falsely *alleged,* that an understanding has been arrived at between us, and pledges made which make me his man." And, he asked rhetorically, wouldn't this "lying interpretation be used in answer to the claim that I am free from any alliances? Might not the friends of other candidates claim that one who was proclaimed as a free candidate, and yet had an understanding with Mr. Manning, or his friends, ought not to be nominated? What would be the effect of such an appeal on the convention, or afterward on the election?" There ought not, of course, "be any foundation for apprehensions of this kind," but Cleveland could not "rid myself of these reflections." He concluded by asking Apgar, "as one who has kindly said that he favors my nomination, whether it is not more likely to occur, and whether, if it does, the chances of our election will not be better, if this visit is not made as you suggest."[12]

The letter was shrewd—indeed, masterful—artifice on Cleveland's part, the sort of thing a consummate politician like Manning could appreciate (as he in fact did). Cleveland had by now concluded that his being elected governor was if not probable, then at least possible. To call upon Manning now would earn him the hostility of Tammany Hall, which was congenitally incapable of cooperating with the party's Albany-based branch. Also, such a meeting would raise suspicions in the Slocum camp, without whose goodwill a squabble for the nomination could be suicidal for the party. For now, Cleveland would thoughtfully assess his position. He asked those acting in his behalf to do likewise.

Meanwhile, he moved quietly to have his lieutenants canvas the upper part of the state. Moving not so quietly were the local Democrats and pro-Republican Independents, whose ambition to send the mayor of Buffalo to Albany was by now the worst-kept secret north of Manhattan Island. In the capacious garden of Buffalo reform Republican leader George Urban, Cleveland met somewhat covertly with his advisers and boosters to plan pre-convention strategy.

Manning and the party hierarchy at Albany were pleased; so much so, they solicited Cleveland's input on the choice for lieutenant governor. As he was from Buffalo, Cleveland suggested, it would be unwise to have the second man on the ticket from the same general area. Mayor Hill of Elmira was to him acceptable. Only a Cassandra could have foreseen that Cleveland thereby gave a big boost up the political ladder to the man who was to become in time his most implacable political foe.

Cleveland realized he could never win without organizational backing; that he must appeal, if at all humanly possible, to all factions of the party, in particular the all-powerful, consistently cantankerous Tammany Hall. Equally vital, he must show the Independents and reform Republicans he was a man for all parties. By the time the state nominating convention met at Syracuse on September 21, his troops, with Cleveland operating behind the scenes, had succeeded in doing just that. Remarkably, he won the nomination without incurring any political debts. He had played the game well, throwing out hints of cooperation with the quarrelsome factions without committing himself to any "deals." Cleveland may have been a new kid on the political block, but all agreed that only a fool would dismiss the kid as a political neophyte.

After winning the nomination and meeting at last with Manning (each felt an immediate admiration and respect for the other), Cleveland paid the obligatory courtesy call on Tilden. Though he disliked Tilden for a number of unsavory stunts he'd pulled as an attorney and for his shady political allies in Erie County, Cleveland did admire the old man's intellect and legal mind, and, above all, his courage as a reform governor. According to a confidant, Tilden found the party's nominee to be "of somewhat coarse mental fibre and disposition," but "of great force and stubbornly honest in his conviction." Later asked, "What sort of man is this Cleveland?" Tilden replied, "Oh, he is the kind of man who would rather do something badly for himself than to have somebody else do it well."[13]

Consonant with his pledge to the people of Buffalo not to ignore his mayoral responsibilities, Cleveland did not campaign actively. The voters seemed not to care. He won by a 192,854-vote majority, surely no mean achievement for a man who until recently had barely been known outside his own county. Not only did many Republicans abandon Arthur's hapless puppet for his Democratic opponent, so did many party leaders, along with many hard-core Republican newspapers. Further help—perhaps the most crucial—came from a totally unexpected source: thousands of James Gillespie Blaine partisans. Because they hated Arthur and would not support Folger, but could not bring themselves to cross party lines, this powerful Republican faction sat out the election. In light of how the man they helped to elect governor of New York would wreck their champion's presidential ambitions two years later, Blaine's people would have been well advised to go with Arthur's man.

In a letter to his brother William on election day, Cleveland admitted to being "troubled" over being able to "well perform my duties, and in such a manner as to do some good to the people of the State." He knew himself to be "honest and sincere in the desire to do well." But the question was "whether I *know enough* [emphasis in the original] to accomplish what I desire." He vowed to define the office he had just won as "a business engagement between the people of the State and myself, in which the obligation on my side is to perform the duties assigned me with an eye single to the interest of my employers." He concluded on a poignant note: if their mother were alive he "should feel so much safer." He added, "I have always thought her prayers had much to do with my success."[14]

Discovered alone in his office next morning by a friend, the governor-elect remarked, "I have only one thing to do, and that is to do it right." Then he added after a moment, "Let me rise or fall, I am going to work for the interests of the people of the State, regardless of party or anything else."[15] Here was a remark the more skeptical voter might expect from even the most sanctimonious politician riding the crest of victory. Coming from Grover Cleveland, it had the resonance of a sacred vow.

9

A laundry list of promises

Cleveland resigned as mayor, turned his law practice over to Bissell and Sicard, and left for Albany on the last day of 1882 for his inauguration the following morning. At Manning's suggestion, he took on Daniel Scott Lamont as his political amanuensis. A protégé of Tilden's, Lamont was also a favorite of Manning, for whose newspaper, the *Albany Argus*, he was a reporter (he later acquired a financial interest); he had also been clerk of the New York Assembly and chief clerk of the New York Department of State. The thirty-one-year-old Lamont and forty-five-year-old Cleveland formed an immediate mutual admiration society that would end only with Lamont's death twenty years later. As military secretary to the governor with the rank of colonel, and, when Cleveland went to Washington in 1885, as his private secretary, Lamont functioned as faithful friend, candid critic, and closest confidant, in addition to acting as Cleveland's buffer with the press.

Cleveland's inaugural address, which Lamont helped polish, contained a laundry list of promises to the people of New York State: honesty, economy, and the application of sound business principles to the management of government; and reforms in the state militia, the insurance and banking departments, and the harbormasters' system in New York City. Also, he stressed a twofold theme dear to his heart that as President he would expand to the national level: reforms in the civil service and taxation. The promises may have sounded platitudinous, but Cleveland sincerely believed them to be what the times demanded and what he felt he could best deliver on.

Observers were impressed by Cleveland's abhorrence of the spoils system that was Andrew Jackson's bequest to American politics. None of his Buffalo friends were rewarded with appointments. Robert L. O'Brien, Cleveland's stenographer during his second presidency, recalls how one day while leaving a meeting of party leaders called to unite behind Cleveland in his third (1892) bid for the White House, Tammany boss Richard Croker remarked, "[Our] situation is not too bad. This man never does anything for his friends. But we are not his friends; he may do something for us!"[16]

Patronage appointments went to qualified men familiar with the routine and responsibility through serving in the office. Example: Cleveland named to be Superintendent of Insurance, an office traditionally reserved for retiring a political debt, a man who started in the department as a messenger and worked himself up by aptitude and rectitude. The exceedingly vocal chorus of disapproval to this and similar appointments was made up of office-seekers who followed the traditional line that political plums were obligatory recompense for services rendered. Cleveland ignored them.

His first act as governor, a purely symbolic one, was to open the Executive Mansion to all visitors, even sightseers. If, however, they sought reward for their decisive contribution (usually imagined) to his election, Cleveland's eyes would form themselves into narrow slits and his tone of voice become gelid. "I don't know that I understand you," he would say. If the offending party failed to get the message, Lamont saw that he did, along with the door.[17]

Cleveland won great respect by upholding the people's rights against the unjust demands of corporations; conversely, he was prepared to risk popular opprobrium by defending the rights of corporations when the people, misled by demagoguery or ignorance, agitated unjustifiably against them. Corporations, he believed, were "created by the law for certain defined purposes" and "restricted in their operations by specific limitations. Acting within their legitimate sphere they should be protected; but when, by combination or by the exercise of unwarranted power, they oppress the people, the same authority which created should restrain them, and protect the rights of the citizen."[18]

A preternaturally suspicious man, he accepted nothing on faith, pondering with great care each bill the legislature submitted for his signature. Those he believed to be in the public interest, he signed; those he believed to be otherwise, he vetoed; those he believed to be potentially good if properly framed, he sent back annotated with suggested emendations and the promise of his signature if they were incorporated. By the end of his first year he had racked up forty-four vetoes, having personally examined all the facts pertaining to each.

He refused to delegate such labors, a trait he would take into the White House. As a result, he dissipated time and energy on details which other executives usually leave to subordinates. But he considered the labors justified, particularly when dealing with appeals for executive clemency. Of 449 such appeals during his first year in office, all of which Cleveland reviewed in detail, he pardoned thirty-nine, commuted seventeen, granted one respite, and denied 181; the rest he carried over into his second year for further review. In crimes less than capital in nature, Cleveland never hesitated to temper justice with benevolence. He pardoned a county treasurer imprisoned for minor malfeasance on condition that he abstain from liquor for five years. And he pardoned a forger who had served only half his sentence when extenuating circumstances were brought to his attention. Very little escaped this governor's notice. Where human welfare was involved, it was addressed expeditiously, as in this letter to the Superintendent of New York Prisons two months after his inauguration:

> I deem it proper to call your attention to the provision of section 108 of the Laws of 1847, which prohibits the infliction of blows upon any convict in the State prisons or by the keepers thereof, except in self-defense or to suppress a revolt or insurrection; and also to chapter 869 of the Laws of 1869, abolishing the punishments commonly known as the "shower bath," "crucifixion yoke," and "buck." . . . I respectfully desire to avoid any injurious interference with the maintenance by prison authorities of efficient discipline, but I insist that, in the treatment of prisoners convicted of crime, the existing statutes of the State on that subject should be observed.[19]

Change of office did not mean a change in Cleveland's lifestyle. Though he now resided in a grand mansion on a hill a mile south of the Capitol, his tastes were still simple. Indeed, he did not want to occupy the mansion at all. According to William E. Dorsheimer, a close friend and author of his 1884 campaign biography, Cleveland originally planned to reside at a hotel. His friends argued that doing so would offend the people of the state, who had provided an official residence and desired to see the man they had elected governor "hedged about with the dignity which is part of his great office. Also on the grounds of expediency we showed him that it would be a mistake, for he would be overwhelmed in the easy approach hotel life would afford." Cleveland agreed to occupy the mansion. Dorsheimer thought it was "the argument of expedience, rather than the other [that] swayed him."[20]

Other than the rent and furnishings provided by the state, all expenses came out of the governor's $10,000 yearly salary. Cleveland made a few alterations, such as installing a billiards table, and converting an upper hallway, always breezy in the summer, into a makeshift office for Sunday work. One of his sisters, usually Susan until her marriage, served as housekeeper, and William Sinclair, the mulatto manservant from his Buffalo days who would serve him through the White House years, saw to details.

As governor, Cleveland's routine rarely varied: He arose at seven, had breakfast at eight, walked to the capitol, and was in his office by nine. At twelve-thirty he walked home for lunch, returned to his office an hour later, and worked till five. After an hour's chat with friends he encouraged to drop by, he walked home for dinner. (Cleveland dined out socially only when obliged to by virtue of his office.) The fare was plain; at times the economy-minded Sinclair served leftovers from official receptions. On evenings when there were no social obligations, Cleveland returned to his office, where he usually worked with Lamont from eight-thirty to almost midnight, when he would break off with the stock line "Well, I guess we'll quit and call it half a day." Some evenings he stayed on to write letters to close friends back in Buffalo or to his siblings, but usually he went straight home, accompanied to the door by Lamont or some friend who had dropped in for a brief chat. After a few hours of sleep, the routine was commenced anew. According to a local news reporter, "The eyes of the large man look glassy, his skin hangs on his cheeks in thick, unhealthy-looking folds, the coat buttoned about his large chest and abdomen looks ready to burst with the confined fat. Plainly he is a man who is not taking enough exercise; he remains within doors constantly, eats and works, eats and works, and works and eats. . . . There was not a night last week that he departed from the new Capitol before one A.M. Such work is killing work."[21] Not so for Cleveland, who, in the bargain, believed that when it came to hard work, all public officials should emulate him. In his second State of the State Address he rebuked the legislature for recessing too often.

Cleveland's practice of toiling on the Sabbath did not find favor with the pastor of the Fourth Presbyterian Church, where he had a pew. Learning that he was sorry not to see the governor at services more often, Cleveland told the messenger with a grin and wink of an eye, "Tell him that an ass fell into a pit."[22] Perhaps the pastor would himself have fallen into a pit if he knew that sometimes, on Sunday evenings, to atone for having ignored the Lord of late, Cleveland would drop into the city's Roman Catholic cathedral. But it was propinquity, not a newly cultivated attraction to Rome, that drove him there whenever he felt the need to assuage a fleeting guilt pang or two. The cathedral was within a stone's throw of the Executive Mansion.

Though he had little time for reading other than official papers,

Cleveland occasionally made time to read for his own pleasure: mostly history and biography, and poetry, which, with his congenital retentive memory, he memorized and repeated verbatim by the page. Manning's *Albany Argus*, commenting on Cleveland's prodigious memory, marveled that the "music and rhythm" of the printed word "charmed his mind. Long after he has forgotten who the author of some noble and diverting verse is . . . he can repeat them with correctness and admirable feeling if only some event or some incident in conversation makes them apposite."

As a kind of safety valve, Cleveland occasionally went off with a friend or two for a few days of fishing or duck-hunting in the Adirondacks. On even fewer occasions, he took a fishing holiday of a week's duration. Sunday afternoons were frequently given over to a session of draw poker with a twenty-five-cent limit. Should anyone remark on the incongruity of a minister's son celebrating the Lord's Day by feeding the kitty, he had a stock defense: "My father used to say that it was wicked to go fishing on Sunday, but he never said anything about draw-poker."[23]

10

The Veto Governor

The Veto Mayor of Buffalo was soon the Veto Governor of New York. (And, in due time, the Veto President. Among the hundreds of bills he refused to sign over two administrations were forty-nine he pocket-vetoed on the morning he surrendered the White House to McKinley on March 4, 1897.) Though he gladly signed a number of bills whose enactments were long overdue, it was by the bills he did not sign that Cleveland's governorship was defined. Never mind that his decision in all instances was the right one; people who see a piece of legislation they hope to exploit for personal gain about to go down the drain are rarely concerned with whether it is right or wrong, only with whether it passes or fails. Among a number of bills Cleveland vetoed despite their hometown connection was one to reorganize Buffalo's fire department. He believed it to be a partisan boondoggle. That a few of his friends supported the legislation, and stood to benefit by it, he dismissed as not worthy of consideration. Some vetoes were of bills he favored but believed to be a violation of his social contract with the people, such as one that would have let county supervisors erect soldiers' monuments. Cleveland insisted that all public monies raised by taxation were meant solely for "the safety and substantial welfare of the public"; monuments, however "worthy and patriotic," should be underwritten by charitable donation or popular subscription. He hoped that "due regard to fundamental principles and the support of the [state] Constitution will prevent the passage of a bill of this nature in the future."[24]

Of all the criticism Governor Cleveland caused by his vetoes, none was as clamorous or had such far-reaching significance as that of the five-cent fare bill. This measure to cut in half the dime fare on New York City's Manhattan Elevated Railroad typified what politicians refer to as "vote-getting legislation." Such legislation is intended to give the voter more for his money in the area of public services, thereby endearing him to his elected representative for having effected it. Among the bill's most impassioned supporters were Tammany boss John Kelly and Theodore Roosevelt: the former a political boss of the old school, the latter a twenty-five-year-old rising star of the Republican party and a leader of its reform wing.

The line was owned by Jay Gould, most nefarious of the railroad robber barons. Though a crony of Gould's, Kelly supported the bill for the obvious reason: to show his New York City supporters, all from the laboring class, that he would forgo even personal friendships in the interest of reducing their cost of living. Roosevelt, who hated Gould (and Kelly), also hoped to endear himself to his nonaristocratic constituents for the same reason. His main purpose in supporting the bill, though, was to reduce Gould's profits, which, it was generally conceded, were being stashed away for purposes of tax evasion.

Cleveland agonized over the bill even before it landed on his desk. He was all for lowering the fares, and cutting into Gould's profits. But, as he found after a characteristically painstaking study of the facts and the law involved, the proposed legislation was unconstitutional. He was "not unmindful that this bill originated in response to the demand of a large portion of the people of New York for cheaper rates," Cleveland said in his veto message. But Gould's line was serving a public need which previous railroads had failed to meet, and fulfilling its charter obligations. If Gould's profit was unreasonable, or if he was abusing his contractual rights, he must be dealt with *legally,* not *legislatively.* "The State," Cleveland insisted, "should be not only strictly just, but scrupulously fair, and in its relation to the citizen every legal and moral obligation should be recognized. This can only be done by legislating without vindictiveness or prejudice, and with a firm determination to deal justly and fairly with those from whom we exact obedience." Translation: Gould may have been a swindler, but he was as deserving of protection before the law as any paragon of virtue.[25]

"Before I was married," Cleveland later told Richard Gilder, "I used sometimes to talk to myself when I was alone, and after the veto, that night, when I was throwing off my clothes, I said aloud: 'By to-morrow at this time I shall be the most unpopular man in the State of New York!' " Next morning, he refused to look at the morning papers. He later recalled: "I didn't think that they had anything to say that I cared to see. I went through my morning mail with . . . Dan Lamont, pretending all the time that I didn't care about the papers, but thinking of them all the time, just the same. When we had finished I said as indifferently as I could, 'Seen the morning papers, Dan?' He said, 'Yes.' 'What have they got to say about me, anything?' 'Why, yes, they are all praising you.' 'They are? Well, here, let me see them!' I tell you, I grabbed them pretty quickly, and felt a good deal better."[26]

Editorial writers were quick to grasp what it took the public a while to accept: it was the *method* of the proposed bill that Cleveland opposed, not the bill itself. Only later would it come out that Cleveland used his influence behind the scenes to have the assembly revise the railroad's charter to allow for the five-cent fare. In going to the crux of the matter, Cleveland gained the respect of every honest politician, party affiliation notwithstanding. For they, like the objective newspapers on both sides of the politically ideological line of demarcation, appreciated that in ignoring the political dangers inherent in defending the people for their own good he was acting as a leader whose obligation it was to give the public what best served their interests constitutionally.

Among the first to support the veto was Roosevelt, who had "to say with shame" that in voting for the bill he had "weakly yielded, partly to a vindictive spirit toward the infernal thieves and conscientious swindlers who [controlled the] railroad [and] partly in answer to the popular voice of New York." Much as he despised Jay Gould and all his associates ("common thieves . . . part of that most dangerous of all dangerous classes, the wealthy criminal class"), Roosevelt concluded: "Now, anything the people demand that is right it is most clearly and most emphatically the duty of this Legislature to do; but we should never yield to what they demand if it is wrong. . . . If the people disapprove our conduct, let us make up our minds to retire to private life with the consciousness that we have acted as our better sense dictated."[27]

It was around this time that the two future Presidents, each the paradigm of his respective party between the Civil War and First World War (Lincoln and Wilson always excepted), formed a collegial relationship whose hallmarks were mutual admiration and mutual respect. One example of how this relationship benefited the public: Roosevelt moved the civil service reform bill, which Cleveland was eager to see passed, out of the judiciary committee, where its opponents, the Tammany-controlled downstate Democratic delegation, caused it to languish, and had it quickly passed. The relationship got derailed when Roosevelt learned Cleveland was preparing to veto a number of his bills for regulating New York City. Political journalist William Hudson, who happened to be present during their celebrated confrontation, has described Roosevelt's reaction on learning—from Hudson himself—of the proposed vetoes:

"He mustn't do that! I can't have that! I won't let him do it! I'll go up and see him at once!" With Hudson in hot pursuit, Roosevelt rushed off to the executive office, where the governor was tackling a mountain of paperwork. Hearing Roosevelt out, Cleveland patiently explained that the bills were admirable in intent, and he would like nothing better than to sign them. But they contained a number of inconsistencies that would render them legally ineffective. For instance, in the tenure of office bill one clause specified two different terms for the same officer. Also, some of the language was incomprehensible even by legal standards, though, as Cleveland hastily assured Roosevelt, a simple line-editing would make them logical and thus acceptable. But he could never sign the bills in their present form.

Whereupon Roosevelt threw one of his celebrated temper tantrums. All that mattered was "principle!" he fairly shrieked in his inimitable high-pitched voice. Besides, he raged, it was too late—and quite irrelevant—to worry about mere details. "You *must not* veto those bills!" he screamed. "You *cannot! I can't have it,* and I *won't have it!*"

Cleveland could give as well as take. "Mr. Roosevelt, I am going to veto those bills!" he roared back, slamming down a ham-hock fist on the desk with such force that Roosevelt fell back into a nearby chair, from which he muttered a feeble "Outrage!" Cleveland, who had already resumed his work, ignored him. The interview was ended. Much to Roosevelt's mortification and fury, Cleveland vetoed the tenure of office bill. The others he signed—after they were tidied up to his satisfaction. He later said of Roosevelt, "There is a great sense in a lot that he says, but there is such a cocksuredness about him that stirs up doubt in me all the time. Then he seems to be so very young."[28]

Unfortunately, the whole business ended the political partnership of this political odd couple, though they did continue to labor conjointly in the cause of reform and to share a mutual respect. After Roosevelt succeeded the murdered McKinley, Cleveland told his unofficial Boswell, George Parker, "Roosevelt is the most perfectly equipped and the most effective *politician* [emphasis added] thus far in the presidency. Jackson, Jefferson and Van Buren were not, for a moment, comparable with him in this respect." On learning of Cleveland's death, Roosevelt said, "I always regarded him as a freshman regards a senior." When leaving instructions to his official biographer, John Bucklin Bishop, toward the end of his own life, he said: "I wish you would put in all the letters of mine to him. I was very fond of the old fellow."[29]

The most significant consequence of the five-cent fare bill veto was that it perpetuated the hostility between Cleveland and Tammany Hall that at times threatened to inflict on the Democratic party what Humpty Dumpty inflicted on himself through egregious carelessness. Tammany's power and influence cannot be overstated. It worked hand in hand with men like Jay Gould, who bought legislators as if Albany were a bargain mall. And it delivered—through means more foul than fair—inordinately large blocks of votes, a plenitude of them illegal, to whomever their current boss granted his personal imprimatur.

Founded as the Society of St. Tammany or Columbian Order a few days after George Washington's inaugural, Tammany's purpose was to counter the influence of the aristocratic and propertied elements and thus represent middle-class opposition to upper-class pretensions. It was named for Tamanend, a colonial Delaware Indian chief known for his wisdom, benevolence, and love of freedom. ("Saint" was an intended anti-Catholic derision.) Officers took Indian titles; its chief was Grand Sachem, his underlings sachems; the society was known as the Wigwam (though more popularly as the Hall). Membership was at first restricted to "native-born patriots," as Tammany did not wish to fraternize with the lower economic groups, especially the Irish Catholic immigrants who poured into New York during this period. All that changed in the evening of April 24, 1817, when hundreds of them tried literally to pull down the Wigwam. In the interest of self-preservation, the rules of membership were changed. Within a few years the immigrants were sharing parity with the propertied element. Within a few more years, they were in the majority—and in control.

Letting in the immigrants proved over time to be a propitious move. They helped their economically and politically deprived fellow braves, along with those who came in their wake, to obtain naturalization. By thus increasing its numbers, Tammany increased its strength and political influence. Every naturalized citizen represented a vote—at times, two or three. Ironically, these braves became the chiefs who went on to become a—perhaps *the*—paramount factor in transmuting the gold of Tammany's initial good name and intent into the dross of political venality.

Tammany's venality realized its apotheosis in the person of William Marcy Tweed, the "boss" who supervised the plunder of New York City to the tune of more than $200 million, truly a cosmic sum for the times. Though Tweed died in jail, most of the money was never recovered; since this predated the popularity of secretly numbered Swiss bank accounts, it is believed to have wound up in the pockets of a number of Tweed confederates. Succeeding Tweed as Grand Sachem was Boss John Kelly, who would take pride of place among Grover Cleveland's *bêtes noires.*

A product of New York City's Lower East Side, Kelly came to the political fore with the rise of the short-lived avowedly anti-Catholic, anti-immigrant Know-Nothing party. His opposition won him the support of New York's large Irish and German populations, which rewarded him with a seat in Congress. Advancing steadily in Democratic politics, Kelly confirmed his hold on the predominantly Democratic Irish Catholics by marrying a niece of the nation's senior Roman Catholic prelate. He also made a sizable fortune, though it has never been established precisely how. Succeeding Tweed as Grand Sachem in 1878, Kelly preached the gospel of reform; indeed, he persuaded the leading Democratic reformers of the day—most notably Samuel J. Tilden—to join the Wigwam. But Tilden and the other reformers soon realized Kelly was one of those people to whom the idea of practicing what they preach can be at times downright ridiculous. They left the Hall and relocated to Albany, where they took over the New York State Democracy. Kelly led Tammany in cultivating an undying hatred of Tilden and, by extension, the entire Albany-run state organization.

The prospect of Grover Cleveland's becoming governor did not thrill Kelly and the other sachems; they much preferred someone from downstate and not so obsessed with the idea of reform. But they supported him in the interest of party unity and delivered the all-important New York City vote. In so doing, they assumed Cleveland would dance to their piping. After all, they reasoned, so many state legislators did. When it became obvious that they'd misread the man, Kelly and the other sachems felt they had no choice but to cut him down to size. As Kelly quickly learned to his chagrin, such a task was easier said than done. A plethora of Tammany-backed bills succumbed to Cleveland's veto—though not because the sachems backed them but because he deemed them totally unacceptable. Exacerbating matters, Cleveland shared the Tilden group's implacable hostility toward Tammany; mention of Kelly's name summoned to his mind memories of the Civil War Draft Riots, the Tweed Ring, and all other manifestations of "political gangsterism by an ignorant, venal Irish element that offended his own Anglo-Saxon tradition."[30]

Cleveland was open to some kind of *modus vivendi* with Tammany for the party's sake. Tammany wasn't. And unlike some of his presidential successors, who would do anything necessary to court their party's embarrassing wing—George Bush's and Ronald Reagan's shameful pandering to the Christian fundamentalist right comes most readily to mind—Cleveland refused to play the political whore, party consequences be damned! Tammany was interfering with his responsibilities as governor. It must be precipitately thrust aside. Ironically, while Tammany's hostility weakened Cleveland's strength in New York State it added to his strength in the rest of the country; this was particularly true in the West and South, where Kelly and his faction were held in the same regard that a cobra is held by a mongoose.

11

An exercise in circumlocution

Though he did not entertain the idea of seeking the White House, it would be fatuous to surmise that Cleveland did not at least share the view of his many friends and admirers that the possibility might be worth entertaining. But that possibility, he assumed, was chimerical at best. It was a political axiom of the times, grounded in historical fact, that no Democrat could be elected President of the United States without carrying New York State. The axiom had a corollary: the Democracy's chances of carrying the state without Tammany support were exiguous in the extreme. Tammany Hall was John Kelly's realm. And the realm was, metaphorically speaking, surrounded by a sign that read "Grover—Up Yours!" Democrats controlled the legislature, and demographics gave the Tammany-controlled downstate delegation inordinate power over their upstate political coevals.

Tammany had done its damnedest to get the five-cent fare bill passed. Leading the campaign was Kelly's point man at Albany, Senator Thomas Grady. For Tammany, the Cleveland veto was unforgivable. Vowing to bring him to heel, Kelly ordered Grady to join forces with the Republican opposition and thwart the balance of Cleveland's reform package then before the legislature. On the closing day of the session, two bills Cleveland favored (to regulate the duties of the harbormasters and reduce the operating costs of the immigration commission) were passed, and he wasted no time on nominations necessary for implementation. Grady managed to "hang up" the nominations, thus postponing the reforms until the next legislative session.

The resultant chorus of denunciation, not only by Cleveland loyalists but by the major downstate newspapers, drew from Kelly an I-swear-to-God avowal that Grady had acted without Tammany's advice; Tammany "heartily" disapproved of what Grady had done, and Kelly promised to "properly rebuke the Senator" the minute he returned home from Albany. Furthermore, Kelly wanted it "perfectly well understood" that Tammany was "in total harmony with

Governor Cleveland's reform program" and was "most anxious to make his Administration a whopping success." Kelly's avowals came as no surprise. What came as a surprise was how he managed to articulate them with a straight face.

Kelly's announcement ten days later that Tammany would renominate Grady for the state senate in the fall elections elicited from the governor the first of a string of letters that would pepper his political career: letters that were, at first blush, imprudent, ill-advised, and better burned than posted, but that Cleveland went ahead and sent anyway—which, more often than not, led to his political advantage. Writing in confidence to Kelly, the governor allowed as how he was

> anxious that Mr. Grady should not be returned to the next Senate. I do not wish to conceal the fact that my personal comfort and satisfaction are involved in the matter. But I know that good legislation, based upon a pure desire to promote the interests of the people and the improvement of the legislative methods, are also deeply involved.
>
> I forbear to write in detail of the other considerations having relation to the welfare of the party and the approval to be secured by a change for the better in the character of its representatives. These things will occur to you without suggestion from me.[31]

The Tilden-Manning factions, backed by the strong Erie County faction and just about all the other Democratic bosses around the state, not excluding the more cautious Tammany sachems, had been seeking to effect if not a reconciliation then at least a Mexican standoff between Cleveland and Kelly in the interests of party harmony. To borrow a choice Lyndon Johnson metaphor, they preferred to have John Kelly inside the tent pissing out, while Kelly preferred to be outside the tent pissing in. When Dan Lamont, insisting that tangling with Kelly could be politically suicidal, urged against sending the letter, Cleveland said with characteristic determination and finality: "Well, I'm going to!" Clearly separating himself from the Kelly crowd would enhance his standing among the Democrats beyond New York's borders.

The letter was the start of Grover Cleveland's career as a national figure. Until then, only New York was aware of his boldness in taking on so powerful and so despised a politician and machine as John Kelly and Tammany. Now the entire nation was privy to the knowledge. Perhaps if he had realized that beneath Cleveland's placid exterior there lurked a formidable political foe, Kelly might have left well enough alone. Perhaps not.

Kelly, every bit as canny as Cleveland, told no one of the letter, nor did he reply to it. Instead, he maneuvered to have Grady nominated from his old assembly district. But district leaders decided Grady was unelectable and put up their own man. Kelly next went to the contiguous district, but its leaders already had a candidate. When they refused to drop their man, and no other district would have him, Grady wisely announced his retirement—"a retirement," Cleveland chortled, "which was forced by the fact that he could not be elected."[32] As an act of retaliation, and much to the glee of a grateful Republican opposition, Kelly now sent a copy of the "Grady Letter" to Joseph Pulitzer's *New York World*, which published it but with the name of the recipient deleted—as per the recipient's agreement.

With its typical flair for the sensational—which is exactly what Kelly had counted on—the *World* played the letter up as an outrageous attempt by the governor to encroach upon the people's constitutional right to choose their own representatives. Alongside the letter it ran a hysteria-laden screed from Kelly: "All the disaffection existing in the Democratic party today in this country has its root and center in the brain" of Governor Cleveland; he had allowed "his personal spite towards Senator Grady to get the better of his judgment," though Grady had done nothing "to merit such a spirit of revenge."[33] Cleveland declined all public comment except to confirm that the letter's unnamed recipient was Kelly. Meanwhile the two rival Republican factions, the Half-Breeds and the Stalwarts, made their (transitory) peace, and on Election Day the Democrats' long-held control of the state legislature was broken (by margins of six in the senate and eighteen in the assembly).

There is no doubt that Kelly's handling of the letter was responsible in great measure for the election results. Of greater consequence, the breach in Democratic ranks was irreversible. Kelly could not have cared less. So far as he was concerned, Cleveland had caused him to lose face in the eyes of New York's political operatives by making it impossible for him to get Grady returned to Albany. Kelly's hatred of Cleveland was now absolute. He published the Grady Letter in his Tammany house organ, in facsimile, under the headline "How Harmony Fell Through in New York," and had the piece replicated in all Tammany organs throughout the state, along with an editorial expressing "indignation" and "shock" that the state's executive branch would "dare tell the good people of New York how to select their representatives." At the same time, he openly attacked and sought the defeat of four leading Democratic state senators from outside New York City and a few Democratic assemblymen. Grady got into the act with a vulgar speech to his fellow Tammanyites in which he charged that Cleveland had been bribed to veto the five-cent fare bill, a large sum of untraced cash having been transferred to him through his law partners Bissell and Sicard. It was a charge not even the Republicans took seriously.

Cleveland, again characteristically in comparable situations, remained silent. He would not come down to Kelly's level and engage in a public brawl, even though it meant defending himself, and his two close friends, against such arrant calumny. Not yet, that is. He knew, as Daniel Webster once said, "There are blows to be taken as well as blows as to be given." In late November, Cleveland received a news reporter sent to get his version of events. By now he was ready and eager to give them. Finding the governor "vigorous and buoyant," the reporter opened, "This letter of yours to Kelly has caused a great deal of talk."

> "I hold," said the Governor, "that it was the proper thing, under the circumstances, to send that letter."
>
> "You think Grady was not a proper representative to send back to the Senate?"
>
> "I do, most assuredly," Mr. Cleveland answered. "His action in the Senate has been against the interests of the people and of good government, and his ready tongue gave him power to be of great aid to bad men. I believed that the Democratic party could not afford to endorse such a course, and that his rejection would be a great benefit to the party and to the people. What's the use of

> striving for the Senate, County Democrats argue, and have Grady holding the balance of power to sell out to the Republicans?"

Asked whether he still believed the Grady Letter should have been sent, the governor replied:

> Most undoubtedly. [It] was written in the interest of the people, to better the representation in the Senate of this State. . . . It is unfortunate for the Democratic party that this "boss" system exists. While it does exist it became a necessity—a disagreeable necessity, I assure you—for me to recognize it, and consequently to address that letter to Kelly. However, the time is fast approaching when this odious system will be swept away and the voice of the people alone be recognized as potent in determining nominations to public offices.

After a brief pause, Cleveland supposed that the will of the people had nothing to do with the Grady nomination. "It began and ended with the will of Mr. Kelly, and his election after nomination depended upon the same power, bounded only by the trades and dickers that could be made with the so-called leaders, and the freedom of the field from other candidates." This was not a condition consistent with true democracy, nor was it a condition most favorable to good government, Cleveland wanted it emphasized. But he "had nothing to do with creating it. I entirely conceded it as I found it and wrote to the man who had the whole matter in his keeping. . . . If this be treason I can't see how I can escape its consequences."[34]

Cleveland not only capably presented his side of the story, he won over even more believers to his view that the limits to the power of the John Kellys of this world are finite, as are the limits to how much must be feared from tilting lances with them. Of greater consequence, though it was not his specific aim in doing so, writing the Grady Letter, along with the political dust its recipient kicked up, advanced Cleveland to the short list of Democratic possibilities for the forthcoming presidential race.

Short list or long, the call was one that Cleveland at first seemed unwilling to heed. Four months prior to the nominating convention, he was sounded out by Charles S. Fairchild, one of the party's leading strategists and financiers. Acting on Manning's behalf, Fairchild wrote to inquire if Cleveland would accept the nomination.

Cleveland's letter of reply began with the avowal that he had "but one ambition [and that was] to make a good Governor and do something for the people of the State and, by such means, benefit the party to which I belong." Though he now felt a "desire to retire from public life at the close of my present term," he was prepared to make "every allowance for a change of sentiment," as it was "absolutely certain that an endorsement by the offer of a second term" would "satisfy every wish I can possibly entertain, at all related to political life." Here Governor Cleveland was admitting "frankly not only what I don't want, but what possibly I may want." It was his "expectation," he added hastily, "that I shall be able to somewhat prepare the way for better things," and then "be relieved as one who has performed his purpose in political affairs." With this he would "be content."[35]

Was Cleveland circumlocutorily sending to party chieftains the sort of message a proper Victorian maiden might send to the suitor of her choice: "If you ask me, I shall be yours"? Probably not. Unable in all honesty to see himself as a contender for the presidential nomination, he was letting it be known he wanted a second term at Albany, to finish what he had started in his first term.

12

"Yes, I believe things are coming my way"

It had been quite a start. Under Cleveland's administration—and it was just a year old—the state's most equitable, most comprehensive civil service program was now in place. The abhorrent tradition of imposing political assessments on state employees was now prohibited. The selling off of forest lands at the source of major important streams was now illegal, thus obviating disaster to commerce on the waterways. Insurance companies were now subject to state control and supervision, to the advantage of policyholders. Sound business principles had been introduced in the construction and care of public buildings, among them a new state capitol, guaranteeing prevention of waste and extravagance. A law had been passed ensuring better administration of the immigration bureau and elimination of traditional abuses. A court of claims had been set up in which the demands of a citizen against the state could be properly determined. These achievements, said Cleveland when he opened the 1884 legislative session, "and others of less importance and prominence, may be cited in proof of the fact that the substantial interests of the people of the State have not been neglected."[36]

Weeks later, when friends predicted Cleveland's nomination for the presidency, he replied: "Go away, boys, and let me do my work as governor. You're always trying to get me into a scrape."[37] Cleveland was not being coy. His first concern was completion of his reform program, a concern now intensified by the realization that the Republican majority, in collusion with the Tammany-controlled New York City delegation, could easily override any veto; could even, for that matter, sabotage the entire program.

Still, as mention of his name in connection with the coming campaign increased, Cleveland began to suspect ("fear" would be too strong a word here) that the choice might not be his alone to make. Just three days before the state convention called to select delegates-at-large to, and map strategy for, the national convention in Chicago, journalist Frank W. Mack, in an interview with the governor, remarked that the nomination seemed to be coming his way.

"Yes," Cleveland muttered, more to himself, after a long moment; "yes, I believe things are coming this way . . . and I feel certain now that I cannot escape it." After another pause he asked, "Can you understand me—might anybody understand me—when I say that, if I were to indulge my personal impulse at this moment, I would go away into some forest, hide in some fastness where no man could reach and where this awful burden might never find me?"[38]

Based on his behavior during this period, one may, without appearing to be unduly cynical, question just precisely how far into that metaphorical forest Cleveland was prepared to go. As early as the preceding December he had been speaking out in newspaper interviews on national issues. Was he beginning to entertain hopes for the presidential nomination after all? Or was he merely taking pains to assure his continuance in the governorship?

Cleveland was a political realist. Despite the agitation for his nomination among the state's party elders and in the pro-reform newspapers, he realized his selection by the run-of-the-mill Democrats was, at the very best, a long shot. He had been governor little more than a year, hardly enough to win him a national following. Available for the nomination were a number of eligible—and eager—prospective candidates with many years' administrative experience on the state and national levels. As the convention neared, two men emerged as front-runners: Delaware's Thomas F. Bayard (Cleveland's preference) and Allen G. Thurman of Ohio (Tammany's choice). Bayard was from a minor state, and had defended secession in 1861. Thurman, who was nearly infirm, espoused fiscal policies totally out of sync with those of the Democratic majority, and his being championed by John Kelly did not go down well with party leaders nationwide, let alone statewide.

By 1884, the Democrats were not so much a national party as a mutually antipathetic group of state and sectional confederations that met quadrennially in hopes of capturing the White House. Will Rogers's great quip would have been as appropriate in Cleveland's day as it was in his own (and, indeed, in *our* own): "I belong to no organized political party. I'm a Democrat." What was needed was a man around whom the fragmented party could rally.

State Democratic leader Daniel Manning suspected Cleveland just might be that man. He was free from the taint of factional quarrels, he had no ties to any machine, and he had a proven reputation for honesty and incorruptibility, not to mention that remarkable record in only one year at Albany. In the spring of the year, Manning lined up the party behind a Cleveland candidacy, reasoning that the comparatively inexperienced governor stood a better chance than any of a dozen or so more seasoned men, all of whom, like Bayard and Thurman, were burdened with at least one or two more pieces of political baggage that could be transformed by the opposition into steamer trunks of political embarrassment.

Less than two weeks before the Chicago convention was to get under way, Cleveland in a letter to Manning reflected a sense of inevitability about the nomination. After reiterating the by now familiar avowal that he was "entirely content to remain at the post of duty which has been assigned to me by the people of the State of New York" and that he had "not a particle of ambition to be President of the United States," Cleveland pledged that if selected as the nominee, "my sense of duty to the people and my party would dictate my submission to the will of the convention." There was, however, one point on which the will of the convention could never dictate his submission: he would not, "in any condition of affairs, or under any imaginable pressure, deem it my duty to relinquish the trust which I hold for the people of my State [i.e., the governorship] in order to assume the duties of the Vice-Presidency."[39]

When the party gathered at Saratoga to select delegates for the national convention, Cleveland's backers came prepared to settle for nothing less than a delegation committed to his nomination for the top spot. Faced with bitter defiance from Tammany and its satrapies throughout the state, though, the best they could manage was an uninstructed delegation bound by the unit rule to vote for the governor as a favorite son on the first ballot. Manning suggested that they not fight for any more at this time. Get past the first ballot at Chicago, he advised, and take it from there. Tammany, he argued, would be in a weaker position at Chicago to create its unique brand of havoc than here at Saratoga. The Wigwam, for its part, was so confident of eliminating the governor after that first ballot that Kelly magnanimously supported a resolution Manning demanded that approved Cleveland's record-to-date at Albany!

A week prior to the convention, Manning sent William Hudson to Chicago to open Cleveland headquarters at the Palmer House and prepare to receive arriving delegations. Hudson carried a list of the New York delegates, arranged in three groups: those certain to support Cleveland, those sure to oppose his nomination, and those considered to be "doubtful or undeclared." Manning knew that without the last group "we cannot hope to make a successful presentation of the Governor's name." He ordered Hudson to discern "the conditions surrounding them, the influences, political, commercial and moral . . . and if they are inclined to be against us, find out why. We must subject them to pressure [but] first we must learn the sort of pressure that should be applied."[40]

At Chicago, Hudson found Kelly, Grady, and the other Tammany leaders already at work trying to undermine Cleveland. Cornering delegates and news reporters in the bars, hotel lobbies, and public toilets, on street corners, and on the convention floor itself, they falsely charged him with being an anti-Catholic, antilabor chronic dipsomaniac. They also "guaranteed" he could not possibly carry his own state. So resolved were they to stop Cleveland they urged that as a compromise the nomination go to Ben Butler and his Greenback-Labor party. Organized in 1878, and calling for such innovations as an eight-hour day and restriction on Chinese immigration, the Greenbackers did surprisingly well in their first Congressional elections, winning fourteen seats. But membership declined drastically, and the party's poor showing in the 1884 elections would hasten its collapse. Its choice of a standard-bearer was not the wisest. Known as "the Beast of New Orleans" for his heinous tactics as military governor of that city during the Civil War, and said by Abraham Lincoln to be "as full of poison as a dead dog," Butler was one of those men who have no difficulty counting their true friends on the fingers of one hand.[41]

On the Republicans' side, a few weeks previously they had rejected Chester Arthur, seeking the presidency in his own right although he was entering the terminal phase of Bright's disease (a closely guarded secret). His unanticipated conversion to reform after succeeding Garfield had alienated the conservative Stalwarts, his natural support base, while the Half-Breeds continued to distrust him for his pre–White House record on a litany of offenses, e.g., making a whopping illicit fortune as customs collector for the Port of New York. Instead, the party had turned to James Gillespie Blaine, leader of the Half-Breeds. Known to his admirers as the Plumed Knight, Blaine boasted a record in Congress that included three terms as Speaker of the House and a subsequent term in the Senate. He could also boast (if boast be the word) a reputation for having raised the concept of "conflict of interest" to an art form. Twice his party denied Blaine the nomination—preferring Hayes in 1876, and, four years later, Garfield (whom Blaine served as Secretary of State, as he would Benjamin Harrison). When he won the 1884 nomination, almost by default, a small but influential group of Independents bolted the party and organized the so-called Mugwumps.

First used by John Eliot in his Indian Bible, "Mugwump" is a corruption of *mogkiomp*, the Massachusetts Algonquian dialect word for "big man." *New York Sun* editor Charles Dana is credited with the word's coinage as political slang, to indicate one who practices party dissidence. It first appeared in that context on March 23, 1884, in the *Sun.* Maverick Republicans one and all, the Mugwumps were "virtually a new party—from 1884 to 1897 a Cleveland party. They were able to decide at least one national election [that of 1884], and their faith was to be a leavening force in politics for a long generation."[42] Mostly from Boston and New York, all from the patrician class, all prominent nationally, they included political and social reformer Carl Schurz, their self-anointed spokesman; Harvard University president Charles W. Eliot; Edwin L. Godkin, editor of *The Nation*; George W. Curtis, editor of *Harper's Weekly* and president of the Civil Service Reform Association; Charles Francis Adams, son and grandson of the Presidents, and one of the leading intellectuals and political thinkers of the time; Thomas Wentworth S. Higginson, Unitarian minister, author, and one of the earliest leaders of the abolitionist movement, and his fellow New England Unitarian James Freeman Clarke; Boston politician and educator Josiah Quincy; and immensely popular preacher Henry Ward Beecher. In fact, about the only major Republican reformer not to go with Cleveland was Theodore Roosevelt. Though he considered Blaine "a bad man," Roosevelt decided, admittedly against his inclination, and, as he conceded, against his political interest, to support the Plumed Knight because "the future of the country is safer under control of the Republican party."[43]

The Mugwumps saw their mission as a geminate one: the defeat of James Gillespie Blaine for the presidency, and an end to what they considered the corruption of the entire political system by wealthy parvenus, patronage-oriented politicians, and boss-run machines. They viewed the moral corruption permeating American politics as the root cause of the nation's ills, and James Blaine as its paradigm. They did not see themselves as an alternative to the two-party system; they were "not an organization but a mood."[44] They were convinced that political morals were more important than legislative issues; that the greatest peril the American people faced was political corruption; and that in the coming election voters must select their next Chief Executive on the basis of the candidate's character and integrity, not on the basis of obsolete political slogans. Perceived by many Americans as an avowedly elitist lot, they were mocked (primarily by Republican regulars) as a coterie of political eunuchs who fondled their silk-stocking airs and moral self-righteousness as an abbess might fondle her beads. One popular quatrain of gibberish they inspired:

> Oh, we are the salt of the earth,
> and the pick of the people too;
> We're all of us men of worth,
> and vastly better than you![45]

While the Mugwumps hardly considered Grover Cleveland "one of us" classwise, they did consider him, party notwithstanding, the only man then before the public capable of initiating the new, cleaner era in American politics that they believed to be their sacred cause and *raison d'être.* After Blaine won the nomination, the avowedly Republican *New York Times* (June 8, 1884) ran three columns of letters from "prominent and responsible Republicans" (for which read Mugwumps) urging the Democrats to nominate Cleveland. Within days, *Harper's Weekly,* one of the nation's most influential magazines, came out against Blaine. A week before the Democrats met at Chicago, it ran an editorial by George Curtis in which, speaking for his fellow Independents, he asserted Cleveland was inarguably the strongest candidate the Democrats could field, "not because of his party, but despite of [*sic*] it."[46]

The Blaine camp—which is to say the mainstream Republican party—hit critical mass when a number of reform committees in Boston and New York, the base of Mugwump strength, initiated communications with anti-Blaine factions nationwide to organize support for the Democratic ticket—with one condition: the ticket must be headed by Grover Cleveland. Tammany Hall merely hated the New York governor; pragmatic Republicans feared him. The two factions now united in what amounted to a loosely knit alliance dedicated to stopping Cleveland's nomination, concentrating their efforts on the heavy Irish vote by trying to portray him as Catholicism's greatest tribulation since Martin Luther.

The Democrats arrived at Chicago on July 8. Prominent among them was the Tammany delegation of six hundred under Boss Kelly's personal command. It was obvious even to the deaf and the blind that he had come for the specific purpose of stopping Cleveland. Kelly went on record as being "d——d!" if the party was going to nominate a man who abhorred the traditional spoils system; a man, moreover, who was dedicated to reform on every level. Most of the Kelly troops were not delegates, but minions come to sow discord. Chairman Manning arranged that the front seats on the convention floor go to the Cleveland people. In addition, he had the galleries loaded with anti-Tammany people.

As was customary among potential presidential nominees until the advent of Franklin D. Roosevelt, the first candidate to accept his party's nomination in the flesh, Cleveland did not attend the convention. But, lest he still be at this late date a stranger to some of the party regulars, especially those at far remove from Albany, a word portrait that ran in a sympathetic Boston paper was given wide currency:

> Cleveland [he was then forty-seven] is stout, has a well-fed look, is indeed a good liver, has the air of a man who has made up his mind just how he ought to behave in any position where he may find himself. He is getting bald; he is getting gray—though his white hair does not show conspicuously, as his complexion is sandy.
>
> He dresses well, carries himself well, talks well upon any subject with which he is familiar, and upon subjects with which he is not familiar he does not venture to talk at all. He has the happy faculty of being able to refuse a request without giving offense.
>
> It has been [the reporter's] fortune to see him several times during the past winter upon business in connection with some of the State institutions. He has impressed me always as one heartily desirous of getting at the bottom of any matter he may have in hand, and of acting wisely on it.[47]

After a series of failed maneuvers by Tammany to delay the nominating process until they could, if possible, erode Cleveland's strength, Grady moved that the convention release the New York delegation from the instructions imposed upon it at Syracuse. The motion was defeated resoundingly, and Cleveland's friend Dan Lockwood then put his name in nomination. Lockwood's words added up to formula rhetoric. It was Wisconsin politician General Edward Stuyvesant Bragg, in seconding the nomination, who delivered the convention's most memorable line: "They love Cleveland for his character, but they love him also for the enemies he has made!"[48]

The first ballot tally showed Cleveland 392, Bayard of Delaware 170, and Thurman 98, with the balance distributed among former Speaker of the House Samuel J. Randall of Pennsylvania and Indiana congressman Joseph E. McDonald, plus a smattering of favorite sons. That night Kelly covertly organized a stampede for Governor Thomas A. Hendricks of Indiana by conspiring with the sergeant-at-arms to pack the gallery for the next morning's session with men pledged to cry "Hendricks for president," and have the popular Hoosier appear on the convention floor just before the second ballot was taken. Hendricks, who had served in both houses of Congress, where he was a constant critic of every previous major policy, had been nominated for the presidency by every Democratic convention from 1868 on except that of 1872.

Learning of the plot, Manning sent his adjutants to alert every anti-Tammany delegate. When Hendricks appeared before the convention the galleries rang with shouts and applause—but the delegates on the floor remained mute. The Hendricks boom went bust.

On the second ballot, Randall's friends withdrew his name and McDonald's Indiana delegation threw its support to Hendricks; Illinois announced its 38 votes for Cleveland, and New York added its 72 over Tammany's frenzied objections. When the roll call ended, though Cleveland's strength was formidable he still lacked the required two-thirds majority. All the delegations now fairly tripped over one another in the rush to switch their votes and hop on the bandwagon. The revised ballot gave Cleveland 683 votes, 136 more than the number needed for nomination. Kelly and his troops sat in total dejection as delegates and observers joyously echoed Governor Bragg's tag line, "We love him for the enemies he has made!" When order was restored, the highly popular Hendricks was nominated for the vice presidency by acclamation. The convention was adjourned after a lusty rendition of "Praise God from Whom All Blessings Flow."

How Cleveland back in Albany received news of his nomination:

> It was 1:45 A.M. when General Farnsworth [of the state militia] heard what he supposed to be a cannon shot. He held up his hand, exclaiming, "Listen!" The wind was westerly, but the next and succeeding shots were distinctly heard, and it was known that Cleveland was nominated, the first [telegraph] dispatch to the Governor being received a few moments later.
>
> General Farnsworth . . . jumped up and exclaimed: "They are firing a salute, Governor, over your nomination."
>
> "That's what it means," added Colonel Lamont.
>
> "Do you think so?" said the Governor, quietly. "Well," he continued, "anyhow, we'll finish up this work."
>
> The work was resumed. . . .
>
> In a couple of minutes the telephone rang, and a voice said:

"Tell the Governor he has been nominated on the second ballot." Lamont repeated the words.

"Is that so, Dan?" said the Governor, as his face brightened up for the first time. "By jove, that is something, isn't it?"

All present at once tendered their congratulations. Suddenly the Governor said: "Dan, I wish you would telephone the news to the Mansion. Sister [Rose, his official hostess now that Susan had married] will want to hear it. . . ."[49]

That night, the nominee reviewed a parade of some five thousand marchers and then gave what became known as his "Serenade Speech," his first message as a national figure:

> Fellow-Citizens: The American people are about to exercise, in its highest sense, their power of right and sovereignty. They are to call in review before them their public servants and the representatives of political parties, and demand of them an account of their stewardship. Parties may be so long in power, and may become so arrogant and careless of the interests of the people, as to grow heedless of their responsibility to their masters. But the time comes, as certainly as death, when the people weigh them in the balance.
>
> We believe that the people are not receiving at the hands of the party which for nearly twenty-four years has directed the affairs of the nation, the full benefits to which they are entitled, of a pure, just and economic rule; and we believe that the ascendancy of genuine Democratic principles will insure a better government, and greater happiness and prosperity to all the people.
>
> I am profoundly impressed with the responsibility of the part assigned to me in this contest . . . and I pledge you that no effort of mine shall be wanting to secure the victory which I believe to be within the achievement of the Democratic hosts.[50]

PART III

1884

13

What should have been the focus

Unanimity of opinion is lacking as to whether the 1884 presidential campaign was the dirtiest in American history. Others, it can be argued persuasively, were dirtier. Among them the 1824 contest between Andrew Jackson and Henry Clay, when Jackson's wife was accused of bigamy, and four years later, when it was claimed Jackson was the son of a whore by a lascivious mulatto, while Louise Adams was not only illegitimate and the Adamses had not only enjoyed premarital sex, but John Quincy Adams, while U.S. Minister to Russia, had pimped for Czar Alexander; the 1972 campaign, with its "dirty tricks"; the 1988 race, with Willie Horton. The 1884 canvass was, though, the only one in which the morality of both candidates was dwelt upon to the near-exclusion of honest, intelligent debate on the issues. Indeed, more than mud-slinging, it was libel-slinging, with the Republicans branding "Grover the Good" as a "gross and licentious man," "a moral leper," and "a coarse debauchee who would bring his harlots with him to Washington."[1] Before we examine what became that contest's focus, let us examine what should have been the focus.

The Democrats in their party platform called for reform of the federal land-sales policy, reduction of federal taxes through the lowering of import duties, and tighter controls on monopolies. The Republicans called for high tariffs, domestic market expansion, and an international standard for the relative value of gold and silver coinage. Also, they demanded more federal involvement on the local level, whereas the Democrats favored "the preservation of personal rights" and "the reserved rights of the states."[2]

The two candidates differed in style. Blaine, the more polished speaker of the two—he was, in fact, one of the leading orators of the day—stumped the country. Cleveland, on the other hand, remained at his desk in Albany throughout most of the campaign, limiting his speeches to one at Bridgeport, the other at Newark. He was the first to admit that he lacked any aptitude for extemporaneous speaking. ("I have never been a stump speaker and do not think I should be a success in that role.")[3] Just as he would never extemporize publicly on any topic in which he was not well versed, neither would he let himself appear publicly at a disadvantage.

The candidates differed not only in strategy but in objectives. Blaine emphasized the high tariff, stressing the theme in those parts of the Democratic South that were becoming industrialized and would be attracted to protectionism. In New York, New Jersey, Indiana, and Connecticut, traditional "swing states," where most of the nation's Irish Catholics lived, he appealed to that powerful voting constituency by demagogically peppering his demand for tariff protection with its implied distrust of the British system of free trade.

Cleveland, conversely, emphasized the honest administration of public affairs and an end to prodigious government spending. His stand on the tariff, one of the most controversial issues of the day, was curious. Curious in that as President he would be so assertive on lowering duties, yet as presidential candidate he was presumably uncertain of where he stood on the issue. "Presumably" is the operative word here. It may be that he sensed the inherent danger of the tariff as a campaign issue, and therefore thought it prudent to straddle the topic, alluding to it only indirectly while appearing to favor a reduction, and in many cases elimination, of all import taxes. It would seem, in retrospect, that he knew what his position would be, once in office. But first he must get elected.

In his letter accepting the nomination, Cleveland called for a constitutional amendment limiting the presidency to a single term. He believed this would inhibit an emulous politician's temptation to curry the favor of an army of officeholders instead of being a public servant. In the social sphere, he dedicated himself to civil service reform and government economy, advocated legislation to promote the welfare of the working class, and, in a brief passage, criticized alien immigrants who had no intention "to become Americans." Other than the one-term presidential point, which he wisely dropped as sounding like mere electioneering palaver (which may well have been his intent), Cleveland fell back on the other themes in his Bridgeport and Newark speeches. He dismissed the Republicans as "a vast army of office-holders" rich in money and influence who had been too long in power and become corrupt to the core, and condemned their continuing to ignore the economic and, yes, even moral perils of a bloated Treasury surplus that had resulted from a decades-long policy of high-tariff protectionism.[4]

Besides the Democrats and Republicans, five other parties fielded candidates, but only two—the Greenbacks and the Prohibitionists—received attention. Secretly subsidized by the Republican National Committee to siphon off Democratic votes, the Butler-led Greenbackers' canvass was a fiasco, and their presumed threat to Cleveland never materialized. The Prohibition party, led by former Kansas governor John P. St. John, was a major impediment to Blaine, mainly in upstate New York. Most of St. John's followers were former Republicans who may have detested both Cleveland and the Democrats but had no intention to support either Blaine or his party, whom they hated in equal measure. That hatred derived mainly from the humiliation inflicted at the Republican National Convention upon Frances E. Willard, head of the WCTU, who was permitted to present the platform committee with a petition in support of the temperance cause, signed by twenty thousand of her co-"dries." After she was politely bowed out, someone wondered derisively what to do with the petition. This evoked gleeful shouts of "Kick it under the table!" There it was found when the convention adjourned—covered with the stains of tobacco juice.

The Democrats' failure to win the White House after 1856 was due to the legacy they still suffered from a Civil War for which popular judgment held them responsible. The Republicans exploited this in every election, claiming to have single-handedly saved the Union, freed the slaves, and preserved the Republic—over which, as a consequence, they believed themselves entitled to preside in perpetuity. They conveniently disregarded the many Democrats who also sacrificed their lives to "the cause," and the many outstanding chieftains like Sherman, Meade, and Sheridan who were Democrats. Also conveniently overlooked by the Republicans—something they took pains to ensure was overlooked by the public—was that Lincoln's second nomination came not from the Republican party, but from a coalition Union convention composed of Republicans and Democrats.

The 1884 campaign's dominant issue was Blaine's integrity. ("The Republican National Convention has with brutal directness . . . forced upon the country . . . a man whose unclean record it cannot deny and dare not face," thundered paramount Mugwump Carl Schurz.)[5] Blaine's record redounded to Cleveland's advantage, as did three added factors—the Prohibitionist vote; lingering distrust of the Republican party in the South, a bitter heritage of Reconstruction; and a short business recession that year that generated popular discontent with Republican fiscal policies. Working to Cleveland's disadvantage was the split among New York Democrats caused by the Tammany revolt.

Tammany's importance for the New York votes it controlled was exceeded only by its influence on Irish-Americans throughout the country. Winning the Irish vote, estimated at close to a half million, was seen as critical to the Republicans. Much was made of the facts that Blaine's mother and sisters were practicing Irish Catholics, with one sister the mother superior of an Indiana convent; that he was outspoken in support of such Hibernian causes as the Irish Land League, which was then trying to abolish absentee English landlordism in Ireland; and that, as Garfield's Secretary of State, he had been openly antagonistic to the British government. Although the Irish announced in great numbers for Blaine, some, like the bishop of Albany, resented the Republican effort to drag the church into politics and encouraged the election of the Democratic candidate.

Along with other anti-Cleveland Democrats, and encouraged by the Republicans, Tammany supported Butler's Greenback candidacy in hopes of denying Cleveland the important New York and New England vote; it was there that what strength Butler had was concentrated. Tammany boss Kelly also pursued the preposterous delusion that Cleveland might be forced to abandon his candidacy. He hoped to see the candidate replaced by Allen Thurman, whereupon, he posited, all the other anti-Cleveland groups, led by Ben Butler and the Greenbacks, would line up behind the exceptionally inept Thurman.

In this bizarre scenario, Kelly had the support of the *New York Sun*, which demanded, on more than one occasion, that Cleveland drop out of the race.[6] Kelly was brought back into line by Cleveland's running mate. A traditional machine man, Hendricks managed to make Kelly, a personal friend, appreciate the political facts of life. This despite Cleveland's refusal to make any concession for the Tammany chieftain's support: "I had rather be beaten than to truckle to Butler or Kelly. I don't want any pledge made for me that will violate my professions [i.e., his political and philosophical beliefs] or betray and deceive the good people that believe in me."[7]

From the outset it was obvious Cleveland would receive the preponderance of reform votes, regardless of party affiliation. This, plus the lack of anything about his political career they could criticize, and the added fear that drawing the public's attention to his successes at Albany could prove counterproductive, caused profound trepidation in the Blaine camp. Their Democratic opponent was beyond reproach. Not only had he acquitted himself admirably as mayor of Buffalo and governor of New York, he had never manifested so much as a hint of demagoguery, never permitted himself to be dictated to by party machines. Why, he had even publicly defied Tammany Hall!

When the Republicans realized that no amount of ingenuity could make a case against Cleveland, they trotted out one of the oldest political ploys, one still very much with us: crass appeal to target groups on the bases of economics, racism, and/or regionalism. They warned southern blacks that electing a Democratic President would lead to the immediate restoration of slavery—a threat, it is pleasant to record, that the new generation of blacks had the good sense to dismiss out of hand.[8] Also doomed to failure was the Republican attempt to portray their opponents as the enemy of the workingman and perpetrator of economic as well as social elitism.

Singled out for special targeting were the thousands of Union veterans, whose Grand Army of the Republic was one of the nation's most powerful voting blocs. They were warned that a Democratic victory would mean a cessation of all pensions and increased anti-veteran hostility, whereas a Republican victory would engender an increase in benefits. At the same time the Republicans, enjoying the advantage of incumbency, politicized the Pension Bureau and poured a small fortune into mobilizing veterans' support, which the Mugwumps rightly described as "disgraceful, being nothing less than the [Pension Bureau's] use . . . with all its power and influence, as a bribe for votes." Thousands of veterans who might have gone for Cleveland now believed that only a Blaine victory would guarantee their pensions.[9]

Hoping to humiliate Cleveland, Blaine called for a public debate on the tariff issue as well as any other issue he might wish to cover. Cleveland wisely declined. One might go into court with a memorized speech and win a case; but one dared not go into a public debate thus armed. Knowing Cleveland's weakness as a campaigner, and adumbrating the Rose Garden Strategy their spiritual heirs would follow a century later in Jimmy Carter's reelection bid, his handlers explained it was more important for the governor to remain at his desk in Albany. The public bought it.

Yes, there were more than enough issues of public concern to suffice for two campaigns. But the 1884 campaign was marked not by an exchange of political ideas but by an exchange of political filth. The exchange did not originate with the standard-bearers, but with their partisans. Once the oral manure started flying, both sides hastily added the professional expertise that spelled the difference between its being allowed to die a quick, localized death and receiving the widest possible airing in this era of comparatively primitive communications.

14

"Ma! Ma! Where's my Pa?"

It started on the Republican side, ten days after Cleveland's nomination. The man who got it going was one of those insufferably sanctimonious ecclesiastics—a breed doubtless as old as the very concept of organized religion—who believe they are divinely obliged to make the entire race march to the beat of their own very much out-of-tune drummer. He was the Rev. George H. Ball, D.D., pastor of Buffalo's Hudson Street Church and a Republican loyalist. While the basic facts were not created out of whole cloth, as much cannot be said for Ball's interpretation.

In late July, under the headline "A *Terrible* Tale: A Dark Chapter in a Public Man's History," a leading Buffalo paper carried Ball's account of how Cleveland had "accomplished the seduction" of a comely widow, one Maria Halpin, by whom he had sired a child, now aged ten. Bringing what was by now stale news before the public at this point in time was defended as an issue "not between the two great [political] parties but between the brothel and the family, between indecency and decency, between lust and law, between the essence of barbarism and the first principles of civilization, between the degradation of women and due honor, protection and love to our mothers, sisters and daughters." Professing to speak for "an investigating committee of ministers," Ball allowed as how

> the woman, so far as known, had borne an irreproachable character up to that time; that her employers [a popular Buffalo emporium], with whom she had been about four years, had a high regard for her and considered her a virtuous Christian woman; that Mr. Cleveland had taken her to the Lying-in Hospital during her confinement; that the woman became depressed and threatened his life; that he became apprehensive that she might attempt some injury to him or herself and appealed to the Chief of Police, Colonel John Byrne, to keep her under surveillance; that Mr. Cleveland had her taken by force from her room at Mrs. Baker's [boardinghouse] to the Providence Lunatic Asylum [and she] was seen there by Doctor Ring, who did not think her insane; that after several days she escaped and no efforts were made to retake her; that she put her case into the hands of . . . an attorney, alleging kidnapping and false imprisonment; that she finally gave up the child and received $500 from Mr. Cleveland [and] these are matters of common repute in Buffalo, to substantiate which numerous witnesses can be found.[10]

Vowing to obviate the chance of so heinous a specimen as Grover Cleveland inhabiting the White House, Ball expanded his "*Terrible* Tale" into "an epic of moral depravity such as no city in Christendom [let alone Buffalo, New York] has ever witnessed." To "prove" that the Halpin affair was not a single episode in Cleveland's past but simply the aspect of an ongoing lifestyle, Ball swore before God that investigations disclosed "still more proof of debaucheries too horrible to relate and too vile to be readily believed. For many years days devoted to business have been followed by nights of sin." To hear the good reverend tell it, Cleveland was "an artful seducer, a foe to virtue, an enemy of the family, a snare to youth and hostile to true womanhood." Worse, the Halpin case "was not solitary." There were countless others including quite a few "disgraced and broken-hearted victims of his lust now slumber[ing] in the grave." In fact, Cleveland had not "abated his lecheries." Ball doubted he ever would. Or could.[11]

Ball's philippic was, surprisingly, ignored by every respectable eastern newspaper and all but one western paper with any appreciable circulation, and was completely disregarded in the South. But then the *Boston Journal*, the only major New England daily supporting the Blaine candidacy, ran the story on its first page, under hysterical headlines. Why Ball waited until the campaign to resurrect what was basically not only a dead horse but not even much of a secret was "obvious" to Joseph Pulitzer's *World*—which formally charged the national Republican leaders with putting Ball up to it. (Cleveland had mentioned his "woman scrape" to a prominent New York Democrat prior to the nominating convention; and Tammany had spread hints of it around Chicago, but nothing came of them.)

By then, the Cleveland-Halpin liaison had became a national sensation. Not unexpectedly, the Republican press had a field day with it. The influential church journal *Independent* encouraged clergymen of all faiths to interpret the whole business as a sign from on high that Cleveland's defeat had been divinely ordained. Lucy Stone's suffragette organ *Woman's Journal* saw in the Cleveland saga "an affront to decent women." Meanwhile, back in Buffalo the *Telegram*, enjoying a circulation it had never dared aspire to, embellished the Ball charges with a series of fallacious anti-Cleveland allegations that ranged from the venomous to the ludicrous. All were dismissed scornfully as "so improbable and so filthy that they seem to have been hatched by streetwalkers and sold to Dr. Ball for a dollar apiece."[12]

Some well-meaning Cleveland enthusiasts unwittingly added a dollop of credibility to the rumors with their denials. Henry Ward Beecher, for one, declared that the "immoral" governor, whom he much preferred to Blaine (a man he saw as "a-whoring after votes"), had atoned for a sin that many men shared (Beecher himself included—though, suffice it to say, he saw no reason to mention it). Beecher implied that if every man who broke the Seventh Commandment voted for Cleveland he'd be elected by a 200,000 majority—which the Republican *New York Tribune* described prissily as "a call to adulterers to vote Democratic." "I am afraid," wrote Cleveland to a Buffalo friend, "that I shall have occasion to pray to be delivered from my friends!"[13]

Cleveland's best defenders were those who suggested that his behavior while a private citizen was irrelevant when compared with Blaine's dishonest behavior while a public servant. *The Nation* said that the Democratic candidate's "sin" would disqualify him for the presidency "if his opponent be free from this stain, and is good a man in all other ways," adding that the sins of Blaine were totally unacceptable in a statesman, while Cleveland in philandering had only followed in the steps of many great (and randy) politicians. One southern senator took a more earthy approach; when asked his opinion, he said, "What of it? We did not enter our man in this race as a gelding!"[14]

Cleveland had been forewarned of the impending attack in a wire from a Buffalo friend, who asked how he and other supporters should respond. He wired back: "Whatever you do, tell the truth."[15] At his insistence, the telegram was made public. Also at his insistence, so were all the facts. Grover Cleveland believed that if a man owned up to the facts, the falsehoods would quickly dissipate, and the unpleasantness would be quickly forgotten. And that is precisely what happened.

Based on a careful study of the Buffalo and New York City press for the years 1876 and 1884, and Cleveland's letters (including many not published), Allan Nevins has put together a scenario embracing what historians now accept as the true facts of the matter. Nevins's scenario, on which the following account is based, also took into consideration an 1884 Democratic campaign pamphlet that contained the record of a thorough investigation by a panel of prominent Buffalo citizens. The group, which included several clergymen—and more registered Republicans than Democrats—wanted it widely known that its "examination of the general charges which have been made against Governor Cleveland's private character shows that they are wholly untrue. In every instance in which the reports and insinuations have been tangible enough to . . . guide us in our investigations they have been positively proved to be false. The attack upon Governor Cleveland's character is thoroughly discredited when we consider the sources from which it comes."[16]

Maria Halpin was a widow of thirty-one when she arrived at Buffalo around 1871, having left behind two children with her family in

Pennsylvania. Finding employment as a salesgirl in a dry goods emporium, she quickly moved up to head of the cloak department. The qualities that won over her employers—lithesome beauty, pleasing demeanor, fluency in conversational French—won Maria welcome entry into the city's best social circles. On September 14, 1874, Maria gave birth to a son she named Oscar Folsom Cleveland. Grover Cleveland was named as the father. Though admitting to the possibility, Cleveland did not admit to a certainty. One doubts that even God could have established the babe's true paternity. Maria had been passed around—or, more properly, had passed herself around—among "Big Steve's" closest friends, including, as the child's name more than suggests, his law partner, Oscar Folsom. It was generally believed that Maria was herself uncertain who the father was, and that she "selected" Cleveland because he was the only one of the group who was single—and available for marriage.[17] Without conceding paternity, Cleveland agreed to provide for the child. This supports the view of his defenders that he suspected Folsom, who was killed in a traffic accident in 1875, was the father, and gallantly assumed responsibility in order to protect his great friend's memory and spare his widow grief and public humiliation.

While nursing the child, Maria turned (or perhaps *re*turned) to the bottle. Concerned for the child, whose mother was now known to be neglecting him, Cleveland sought the assistance of an old friend, county judge Roswell L. Burrows. After a thorough investigation, Burrows had Maria remanded to an institution for the mentally deranged, where she was persuaded to remain for a short time while legal arrangements were made to have the boy, now a year and a half old, sent to the Protestant Orphan Asylum—to which Cleveland paid the weekly board rate of $5 through Judge Burrows.

When Maria was released soon after, Cleveland gave her funds with which to establish a dress salon in Niagara Falls. A week later she reappeared at Buffalo, claiming to be lonely for her child—lonelier, in fact, than for her first two, back in Pennsylvania. In all likelihood her loneliness derived from the realization that in surrendering the boy's custody to the authorities she surrendered what leverage she had in pursuing her claim on (and possible marriage to) Cleveland. When legal steps to recover her son failed, she abducted him from the orphanage. At Cleveland's urging, Judge Burrows ordered the boy returned. Soon thereafter, Cleveland arranged for his adoption by a western New York family. He went on to become successful in one of the professions (possibly medicine, possibly education; the facts are not clear). Cleveland and young Oscar never met again, or had any contact, even through intermediaries. This apparent indifference was probably due to Cleveland's strong doubts that he was the biological father. As he was known to love and fuss over children, it has been conjectured that if he knew for a fact that he was, he would have kept up some relationship, if only a distant one in light of the boy's fortuitous adoption.

As for Maria, she disappeared from Buffalo—after admitting to her lawyer that Cleveland had never promised marriage. Twenty years later, now remarried, she surfaced in New Rochelle, New York. From there she sent Cleveland, then in the White House, two letters, one of which survives, in which she solicited money under threat of publishing "certain facts" still in her possession. Whether Cleveland submitted to extortion is unknown, but extremely doubtful. Those "certain facts" were never published.

In publicly ignoring the scandal while leaving his defense to such close Buffalo friends as "Shan" Bissell, Charlie Goodyear, John Millburn, and Dan Lockwood, Cleveland charged them all with a policy of "no cringing." They were to indicate his decent and generous assumption of responsibility for the boy, abstain from allegations against any other presumed father, and, above all, deny he ever entertained any loose women, or, for that matter, any woman "in any bad way," in the governor's mansion. Also, they were to be on the lookout for the existence of any letters from him to Maria Halpin—which would be forgeries, and were to be exposed as such.[18]

The scandal's timing, from Cleveland's point of view, was serendipitous. Coming out during the Chicago convention, it would doubtless have prevented his nomination; in the campaign's closing weeks, it would doubtless have cost him the election. But the voters perceived that what was really at issue here was the public integrity and leadership capacity of the two candidates; questions of private conduct were extraneous. As one Mugwump put it, speaking for all Independents, "We are told that Mr. Blaine has been delinquent in office but blameless in private life, while Mr. Cleveland has been a model of official integrity, but culpable in his personal relations. We should therefore elect Mr. Cleveland to the public office which he is so well qualified to fill, and remand Mr. Blaine to the private station which he is admirably fitted to adorn." the *Nation* and *New York Evening Post* editor Lawrence Godkin accused Blaine of having "wallowed in spoils like a rhinoceros in a pool" all his political life and demanded to know which was better suited for the presidency—a man who, like Franklin, Hamilton, and Webster, had been unchaste; or a man who, like the Republican nominee, had sold his official influence for money, and broken his word for purposes of destroying documentary evidence of his corruption.[19] (Godkin was referring to Blaine's role in the Little Rock & Fort Smith scandal, discussed below.)

The Blaine camp neither rebuked nor dissociated themselves from Ball's charges. They did, though, keep the story alive through constant repetition, in cartoons and at public rallies, of the campaign's most remembered doggerel:

Ma! Ma! Where's my Pa?

to which the Democrats would retort,

He's gone to the White House! Ha! Ha! Ha!

15

"A dreadful self-inflicted penance"

"Slippery Jim" (as Blaine was known to his political foes) may or may not have been personally responsible for helping to make Maria Halpin a campaign issue. But that did not curb his delight over Cleveland's public embarrassment and the hope that there'd be no end to it. Much as Cleveland detested Blaine, though, and found it easy to believe every negative thing said about him, he refused to retaliate on a personal level. This became manifest when his backers produced gossip intended to question Mrs. Blaine's premarital virtue by alleging that the birth of her first child followed the recorded date of the Blaine marriage by a mere three months.

Told that an entrepreneur was selling documentation of the charge, Cleveland sent for him. According to William Hudson, who with Dan Lamont attended the interview, Cleveland took the documents and paid the peddler "for his expenses . . . and his good will in the matter," then dismissed him. Without glancing at them, he asked Hudson, "Are the papers all here?" Assured that they were, he added them to others he had received earlier on the same theme, tore them into small bits, and then had a servant burn them in the fireplace, "standing over him to watch the process." When they all had gone up in smoke, Cleveland walked back to where Lamont stood and said, "The other side can have a monopoly of all the dirt in this campaign."[20]

The entrepreneur sold his tale to a local newspaper, where it might have died if the *Indianapolis Sentinel* hadn't picked it up and, through the combined efforts of the Democrats and their Mugwump allies, aired it nationally. Barely managing to suppress its suspiciously inflated indignation, the *Sentinel* proclaimed there was "hardly an intelligent man in the country who has not heard that James G. Blaine betrayed the girl whom he married . . . at the muzzle of a shotgun. If, after despoiling her, he was craven to refuse her legal redress, giving legitimacy to her child, until a loaded shotgun stimulated his conscience—then there is a blot on his character more foul, if possible, than any of the countless stains on his political record."[21]

One is almost tempted to pity Blaine (pity for his poor wife is a given) for the way he handled—rather, mishandled—the whole business. He sued the *Sentinel,* charging that there had in fact been *two* marriage ceremonies. In 1850, he claimed, when he was twenty years old and living in Kentucky, they had just become engaged when he was suddenly summoned to Pennsylvania by the death of his father. "It being very doubtful if I could return to Kentucky, I was threatened with an indefinite separation from her who possessed my entire devotion. My one wish was to secure her to myself by an indissoluble tie against every possible contingency in life, and, on the thirtieth of June, 1850, just prior to my departure from Kentucky, we were . . . united by what I knew was, in my native [actually, adopted] state of Pennsylvania, a perfectly legal form of marriage."[22] A second marriage was performed six months later, but the date was kept secret "for obvious reasons" (the words are Blaine's). Three months later their child was born. The marriage turned out to be a long and happy one.

Had Blaine emulated Cleveland's directive to his supporters when under fire to "tell the truth," it probably would have ended then and there. But Blaine's enemies saw too many evasions in his accounting of the facts and bombarded the newspapers with letters demanding answers to such questions as: Why did he keep the first marriage secret till his wife was in her sixth month of pregnancy? And why was he vague about details of the first wedding, who were the witnesses, and why was there no record? Compounding matters, Democratic lawyers challenged Blaine's interpretation of the differences between Kentucky and Pennsylvania laws.

The hostile press kept the story alive—not to humiliate Blaine's wife but to underscore Blaine's congenital inability to face any issue honestly. When he asked a political enemy, prominent attorney and New York Republican boss Roscoe Conkling, to speak out in his defense, Blaine found himself on the receiving end of the campaign's most memorable retort: "You know I don't engage in criminal practice!" Cleveland felt enough was enough. For the only time in the campaign he intervened in all the Blaine-bashing, demanding that his managers accept his version of events and put an end to the slander: "I am very sorry it was printed, and I hope it will die out at once," Cleveland told Lamont.[23]

It must be recorded, though, that Cleveland never demanded a cessation of the abusive cartoons on the two marriages (as well as on other Blaine scandals) that were daily fare in the anti-Blaine press—so long as Mrs. Blaine's name or reputation was not a factor. He insisted that the American electorate be reminded they were being asked to elect as President a man whose political morals were of the gutter variety. Blaine's enemies agreed with his friends that he was a highly intelligent and capable politician. Where they could not agree was whether he was easily corrupted or inherently corrupt—as in his involvement with the Little Rock & Fort Smith Railroad, which superseded Maria Halpin as the campaign's major scandal.

In 1869, while Speaker of the House, Blaine ruled favorably on behalf of the Little Rock & Fort Smith by blocking a bill that would have prevented the State of Arkansas from giving it a land grant; by secret agreement he was later allowed to sell the line's bonds to friends in his home state of Maine on a generous commission basis. Seven years later, with a Congressional investigation looming, and anxious that his bid for the 1876 Republican presidential nomination not be compromised, Blaine wrote to Warren Fisher, the line's chief executive: "Certain papers and persons are trying to throw mud at me to injure my candidacy before the Cincinnati convention. . . . I want you to send me a letter such as this enclosed draft. Regard this letter as strictly 'confidential.' Do not show it to anyone." Enclosed, for Fisher to copy in his own hand and return, was the draft of an "unsolicited" testimonial confirming Blaine's innocence in the matter. Blaine ended his cover letter with words that would come back to haunt him: "Burn this letter."

Taken in tandem with Blaine's sworn statement of April 24, 1876, that his "whole connection with the [rail]road has been open as the day," disclosure of such a letter would be damaging beyond measure. For eight years this and other incriminating letters remained a well-kept secret. Then, through the courtesy of Fisher's former bookkeeper James Mulligan, they fell into the hands of Blaine's enemies when he won the 1884 Republican nomination. (Whether Mulligan was motivated by partisan politics or old-fashioned greed has never been determined, and is for our purposes unimportant.) The *New York Times*, one of the first major Republican papers to come out for Cleveland, ran what became known as the "Mulligan Letters" across its front page and charged Blaine with having "exposed himself" as "a prostitute of public trusts, a scheming jobber, and a reckless falsifier."[24]

Blaine's apologists argued that he had simply been engaged in an ordinary commercial transaction, the sort of thing any businessman might have done. Carl Schurz demanded to know why in 1876 Blaine hadn't just bared all his records and correspondence to the investigators, instead of being selective about it. The best the Republicans could come up with was Massachusetts senator George Hoar's unpersuasive defense that "the circumstances were perilous," and Blaine felt "inexpressibly outraged and indignant" at having his correspondence examined by a hostile, Democratic-run Congressional committee. (When the glib Hoar added that even George Washington would have been indignant at such a demand, Schurz responded with the assurance that no " 'Mulligan letters' would have been found among George Washington's correspondence.")[25]

In New York City, the Cleveland forces organized a gigantic parade of "Democratic business men" who marched up and down Wall Street chanting "Burn this letter!" and then stopped on cue to produce an enormous facsimile of Blaine's letter to Fisher, which they then ignited, to the delight of onlookers. In a bold attempt to deflect attention from their candidate, the Republicans now sought to diminish Cleveland's hold on his party's northern wing, and at the same time attract Democratic voters in order to compensate for the defecting Independents.

Their instrument of choice was that good old reliable standby patriotism.

So determined were the Blaine forces to embarrass Cleveland that they went so far as to claim that none of the eligible Cleveland brothers served in the Civil War, that all three had been draft dodgers. Army records prove otherwise. Lewis Frederick joined the 32nd New York Volunteers on May 15, 1861, in New York City, saw heavy action with the Army of the Potomac, was commissioned a first lieutenant (June 23, 1862), and was mustered out with his company on June 9 of the following year. Richard Cecil joined the 24th Indiana on July 31, 1861, saw action under Frémont and Grant, became a second lieutenant, and was mustered out December 4, 1864.

Even these twenty years after the Civil War, Democrats were sensitive to the accusation that so many of them had not done their share in the fight to save the Union. How better to compromise Cleveland, reasoned the Republicans, then to spread the word that he had dishonorably—nay, cowardly—evaded service by sending a convict to fight in his place? The charge was contained in a nationwide circular letter, which quickly made the front pages of the anti-Cleveland press. A copy of the letter, which originated in Buffalo, was sent to the candidate by the vice-commandant of a New York City veteran's group, with the request for a denial to be circulated over Cleveland's own signature.

Cleveland replied next day with characteristic candor to this "political mendacity," dismissing it as "calculated to deceive, and in all prejudicial statements absolutely false." Being at the time assistant district attorney, he "had plenty of opportunity to secure a convict substitute [at] no expense, and, in fact, was urged to do so." However, he refused, and hired instead a sailor "who had just arrived in port and been paid off. I don't know that he was ever arrested, and I am sure he was not a convict." There were, he went on to explain, three men of fighting age in the Cleveland family. (The eldest, the Rev. William, was deferred because of his age, his professional calling, and his being married with children.) "We were poor, and mother and sisters depended on us for support." It was decided that two of them should enlist and the third stay at home to support the family. "We decided it by drawing lots. Two long and one short pieces of paper were put by mother in the leaves of the old family Bible. She held it while we drew. My [two other] brothers drew the long slips, and at once enlisted, and I abided by my duty to help the helpless women."[26] Cleveland insisted that the letter be given the widest possible airing.

The substitute Cleveland found was a quasi-illiterate Pole of thirty-two, George Benninsky (some sources give it as Brinske), who arrived in the United States in 1851 and five years later became a sailor on the Great Lakes; presumably he belonged to Buffalo's large Polish community. After agreeing to serve in Cleveland's place, he was sworn in at Fort Porter on July 6, 1863. Although reports in the opposition press—reports that continued past the campaign and into Cleveland's presidency—told in lurid detail of the wounds and hardships Benninsky suffered and of how Cleveland had callously washed his hands of him, army records show that he served briefly with the 76th New York Regiment on the Rappahannock, where he injured his back, and was then detailed to orderly duty in the military hospital in Washington, surviving the war without having taken part in any major battle as a combatant. As late as three years after the 1884 campaign, Cleveland was asked to defend his not having "done more" for Benninsky. Responding to a letter containing such allegations, he wrote, in part, "When I was at Buffalo on election day in November, 1885, I saw Benninsky for the last time. . . . He told me that he had been sick, and that he was poor and in need [and] without any hesitation or question I gave him five dollars, which he received with expressions of gratitude and immediately left. Never at any time nor in any form has he uttered a complaint to me of my treatment of him, there is no obligation of mine to him that has not been more than fulfilled, and there has not been in my relations with him any omission of duty or kindness which upon any decent theory ought to subject my conduct to criticism."[27]

Whether the Republicans could have gotten more mileage out of the "Draft-Dodging Grover" charge is doubtful. The public seemed satisfied with Cleveland's explanation. Of greater consequence, the Blaine camp was quickly overtaken by an uproar, in part of its own making, that not only cost Blaine New York State, it cost him the election.

With the campaign now focused almost exclusively on Blaine's integrity and Cleveland's morality, what had begun three months before as a political encounter had degenerated into a political circus. As the race entered its final days it became evident the election would be decided by a small margin turning on New York's thirty-six electoral votes. Almost weekly in the state's most populous city, where it was tacitly agreed that the ultimate battle was to be waged, there were mammoth parades by both parties—simultaneously—featuring the cacophony of competing brass bands and human din. Caparisoned in bogus medieval armor, Republicans clanked through Manhattan's canyons howling repetitively for hours on end,

> Blaine! Blaine! James G. Blaine!
> The white plumed knight from the state of Maine!

This invariably drew from rival marchers the hooted reply:

> Blaine! Blaine! James G. Blaine!
> The Continental Liar from the state of Maine!

One prejudiced daily called to the attention of native-born New Yorkers the joyful tidings that in one such demonstration "[t]here were no newly arrived immigrants in [the Blaine] line, as was the case in the Cleveland parade." Another noted beneath the headline "The Greatest Parade in New York's History" that some fifty thousand partisans marched "in the muddy street" for three hours. The campaign in New York was particularly rough on Blaine, described by the *Herald* as "harried and drawn [of] face, blanched to a degree of pallor that was starling."[28]

Small wonder. He had lost the support of the six major New York Republican dailies which had backed Garfield in 1880 but were now solidly behind Cleveland. In doing everything they could, within the parameters of journalistic good taste, to ensure Blaine's defeat, they were joined by the leading periodicals. By far the most aggressive were *Puck* and *Harper's Weekly*, whose respective cartoonists, Bernhard Gillam and Thomas Nast—one could call either the Herblock of his day—did a weekly number on the Republican standard-bearer. Nast depicted him fawning before the hated railroad baron, Jay Gould. Gillam pictured him as the "Tattooed Man," bedecked in a breechcloth as he struggled to hide a flabby body on which notations of his alleged misdeeds and phrases from compromising correspondence like the Mulligan Letters were tattooed. Adding to Blaine's woes, Roscoe Conkling was doing his best to have the state Republican party sit out the election. Never forgotten—or forgiven—was Blaine's attack eighteen years previously when as leader of the party's Half-Breed faction he referred to Conkling, the Stalwarts' leader, as "a grandiloquent swell" with a "turkey-gobbler strut." Of such rhetoric are enduring political enmities spawned.

Still, Blaine was confident of winning. Though the party had written off the South and a few of the northern states, which were solidly for Cleveland from the outset, there appeared to be enough concrete support in the more populous western and northern states—such as New York—to ensure victory. As Election Day approached, it seemed that all Blaine need do to win was show up in New York and take a bow. He need not make a speech. Thanks to Tammany's trashing of their own party's standard-bearer, he need not even open his mouth except to breathe and eat. Democratic leaders were privately prepared to concede him the state.

Had Blaine just coasted that final week, the outcome might have been different and America's political history altered radically. But in seeking to nail down critical New York State, he nailed down his own coffin, as it were, with two glaring gaffes that took place within hours of each other. The first proved to be only damaging. The other proved to be fatal. In both, Blaine was not iniquitous, just imprudent. That does not excuse him. But it does prove how guarded a candidate for public office must be at all times—especially at the eleventh hour.

Given the nation's voting pattern and demographics, and its large concentration of Catholics, New York was the key state in this election. The Irish were obviously not the only Catholic ethnic group; they were, though, the overwhelming majority, so that the terms "Irish" and "Catholic" were used interchangeably. The Irish-born in the United States, according to the 1880 census, numbered 1,855,000, of which 499,455 lived in New York State. The second-largest Catholic group, the Italians, did not immigrate here in appreciable numbers until the turn of the century. Neither candidate could hope to win without carrying the state, short of a miracle. And the probability of Cleveland doing so was not taken seriously—even by Cleveland. To be either pro- or anti-Catholic could be problematic for a candidate, given the strength of the Irish vote and the enmity it engendered among the Protestants (and vice versa). But, as already noted, three factors would seem to counterbalance what problem this might pose for Blaine. These were Tammany's convincing the nation's Catholics that Cleveland was the Antichrist, the Catholicism of Blaine's mother and sisters, and the candidate's openly anti-British bias while Garfield's Secretary of State.

Blaine arrived in New York City seven days before the election for the campaign's final push after stumping throughout the West. Without taking a rest before plunging into a week of hectic political activity, he received a delegation of prominent clergymen in his headquarters at the Fifth Avenue Hotel. Their prominence derived from the fact that all were reform Republicans who had refused to join the Mugwumps. To Blaine it was imperative that he assure them he was the only qualified candidate. In a popular mantra of the day suggestive of the "family values" catchphrase his party would make the centerpiece of their race for the presidency a century down the line, Blaine predicated his acceptability on an unconditional "dedication to Christian values."

Because Blaine was exhausted from weeks of steady campaigning, it was agreed that one Dr. Tiffany would simply offer in the group's name a congratulatory address on the candidate's expected victory at the polls come Tuesday. When a few colleagues objected to Dr. Tiffany's being singled out for the honors, it was decided, after spirited debate, that the honor go to Dr. Samuel D. Burchard, New York City's leading Presbyterian clergyman and at seventy-two the oldest one present. The weary—hence unwary—Blaine did not seem to pay any attention as Burchard, a passionate anti-Catholic who vowed to keep tight rein on that particular prejudice, uttered a remark that brought down upon Blaine the wrath of the political gods before he even realized what had happened.

Hailing the candidate's excellence with great orotundity, Burchard concluded with what was intended as a commitment but sounded suspiciously (at least to Protestants) like a sacred vow: "We are Republicans, and don't propose to leave our party and identify ourselves with the party whose antecedents have been Rum, Romanism, and Rebellion!"

Blaine may not have been paying close attention; nor was anyone else in his entourage, for that matter. But a scout from the enemy camp was. William Hudson, who was at Cleveland headquarters that night, has left an account of what happened: "[W]e heard some one come up the stairs in great haste. In a moment Colonel John Tracey, head of the newspaper bureau, plunged into the room so much out of breath by reason of his haste and excitement that he could not speak, only point to pages of paper he had." Maryland senator Arthur Pue Gorman, Cleveland's campaign manager, took the papers from Tracey and "straightened up with a start" as he read the words "Rum, Romanism, and Rebellion." He then spoke, "his voice cracking like the snap of a whip: 'This sentence must be in every daily newspaper in the country tomorrow, no matter how, no matter what it costs. . . . it must be kept alive for the rest of the campaign!' "[29]

It was.

When the gaffe was pointed out to Blaine next day, he tried frantically to distance himself from Burchard, whom he described as "an ass in the shape of a preacher."[30] But to no avail. Gorman all but forced the remark down the collective throat of every Catholic, particularly in New York and New England, where they were concentrated. Burchard's alliteration was taken as an insult that the Roman Church and the Democratic Party could not accept, and on Election Day, many of Blaine's erstwhile Irish backers registered their disgust at the polls.[31]

But that particular misery lay ahead for Blaine, who capped the day's activities with a "prosperity dinner" that evening at Delmonico's. Its purpose: to epitomize the Plumed Knight (so called for his ostentatious attire and ornate tastes) as "the businessman's candidate" and tap the nation's two hundred richest men in attendance for funds to underwrite the campaign's final push. Its theme: a Republican victory would bring prosperity, but a Democrat in the White House would visit upon the nation a plague of horrors simply too harrowing to be envisaged. Organizer Jay Gould insisted that only the very best viands and wines be served. The dinner came off, albeit unintentionally, as not so much a political event as a paean to plutocracy. Precious few funds were raised, despite Gould's involvement (or perhaps because of it; he was, after all, one of the most hated men in America, even by his coevals). Those attending "were much less generous than had been expected." They were all "willing to have Blaine in the White House, and certainly they did not want to antagonize him as long as there was a possibility that he would be there. They did, though, set a limit to the amount of money they deemed necessary to demonstrate their friendly attitude. Some millionaires even decided that part of their campaign budget should go to the Democrats, whose friendship was also important and from whom there was nothing to fear."

Worse for Blaine—much worse—his enemies among the fourth estate were only too willing to exploit the dinner's extravagance in the midst of a depressed national economy. Pulitzer's *World* ran an outsized cartoon on its front page depicting "Belshazzar Blaine and the Money Kings" dining in splendor on "Monopoly Soup," "Lobby Pudding," "Navy Contract," and "Gould Pie," while off to one side a starving laborer and his wife appealed in vain for crumbs.[32] It cost Blaine the votes of most of the working class.

Cleveland carried Connecticut, Indiana, and New Jersey, plus, as had been anticipated, the solid South. New York, so essential to victory, was at first uncertain. When the Cleveland-bashing *Sun* conceded his election (with profound reluctance), the Democrats launched a series of celebratory bonfires at which they chanted themselves hoarse with:

> Hooray for Maria! Hooray for the kid!
> I voted for Cleveland, and I'm damned glad I did!

But the Associated Press, which received returns by election district instead of by county, insisted victory had gone to the Republicans.

The election remained in doubt for days, with the eyes of the nation focused intently on pivotal New York State. The Democrats panicked when just about all the state's leading dailies but the *Tribune* proclaimed Blaine the winner. Lamont and Apgar took it upon themselves to send, in the name of Manning, telegrams to prominent Democrats in every county:

> THE ONLY HOPE OF OUR OPPONENTS IS A FRAUDULENT COUNT IN THE [SUBURBAN AND RURAL] DISTRICTS. CALL TO YOUR ASSISTANCE TODAY VIGILANT AND COURAGEOUS FRIENDS AND SEE THAT EVERY VOTE CAST IS HONESTLY COUNTED.[33]

When the Republican National Committee declared, "There is no ground for doubt that the honest vote of [New York State] has been given to the Republican candidate," the opposition murmured ominously. The murmuring rose in decibel count as rumors flew that Jay Gould's Western Union was delaying and falsifying returns. Meanwhile, the behavior of predominantly Democratic crowds in all the major cities appears to have justified Blaine's subsequent speculation that a contested election would probably have resulted in civil war.

Law enforcement people nationwide had their hands full. In New York City, Democrats gathered before newspaper offices and warned of dire consequences if Cleveland was cheated out of his rightful and lawful victory. That night an even greater throng moved down to Broadway to Dey Street to threaten violence before the Western Union Building, while yet another mob marched up Fifth Avenue toward the Gould mansion, singing, "We'll hang Jay Gould from a sour apple tree." Indianapolis Democrats staged a gigantic rally that threatened to degenerate into a gargantuan riot. When the *Boston Journal* posted a bulletin "confirming" Blaine's victory a horde of that city's Cleveland supporters threatened to gut the building.

On the third day, Cleveland, who after appearing at a pre-election rally in New York City and then voting in Buffalo had returned to Albany to await returns, wired state committeeman Edward Murphy of Troy, "I believe I have been elected President, and nothing but grossest fraud can keep me out of it, and that we will not permit." Two days later, in the face of overwhelming evidence, the Republicans admitted defeat. Learning that Blaine had conceded, Cleveland told a select group of friends who had sat out the long wait with him: "I am glad of it; very glad. There will now be no trouble. If they had not, I should have felt it my duty to take my seat anyhow."

The Republicans charged that their man won a plurality in New York, and thus the election, but was cheated out of it by anti-Blaine tellers in Long Island City who counted Ben Butler's Greenback votes for Cleveland. Ben Butler did not earn enough votes to swing a cat, much less an election. The charge was never confirmed. Cleveland won a 23,000-plus plurality, one of the smallest in American history. He received a total of 4,875,971 votes to Blaine's 4,852,234; in the electoral college, he won 219 votes to Blaine's 182. As expected, New York proved to be the key state; Cleveland carried it by a scant 1,074 votes. A 600-vote change could well have turned the election in the electoral college.[34]

The best explanation for Cleveland's narrow margin of victory was the evenness in the strength of both parties. The best explanations for Blaine's defeat, besides his lack of credibility, included the short-term 1884 economic slump (invariably a handicap to the incumbent party over our history) and the widespread unemployment and threat of further unemployment that cost the Republicans labor's support; the failure by Republican leaders to reconciliate the powerful Roscoe Conkling (which contributed heavily to Cleveland's win in New York, and hurt Blaine severely in the other northern states); and—perhaps the most decisive factor of all—Blaine's last-minute loss of the Irish Catholic vote.

It is not too much of a stretch to say that Cleveland did not win the presidency, Blaine lost it.

Cleveland's reaction to his election was summed up in a letter to Wilson Bissell as soon as the results were confirmed. He was hurt that the people of Buffalo had believed the Republicans' version of the Maria Halpin scandal and, worse, had given their vote to Blaine, which elicited the rather melodramatic "Elected President of the United States, I feel I have no home *at my home* [emphasis in the original]. As I look over the field," he went on, he was able to "see some people lying [politically] dead whose demise will not harm the country, some whose wounds will perhaps serve to teach them that honesty and decency are worth preserving, and some whose valor, fidelity, and staunch devotion are rewarded with victory and who have grappled themselves to me with 'hooks of steel.' " He knew now who his true Buffalo friends were, and found it "quite amusing to see how profuse the professions are of some who stood aloof when most needed." Expressing a bitterness that was wholly out of character, he intended "to cultivate the Christian virtue of charity toward all men except the dirty class that defiled themselves with filthy scandal and Ballism." He did not believe God would ever forgive them. *He* certainly was "determined not to do so." (At the end of his first presidency, when he was contemplating where to live, Cleveland wrote to a friend that it would most certainly not be Buffalo—"the place I hate above all others.")

Having thus vented his feelings toward his adopted city, Cleveland concluded his letter on a note of determination infused with just a trace of martyrdom: "I look upon the four years next to come as a dreadful self-inflicted penance for the good of my country. I can see no pleasure in it and no satisfaction, only a hope that I may be of service to my people."[35]

PART IV

1885–1888

16

"Henceforth I must have no friends"

Of the eight presidents between Abraham Lincoln and Theodore Roosevelt, Grover Cleveland was by far the best. But best, it must be admitted, of a mediocre lot. Johnson was forgettable. Grant was a political incompetent whose capacity for surrounding himself with self-serving felons may have been his finest achievement. Hayes deserved Henry Adams's evaluation: "a third-rate nonentity whose only recommendation is that he is obnoxious to on one." Garfield, had he lived beyond four months into his presidency, would probably have been little more than a well-intentioned master of indecision. Arthur was a shoddy politician of whom the most laudable thing to be said was that he retired from the White House a (presumed) reformed crook. Harrison, the last President to wear a beard, was rather like the actor from Central Casting who *looks* the role he's been assigned but hasn't a clue how to play it. And McKinley, of whom William Allen White said he "walked among men a bronze statue, for thirty years determinedly looking for his pedestal," was an amiable creation of Mark Hanna, that paramount "king maker" of American presidential politics.

But to judge Cleveland solely on the basis of contrast is not only unfair, it is historically insupportable. Where he stood more than a cut above the others was in a willingness to confront the predominant issues that faced the nation in the postwar period: the conflicts between capital and labor, between hard money and soft money, and between protectionism (high tariff) and reductionism (low tariff). His immediate predecessors addressed some or all of these issues, though none with the readiness Cleveland showed to sacrifice his influence—if need be, his presidency—in pursuit of what he believed was best for the nation. Let it not be inferred that Grover Cleveland was a great President whose greatness has somehow eluded history's notice. He was not. One of the most honorable men ever to reach the White House? Undeniably. One of the most inherently decent men to do so? Undoubtedly. Was his judgment sometimes wanting? Unquestionably. Has history unfairly draped the cloak of obloquy over his shoulders? Beyond a doubt.

The presidential history of our nation is the history of forty-one men and their respective opponents who in seeking—and winning—the White House were motivated by a combination of factors, not the least of them an alloy of delusion and arrogance that he, and he alone, was divinely ordained to succeed where others failed. Some wanted to be President because they had a specific, thought-out program they were eager to share with the nation. Some wanted to be President just to be President. To say Grover Cleveland had to be coerced into seeking the White House, as he himself often suggested with disputable ingenuousness, is absurd. He may not have thirsted for the position; but unlike Sherman when urged by the Republicans to run in 1884, he did not threaten to refuse the nomination if offered it and refuse to serve if elected.

We have seen how Cleveland's becoming President of the United States, like his becoming mayor of Buffalo and governor of New York, owed more to the opposition party's disadvantage than to his own party's advantage. Had the Republicans been able to come up with candidates for those offices acceptable to the party's reform wing, let alone to an electorate demanding reform, Cleveland would have remained a successful well-known attorney among a large circle of nationally little-known people. Having been handed the torch, though, he readily locked into what he saw as a God-given opportunity to implement a philosophy on governance he had transformed into a fixed agenda. To Cleveland the powers of the presidency counted for more than the privileges. He truly believed his being raised to the most powerful office in the land owed more to the Almighty than to the politicians and, ultimately, the voters. Ancillary to this belief was Cleveland's view—a view held by few other Presidents—that he was obliged to labor in the best interests of the majority. Like Samuel Johnson, Cleveland believed it is "our first duty to serve society, and, after we have done that, we may attend wholly to the salvation of our own souls."

A few days after his election, while out strolling with an old friend who had come from Buffalo to join in the celebration, Cleveland remarked, "Henceforth I must have no friends."[1] This aspect of the duality in Cleveland's nature became manifest in the wake of his victory at the polls. Within him now resided symbiotically two antipathetic personalities—the genial and approachable Grover of old, whose amiability seemed inexhaustible; and the formidable Mr. President, a persona he wore like a priceless toga that must never be stained. Let a friend solicit political favor, be it for himself or for another, the congenial, often droll Cleveland at once became frigid and distant. He believed incontrovertibly that "gratifying myself and my friends by the use of public offices, simply because I have the power to do so, would be malfeasance in fact, though I was accused of it nowhere except in my own conscience."

If denying a political favor meant the loss of a chum, even a close one, so be it. Take, for example, Wilson Bissell, his former Buffalo law partner and dearest friend. While refusing Bissell's request for a cabinet post because he had already named two New Yorkers, Cleveland offered him a choice of several posts for which it was felt he was well suited, among them Comptroller of the Currency and Treasurer of the United States. They were largely ceremonial posts, to be sure, but either would have kept Bissell in Washington and available for camaraderie and counsel. Bissell not only refused the offers, he swamped Cleveland with letters redolent of ingratitude.

Cleveland replied that "if, in carrying my present burden, I must feel that my friends are calling me selfish and doubting my attachment to them, and criticizing the fact that in my administration of my great trust I am not aiding them, I shall certainly be very unhappy, but shall nevertheless struggle on. The end will come; and if on that day I can retire with a sure consciousness that I have done my whole duty according to my lights and my ability, there will be some corner for me where I can rest."[2] Bissell got over his pique. (Cleveland was able to make him Postmaster General in his second administration, and he turned out to be one of the best in the department's history.) The bottom line: if he believed a friend to be suitable and appropriate for a given position, Cleveland made the appointment; it was not his intention to be the first American President who preferred to be surrounded by strangers and enemies. But "suitable" and "appropriate" were the operative words here.

Cleveland was deluged with petitions from office-seekers even before leaving for Washington, ranging from the cajoling to the demanding, embracing the blatant and the illiterate. A number were so outlandish as to provide a dash of sorely needed comic leavening. It is in this spirit that the following sampling is offered:

One man sought a diplomatic assignment as he did "not care to lead an idle life," adding that his wife "too, wishes to go abroad as our daughter . . . requires treatment which can be best obtained in Europe." Another desired "a place in the Treasury." Fearful lest he not receive the "answer by return of male, because I need the office quick as I have a wife with seven children for support and I am out of menes and money too," he enclosed "a invelope" in case the President "could not spel my name correctlee."

Men were not the only petitioners. Wrote one self-described "orphan, without kindred—literary by nature" of the fairer sex, "As old father Time rolls his leaden car along, I learn that it behooves a lady left as a landmark of her posterity, 'mid the world's treacherous environments, to turn the leaves that are empowered with intelligence and glistening with embellishment: therefore I am impelled to ask, will our noble President give ear to another applicant for his bounteous aid to position?"

Many of the office-seekers believed their best hopes for impressing the President lay in being totally candid, such as one who wrote: "It is very dull out here. There is nothing to enliven things except the possibility of being impaled alive by a live Indian and I dont want to be impaled. I aint got any money to pay Rail Road fare and I want to get out of this. . . . I voted the Republican ticket last fall but if you think there will be any chance of your being elected another term I will vote for you that is if I get an office." And many were willing to settle for any position available, e.g., "I am a young man which I would like to beter my self. The buisness I am at is Junk buisness, but I would rather have the buisness in the govment, either in the Cabnet or as watch-man."[3]

There were, of course, serious petitions. When a nationally prominent lawyer who had staunchly supported his candidacy sought the attorney generalship, he had the enthusiastic backing of many of Cleveland's Buffalo cronies, including a former law partner who was a close relative of the petitioner. But Cleveland felt he was not the best man for the job. Despite cries of ingratitude, Cleveland held firm, concealing his deeply felt grief at the attacks. Equally grievous was their refusal to realize that their man would have gotten the office without their efforts, had he been deemed worthy of it.

Cleveland left Albany for Washington in the evening of March 2, two days before his inaugural. Consistent with his determination to avoid any action that might be perceived as exploiting his public position for private gain, he refused an offer by a number of railways to provide a train gratis and instead hired a train paid for by members of the Democratic party, himself included. His personal party, a small one of twelve, included "the two Dans"—Lamont and Manning—and their wives, sisters Rose and Mary and her husband, brother William and his wife, and his adult nephews and nieces. Invited by President Arthur to spend the night at the White House, he declined, and checked into the Arlington Hotel. His refusal was not intended as a slight to Arthur; neither, for that matter, was his refusal to meet with anyone of consequence on the Washington scene. Not till he took the oath of office would Cleveland set foot in the White House, or in the offices of the nation's movers and shakers. Chester Alan Arthur, he insisted, was still President of the United States until high noon of March 4.

Because he remained in seclusion, and was, besides, a stranger in town, most of official Washington did not get their first look at the incoming Chief Executive until moments preceding the inauguration, when he entered the Senate Chamber on Arthur's arm to conclude the rite of transition. The initial impression he made was a rather negative one. According to famed Populist senator Robert M. La Follette, whose account of the occasion reflected the consensus, "The contrast with Arthur, who was a fine handsome figure, was very striking. Cleveland's coarse face, his heavy inert body, his great shapeless hands, confirmed in my mind the attacks made upon him during the campaign." La Follette added, though, that he soon cultivated a deep respect for Cleveland and came "to admire the courage and conscientiousness of his character."[4]

Cleveland's Inaugural Address, which he wrote himself (as he did all his speeches), was delivered like one of his Buffalo courtroom summations: from memory, forcefully, and without hesitation or faltering, as he stared straight ahead, hands clasped firmly at the small of his back. What it lacked in eloquence was compensated for by its nobility of sentiment and intent. He would "endeavor to be guided by a just and unrestrained construction of the Constitution, with a careful observance of the distinction between" those powers granted to the federal government and those reserved to the states or to the people, "and by a cautious appreciation of those functions which by the Constitution and laws have been especially assigned to the executive branch of the Government." He promised not innovation but an administration dedicated to effecting needed reforms and a new spirit of public service.

He vowed to labor for sound currency and its implied elimination of free-silver coinage; for a revision of the revenue system through a downward tariff revision in order to "relieve the people of unnecessary taxation" yet with "a due regard to the interests of capital invested and workingmen employed in American industries [while at the same time] preventing the accumulation of a surplus in the Treasury to tempt extravagance and waste"; and for his most immediate goal, the promised civil service reform: "Our people have the right to protection from the incompetency of public employees who hold their places solely as the reward of partisan service, and from the corrupting influence of those who promise and the vicious methods of those who expect such rewards; and those who worthily seek public employment have the right to insist that merit and competency shall be recognized instead of party subserviency or the surrender of honest political belief."

The federal government, he stressed, was still and always would be for all the people, not for special interest groups. He urged that "all animosities of partisan strife" engendered by the recent campaign give way to sober concern for the general welfare. He spoke of the need to eradicate the sectional rancor that still remained a legacy of the Civil War. He promised a balanced, equitable economy and noninvolvement in foreign affairs. He called for a shift in government policy concerning two specific groups: future settlers in the trans-Mississippi western territories (an area of the original Louisiana Purchase today comprising more than a dozen states) and the autochthonous Indians. He was resolved to protect the public domain "from purloining schemes and unlawful occupation" and called for legislation to guarantee that the Indians "shall be fairly and honestly treated as wards of the Government and their education and civilization promoted with a view to their ultimate citizenship." He also called for repression of the polygamy practiced by the Mormons in the trans-Mississippi Western Territories, which he found to be "destructive of the family relation and offensive to the moral sense of the civilized world." And, last but certainly not least, he called for rigid enforcement of already existing laws that prohibited "immigration of a servile class to compete with American labor" who had no intention of acquiring citizenship.[5]

17

At times the pressure was almost unendurable

Some of our most execrable cabinet officers over history have served at the pleasure of our least laudable Chief Executives. If proof is wanted, one need only consider the caliber of some of those who inhabited the cabinets of Buchanan, Grant, Arthur, and Harding, and, closer to our own time, Nixon, Reagan, Bush, and Clinton. Perhaps this is understandable. Be it of a nation or a corporation, unless he has abundant confidence and does not fear comparison a leader of limited cerebral aptitude can no more be expected to surround himself with men of intellect than a morally pusillanimous man can be expected to surround himself with morally puissant underlings. Our outstanding Presidents, especially in the early decades of the Republic, almost without exception appointed men who may have been lacking in proficiency but at least performed adequately. Conversely, our least outstanding—in some cases our most downright deplorable—Presidents invariably chose men who proved to be intellectually as well as morally dysfunctional.

In selecting his cabinet, Grover Cleveland, like Franklin D. Roosevelt, had enough self-confidence to surround himself with men who might "threaten" a weaker, less secure Chief Executive. Though not of equal competence—one or two could be accused of verging on the prosaic—none abused his office; and none induced the suspicion that a criminal investigation into his official conduct might be indicated. Cleveland took into consideration a geographical balance, consistent with his determination to achieve the reunification that still eluded the nation twenty years after the Civil War. And by geographical balance, he meant not only North and South, but East and West; the two regions had become mutually antipathetic as America pushed beyond the Mississippi demographically as well as geographically.

Prior to inauguration, Cleveland ordered his supporters not to make any political promises or enter him into any binding bargains. As he prepared to take the oath of office, he discovered that bargains had already been made which he now felt honor bound to fulfill. Fortunately, they worked out for the best. This was especially true of Thomas Francis Bayard. Scion of a distinguished Delaware political family, Bayard had won from party leaders the promise of a major cabinet post in exchange for having his supporters switch to Cleveland at Chicago. Cleveland realized, promises notwithstanding, that Bayard was ideal for Treasury, the one post Bayard coveted. The two shared identical views on currency and the tariff; and sixteen years in the Senate, where he had a reputation for fiscal soundness and conservatism, gave Bayard the experience and clout as a Washington insider that would be invaluable to a President coming on the scene as a Washington outsider. But party leaders had another man in mind for the post. Cleveland gave Bayard the only other major portfolio, Secretary of State. Though Bayard accepted reluctantly, convinced he was not the best man for the job, he went on to acquit himself admirably.

So, too, did the man believed by the party elders to be best suited for Treasury, Daniel Manning. The New York State Democratic leader had risen from ragged newsboy to man of great wealth and political savvy with a firm command of sound fiscal principles. Critics charged him with demanding the post as payment for his critical role in Cleveland's winning the presidency. The charge will not wash. His appointment was urged not only by Democratic leaders, but by men, including Republicans, who reflected the broadest spectrum of political opinion—bankers, lawyers, politicians, and journalists. Also, Cleveland knew that Manning, like himself an advocate of tariff reduction and sound money (maintaining the gold standard), was a paradigm of honesty and moral rectitude, despite his many years in the political trenches. Of all he achieved at Treasury, Manning would be most lauded for ending the tradition of undervaluing imports, a shifty practice that benefited foreign manufacturers and domestic importers at the expense of the Treasury and, by extension, of the American taxpayer. He also initiated a number of administrative reforms that made his the best-run executive department.

For his Secretary of War, Cleveland chose William C. Endicott, a former justice of the Massachusetts Supreme Court, who had just lost the race for governor. That he was the right man for the post was borne out in Endicott's sound handling of the office. In his choice of William Vilas to be Postmaster General, Cleveland wisely blended the necessities of managerial talent, political clout, and regionalism. Vilas, from Wisconsin, was an esteemed national figure whose political strength lay in the Northwest, where the Democrats had only recently made inroads they were anxious to consolidate and exploit.

Cleveland encountered much criticism when he insisted on William C. Whitney of New York, a leader of the core group that engineered his nomination, to head the Navy Department. Party leaders distrusted the financier and sportsman, but Cleveland was impressed by his record. As Tilden's lieutenant he had helped bring down the infamous Tweed Ring; as New York City corporation counsel he saved the taxpayers millions by contesting fraudulent claims. Among Whitney's many achievements as Navy Secretary, pride of place went to a major shipbuilding program which guaranteed the nation's protection and prominence, now that the United States was a two-ocean power.

Cleveland's most controversial appointments were for Interior and Justice. Here he selected men who had served in the late Confederate government. His choice for Interior, Lucius Q. C. Lamar of Mississippi, had drafted that state's Ordinance of Secession in 1861 and served two years in the Confederate army. But, having wisely accepted the South's loss, he was lauded on both sides of the Mason-Dixon

Line for his labors in the cause of reunification. News of the appointment generated a flood of protest, mainly from one of the nation's most powerful voting blocs, the Grand Army of the Republic, with more than 300,000 Union veterans. Cleveland was less concerned with the GAR's sensibilities than with reuniting the country. Lamar built a praiseworthy record at Interior and, after 1888, on the United States Supreme Court, where his temperament and intellect made him the right man for the right job at that particular moment in the Court's history.

Cleveland's other southern appointment, Augustus Garland of Arkansas to be Attorney General, incurred greater protest than Lamar's. Like Lamar, Garland had accepted the war's verdict and gone on to become a powerful force for reunification through service in both houses of Congress. As Attorney General he was criticized, and rightly so, when it became known that he owned stock in a company involved at the time in patent litigation before the government (the details of which we shall examine in their proper chronological sequence). While he proved to be Cleveland's weakest cabinet officer, Lamar was also one of his most capable administrators.

All were given broad latitude in running their departments, with the tacit understanding that as loyal lieutenants they would conform with overall policies the President set for the executive branch and would avoid intramural dissension. In return, all were assured of the President's support when it came to Congressional opposition, aggrieved office-seekers, critical subordinates, and the like. At meetings, all were encouraged to speak their minds, and freely, on any and all matters. No votes were taken, however. Cleveland believed that in a cabinet there are many voices but a single vote. He would hear each man out and then alone make the final decision. On one point he was adamant: there would be no "kitchen cabinet," or inner circle of advisers. Cleveland was determined to avoid even the slightest suggestion of a return to the style of Grant and his disreputable Stalwarts.[6]

Of 126,000 federal employees, 110,000 were not as yet civil service but political appointees, to be selected by, or in the name of, the President. As this President perceived patronage, the primary goal was to select appointees from a group of competent persons, by competitive examination. Winnow the incompetents, he insisted, and he could still satisfy the reformers as well as the Democratic office-seekers without having to replace Republican holdovers who had demonstrated fitness and aptitude for their jobs, especially if it meant replacing them with Democratic hacks. But as leader of a party out of office for a generation, Cleveland knew that to be rigidly nonpartisan when it came to distributing patronage was to risk derailing his presidency before it left the station. For the most part, he filled thousands of offices without suffering public criticism or personal misgiving. On those occasions when he erred grievously he would, in the light of new evidence, reverse himself without caring whom he might offend.

The executive branch inherited by Cleveland had become a cesspool of inefficiency and corruption. Some departments were meagerly staffed: State, Navy, and War, which shared what is now the Executive Office Building a block from the White House, suffered telephone service that wasn't much above the level of the primitive, and only a few on their staffs were equipped with typewriters. By contrast, at the Bureau of Printing and Engraving, 539 of the 958 clerks were redundant. There the Republicans had introduced the custom of increasing the number of temporary employees for political purposes. The situation was magnified at Treasury and the Post Office, where more than half the workers, all temporary, were placed on and removed from the rolls at the pleasure of the Secretary.

Securing funds for the awarding of patronage was as novel as the system itself. All $1,600 and $1,800-yearly permanent positions that fell vacant through attrition were left unfilled and the salaries were allowed to accumulate, to be divided among patronage dispensers in a unique manner. Instead of hiring one $1,800 clerk as a permanent replacement, three would be hired at $600 each—"on the lapse," as the practice was called. In one instance, thirty-five men were hired for eight days at the close of a fiscal year so as to sop up those lapsed funds, which would otherwise have reverted to the Treasury.

Another ploy to spread jobs around, and thereby satisfy the demands for reward by lower-echelon party loyalists, was the so-called rotation system. A worker would be dropped after a while—say, a month, or a few weeks, or even a few days—to make way for another, and go into the rotation for yet another position. This systematic distribution of spoils was customarily practiced away from the nation's capital and the notice of honest observers. Just about every post office, customs house, internal revenue collector's office, and navy yard around the country played the game. The customs collector for the Port of New York, it was learned, removed on average one employee every three days; one of his more expert successors removed 830 of 900 subordinates at the rate of three every four days.

Yet another repugnant practice elevated by the Republicans to a fine art that Cleveland insisted be terminated forthwith was the raising of "assessments" for party purposes. By this gimmick, officeholders were systematically "encouraged" by party heads to pay a fixed portion of their salaries—usually 2 percent—into the campaign treasury. Such donations were treated as a request, though it was hardly a secret that failing to honor the request was treated as almost a crime against humanity. Cleveland made it known that the new Civil Service Law of 1883—the so-called Pendleton Act—was to be enforced scrupulously. The Pendleton Act, which introduced competitive examinations, brought certain categories of federal employees within a merit system and protected civil servants from compulsory political assessments.

Cleveland also made it known that in staffing the executive branch, notwithstanding the traditional meting out of patronage, he would not only enforce the terms of the Pendleton Act, he would observe its spirit in dealing with the huge class of competent holdover Republican employees who were "not within the letter of the Civil Service statute" but so "disconnected" with the incoming administration that they stood in danger of being removed during their terms on merely partisan grounds.[7] All such holdovers were put into one of two categories: efficient workers, who were to be kept for their full terms, and inefficient ones, who were to be removed.

Also enunciated by Cleveland to serve as a warning to spoils-hungry Democrats: party service must not be a criterion for appointment to office, which was to be based solely upon careful inquiry as to fitness. When a delegation of Democrats urged that he name one of them to an office which Cleveland knew was being administered efficiently by a Republican, they were cut off with the frigid observation "Why, I was not aware that there was a vacancy in that position." Another delegation was silenced with the blunt suggestion that they go home and read up on the 1867 Tenure of Office Act, which prohibited arbitrary removal of federal officeholders appointed with the advice and consent of the Senate. (A prohibition, by the way, that would come back to haunt Cleveland.) Yet another delegation in quest of spoils was told by a testy Cleveland that the commissions of the Republican incumbents they hoped to replace had some time to run, and he had heard nothing negative about the men. ("And if you see him once and look at that face and jaw," one of those present later recalled, "you will believe he means what he says!")[8]

It is testimony to the promise of what Cleveland would bring to the presidency that he managed to staff the upper echelons of his administration with capable men and still please all factions who had supported his candidacy, Independent Republican as well as Democratic. He came to grief on only one. Unfortunately, this one led to his international embarrassment. At the urging of America's senior Roman Catholic prelate, Archbishop (later Cardinal) James Gibbons of Baltimore, Cleveland nominated Anthony M. Kelly of Virginia as U.S. Minister to Italy. Cleveland (but surely not Gibbons) was unaware that when attending a public meeting in 1871 called to protest the end of the Pope's temporal authority, Kelly excoriated the Italian government as a usurper. His rather indelicate comments regarding King Victor Emmanuel and the recently achieved Italian unification were now dragged out by the Republican press for a public airing. Rome refused to receive Kelly, the appointment was rescinded, and Cleveland committed an even bigger gaffe by nominating him to be U.S. Minister to Austria.

Proper advice from his State Department might have spared Cleveland the added embarrassment that soon ensued. But such advice was not forthcoming. Austria rejected Kelly, not out of concern for Italy's sensibilities—both nations enjoyed close relations after generations of Austrian control of Italy's northern provinces—but because those relations had become quite strained of late, due to irredentism on both sides of their common frontier. Rome and Vienna both feared that some "incident" might bring them to war. For the Austrians to accept as American envoy a man whose insolent allusions to Italy were the talk of every European chancery would have been interpreted by the Italians as the "incident" both nations dreaded. When Austria rejected Kelly's appointment he tried to save face with the charge that since Mrs. Kelly was Jewish, he would not be accepted in Vienna's social and diplomatic circles. Cleveland had Bayard announce that the United States would tolerate no "religious tests in such a matter." But this was lost amid the tumult of a deplorable muddle that should not have been allowed to arise.[9]

Despite such gaffes, in organizing his administration Cleveland successfully branded as misguided Cassandras all those who professed to see in him "a conundrum in the flesh," "a tool of the New York gang," "a man without ideas." At times the pressure was almost unendurable. Even before entering the White House he described "this dreadful, damnable office seeking" as a "nightmare."[10] If he believed the "nightmare" was about to end, he was sadly mistaken.

It was only about to begin.

18

"Good government is the main thing to be aimed at"

Other than the reaction of extremist northern Democrats over the Lamar and Garland appointments, Cleveland emerged fairly unscathed from the top-tier selection process. It was in filling the thousands of second-level positions nationwide—postal and customs inspectors, judges and district attorneys, and the like—that he came to grief. Here he came up against the quadrennial "rotation of office," as this awarding of spoils by every new President was known. Cleveland was optimistic about negotiating the shoals that separated the Scylla of Patronage and the Charybdis of Reform. It would prove to be a misplaced optimism.

The spoils system, whereby the lion's share of federal jobs went to the winning party, was begun forty years into our nation's history when Andrew Jackson established the precedent of sharing the fruits of victory with his fellow Democrats. It quickly became accepted tradition for his presidential successors. (The term originated in a remark by statesman William Marcy while defending Martin Van Buren's controversial appointment as U.S. Minister to Great Britain. He claimed to see nothing wrong in the unwritten rule that "to the victors belong the spoils of the enemy.") The tradition had its detractors, notably John Calhoun, who insisted that when offices were bestowed in recompense for political favors, the tendency was "to convert the entire body of those in office into corrupt and supple instruments of power, and to raise up a host of hungry, greedy, and subservient partisans, ready for every service, however base and corrupt." Much as Calhoun and others railed against the system, they could offer no alternative.

In 1871, Congress created the Civil Service Commission to devise and oversee rules pertinent to federal employment. Henceforth, certain appointments hitherto awarded as spoils would be made solely on the basis of competitive examination, and, furthermore, appointees would be given tenure. As incumbent President, Grant was to name its first members. But Grant was so intimidated by the uncanny ability of the spoilsmen surrounding him to "prove" through remarkably tortuous logic that their system of dispensing patronage was both right and logical that he suspended the commission's operations—placing the blame on his opponents in Congress for refusing to allocate adequate funding. Out of this was born the National Civil Service Reform League, dedicated to educating the nation on the need for reform.

While the movement was bipartisan, it was the Democrats who took the lead in expounding its philosophy. A plank in their 1876 campaign platform stated: "Reform is necessary in the Civil Service. Experience proves that efficient, economical conduct of the Government business is not possible if its Civil Service be subject to change at every election, by a prize fought for at the ballot box, be it a brief reward of party zeal, instead of posts of honor, assigned for proven competence and held for fidelity in the public employ." Four years later they used even more potent language: "We execrate the course of . . . making places in the Civil Service a reward for political crime, and demand a reform by statute which shall make it forever impossible for the defeated candidate to bribe his way to the seat of the usurper by billeting villains upon the people." After Garfield's assassination by a disappointed office-seeker the cause of reform was advanced light-years with passage of the aforementioned Pendleton Act.

On December 20, 1884, while winding up his affairs in Albany, President-elect Cleveland was asked by the National Civil Service Reform League to issue a statement on the subject. In a letter to the league's president he "pledged" himself to civil service reform. He was not "unmindful" of the fear among many Americans that the advent of a Democratic administration after twenty-four years of Republican control might "demonstrate" that the "deeply rooted" abuses endemic in the civil service were "ineradicable." Too, he was "not sure that all those who profess to be the friends of this reform" would "stand firmly among its advocates" when they found it "obstructing their way to patronage and place." But he wanted it understood that "no such consideration shall cause a relaxation on my part of an earnest effort to enforce this law."[11]

Cleveland promised to operate on the conviction that "[g]ood government is the main thing to be aimed at. Civil Service Reform is but a means to that end." But he could not promise the impossible. He knew that the reformers would settle for nothing less from him than miracles of healing. He also knew that the age of miracles, like the age of dinosaurs, had passed. His first clash, with the Mugwumps, was initiated—as were all clashes involving the Mugwamps—by Carl Schurz, who had insisted from the outset that qualified holdover Republicans not be ousted from office in favor of Democrats, even qualified Democrats.

At issue was the disposition of Henry G. Pearson, Republican postmaster of New York City. Schurz hinted strongly that if he removed Pearson, Cleveland would make enemies of the Independents and, what's more, inspire Democratic spoilsmen to make yet more exorbitant demands.[12] Schurz had no way of knowing (Cleveland preferred to play this sort of thing close to the vest) that if Pearson was as capable as his backers claimed, he would be kept in the office. If not, out he'd go. Given the ensuing controversy, and its outcome, Cleveland was justified in wishing Schurz had cut him a little slack.

Pearson, a Garfield appointee, was one of those meritorious civil servants whom corrupt ones love to hate. In hopes of ousting him, his enemies impugned Pearson as a perfidious man unfit to clean public toilets, much less oversee the nation's largest post office. Responsible leaders from both parties joined in requesting his continuance in office. Tammany, on the other hand, lobbied Cleveland to replace him with one of its own, going so far as to warn that failure to do so would cost the party at least ten thousand votes in the next Congressional elections. Cleveland promised to examine the case personally. In so doing, he found Pearson to be deserving of reconfirmation. Next, he sent to the newspapers a crafty pseudonymous letter from "a gentleman very near the President" saying that Pearson's job performance record was "a complete illustration of the successful application of civil service reform principles to an immense governmental establishment." To retain him in the office he had so expertly managed insured "faith and confidence" in the reform movement—which would "receive a shock from his removal." Addressing the fear that his reappointment might cause great discontent in Democratic ranks, the "gentleman very near the President" asserted he knew for a fact that the President wished to go on record as affirming that "the Democratic party is neither hypocritical, unpatriotic or ungrateful—they will understand the whole matter and be satisfied."[13]

They did, and they were.

Except for the spoilsmen.

Cleveland had already filled 13,500 offices that fell within the guidelines of the Pendleton Act. There still remained 41,000 fourth-class postmasterships and another 5,000 assorted posts whose Republican incumbents must either be retained or replaced. Running through the entire process like a Wagnerian leitmotif were cries of "hypocrite" and "traitor!" The first epithet came from, ironically, Republicans who not only had supported Blaine but had trashed Cleveland while he was governor. Crying "traitor!" were Democrats who not only insisted they deserved to fill vacancies but demanded he create vacancies where none existed. It added little to Cleveland's sense of well-being that a growing faction in his own party, many of them civil service reformers, reproved him as a closet spoilsman who had betrayed their trust by filling a number of the low-level offices with out-and-out partisan hacks.

In fact, he was doing just that, though not consciously. Obviously no President is expected to act as his own headhunter in filling all the offices that fall under his purview. For that he must depend upon colleagues, to whom he delegates the actual selection of appointees, subject to his approval, which, save for those involving major posts, is usually pro forma. A number of highly placed Cleveland people, doubting he would learn about it, made so many partisan removals—an alarming number of them more qualified than the men replacing them—it took no leap of faith for his critics to charge that the Democrats were no more dedicated to reform than the Republicans. When it came to his attention that many men in high office, including Vice President Hendricks, were lending their clout to undesirable applicants, the President began to wonder just who in his official family he could trust.

He doubled his efforts to be scrupulously fair. Obviously, Democratic candidates were given precedence over Republican holdovers when both were equally qualified, and incompetent holdovers had to make way for competent Democrats. But he adamantly refused to supplant qualified Republicans with Democrats whose talents were limited to demanding the spoils of victory. A number of major newspapers nationwide, siding with the Democratic spoilsmen, followed the line laid down by Pulitzer's *New York World:* Cleveland "must remember the obligations which an Administration elected by a great historical party owes to that party."

To support this view, Pulitzer reprinted Jefferson's famous 1801 response to the people of New Haven, when on being admonished for removing a popular customs collector to make way for his own appointee, he replied that removals of this order were necessary, as the public service was a federal responsibility, and "few die and none resign." Even zealous Cleveland loyalists like Manning and Whitney, who wished he would occasionally be less the reformer and more the pragmatic politician if only to get those thousands of offices filled, confided to friends they supported Pulitzer's editorials. Not reticent when it came to airing his views was Illinois politician Adlai E. Stevenson, First Assistant Postmaster General, who in a statement to the press said: "Although it is daily asserted that hundreds of postmasters are being appointed, yet the six months which have elapsed since Mr. Cleveland's accession finds only between ten and twelve per cent of the offices occupied by Democrats." Cleveland declined to rebuke Stevenson. He was only speaking the truth.

The more judicious reformers knew that in doing his best to honor his campaign pledges, Cleveland must surmount a number of hurdles. Most important of these was an obligation to work within the limitations of his constitutional power and not alienate his party and, by extension, the Democratic-controlled House of Representatives. He found comfort—and a touch of self-satisfaction—in George Curtis's praise for the course he was pursuing "amid immense perplexities and difficulties." Since inception of the spoils system, Curtis said, "no President has given such conclusive evidence both of his reform convictions and of his courage in enforcing his convictions as Grover Cleveland."[14]

But comfort is evanescent, often lasting little longer than the slaking of a homeless man's hunger after Christmas dinner at the local mission. Just as it was not lost on Cleveland that his critics included many from within his own party, it was not lost on Cleveland's friends that his penchant for cultivating enemies among the journalists might indicate some inexplicable compulsion to self-destruct politically. Hostile editors, not quite used to an independent-minded President who refused to accommodate them, resorted to the tried but true tactic of Us against Them.

Cleveland played right into their hands with a surfeit of castigating letters. Typical was his reply to the editor of a pro-Democratic humor magazine who sent him for comment an antagonistic clipping that caused Cleveland "much annoyance." Terming the charges not only rubbish but, worse, libelously spurious, Cleveland overreacted: "I don't think there ever was a time when newspaper lying was so general and so mean as at present and there never was a country under the sun where it flourished as it does in this. The falsehoods daily spread before the people in our newspapers, while they are proofs of the mental ingenuity of those engaged in newspaper work, are insults to the American love for decency and fair play of which we boast."[15] Here was yet another of the many letters Cleveland wrote over eight years in the White House that his backers wished he had burned instead of mailing. For a President, to react is permissible, to overreact is reckless. Unfortunately, Cleveland was thin-skinned and insisted on having the last word, even when it was pointed out that he was expending needless energy, wasting valuable time, and, even worse, alienating people he should have been cultivating.

For their part, contentious editors deceived the public as to the true nature of their President by rehashing, and thereby keeping in the minds of the people, the anti-Cleveland slanders of the 1884 campaign. In so doing, they reinforced the negativism of Cleveland's critics, who either failed to perceive what he had actually promised, were genuinely misinformed about his actions, or deliberately chose to distort his accomplishments. The upshot was that Cleveland soon lost the confidence of the reformers with his refusal to be a zealot in the pursuit of their cause. And in refusing to play by their time-honored rules, he forfeited the confidence of the Democratic party regulars. To Wilson Bissell he wrote of this vexatious period (he was now in the ninth month of his presidency), "The d——d everlasting clatter for offices continues . . . and makes me feel like resigning, and HELL is to pay generally!"[16]

Most exasperating of all the "d——d everlasting clatter" was the Bacon-Sterling controversy.

E. L. Hedden, customs collector for the Port of New York, a Democratic appointee, replaced a Republican, Captain Bacon, as chief weigher of the Brooklyn Customs District with a Democratic ward heeler, George H. Sterling, without requiring that Sterling take a competitive examination. (The Civil Service Commission had ruled that an examination was not necessary for appointment to the post, which Bacon had held for sixteen years.) Sterling was a confederate of Bill McLaughlin, "boss" of the Brooklyn Democratic machine, who was in turn a political lieutenant of David B. Hill, Cleveland's successor at Albany. Hill, now on his way to becoming New York's dominant political figure, had already assumed leadership of the party's Tammany-led antireform wing. A mayoral campaign was under way in Brooklyn (then still a separate city), and the customs post in question was important because of the number of waterfront laborers whose votes were coveted.

On September 16, the National Civil Service Reform League asked Edward M. Shepard, president of the Young Men's Democratic Club of Brooklyn, to apprise Cleveland of just how unfit Sterling was for the job. Shepard wrote Cleveland: "I do not know Mr. Sterling personally; but he is certainly widely supposed to be a corrupt man." Sterling's "experience as a weigher, if he ever had any, was very long ago and [does] not qualify him to supervise three hundred men." Also, he was "a liquor-dealer, whose associates are reputed to be of a very rough character." Shepard enclosed several pages of testimony to Sterling's moral and professional failings and implored that Cleveland "without delay and in the most emphatic ways" revoke the appointment and restore Bacon (as the major newspapers and journals were demanding), even though he was a Republican, "unless there be proven charges against him."

In defending the change, Hedden argued that civil service regulations had not been violated; that Bacon's behavior in office had been unacceptable and included lending his office to political exploitation; and that Sterling was "a man of integrity, and particularly skilled in the work of the office to which he was appointed." Cleveland ordered the revocation of Sterling's appointment pending a final decision, and asked his brother-in-law, E. B. Yeomans, to visit Brooklyn and ascertain the true facts. Meanwhile, he requested that Shepard "enquire concerning [Sterling] and his associates and all that will aid me in making up a judgment and write to me the result of your investigation. . . . You can readily see that I am not in a position to act now on general denunciation."

Shepard complied, admitting that his first impressions had been wrong: further careful investigation had convinced him Sterling was "a man of considerable native vigor and brightness," with a practical knowledge of what the job entailed, and was "perfectly competent to direct gangs of men." As for Bacon, "although personally an upright and intelligent man," he left a lot to be desired as a supervisor of men, and what was more, he had exploited his position to sanction "partisan [Republican] employment in the politics of Brooklyn."[17] Yeomans's report was also generally favorable to Sterling and supported his replacing Bacon.

Though convinced nothing had been proved against Sterling to justify his rejection on personal grounds, Cleveland was swayed by arguments of the civil service reformers that letting him replace Bacon would adversely affect the entire reform movement. After consulting with the commissioners, he agreed that weighers should be subject to competitive examination. An examination was held, and Sterling placed twenty-second out of forty-five candidates. (The job went to the man who placed first.) Boss McLaughlin's Brooklyn Democrats, with the support of their Tammany brethren across the East River, passed an agglomeration of resolutions denouncing this "mean and cowardly treatment of Mr. Sterling," which they forwarded to "the Mugwump President," with copies to "the vacillating Secretary of the Treasury, and the weak-minded Collector, Hedden."

And on that note, the affair was ended.

But its repercussions had only begun.

Tammany declared war on what they dismissed contemptuously as the "Snivil Service Reform Act," to the degree that New York newspapers insisted the Democrats either denounce reform openly or treat it as one would treat a mad aunt residing in the basement. Doing his best to steam up the Democrats against their man in the White House was Tammany's leading orator, Bourke Cockran. He declaimed a harrowing depiction of the undoing of equality for one and all if the nation were to permit that "pernicious system . . . that erects and creates irresponsible boards of commissions to control or limit the powers conferred by the Constitution on the people."[18] Cockran had little difficulty convincing the faithful. They were fed up with reform.

And they were fed up with Cleveland.

The New York State Democratic gubernatorial nominating convention was approaching, and the party hierarchy felt that in light of the acrimony caused by the Bacon-Sterling controversy, the President should soft-pedal his views on reform. By way of response to what he considered a gross impertinence, Cleveland committed another of his characteristically self-damaging acts: ignoring the fences that separated him from the powerful men in his own party, instead of mending them. It was on occasions such as this that party sages wondered whether Cleveland might not be politically suicidal, if not, indeed, clinically certifiable.

He was neither. He was, though, a bit naïve. Nothing or no one could dissuade Grover Cleveland from the conviction that if what he did was in the best interests of the nation he had been called upon to lead, his course must not be stayed. Not that he believed, in Henry Clay's words, that he'd rather be right than President. Rather, he believed, to paraphrase the words of Cicero, that he would rather be wrong, by God, with Plato than be right with those goddam Pythagoreans.

Ignoring the advice of the Democratic leadership, Cleveland chose to swim against the rising tide of intraparty animosity, instead of seeking a safe harbor, secure in the knowledge that every tide which comes in must eventually go out. Disregarding warnings from Manning and the others that to do so would prove calamitous, Cleveland picked a pivotal moment during the convention to make public his letter of September 11, 1885, accepting the resignation of Dorman Eaton as Civil Service Commissioner. In the letter Cleveland reiterated his categorical commitment to civil service reform and his determination to ignore all obstacles toward that end—even obstacles thrown up by Tammany and all the other irresponsible party regulars.

The letter evoked more attention than the convention itself and set Cleveland on a collision course with the powerful New York faction that would last throughout both his presidencies. Hill, whom Tammany and the spoilsmen determined must succeed Cleveland in the White House, won the gubernatorial nomination. This prompted the Cleveland Republicans to support Hill's Democratic rival. Joining these defectors were an alarming number of Democrats who now believed Cleveland opposed Hill's election. Alton V. Parker, chairman of the party's executive committee, wrote a letter begging Cleveland to realize that only his support would avert a Democratic disaster at the polls. Ever the loyal party man, Cleveland announced his support for the Hill ticket. He even kicked in the heady sum of $1,000 for the campaign fund—though he knew the Hill people were out to bring him down eventually.

But Cleveland couldn't leave well enough alone. In a cover letter containing the contribution, he spoke his mind, in his characteristically circumlocutory fashion: "If I thought that you needed any advice I should strongly urge upon you to enjoin upon any person pretending to desire the success of the ticket, and at the same time howling about the Administration and claiming that it should 'speak out,' that campaigns are successfully fought by pushing the merits of candidates and principles, and not by a foolish attempt to discredit an Administration which is doing all that is possible to assist the canvass." As for "professed friends of the ticket who are constantly drumming at the Administration," their motives should not be misunderstood "and they should not be permitted to conceal their misdeeds by the cry of 'stop thief.' You see," the letter concluded, "I do not claim any decent treatment for myself, though I am not able to see where I have forfeited it."[19]

Here was yet another of those letters that Manning and the party pros wished Cleveland hadn't sent. Hill's stunning success at the polls—his plurality over his Republican opponent exceeded by tenfold Cleveland's over the Blaine in 1884—was a victory for the Democrats, though hardly for the President. A faction dancing ominously to Hill's piping and committed to perpetuating the spoils system was tightening its grip on the party.

Cleveland's logical course would have been to concentrate less on the Hill machine and more on building a countervailing machine of his own from among loyalist office holders. But he chose not to be logical, to the disbelief of the professional politicians, the delight of the reformers, and the dismay of his closest advisers. In his best throwing-down-the-gauntlet style, he issued an executive order enjoining all federal officeholders ("agents of the people, not their masters") to "scrupulously avoid in their political action, as well as in the discharge of their official duty, offending by a display of obtrusive partisanship their neighbors who have relations with them as public officials." They must "constantly remember that their party friends from whom they have received preferment, have not invested them with the power of arbitrarily managing their political affairs." Nowhere should their influence as federal employees "be felt in the manipulation of political primary meetings and nominating conventions"; to do so would be "indecent and unfair." Individual interest and activity in political affairs were by no means condemned, however. Civil servants were "neither disenfranchised nor forbidden the exercise of political privileges." But their privileges did not extend to "pernicious activity by office-holding."[20]

Such an executive order amounted to a gag order, and it fairly screamed for a test case. One was not long in coming. When it did, the habitually wary Cleveland acted in a blatantly subjective manner that is almost too embarrassing to record; moreover, it exposed him to a nationwide barrage of insult and derision for which he had only himself to blame. These are the facts:

During the 1886 Congressional elections campaign, two federal district attorneys made political speeches: M. E. Benton of Missouri, a Democrat, and W. A. Stone of Pennsylvania, a Republican. Cleveland suspended them both summarily for violating his executive order. When Benton sought reinstatement on the grounds that his speeches had not conflicted with his official responsibilities, Cleveland assented. When Stone sought reinstatement for the same reason, Cleveland ordered his suspension upheld. The anti-Cleveland press had a field day. Here, cried the critics, was brazen partisan discrimination by a man who always claimed that sort of thing to be abhorrent. By way of response, the White House pointed out that Stone had been retained in office despite his having been an active anti-Cleveland spokesman during the 1884 campaign. But making political speeches was a violation of the directive. Ergo, his removal was justified.

Cleveland assumed that Benton, being a Democrat, had defended the administration in his recent speeches. ("I did not intend to condemn the making of a political speech by a Federal official . . . if the speech itself was decent and fair," Cleveland wrote him after deciding on his reinstatement.)[21] Not only was Cleveland waffling here, but worse: Democrat Benton had in fact attacked the President in terms that few Republicans had come up with. The editor of one midwestern journal who heard the speech noted that Benton dismissed his own party as the "poor and ignorant party of this country—the great barefooted, unwashed, dirty-socked party." In addition, he did not agree with Cleveland on a number of ideas, especially "Civil Service humbuggery" and "his ideas on finance," which Benton alleged that Cleveland got "from the gold bugs of Wall Street," whom he characterized as "leeches that suck the blood of the honest yeomanry of the West, like vampires."[22]

When it was revealed that the Republican Stone, on the other hand, had abstained from any criticism of either the President or his party, the reformers were appalled. Carl Schurz wrote Cleveland that his handling of the case was "not a mere mistake as to the character or qualifications of a person, or an error owing to misinformation." It represented "a retreat from a position of principle—a back-down apparently for partisan reasons or under partisan dictation."[23]

Clearly, Cleveland's mistake was not in refusing to restore Stone, but in restoring Benton without first ascertaining that he had been "decent and fair." Cleveland apologists averred that he had been so overwhelmed with the whole patronage problem and the many other problems demanding his attention that he had either failed to do his customary homework or fallen victim to bad advice, and, being only human, he was susceptible to the occasional blunder. The party professionals, however, wisely remained silent, and waited—and prayed—for the storm to blow over.

So did Cleveland, who would have been better off compromising a tad on the whole patronage issue, instead of letting it make extravagant demands on his time and energy. Such a course might not have been politically correct but it would have been politically expedient. Furthermore, what censure he would have faced in doing so would have been no greater—and probably a good deal lesser—than what he endured in taking the high moral ground.

Because Congress was now caught up in a much greater struggle with the President to exploit it, the Stone-Benton storm blew over sooner than even the White House dared anticipate. That greater struggle was over Cleveland's determination to restore the independence of the executive branch.

It was one struggle that the legislative branch was determined he not win.

19

On a collision course with the Senate

Since early in the century a succession of assertive Congresses and compliant Chief Executives had put the White House in danger of becoming handmaiden to Capitol Hill. The problem can be traced to three words: "advice and consent," a concept and crucial role in effective governance dating back to Norman England, when it served to keep the sovereign in check. All actions in the management of the kingdom were subject to the "advice and consent" of whatever body was empowered to bestow it, clerical or laical. The formula was brought to America by the first English colonists and incorporated into the legal charters of six of the original colonies. When the framers of the Constitution gave to the President the authority to "appoint ambassadors, other public ministers and consuls, judges of the Supreme Court, and all other officers of the United States whose appointments are not herein otherwise provided for, and which shall be established by law," they stipulated that such appointments be "by and with the advice and consent of the Senate." Over time, "advice" lost its independent meaning and "consent" remained the operative word. Thus did the Senate retain the authority to check the President's power of appointment (though not the authority to share it).

Left unanswered was the question of whether the President required senatorial consent to remove from office anyone whose original appointment had required such consent. In the early decades of the Republic the power of removal was held to be uniquely the President's. When Jefferson came to office he found the government bureaucracy packed with Federalist holdovers. "If a due participation of office is a matter of right, how are vacancies to be obtained?" he demanded. We are already familiar in these pages with the New Haven incident and his rationale: "Those by death are few, by resignation none. Can any other mode than that of removal be proposed?" Jefferson resolved the dilemma by removing thirty-nine incumbents without tolerating any discussion on the matter. Simply ignored over the succeeding three presidencies was the question of what role, if any, the Senate was empowered to play in the removal of appointees whose appointments it had played a constitutional role in effecting.

Then came Andrew Jackson. Unable to strike a deal with the Senate to make way for some of his loyalists on the federal rolls, Jackson resorted to the simple expediency of wholesale removal of other-party incumbents (more than two thousand in his first year alone). Faced with this powerful Chief Executive and the spirit of anti-elitist democracy he unleashed on the nation, the Senate backed down. But under Jackson's impotent successors, it was able to encroach upon the authority of the executive branch, through intramural horse-trading. It mattered not that removals and nominations were still the prerogatives of the executive branch. Confirmation was the prerogative of the legislative branch—specifically, the Senate. Presidents now found themselves in the unique position of having to make their nominations conform to the demands of its members and their respective political machines. (The reader should bear in mind that until passage of the Seventeenth Amendment, in 1916, United States senators were elected by the state legislatures.) By manipulating this so-called "courtesy of the Senate," that body extended its inherent right to confirm major presidential appointments to cover removals from office. Their reasoning: before they could be sure a man was worthy of confirmation, they must ascertain the propriety of his predecessor's removal.

This subtle infringement on traditional executive powers culminated in the aforementioned 1867 Tenure of Office Act, giving the Senate control over all appointments and removals covering specific posts, with the result that the President now required legislative authorization for many appointments which came under his exclusive constitutional authority. These included cabinet and subcabinet officers, postmasters, federal district attorneys and marshals, customs and internal revenue collectors, foreign service officers, and public lands and Indian affairs commissioners. His power of removal was limited to suspension for "misconduct or crime." Were the Senate in recess at the time of a removal, the charges had to be reported to that body, accompanied by all applicable evidence and reasons for the action, within twenty days after Congress reconvened. If the removal was denied senatorial approval, it was voided and the incumbent immediately reinstated. By tossing this wrench into the Constitution's checks-and-balances mechanism, Congress fulfilled the prophecy of jurist James Wilson, who on signing that document said: "The President will not be the man of the people, but the minion of the Senate."

Within two years of its passage, public pressure and presidential indignation stripped the Tenure of Office Act of its most heinous provisions. Out went the requirement that the President provide the Senate with "evidence and reasons" for removal. Also, the precondition limiting causes of suspension to criminal acts and misconduct was replaced with the broader provision that such action by the President was allowable "in his discretion." Yet, the revised act failed to restore the full freedom of removal that had been held by early Presidents. Though free to replace instead of merely suspend federal officeholders, the President now had to make nominations for all vacancies within thirty days of the start of each Congressional session. If the Senate rejected a nomination, he had to make another, and, if need be, yet another, and thus proceed until the obligatory "consent" was granted.

Cleveland's immediate predecessors demanded total repeal of the act, which legal experts held to be unconstitutional, even in its altered form. But the issue had never come before the courts, and the Republican-controlled Senate during the Hayes–Garfield era declined to consider a twice-reiterated demand by the Democratic-controlled House for judicial review.

Despite warnings from advisers to tread cautiously, Cleveland moved aggressively in his determination to preserve what was to him a prerogative of the executive branch, with not a care as to what it might cost or whom it might offend. Aware he was on a collision course with the Senate, he nonetheless plowed ahead. In his first ten months, he submitted the names of 643 holdovers he wanted removed from office. A number had performed adequately, but he had a list of Democrats he was confident could perform just as adequately, if not better. Most were suspended for "gross and indecent" partisan conduct. (For instance, he had learned that a number of the post offices were being used as headquarters for local Republican party committees.) Some of the suspensions were ordered because of official malfeasance.[24]

Various Senate committees requested heads of the appropriate departments to submit reasons for the removals. Cleveland ordered noncompliance. The Senate had the constitutional right to "advise and consent" on appointments, he conceded; but it had no right to demand such "justification." Did not the Senate realize, he asked with heavy irony, that the "evidence and reasons" clause in the original Tenure of Office Act had been knocked out by the 1869 revision? The Senate realized this. The Senate also realized it held a perfectly legal wild card, which it now threw onto the table: it refused to take action on removing the 643 holdovers, thus blocking the replacement nominations in committee.

Their intent here was obvious: to force Cleveland to repudiate his reform pledges, thereby discrediting the Democrats and increasing the strength of the Republicans, who controlled the Senate and were determined to win control of the House in the upcoming elections. What was needed to break the deadlock and resolve the issue once and for all time was a test case.

That case came in December, and resulted in what was probably Cleveland's greatest achievement: retrieving for the executive branch many of the prerogatives that had fallen to the legislative branch through a succession of presidential mediocrities. For that reason, an examination of what was one of this nation's major constitutional crises of the late nineteenth century is warranted.

It began the previous July when Cleveland suspended George M. Duskin, U.S. attorney for the Southern District of Alabama, and a Republican. Named to succeed him was a qualified Democrat, John D. Burnett. As a test case it was a curious choice; neither the President nor the Senate seemed to have noticed (or perhaps to have cared) that Duskin's term was due to expire in a few days, thus rendering his removal academic. Still, it served the desired purpose.

Because Congress was in recess, Burnett took office pending confirmation of his nomination, which Cleveland submitted to the Senate when it returned from recess on December 14. Twelve days later (six days after Duskin's term expired) the Senate Judiciary Committee asked Attorney General Garland for all documentation covering Duskin's removal and Burnett's nomination. Garland complied in regard to Burnett, but said the President had enjoined him from transmitting any documents relating to Duskin. A month later, the committee obtained a Senate resolution directing that Garland forward at once copies of all documents and papers filed with the

Department of Justice as of January 1, 1885 (two months before Cleveland's inauguration, it should be noted), relating to the management and conduct of the office in question.

Here was a case of casting a trawler's net to snag a minnow. And the President had absolutely no intention to bite. Three days later, in a challenge to battle, he had Garland remind the committee that all documentation regarding Burnett's fitness had already been sent; as for all those other documents requested, it was "not considered that the public interest will be promoted by a compliance with said resolution."[25] The committee reacted by prevailing upon the Senate to censure the Attorney General—and by extension the President—for refusing compliance.

What began as an exchange of messages between a Senate committee and the head of an executive department had escalated into a major national debate over whether a President could or could not remove federal officers without senatorial interference. This particular President, while recognizing the obligation of the executive branch to avoid encroachment upon the constitutionally defined powers of the legislative branch would settle for nothing less than restoring for himself and his successors what he considered the constitutional prerogatives of his office ("preeminently the people's office").

"The only thing that gives me any real anxiety," Cleveland confided to a Boston reporter at the height of the controversy, was that the people might "get a false idea of my position, and imagine that I have done anything which I have the least ground to cover up." He had "nothing to conceal"; he was "conscious that in exercising the power of suspension" he had "in every case been governed by a sense of duty and a regard for the good of the public service." Too, he wanted it made clear that "any and every proper inquiry, made in good faith and with a regard to the courtesies that have always prevailed . . . would have been answered." But that, he insisted, was not what the Senate now sought, and he added, in his best desk-thumping style, "I shall not submit to improper dictation!"[26]

There was also a personal factor involved here. Having inherited a federal bureaucracy estimated at 95 percent Republican, Cleveland wanted to replace incompetent Republican incumbents with competent Democrats, at the same time ridding himself of a sizable number from an opposition party bent upon disrupting, if not sabotaging, his administration. But then, any President, regardless of party, would want the same thing.

As reports of imminent bloodletting between the White House and Capitol Hill spread, fueled by newspaper speculation, Cleveland was deluged by a flood of letters, some loaded with advice ranging from the solicitous to the judicious. Historian and legal scholar James Schouler, perhaps the century's foremost authority on the Constitution, wrote that he considered Cleveland's stand "to be just, constitutional, and public." He did not see how "any papers bearing upon such cases could be furnished as a rule, without requiring some further explanation of reasons."[27] Others, more cautious, pleaded that a constitutional fight be avoided, warning that the Senate was not about to compromise, let alone retreat so much as a millimeter. As always when confronted with strong conflicting views on an issue, Cleveland respectfully heard out one and all and then acted as he deemed appropriate.

On March 1, 1886, he sent a cleverly worded message to Congress that covered the entire question of presidential appointments and removals: "Duskin's suspension, and all the others, were my executive acts based upon considerations addressed to me alone and for which I am wholly responsible. My oath to support and defend the Constitution, my duty to the people who have chosen me to execute the powers of their great office and not to relinquish them, and my duty to the Chief Magistracy which I must preserve unimpaired in all its dignity and vigor compel me to refuse compliance." He denied the Senate's right "to review or reverse the acts of the Executive in the suspension, during the recess of the Senate, of federal officials." He was "not responsible to the Senate" in this regard; he was "unwilling to submit my actions . . . to them for judgment." The power to remove or suspend such officials, he insisted, was defined by the Constitution, which expressly provides that "the executive power shall be vested in a President of the United States of America [and] he shall take care that the laws be faithfully executed." Therefore, Cleveland argued in summation, the Tenure of Office Act was unconstitutional.[28]

The Senate debated Cleveland's message for two weeks, the Republican majority attacking, the Democrat minority defending. Then, by a vote of 32 to 25, the Attorney General—and, by implication, the President—was formally censured for withholding the documents demanded by the Senate, an action seen as "subversive of the fundamental principles of the Government." The President's response: since Duskin's term of office had already expired, the only issue was Burnett's confirmation. And since no reason to remove him arose, the censure was meaningless and the Senate had no choice but to confirm him in the office!

Congress capitulated—though after a respectable period of time, so as not to lose face altogether. Thus did a major constitutional crisis end, like Eliot's world, not with a bang but with a whimper. A bill to repeal the Tenure of Office Act was introduced on July 21, 1886, and passed the Senate on December 17 by a vote of 30 to 22, with four Republican senators joining the Democrats to effect the requisite majority. It found easy acceptance in the Democratic-controlled House of Representatives, and with Cleveland's signature on March 3, 1887, the removal process was returned to the status that had lasted from the terms of George Washington through Abraham Lincoln. With Cleveland having restored the constitutionally established bounds of executive power, Presidents were again free to deal with subordinates without senatorial hindrance.[29]

20

Civilization, citizenship, assimilation

Of the many controversial issues Grover Cleveland dealt with over the course of two presidencies, one that resonates to this day is the status of the Native American—or, to use the term current until fairly recently, the American Indian. The first problem to confront him, it was triggered by an executive order of President Arthur just five days before leaving office.

"The concern of the people demands that the Indians be fairly and honestly treated as wards of the Government," Cleveland said in his Inaugural Address. This involved "efforts for the improvement of their condition and the enforcement of their rights," the ultimate object being their "civilization and citizenship." He was confident that "the red man" would "readily assimilate with the mass of our population" if the white man helped him keep "pace in the march of progress."[30]

Thus did Cleveland establish his determination to rescue the Indians from depredations by the white speculators, ranchers, and railroad entrepreneurs who coveted their land, and then to help them evolve into good American citizens. In return for being taught the English language, educated in American ways, and protected by the federal government against those bent on stealing their land and rushing them along the path to extinction, the Indians were expected to abandon such "outmoded tribal ways" as peregrination throughout traditional "happy hunting grounds" and settle down as freehold farmers on federal lands to be given them in severalty.

Cleveland believed being President made him a kind of court-appointed guardian to these "wards," who he regarded as uncivilized yet educable children who could be transformed into viable, productive citizens under such guardianship. This judgment figured prominently in his first, second, and fourth Annual ("State of the Union") Messages to Congress. He saw among the Indians a diversity of traits. Some were "lazy, vicious and stupid," others "industrious, peaceful, and intelligent." Some had "mastered the art" of self-government, others still continued in the squalor and "savagery of their natural state." They must be taught the white man's ways, as "barbarism and civilization cannot live together"; it was "impossible that such incongruous conditions should coexist on the same soil." They were part of "the white man's burden"; "the paths in which they should walk must be clearly marked out for them"; they "must be led or guided" until "familiar" with the conventions of citizenship. Once the process was complete, "the curse [would] be lifted, the Indian race saved, and the sins of their oppression redeemed."[31]

Cleveland's approach to the problem—civilization, citizenship, assimilation—was commendable. Not so commendable was his approach to the Indians' culture. He insisted that English be the sole medium of instruction in all government-operated Indian schools: "It will not do to permit these wards of the nation, in their preparation to become their own masters, to indulge in their barbarous language because it is easier for them or because it pleases them."[32] Seen from today's perspective, this attitude was antagonistic to tribal tradition. Possibly racist. Certainly elitist. But regardless of how he is to be judged by today's standards, by the standards of a century ago Cleveland was dedicated to improving the Indians' lot.

No previous President was so determined to ameliorate the

appalling injustices that had been (as they continue to be to this day) inflicted upon these people by the white man under the odious shibboleths "civilization," "progress," and "eminent domain." America's first century as a nation was punctuated by countless Indian wars and close to four hundred treaties between various tribes or tribal confederations and the federal government. Practically all those treaties were broken by the white man as being antithetic to his plans for ultimate control of all the land that lay between the Atlantic and the Pacific.

In his penultimate Annual Message to Congress, George Washington counseled that "to enforce upon the Indians the observance of justice, it is indispensable that there shall be competent means of rendering justice to them." Similar sentiments were expressed by Washington's successors (except Andrew Jackson). Still, Congress consistently failed to respond in any meaningful way. At times one chamber would propose equitable legislation, but the other chamber would fail to assent. In 1871, Congress legislated an end to treaty-making: from that time forward, "no Indian nation or tribe . . . within the United States" would be "acknowledged or recognized as an independent nation, tribe or power."

As American settlers moved westward toward the Mississippi, creating new states, the resident autochthons were promised that if they accepted relocation beyond the Father of Waters, the lands we know as the Great Plains that had been set aside for them by the federal government would be theirs in perpetuity. With the promise came a caveat: remaining in their old homes east of the Mississippi would put the tribes under control of the states in which those homes lay; and thus outside the jurisdiction of a more benevolent national government, whereas by relocating in the trans-Mississippi territories they would come under the protection of the "Great White Father."

The tribes relocated, and as promised, they were allowed to enjoy independent sovereignty in their new homes. Some, notably the Creeks, Cherokees, Choctaws, Chickasaws, and Seminoles, for whom the Indian Territory was set aside, showed a faculty for self-government and united as the Five Civilized Tribes. A fertile area of some 45 million acres, the Indian Territory encompassed present-day Oklahoma north and east of the Red River and present-day Nebraska and Kansas. A number of other tribes settled alongside the original five, though each retained its own government. In 1854 the area was reduced by the creation of the Kansas and Nebraska territories. As the United States moved westward under the rubric of Manifest Destiny, pressure mounted to abolish the Indian Territory—or as it was by then known the Oklahoma Territory. (The process, begun by Benjamin Harrison, culminated in 1912 with Oklahoma's admission into the Union.)

Over the years before Grover Cleveland reached the White House, though, the popular notion of a savage people functioning as a separate polity gave way to the conviction that the Indians were—and must ever remain—under direct federal control. On the very day before his inaugural a law went into effect establishing federal jurisdiction over all land ceded by treaty. This gave added poignancy to the Indians' definition of Heaven as "the place where white men lie no more." Even before departing Albany for Washington, Cleveland had been determined to regain and secure for the Indians the rights they had been granted by treaty only to have them abrogated. Paramount among them was the right to occupy their reservations free from the threat of white invaders. But Cleveland was a realist; he knew this was easier said than done. Arriving at Washington, he learned of an added complication:

Just four days earlier, President Arthur had issued an order opening the Winnebago and Crow Creek lands for white settlement on the first day of the following May. The land—which the government had ceded by a treaty it subsequently abrogated—consisted of 494,778 acres on the east bank of the Missouri River in the Dakota Territory, valued at around $1.5 million. Arthur's order resulted in all likelihood from an act of collusion between greedy land speculators and their allies in the Interior Department. That there was no significant public outcry was doubtless due to the feeling among many whites, dating from colonial times, that America's first known inhabitants had no rights worth honoring, and besides, the western reservations given them under benefaction were much larger than they actually needed.

By March 5, 1885, Cleveland's first full day in the Oval Office and nine weeks before the designated day, two thousand settlers had moved into the territory, a quarter of the claims had been taken, and houses were already under construction. Larger numbers, respecting the opening date, massed along the border in the tens of thousands, champing at the bit. Cleveland ordered federal marshals sent to remind the invaders that they were trespassers and therefore obliged to gather their personal property and withdraw. The trespassers responded with defiance: they were staying, and would defend themselves and their property with arms. Meanwhile, eighteen U.S. Army companies moved into position on the territory's border, with instructions to prevent, by force if necessary, any other settlers from moving in.

The situation intensified when some of the Indians began to slaughter the cattle and terrorize the unlawful ranchers. The ranchers demanded federal protection. Determined to know all the facts before deciding how best to proceed, Cleveland ordered General Philip Sheridan, the army's senior commander, to investigate personally and suggest a course of action. Sheridan reported that the cause of the disorder lay in the grazing leases between the ranchers and the Indians. These were contracted on an individual basis without government consent, though all parties knew the leases were illegal without such consent. Four million acres—nine-tenths of the acreage set aside for the Indians—had been leased at between one and two cents a year per acre. Two hundred thousand cattle grazed land on which owners paid no taxes and maintained no roads. Furthermore, the Indians, few of whom could read what they had signed, now learned they were liable for any loss or injury to the cattle, with the value of losses to be deducted from the rentals. Should any livestock break a leg or come down with colic, or just drop dead, all financial liability devolved upon the lessor—who, theoretically, could wind up having leased the land for nothing, or, even worse, paying the lessee for the leasing rights!

Cleveland was appalled to learn that the white man's cupidity, in tandem with the red man's ignorance, was gulling the nation's "wards" out of all the equitable and lawful rights granted them by the federal government. On April 17, just five weeks into his presidency, he formally rescinded Arthur's order by executive proclamation. The proclamation was hailed nationwide, and not only by the Indians. Sympathetic whites lauded the latest Great White Father for initiating an honorable phase of the "century of dishonor"—the name given to America's dealings with the Indians by activist author Helen Hunt Jackson.

Despite Cleveland's threat that "all the power of the Government will be employed to carry into proper execution the treaties and laws," the ranchers treated his proclamation as nothing more than a political grandstand play. Hoping to exert pressure, they rushed a delegation to Washington, sure that the President, presumably desirous of a second term in the White House, would never oppose them and those they represented for the sake of a few thousand politically impotent savages. Cleveland received the delegation courteously and had them plead their case. After reminding him of the extent of their fiscal interests and political influence, they bemoaned the hardships they faced if forced to leave the territory. Cleveland's reply:

They had spoken too much about their interest, but not a word about the public interest. And it was the public interest that he represented, and would continue to represent. They had elaborated on hardships which they themselves had created, but had spoken not a word about the rights they had violated. They had sacrificed the public peace and public honor to enrich themselves at the expense of the Indians. They had made no effort to obey the law, but had labored indefatigably to breach it. Then, without allowing them to respond, he precipitately ended the interview. There was nothing more to be said. His policy was irrevocable and irreversible. They had already wasted twelve of the forty days given them to evacuate the land in this ill-advised attempt to get him to back down. They had best get started without further delay.

Eastern investors joined the western ranchers in protesting what they saw as the inadequacy of a mere forty days' notice; they feared that many if not most of the cattle involved would die from being forcibly driven off the disputed land. Cleveland held firm, and the fears came to pass. The herds reached ranges of the Southwest, already overgrazed, just as the region was about to suffer one of its bitterest winters in recorded history. By the following spring, over 80 percent of the stock had perished. It must be admitted that while Cleveland took the proper and honorable course, he went about it recklessly and harshly. There is some evidence that in retrospect even he regretted having acted peremptorily in denying the ranchers sufficient time to evacuate the land. But, in his defense, Sheridan had warned that only prompt action would avert an outbreak of hostilities, a judgment seconded by the local government agent for Indian affairs.

Conditions that formerly protected the Indian lands from encroachment by the whites were becoming subsumed in the march of progress. New states were transforming the area contiguous to the reserved lands, and the tendency to overrun and settle these lands was both inevitable and compelling. It was no longer possible for the federal government to keep its citizens out of these territories, advised one Indian commissioner. "It has been demonstrated that isolation is an impossibility, and that if possible it could never result in the elevation of civilization of the Indian."[33] When a delegation from the Mohonk Conference visited him to urge action, Cleveland rued that whatever he might do to resolve the problem would "only make it a beginning." (The Mohonks were a group of clergymen, educators, legislators, government officials, and other reformers who met annually from 1883 to 1912 at Lake Mohonk, New York, to recommend policies intended to assimilate the Indians into the mainstream of American life.) Still, he wished to do "the most useful thing that now can be done." The delegation requested that he seek legislation empowering the federal government to grant lands, along with American citizenship, to any tribes it deemed ready.

Before Cleveland could decide on the most practical course consonant with this suggestion, reports reached him that some of the tribes were planning to secure by combat the rights he hoped to secure for them by peace. Warned by the Indian agent at Santa Fe, "An Indian war is as sure to come next spring as that the sun will shine tomorrow," Cleveland ordered General Sheridan to prevent any confrontation between the Indians and the American troops concentrated in the area. At the same time Sheridan was to request of the Indians "a statement on their part, as to any real or fancied injury or injustice towards them, or any other causes that may have led to discontent, and to inform yourself generally as to their condition." Any and all complaints, he was to tell the Indians, would be fully examined by the authorities in Washington, "and if wrongs exist they shall be remedied." Additionally, the ranchers and other settlers were to be "fully assured" of the government's resolve to "enforce their peaceful conduct, and by all the power it has at hand." They and the Indians were to be assured that the government would "prevent and punish acts of lawlessness and any outrages upon our settlers."[34]

Before Sheridan could act, lawlessness and outrages were under way by both sides. The situation was escalated by the Apaches, predominant for three hundred years in northern Mexico, Arizona, and New Mexico. Led by their legendary chief, Geronimo, they left their reservation in small bands and slipped across the borders, leaving in their wake an accretion of murder, arson, and pillage. On April 20, Cleveland had the War Department issue Field Order No. 7—and the last of the Indian Wars got under way.

For months, federal border troops ranged over a wide area in quest of the Apaches, even descending into northern Mexico on the supposition that they had fled there. On July 13, they stumbled upon and overran Geronimo's camp in a surprise raid. He and his braves were relocated to Florida, and later to Alabama. (Contrary to agreement, they were denied permission to take their wives.) Peace came to New Mexico, Arizona, and the entire Mexican border area. By waging a small war vigorously, Cleveland had prevented a greater war.

On February 4, 1887, Congress passed the Dawes Severalty Act (named for its author, Henry L. Dawes of Massachusetts, chairman of the Senate Indian Affairs Committee), which called for the allotment, on a family and individual basis, of lands previously held as tribal property. The President was authorized (but not required) to allot the land in fixed quantities: a quarter section (160 acres) to each head-of-family, plus a one-eighth section to single adults and orphans and a one-sixteenth to each dependent child. The lands were to be considered inalienable, and held in federal trust for twenty-five years, after which full title would be given. Those who accepted would have citizenship conferred upon them. What Congress had enacted was an opportunity and little more. Success or failure would depend on how its provisions were carried out. And the most critical provision was the distribution of the land. Cleveland promised that in naming land agents, he would consult with men empathetic to the Indians and sensitive to their needs. He feared the obvious: an unscrupulous agent could easily assign the least hospitable, least productive acreage and sell the best to covetous white speculators, who alit upon the scene like checkbook-bearing vultures. (Thus echoing Dawes's cynical fear: "Hunger and thirst of the white man for the Indian's land is almost equal to his hunger and thirst after righteousness.")

True to his word, Cleveland interviewed numerous missionaries and teachers whose resolve to protect the Indians' best interests was established, before designating twenty-seven reservations for this first experiment in severalty. More would be set aside, if necessary. Surprisingly few tribes favored the change. Most resented the allotment agents, who they feared would inflict on them American citizenship and loss of their nomadic tradition as a prerequisite to accepting as a gift land that was once theirs and subsequently taken away. They considered severalty inimical, if not fatal, to their ancient tribal system. More often than not, the sight that greeted agents entering a reservation was the backs of Indians heading for the woods under full steam. Nevertheless, the allotment proceeded, slowly.

The Dawes Act did not resolve the overall problem, which was intensified by the reality that the very legislation which ended effectively the Indians' resistance to the white man's westward expansion had confined them to reservations and put their traditional tribal system in jeopardy. It was, though, a giant step in the right direction, one taken by no other American President.

21

Spoliation of the American West

Another problem Cleveland inherited from his predecessors was the wholesale spoliation of the American West—specifically, the approximately one million square miles in public domain that comprised the eight great territories of the trans-Mississippi West. For more than twenty years a corrupt clique of railroads, cattle barons, lumber companies, surveyors, and western politicians had eyed these lands like a group of starving swine eying a slops-laden trough. In 1862 the area was thrown open to settlers by the Morrill Act. Meanwhile, large land grants had been, and were continuing to be, made to railroads and agricultural colleges. (These were the "land grant schools" from which grew today's state universities.)

By the time Congress halted the program in 1871, the railroads had received over 160 million acres, more than a quarter of the entire area. Many kept the grants despite forfeiture clauses calling for reversion to the government if certain conditions were not met, such as agreement to extend trackage. Under six Republican administrations the railroad barons ignored these forfeiture clauses. When Cleveland entered the White House the area subject to forfeiture was equal to New York, New Jersey, Delaware, Maryland, Pennsylvania, and Virginia combined. He saw to it that the Interior Department eventually returned the land to the public domain.

Yet another evil Cleveland inherited was the abuse of so-called indemnity lands. The railroads were granted strips of land along proposed routes which in many cases contained parcels already in private hands. As indemnity, they were permitted to select added tracts within certain fixed limits beyond their grants. It was not unusual for newly arrived homesteaders to settle on these tracts, ignorant of the risks involved. Soon the railroads would hastily dispatch agents to lay claim to acreage, much of which had by then been put into productive cultivation by the innocent settlers—and go on to lay claim to contiguous parcels of land which were available for homesteading. An added horror: acquiescent officers in the Arthur Interior Department, pressured by the railroads, withdrew abundant tracts of available land from distribution, making them unavailable to potential settlers—whereupon the railroads picked the best of these lands as their indemnity.

A further loss of these government lands was due to fraudulent surveys. Because the Interior Department allowed the state and territorial surveyors-general to award contracts for public-land surveys to their deputies, there was an increase in duplicity and deceit. Syndicates were organized that got control of all surveying contracts and thereby succeeded in cheating the government out of valuable land rights. Large lumber and cattle corporations were left free to exploit the system for their own benefit.

And then there was the devious land-grabbing by predatory lumber and ranching corporations. When their local agents took on hired help such as cowboys or lumberjacks, they had them file homestead papers on the best timber or grazing lands. These were then sold or given to the employers. When the legitimate homesteader arrived to establish a claim in the area, he found the best land already in the hands of the corporations. It is estimated that over five thousand cases of perjury or subornation of perjury were verified, and collusion among state and territorial officials reached the magnitude of a major epidemic throughout the western public domain. Often, when the barons could not seize the land, legally or otherwise, they resorted to stealing its product. One well-financed corporation, allegedly fronting for the Northern Pacific, was the Montana Improvement Company, organized in 1883 with a capital of $4 million to exploit the forests of Montana and Idaho. The company not only plundered government lands, it bought witnesses and audaciously mocked all threats of prosecution. Elsewhere throughout the West, valuable woodlands bordering rivers and creeks were razed.[35]

It was the railroads that were most imaginative when it came to despoiling the West. A case in point was the New Orleans, Baton Rouge & Vicksburg Railroad Company. Years before, Congress had made a large land grant to the line, but with a time limit for development, which expired while the roadbed was still under construction. The grantee sold its claim to the New Orleans Pacific Railroad Company, which filed selections of more than one million acres between New Orleans and Shreveport, despite protests by area residents.

On the Friday before Cleveland's inauguration, Arthur's Interior Secretary ordered an additional force of clerks to accelerate preparation of necessary patents. Laboring night and day, they actually issued patents for 680,000 acres as Arthur was escorting his successor to the Capitol for his swearing-in.

While Congress debated the subject, the successor immediately set a new policy in motion. Moving simultaneously on many fronts, he had Interior Secretary Lamar halt further issuance of patents, initiated an investigation of all fraudulent claims, and suspended action in the General Land Office on all entries in most of the western domain. This sudden partial halting of the public-land program evoked widespread condemnation. Cleveland insisted the move was imperative until further precautions could be taken to protect the public's interest. He then ordered the hasty dispatch of forty-two special agents to the area. Over the succeeding fiscal year they exposed more than three thousand cases of suspected fraud, some quite sensational. On one tract alone, 4,300 homestead claims had been certified for patents where fewer than a hundred settlers were cultivating the soil.

Even more outrageous, and to Cleveland particularly appalling, were numerous instances of homesteaders being driven from their rightful land by the corporations, which employed goons on contiguous homesteads to cut the settlers off from water and access to market for their goods.[36]

The railroads and other large corporations were not the only targets of Cleveland's wrath. Launching an attack against ranchers who were fencing in public lands and water courses, he issued a proclamation denouncing these unlawful enclosures and ordering government agents to demolish them. (One rancher had to remove thirty-four miles of fence.) In addition, he ordered steps taken to clean up the surveying system. Men who destroyed physical points of reference by which a proper survey was assured were punished; soon these surveying "rings" were put out of business. Also done away with was the pseudo-homesteading by newly hired cowboys and lumberjacks described above. In addition, widespread timber thievery was halted by vigorous patrolling. Corporations found guilty both in the civil and criminal courts of having engaged in such practices were run to ground; during 1885 alone the Interior Department recovered a total of $3 million.

Cleveland's praiseworthy record in protecting the American settler against avaricious individuals and corporations is ignored. Perhaps it should be recalled, in light of what today's generation of rapacious developers is doing to the environment and endangered wildlife. If nothing else, it might raise our consciousness when next we enter the election booth.

22

The currency issue splits the nation

Two great issues that confronted the United States in the post–Civil War period, tariff and currency, ran like connectives through Cleveland's eight years in the White House. The issue of high tariff versus protectionism will be dealt with as we approach the end of Cleveland's first administration, where it properly belongs.

Of the two, the currency issue was more divisive; it split the nation along geographical lines as did slavery in the years leading up to the Civil War. It wore many hats—silver, free-silver coinage, monometallism, bimetallism, hard money versus soft money—yet had but one head. No issue had so profound an effect on Grover Cleveland's White House career as did the attempt by a powerful majority in

Congress to establish silver as a basis for the nation's currency—if need be, over his politically dead body. Pitting him against his own party on Capitol Hill, it made Cleveland's first administration an adventure in stress, destroyed his hopes to succeed himself in 1888, won him reelection four years later, and drove him from the White House in 1896.

Might Cleveland, the proponent of hard money—maintaining gold as the nation's primary medium of currency—have been less intractable, or more politically correct, on the issue, if only out of self-preservation? We can answer that with an emphatic no, given his absolute commitment to maintaining the gold standard, which he saw as the nation's only hope for avoiding fiscal havoc. Many chroniclers of the period argue persuasively that Cleveland's single greatest service to the nation was his obdurate defense, against massive assaults, of an inherently sound financial system.

Few students of our nation's history are unfamiliar with the celebrated speech by William Jennings Bryan, that implacable leader of the free-silver, or soft-money, movement, before the 1896 Democratic Natural Convention in Chicago, when he brought down the house with its ringing coda: "You shall not crucify mankind upon a cross of gold." As oratory, it was exemplary. As economic theory, it wasn't. Cleveland knew that. He'd been saying so all along. But by then the currency issues had made enemies of these onetime Democratic allies. And Bryan, being one of those fundamentalists who demand that mankind accept as irrefutable its lineal descent from Adam and Eve, was not willing to consider, let alone embrace, his enemy's judgment.

Root cause of the issue was the Bland-Allison Silver Coinage Act of 1878, which called for the United States Treasury to purchase monthly between $2 million and $4 million in silver bullion at market price and coin it into silver dollars, for use as legal tender in all debts. Behind the bill were western representatives in whose states silver was mined profusely; they were abetted by a powerful southern bloc who saw in bimetallism a corrective to the powerful anti-silver eastern financial establishment. (Once Bland-Allison went into effect, these so-called silverites, unwilling to accept the old maxim that half a hog is better than no hog at all, sought to replace it with a bill calling for unlimited coinage of silver. This failed, as did an attempt by the gold-standard or hard-money forces—the monometallists—to repeal Bland-Allison altogether.)

One does not require a degree in economics to appreciate the intrinsic danger of a government forced to suffer the interchangeability of silver dollars with the more valuable gold ones. Under this plan, the silver dollar was worth only 80 percent of the value of gold in a gold dollar; yet, it could be used in place of, even exchanged for, a gold dollar at par. One could—many in fact did—exchange silver dollars for gold dollars and hoard the more precious of the two metals against a dramatic rise in their value. To their credit, Presidents Hayes, Garfield, and Arthur, though they could not get Bland-Allison repealed, at least mitigated its effect somewhat by limiting the purchase of silver bullion to a permissible minimum. But such action merely wounded the beast; and all the world knows how beasts react when wounded.

By the outset of the Cleveland presidency, federal mints had turned out more than 215,750,000 silver dollars. Not only was this much more than the country needed, it was much more than the country could absorb. Despite efforts over the preceding three administrations, only $50 million in silver was in circulation with $165,700,000 sitting in government vaults, while $2 million in gold was being paid out every month for the requisite purchase of silver to be added to the idle mass. A firm believer in Gresham's Law ("In the long run, cheap money drives dear money out of circulation"), Cleveland, supported by discerning economists and Wall Street bankers, was convinced that with continued coinage, cheap silver dollars would over time displace gold as the nation's sole monetary medium, resulting not only in calamitous inflation at home but in damage to our credit and trade abroad, where the gold standard prevailed.

On February 2, 1885, Abram Hewitt, chairman of the House Ways and Means Committee, wrote to President-elect Cleveland that the nation was "in the presence of a great peril." Receipts of the New York Custom House were now primarily in silver certificates. The stock of gold in the Treasury was being exhausted, and could not be replenished "except through practical purchase, which will soon put gold to a premium—already the banks and trust companies are hoarding gold, or investing in sterling exchange." The Arthur administration was "striving to maintain gold payments until the 4th of March [Cleveland's inaugural day], so that the inevitable suspension shall take place under a Democrat Administration." At the urging of the outgoing Secretary of the Treasury, "the Republican presidents of the United States banks . . . have agreed to take silver certificates at the New York Clearing House, so far as may be necessary to keep up the balance of gold in the Treasury to the point needed to avoid suspension."[37]

Despite attempts to force the vast amount of silver mandated by Bland-Allison into general circulation, much of it had actually gone into the channels of trade; as a result of the business depression of 1884 it was coming back to the Treasury. Obligations due the government were being steadily paid in this coinage, while gold was being withdrawn from government vaults through the use of both silver dollars and legal paper specie ("greenbacks"). This put the government in the shaky position of having to accept silver from its debtors while paying out gold to its creditors. To avoid wrecking its credit, the government had to keep its silver money and gold money at par while maintaining a reserve of at least $100 million in gold, the floor established by Congress in 1882 to protect redemption of the greenbacks. Hence Hewitt's charge that this reserve was gravely threatened and his warning that the nation's precarious fiscal posture spelled total disaster for the incoming administration.

Hewitt and other sound-money men insisted that legislation to halt the further coinage of silver was crucial, lest the gold reserve drop below $100 million, at which point specie payments would have to be halted by law. He drafted a rider calling for suspension of silver coinage to a pending civil appropriations bill and demanded that Cleveland come out in its support. Meanwhile, on February 11, ninety-five Democratic congressmen representing the pro-silver West and South expressed the hope that the President-elect would not yield to those calling for suspension of silver coinage.

As Inauguration Day neared, Samuel J. Tilden led the Gold Democrats in pressuring Cleveland to state publicly his determination to maintain the gold standard; specifically, to seek repeal of the Bland-Allison Act and thus end the coinage of free silver, which they saw as one of the profoundest perils facing the nation. To Cleveland such a declaration seemed unnecessary; he was already committed to such a course. Still, he felt obliged to honor the request, which, after all, was reasonable enough. Preoccupied with writing (and memorizing) his Inaugural Address, putting together his cabinet, and otherwise preparing for the move to the White House, Cleveland, who preferred to write his own letters, agreed to Tilden's suggestion that the letter be composed by former *New York World* editor Manton Marble, the letter then to be signed by Cleveland as his own. The letter, addressed to "members of the Forty-eighth Congress," was published February 24, 1885.[38]

For all its effect, it might as well have been written in no known tongue. Two days later, by a coalition of 118 Democrats and 52 Republicans against 54 Democrats and 64 Republicans, Congress defeated decisively Hewitt's proposal to suspend silver coinage. Thus did the first post–Civil War Democratic President receive a humiliating rebuke by his own party even before taking the oath of office. Still, the letter served notice that Cleveland would oppose unyieldingly any and all inflationary schemes. Immediately upon assuming office he ordered strict protective measures. These included discontinuation of Arthur's bond redemption policy, thus allowing federal revenues to accumulate in the vaults; and the authorized disbursement of greenbacks where possible in lieu of gold coin or silver certificates. He also had Treasury Secretary Manning arrange for the New York Clearing House to keep intact its current stock of gold and, if possible, augment it, and secretly had three leading New York banks accumulate more than $25 million in the precious metal. By resorting to such prompt and radical measures, and facilitated by an unexpectedly favorable upturn in business, Cleveland in his first year alone increased the gold reserve from $125 million to $151 million, preventing a possibly fatal assault on the nation's economic well-being.[39] As if that were not enough for the silver faction to swallow, in his first (1885) year-end Annual Message to Congress, Cleveland called, as promised, for repeal of Bland-Allison.

When Congress returned from the Christmas recess, in January 1886, the silver bloc went on the offensive. In the Senate, the powerful Democratic senator from Kentucky, James Beck, denounced the administration's policy as "locking up so much money in the Treasury" that if a cyclone struck it would be scattered to the four winds, the people would run to gather up the currency, and "that would be better than the Administration's course." In the House, Cleveland and Manning were accused of being "subservient" to Wall Street and practicing "a gross deception" on the nation by predicting a financial crisis of calamitous proportions that was no more than a "transparent cheat" to benefit "the money-changers and creditor classes."[40]

Cleveland's reaction was to blow an opportunity and, worse, commit a blunder of epic dimensions. Instead of getting behind a program of curative financial legislation—prospects for accomplishing much in support of his position at this time were unusually bright—Cleveland took the position that it was his duty to "keep right on doing executive work. I did not come here to legislate."[41] Next, believing that in its prediction that he would take a strong line with Congress the *New York Herald* had misrepresented him to the public, he committed yet another blunder by speaking out.

The *Herald* was "in error," he informed White House reporters on January 4, for "the most important benefit that I can confer on the country by my presidency is to insist upon the entire independence of the executive and legislative branches of the government." According to the Constitution, he went on didactically, the President was obliged only to make recommendations from time to time to Congress. And he wanted it known that this President meant to be a strictly constitutional one. Asked if he thought Congress would follow his recommendations on Bland-Allison, he said he had no way of knowing. The subject was beyond his control. Moreover, he had no desire to influence Congress in any way; it was enough that he had fulfilled his constitutional obligation by calling its attention to the problem.[42]

The nation was floored by Cleveland's nonconfrontational policy. The *Herald* ran the interview under the headline "Belief That the President's Non-Interference Will Disorganize Parties—Democrats Without a Leader." Silverites were beside themselves with joy. Administration loyalists were beside themselves with despair. The overall tone of his 1885 Annual Message, the strong language he would sometimes use when addressing recalcitrant congressmen, his reputation as a man of unwavering convictions—these had led the silver lobby to fear, and his loyalists to believe, that Cleveland was a determinist in the tradition of Andrew Jackson when it came to initiating legislative programs. Now it was those very loyalists who believed they had what to fear. Said one anti-silver congressman, speaking for all the others, "If only Mr. Cleveland had been content to say nothing, he had the game in his own hands. The opposition to his [hard-money] policy was melting away like snow in a thaw. He need not have done anything, if only he had said nothing. We should presently have had a united party, confident and happy, with him as our natural and proper leader. It makes me sad—for what he so needlessly said is a direct invitation to confusion and discord."[43]

As late as July 1886, Cleveland continued to be "not at all inclined to meddle with proposed legislation while it is pending in Congress," as he told Samuel J. Randall.[44] Randall was leading the House opposition to the Morrison Resolution, which required the Treasury to utilize all its reserves in excess of $100 million in the redemption of government bonds. This was the sort of thing that Cleveland feared would imperil the gold standard. Yet here he was limiting himself to urging that Congress vote in line with his wishes on the resolution. It was rather like asking a deaf puppy to stop chewing on the furniture.

Now spared the threat of an antagonistic President bringing the prestige of his office to bear against them, the silverites in Congress resumed the offensive. Though all their attempts failed, they at least managed to force the pro-Cleveland faction into a Mexican standoff by the time Congress adjourned in August: the President had failed to obtain a repeal of Bland-Allison, and the western silver men had failed to enact an unlimited coinage bill. The standoff was to continue for the remaining two and a half years of Cleveland's first administration, and come back to haunt him in his second—while a minimum of $24 million would be added yearly to the silver deluge. Meanwhile, Cleveland was subjected to a litany of demagogic charges from both pro- and anti-silver forces in his own party: "one of the grandest conspiracies against the rights of the people ever inaugurated by human greed"; "Wall Street gambler"; "plutocratic rule"; "heartless creditor"; "eastern Shylock."

Such criticism was insignificant when compared to the foreboding provoked by the incessant growth of the Treasury surplus. Having refused to buy bonds during the 1885 crisis, the Treasury now began to redeem those which had reached maturity. By the close of 1886, nearly all the bonds had been called in, and the government had to compete in the open market with other purchasers in order to buy noncallable bonds. This necessitated the payment of exorbitant interest. Moreover, it hardly escaped notice, especially by the millions of wage-earners and farmers, that the large sums they, along with the rest of the consuming population, had paid into the Treasury through tariff and internal revenue and excise taxes were being used to pour heavy unearned profits into the pockets of the investing classes, predominantly in the East. The injustice was obvious even to a blind man.

A mutually unsatisfactory stalemate that owed much to the action—more properly, the inaction—of a President who allowed his political capital to dry up instead of exploiting it slowly evolved into a major problem Cleveland would have to face when he returned to the White House in 1893. And that at a time when he would have to reckon with more problems than any President should have to face concurrently. Given the large delegations of pro-silver men in both houses of Congress, one can argue convincingly, if not conclusively, that Cleveland would have fared no better even had he acted more the Jacksonian infighter and less the strict constitutionalist on the currency issue at this particular point in time. Where he is to be faulted, though, was in defining his duty as President in terms of resistance rather than initiative. That would change in 1893.

Adding to Cleveland's distress during the "silver blizzard," as it came to be known, was the sudden collapse of his Treasury Secretary. While returning to his office from a cabinet meeting on March 23, Manning suffered an attack of vertigo on the steps of the Treasury. Learning he had burst a blood vessel at the base of the brain, Manning offered to resign. But Cleveland would not hear of it. He depended greatly on Manning's friendship and political savvy. After repeated pleas that he be allowed to resign, Manning was asked by Cleveland to turn his office over temporarily to his deputy, Charles S. Fairchild, and take a leave of absence until October; if by then he had not regained his health, his resignation would be accepted.[45] Manning's health was already in irreversible decline. Cleveland reluctantly accepted his resignation in the following February (and chose Fairchild to succeed him).

23

"She is a superior person"

Compared to the elaborate personal support we provide for today's Presidents, the support provided Grover Cleveland and his predecessors was primeval. The entire Executive Mansion staff consisted of but a few dozen clerks and servants. Security was handled by a few detectives, even though the country had suffered two presidential assassinations and the public was allowed almost unlimited access to the mansion. (Established in 1865, to investigate and prevent the counterfeiting of currency, the Secret Service was not charged with protecting the President until McKinley's assassination in 1901.) At first, Cleveland did not even have a stenographer. Dan Lamont made finished copies of his handwritten correspondence, along with performing his many other duties. (An official copyist was later taken on.) A single telephone served the entire mansion. If it rang after business hours when the clerks had left for the day, whoever was within earshot answered—usually Cleveland's servant Sinclair, sometimes Cleveland himself.

Unlike the fastidious Arthur, who favored butlers and valets, Cleveland disdained personal attendants. Sinclair saw to the laying-out and general upkeep of his wardrobe, in addition to serving the household as chief steward and general factotum. He also kept the tradesmen serving the mansion honest: every charge, no matter its insignificance, was itemized and justified. On the first day of each month he went over household accounts with Cleveland, who then wrote checks for payment. No tradesman ever realized so much as a single dishonest penny doing business with Grover Cleveland.

Chester Arthur had spent a considerable sum to renovate the mansion. Exceeding the $30,000 Congressional appropriation by $80,000, it was the largest amount spent on the President's House (as it was still called) since its reconstruction after being burned by the British during the War of 1812. (It did not become the "White House" officially until Theodore Roosevelt's day, although Cleveland used the term as early as 1886, in the May 28 invitations to his wedding.)[46] Despite the funds accorded every incoming President for that purpose, Cleveland made no improvements. One holdover from the Arthur years was the French chef, whose creations Cleveland, an authentic steak-and-potatoes man, loathed.[47] Cleveland begged his successor at Albany to let him have the gubernatorial mansion's longtime cook, Eliza. Eliza came, "that man who cooks" went, and Cleveland was gustatorily content. The official dinners he held each week during the winter social season and the more elaborate state affairs held in the spring were handled by private caterers. Eliza's talents were reserved for the President's private guests, who came and went frequently. These were predominantly friends from his Buffalo and

Albany days, in addition to his siblings and their children, whom the family-oriented "Uncle Jumbo" liked to have about him as often as possible.

Until he married, Cleveland's Official Hostess was his sister Rose. Before assuming these responsibilities, Rose (to "Grove" she was always "Libby") had taught at an exclusive girls' school and published essays on notable female writers like George Eliot. Such was the extent of this no-nonsense woman's erudition that she relieved the boredom of White House receiving lines, which she disliked intensely, by silently conjugating Greek verbs. An ardent feminist long before the term became fashionable, Rose was the antithesis of her traditionalist brother, who insisted: "A good wife is a woman who loves her husband and her country with no desire to run either."[48]

Being the nation's Chief Executive in no way altered Cleveland's habits. Averse to utilizing public property for personal pleasure, he never used the presidential yacht, *Dispatch*. When he went deep-sea fishing, he used a lighthouse tender—and insisted on paying all expenses out of his own funds. A staunch believer in making himself available to constituents, he held public receptions three times a week, at which even casual sightseers were welcome to gawk at, even shake hands with, their President. At these receptions, he remained constantly on his feet, "working the room." This, plus the occasional stroll among the flower beds or to visit the duck pond on the White House lawns, was about the only exercise Cleveland took. He would never abandon an innate disinclination to pursue more energetic forms of physical exercise.

Prior to his marriage, Cleveland kept social engagements to a minimum. He particularly detested public dinners at which he was the guest of honor. This was less because the adulation (or the sycophancy, depending upon the occasion) annoyed him than because of an aversion to making—and listening to—postprandial speeches. Until he married, he invariably spent evenings at his desk, in keeping with a childhood resolution always to finish a day's work before retiring for the night. As during his Buffalo and Albany years, a typical "working day" during his Washington years often ended at two or three the next morning. With marriage, Cleveland willingly abandoned many habits cultivated during his bachelorhood. But an obsessive dedication to work was not one of them.

Fortunately, his wife found this as easy to live with as everything else about him that other wives might have found somewhat off-putting in their mates. But then, unlike most brides, Grover Cleveland's knew everything one could possibly know about her man, since she'd known him literally all her life. Here was one marriage that would produce not a single surprise. Might that explain why it was one of the happiest presidential marriages, if not *the* happiest, on record?

Frances Clara Folsom Cleveland was not only the nation's youngest First Lady, she was one of the prettiest and best-educated. (Cleveland disliked the term "First Lady," and his wife, who cared little for it herself, never used it in self-reference. The first presidential spouse to be referred to as "First Lady" was Dolley Madison on the occasion of her death in 1849. Cleveland preferred "The President's Lady.") While the news media made her a celebrity, Frances did nothing to encourage it, and much to *dis*courage it. Nor did she let all the attention and flattery heaped upon her go to her head. Her popularity set records. Women styled their hair "à la Cleveland," emulated her distinct way of posing for a photo, and hung on her every utterance as if it were received wisdom. Despite all this, her overall demeanor was that of an old-fashioned girl who wished to be no more than a proper and loving wife to a man who happened to be President of the United States, and the mother of his children. She knew her fame was of the reflected-glory variety. She refused to exploit it.

Still, Frances Folsom Cleveland was no insipid spouse, no domesticated doormat. Her natural beauty and innate vivacity were complemented by a streak of independence her husband found utterly charming—probably because she kept it well within the parameters of propriety. She refused to lend her name to any of the controversial "causes" of the day; the American people, she would remind those who needed reminding, had elected her husband, not her. She did send money to support many of those causes, though, such as the WCTU. Having taken a childhood pledge of abstinence, she honored it—after a fashion. She tolerated social drinking in others, and after entering the White House she took to sipping an occasional brandy—though making sure her glass was filled with Apollinaris water at social functions.

Frances was publicly active in behalf of female education and helping women to gain professional employment; her feminist orientation was interracial. She helped to found, and worked to interest other white women in, the Washington Home for Friendless Colored Girls, and she was active in the Colored Christmas Club, which provided food to poor children of color, to whom she personally distributed gifts. (When the Clevelands retired to Princeton after leaving the White House in 1897, Frances became active in opening up educational opportunities for girls "like [those enjoyed by] young men." This led to the founding of New Jersey College for Women, today Douglas College, a part of Rutgers University.) Others who benefited from her moral—and often financial—support were aspiring musicians. Besides possessing a fluent command of French and German (she also read Latin) and proficiency at the comparatively new art of photography, she was a quite talented amateur pianist.

Just as Frances never flaunted her status as the President's Lady, neither did she flaunt her best qualities. She exposed friends and strangers alike to her wit and intellect without causing offense or leaving anyone feeling patronized. She had a whimsical sense of humor and was considerate of all people, race or class notwithstanding. The two qualities once came into play when, during the White House years, she walked into her sitting room one day to discover a few servants dancing while one of them played the piano. She reprimanded them with a stern look and shake of the head—and then joined them.

To those who did not know her personally, Frances came off as a beautiful young woman whose intelligence was seriously open to question. However, Rose Cleveland, whom no man ever accused of disseminating compliments freely, set the record straight when she remarked shortly after her brother's marriage: "My new sister is a woman capable of great development; a much stronger character than appears on the surface. She is a superior person." While Cleveland seconded this opinion, he was rather concerned as to how his twenty-two-year-old bride would fare when it came to entertaining the nation's movers and shakers. "You will find that you get along better in this job if you don't try anything new," he counseled at the start of their marriage. She took his advice. When at her first White House reception Cleveland saw how expertly she handled a large crowd, he beamed, "She'll do! She'll do!"[49] He shouldn't have been surprised. He knew her quite well.

After all, he had dandled her as an infant, bought her first baby carriage, and kept a concerned avuncular eye on her since she was ten.

Frances was the only child of Cleveland's friend and law partner Oscar Folsom and his wife, Emma C. Harmon Folsom. To Cleveland she was always "Frank," a privilege granted no other person. The press dubbed her "Frankie," which she detested and her husband hated. ("I am never called Frankie, and dislike the name very much," she wrote to a Kentucky woman seeking permission to name her newborn child for her. "Will you do me the favor not to call her Frankie, but Frances or [if a boy] Frank?")

"Uncle Cleve," as she called him throughout her childhood, immediately assumed responsibility for Folsom's widow and child following Oscar's death in a carriage accident when Frances was in her tenth year. (Only later was it learned he had named Cleveland the child's legal guardian.) Whether she became surrogate child to this ostensibly confirmed yet paternally inclined bachelor is unknown, and probably unimportant. In the event, he saw little of her for several years. Devastated by Folsom's loss, Emma moved with the child to her hometown of Medina, New York, returning a few years later to Buffalo, where Frances attended the Central School. One of her teachers later recalled that she had a knack for learning things rapidly and "always put a little of herself into her recitations."[50]

Oscar Folsom left his family well provided for, and after a proper coming-out in Buffalo, Frances went off to college. She had by now become endowed—and, in a sense, endowed herself—with the fetching physical and intellectual traits that set her apart from most women of her time (as well as most of her White House predecessors—and successors). She was often compared to the near-legendary Dolley Madison, though it was stipulated that Mrs. Cleveland called to mind only "Queen Dolley's" beauty and charm and grace under pressure, but that, thankfully, she lacked such lesser Madisonian qualities as a brashness that many perceived as vulgarity.

Frank and Uncle Cleve corresponded regularly after he went off to Albany in 1882 and she was a student at Wells College in Aurora, New York, class of '86. (Clever enough to skip her freshman year, she was graduated with the class of '85.) Cleveland made it a point to spend time with the Folsom ladies whenever he visited Buffalo. Both were with him, at his insistence, when he was officially informed of his nomination for the presidency. (Other than Cleveland's acceptance and the inclement weather, the occasion was best remembered for a remark his friend Bissell made. Telling the governor's young aides to be gallant, Bissell, who, like everyone else, was neither prescient about nor conversant with Cleveland and his ward's future plans, said: "If one of you young fellows doesn't take an interest in that pretty Miss Folsom the governor is likely to walk off with her himself!") Did their friendship gradually evolve into love as a matter of inevitability? Or, given the twenty-seven-year disparity in their ages, did Frank see in Uncle Cleve the father she lost at an impressionable age? Let us leave such psychobabble to others, and deal only with historical fact.

The adult aspect of their friendship began in Cleveland's second year as governor; at his suggestion, knowledge of the change in their relationship was confined to just the immediate families. He was determined to spare Frances what notoriety might attach were it known she was being courted by a prominent politician; one who was, in the bargain, old enough to be her father. Too, he wished to spare himself the ribaldry of being labeled "a cradle snatcher" or someone who had "betrayed" his quasi-fiduciary trust by "seducing" his ward.

Frances shared this desire for secrecy, partly for the stated reasons, partly for the sense of adventure it brought. That her college room was subjected to a steady flow of flowers from the governor of New York (on one occasion, even a puppy) raised as little curiosity among her friends as her visit to the White House and the several visits Cleveland made to her in Buffalo while en route to and from fishing expeditions in the Adirondacks. He was, after all, her guardian. Besides, her mother was always present.

In the summer of 1885, which they spent on the New York State farm of Frances's paternal grandfather, she and her mother decided to go abroad for nine months of sightseeing, chaperoned by a male cousin. While they were visiting friends in Scranton prior to sailing, Cleveland wrote a letter proposing marriage. To ensure Frances's privacy as a tourist, it was agreed the engagement be kept secret. The secret almost got out when the President sent his fiancée an affectionate bon voyage cable as her ship was preparing to depart New York harbor. The wireless operator made a copy he contrived, presumably for recompense, to get into the hands of one of the city's papers.

The story was swiftly flashed across a nation already wondering if Grover Cleveland intended to leave the White House a bachelor like

James Buchanan. However, it was assumed he'd sent the cable to the Widow Folsom. "I don't see why the papers keep marrying me to old ladies," he told a friend with mock irony. "I wonder why they don't say I am engaged to marry her daughter!"[51] The White House issued a firm denial to the rumors of a coming marriage, and the story was allowed to die.

It was resurrected just weeks later when Frances wrote from England to a close friend of her engagement. The friend was at a family breakfast when the letter arrived; she began to read it aloud—until she came to the passage admonishing her not to tell a soul. Someone at the table tipped off a friend on the local newspaper, and the press had another field day. This time, the White House declined all comment, the story faded by October, and the President's fiancée was able to enjoy her tour of the Continent. The two agreed that Cleveland's would be the last word on all aspects of the wedding. He, in turn, delegated to his favorite sister, Mary Hoyt, responsibility for arranging all the details. (He believed this to be an area in which their spinster sister Rose, though his Official Hostess, had no experience, let alone expertise. The presumably sapphic Rose, who never married, and settled in Italy with a wealthy widow, with whom she was buried side by side.)

Three days after his forty-ninth birthday, Cleveland wrote Mary, "I expect to be married pretty early in June—very soon after Frank returns. I think the quicker it can be done the better and she seems to think so too." He desired that the marriage be a quiet one "in the direction of sense and proper decency." He did "not feel like extending the attendance beyond" their immediate families and a few close friends. As for the style of reception: "A more democratic and popular thing, and what I would like on some accounts better, would be a public reception; but it seems rather hard to subject Frank to such an ordeal at that time." Cleveland allowed as how he had his heart set upon "making Frank a sensible, domestic American wife, and I should be pleased not to hear her spoken of as 'The First Lady of the Land' or 'The Mistress of the White House.' I want her to be very happy and to possess all she can reasonably desire, but I should feel very much afflicted if she lets many notions in her head. But I think she is pretty level-headed. . . ."

On May 29, 1886, Cleveland sent personally handwritten notes to some thirty cabinet members and close friends:

*I am to be married on Wednesday evening at seven o'clock at the White House to Miss Folsom. It will be a very quiet affair and I will be extremely grateful at [*sic*] your attendance on the occasion.*

Yours Sincerely,
Grover Cleveland

(Announcements of the marriage, and miniatures of the wedding cake, were sent as a courtesy to the five surviving former First Ladies: Julia Gardner Tyler, Sarah Childress Polk, Julia Dent Grant, Lucy Ware Hayes, and Lucretia Rudolph Garfield.)

It was Cleveland who insisted the ceremony and reception be held at the White House, where he could ensure complete privacy from the "impudent inquisition" of news reporters, whom he referred to collectively as "that dirty gang."[52] It was just as well Cleveland left all arrangements in sister Mary's capable hands, as he had to concentrate on the many problems demanding his attention. Of these the most exigent of the moment was the rapidly escalating dissension between capital and labor.

24

The Haymarket Riot of 1886

Industrialization took a giant leap forward after the Civil War, with the introduction of new machines and improvements in transportation and communications. This had a propitious effect on the nation's economic growth as well as its social and cultural growth. Most affected as a group was the laboring class, some advantageously, some disadvantageously. The number of industrial workers had trebled in the quarter century between the outbreak of war and the opening of the Cleveland presidency, from less than three million to some nine million. A rise in living standard was made possible by the expanded use of machinery and the development of more efficient production methods, enabling them to greatly increase their output. By 1885, the purchasing power of skilled laborers had risen 40 percent. Even unskilled workers could provide for their basic needs by practicing fiscal prudence. Labor might not be getting a fair share of the pie, but most workers were considerably better off than their prewar peers.[53]

The growth of industrialization led to added problems for labor. Innovative machinery and business expansion subverted the craftsman's pride both in his work and his bargaining power with management, and, ominously, led to a diminution in harmonious relations between employer and employee. The workday, once coextensive with daylight hours, began to grow shorter in the 1870s; by 1880, only one worker in four put in a ten-hour day. Radicals agitated for eight hours as a fair day's labor. Despite the dramatic rise in the living standard among industrial workers, discontent toward employers became prevalent. This led to a sense of class consciousness on the workers' part, and in turn led them to espouse the burgeoning labor union movement, which dated back to the Jacksonian era but did not begin to prosper until after the Civil War. Workers saw in unions the most effective—perhaps only—means with which to take on the powerful corporate giants.

By the early 1870s, some 300,000 workers belonged to national craft unions (iron molders, cigar makers, printers, etc.), and many new trades were unionized, predominantly in the rapidly expanding railroad industry. An attempt at federation of the unions was now undertaken, in hopes of increasing their power exponentially. The result was the National Labor Union, created in 1866 and doomed to eventual failure when it became obvious that its leaders—all of them visionaries, none of them a pragmatist—were concerned primarily with effecting basic social reforms having little to do with bargaining between labor and management. It quickly evolved into what was in essence a political confederation, the National Labor Reform party; a pitiful showing in the 1872 elections led to its demise.

Enjoying greater success was the Knights of Labor, begun in 1869 by a group of Philadelphia garment workers. At first it attracted few members because of its secrecy, complemented by an elaborate ritual. But in 1881, these trappings were abandoned, and its ranks were opened up to Negroes and immigrants as well as women (a novelty in the trade union movement). Unskilled workers were also accepted as the peers of trained craftsmen; even employers were welcome (save for bankers, lawyers, gamblers, and corporate stockholders). Besides pursuing traditional trade-union goals, the Knights supported such politically controversial aspirations as currency reform, nationalization of natural resources, the curbing of land speculation, abolition of child labor, equal pay for equal work, elimination of private banks—and, of course, the eight-hour day. Such an agenda harmonized with their rejection of the notion that workers must accept the status of wage earners as their lot in life and gave credence to their contention that workers might ascend the economic ladder into the capitalist class through a pooling of resources. "There is no good reason why labor cannot, through cooperation, own and operate mines, factories, and railroads," said Terence Powderly, the movement's second and most effective leader.[54]

Ironically, it was in 1886—the year when it achieved its greatest membership, 702,000, and its greatest influence on the national scene—that the Knights of Labor began the descent into oblivion. This stemmed from a number of internal factors, among them rigid centralization that resulted in a vertical autocracy from top to bottom, factional disputes, mismanagement, and the dissipation of financial resources through a series of unsuccessful strikes. But it was two events, both in 1886, that set the descent into motion: the Knights' failure in the Missouri Pacific Railroad Strike, and the Haymarket Riot—for which it was not held accountable but was condemned by the press and the anti-union general public.

Blame for the labor strife can in no way be imputed to Grover Cleveland, as many in the labor movement attempted to do. Therein lay an irony that was lost at the time on many: this conspicuously pro-business President, a staunch advocate of laissez-faire, took a remarkably liberal position on the plight of the workingman. ("The capitalist can protect himself, but the wage earner is practically defenseless.") In acknowledging a signed copy of Andrew Carnegie's *The Gospel of Wealth,* he told the industrialist: "I have thought for a long time that there must be a way to so weld capital and labor together that the distressing result of their quarrels and misunderstandings would be prevented."[55] The idea of reconciliation between labor and management runs like a motif through Cleveland's public speeches: in accepting the nomination for governor of New York and then the first presidential nomination, and in his first Inaugural Address, to cite but three of many. Arbitration, he maintained, was not only an imperative, it was the only rational means of reconciliation. But arbitration implies a willingness by concerned parties to come together for that purpose.

Cleveland's first priority in every labor dispute was to end the fighting and then get everyone to the peace table.

The year 1886 saw twice as many strikes as in any prior year in American history—ironically, not because times were bad but because they were improving, as the nation came out of the 1884 economic downturn. Nationwide, the laboring class agitated for better wages and working conditions. Riots among the coke workers of western Pennsylvania set the tone at year's opening. When Cleveland entered the White House, more than fifty thousand men were out on strike in the coal mines of Pennsylvania, Maryland, and Ohio and targeted factories in New England and the Alleghenies. The passing weeks saw the nation's collective industrial capacity all but paralyzed by a combination of walkouts and lockouts. What most affected the federal government, however, in light of its impact on the economy, was the action by the Knights of Labor against Jay Gould's extensive railway system in the Southwest, which included the Missouri Pacific and the Texas & Pacific.

Encouraged by success against Gould's Union Pacific in 1884 and the Wabash Railroad in 1885, the Knights surreptitiously established cells throughout the Missouri Pacific system and then forced management to recognize the union. When Texas & Pacific filed for bankruptcy the Knights presented the federal receiver with a litany of demands intended to protect its members against reprisal by Gould. The receiver rejected the demands and then discharged a mechanic at Fort Worth known to be a leading Knight. Five days after the mechanic was denied reinstatement, shop men struck the Texas & Pacific, their brethren struck the Missouri Pacific, and the strike spread rapidly through Illinois, Missouri, Arkansas, Kansas, and Texas.

This walkout by ten thousand men affected six thousand miles of railroad and countless communities along their routes. All freight west of the Mississippi was blocked; effects were soon felt from one end of the continent to the other. Suffering particularly were the farm communities, which depended exclusively on the railroads to move their product to market. Many major cities were left all but prostrate, as vital goods could not be brought in nor items of manufacture shipped out. Perishable goods rotted along the tracks, the cost of on-hand provisions went through the roof, and many flour mills and factories were forced to shut down.

Resentment toward the strikes led to the spontaneous birth of the Law and Order League, whose goal was to break the power of the Knights. When violence broke out, Gould and Powderly entered into negotiations, but these came to naught. On March 26, the governors of Texas, Missouri, Arkansas, and Kansas issued orders that all managers dispatch their trains as usual, and all law enforcement officers provide protection. By way of reprisal the strikers disabled engines, uncoupled freight cars, and otherwise created havoc with the rolling stock. A pitched battle between lawmen and strikers broke out at Fort Worth in which several men on both sides were killed. In mid-April, another confrontation caused more casualties, this one in East St. Louis. Responding to a great public outcry, Congress named a committee to investigate "existing labor troubles."[56] This was followed up by the passage of legislation calling for voluntary arbitration of all railroad disputes, with the government to defray expenses up to $1,000 in each case. By month's end, the strike was broken, and on May 4, it was formally ended, with no more than 20 percent of the strikers being taken back by the Missouri Pacific.

In the meantime, Cleveland had sent a Special Message to Congress on Labor Legislation. The first such action on the subject of labor by an American President, it was not only innovative, it was downright remarkable. "The discontent of the employees is due in large degree to the grasping and heedless exactions of employers and the alleged discrimination in favor of capital as an object of governmental attention," he said in urging that Congress enact laws to arbitrate labor-management disputes. "[T]he value of labor as an element of national prosperity should be distinctly recognized, and the welfare of the laboring man should be regarded as especially entitled to legislative care." He warned that "corporations, which should be carefully restrained creatures of the law and servants of the people, are fast becoming the people's masters." Lest he be accused of pandering to the working class, Cleveland demanded that it "also be conceded that the laboring men are not always careful to avoid causeless and unjustifiable disturbance." Insisting that the American laborer was entitled to "the same recognition from those who make our laws as is accorded to any other citizen," he proposed, as a start, that the government establish a permanent board for voluntary arbitration in all disputes.[57]

Cleveland was hardly astonished when his proposal met with less than spectacular enthusiasm. He knew that compulsory arbitration was unrealistic, unless mutually agreed upon. Nevertheless, he dared rush in where all other Presidents had feared to tread. What he now proposed was more effective than the O'Neill bill passed only days before by the House and awaiting Senate action, which called for settlement of railroad disputes on a case-by-case basis, with each side having recourse to its own special board representing labor and management.

Cleveland proposed that instead of relying on an arbitration panel "chosen in the heat of conflicting claims," the government create a permanent three-man board to adjudicate all appeals; that it be part of the Bureau of Labor, with the power to offer its good services in any dispute, instead of limiting itself to disputes on interstate railroads (creation of a cabinet-level Department of Labor lay twenty-seven years in the future); and that it be authorized to investigate the causes of all labor troubles. Though its decisions would carry no legal weight, Cleveland hoped that its moral authority would prove decisive.

The Senate, eager like the House to court the votes of labor, let both the O'Neill bill and Cleveland's proposals languish in committee while quickly enacting a number of measures of its own creation. Included was one legalizing the incorporation of trade unions (accepted by the House and signed by the President). Others included a bill to grant letter-carriers an eight-hour day. The House then came up with a hearty legislative agenda, and secured its own lock on the labor vote, by passing a long-standing bill that prohibited the importation of contract labor, which became law despite strong opposition in the Senate. At the close of the legislative session the Senate passed the O'Neill bill; it was incompatible with Cleveland's ideas, but he signed it, realizing it was probably the best he could get at the time.

In calling for voluntary arbitration of railway disputes, Congress authorized the President to appoint a commission to investigate any labor quarrel that would function concurrently as a board of conciliation. But that did not resolve the conflict between employer and employee. Just as Cleveland would have to resume confrontation with the tariff and currency issues when he returned to the White House in 1893, so would it be with the labor issue, which came to a bloody climax in the Chicago Pullman Strike of 1894, which would help sink his second presidency.

But first there was that city's bloody Haymarket Riot of 1886.

Occurring eleven days after Cleveland's labor message to Congress, as both houses were deciding how best to address the problem, the riot was precipitated by a lockout of fourteen hundred employees of the McCormick Reaper Company in Chicago. Climaxing weeks of labor agitation in that city, the lockout led to several instances of brutal clubbing of the workers by police. The turmoil was aggravated by a group of anarchists led by August Spies, Sam Felden, and Albert Parsons. On May 1, forty thousand to sixty thousand trade unionists (the figures vary depending upon whose account is taken as definitive) staged an ostentatiously orchestrated nationwide dropping-of-the-tools in a call for an eight-hour day. Two days later, seven thousand McCormick workers clashed with police after being locked out for their part in that action; one man was killed, a half-dozen others were seriously injured. In an overreaction intended to inflame the situation, Spies, in his radical newspaper *Arbeiter-Zeitung*, exhorted, "Revenge! Workingmen! To Arms!" and claimed: "Your masters sent out their bloodhounds—the police—they killed six of your brothers at McCormick's this afternoon!" A mass meeting was called for the night of May 4 in Haymarket Square "to denounce the latest atrocious act of the police, the shooting of our fellow workingmen."

Fifteen hundred workers and their sympathizers gathered at the appointed hour and heard in orderly fashion a series of speeches. Though permeated with the resentment and class feeling one would expect under the circumstances, the speeches were rather temperate in tone. Around ten o'clock, it began to rain and the crowd started to disperse. While the last speaker stood atop a wagon concluding his remarks, a detail of police swooped down to hurry the crowd along. No sooner had the speaker shouted, "We are peaceable!" than a homemade bomb exploded amid the police. Of the more than fifty cut down, seven were either killed instantly or fatally wounded. The police drew their arms and fired randomly into the unarmed crowd as it frantically sought refuge.

Nationwide, the press denounced all anarchists and socialists in the most scathing terms while xenophobes capitalized on the fact that so many immigrant Poles and Germans were in the vanguard of the revolutionary movement. Indictments were handed down on ten of the alleged provocateurs (two were released for lack of evidence). Given the atmosphere, chances that they would receive a fair trial were beyond probability. Men were accepted on the jury who admitted to being prejudiced by news accounts of the riot; the presiding judge was biased against the defendants, both in his conduct of the trial and his charge to the jury.

Because whoever threw the bomb could not be identified, it was impossible to prove the prosecution's charge that he was motivated by the speeches or writings of the defendants. Yet it was the judge's rather syllogistic supposition that because the defendants "generally by speech and print advised large classes to commit murder," and murder had resulted, they were guilty. Four, including Spies and Parsons, were hanged. (Parsons, who eluded capture, walked into court dramatically as the trial began and surrendered.) A fifth committed suicide by exploding a bomb in his mouth. The remaining three were sentenced to prison. (They were pardoned seven years later by Illinois governor John P. Altgeld, who will engage our attention when we come to the sanguinolent Pullman strike eight years later.)

But now let us return to the merry month of May when the President was eagerly anticipating the return of his intended bride.

25

"O, those ghouls of the press!"

Informed by cable that the liner *Nordland* bringing Frances and her mother home from Europe would dock in New York City late in the afternoon of May 27, Cleveland sent Lamont to run interference. He feared that the news reporters, knowing that the President's Lady was aboard, would make her the centerpiece of a three-ring media circus. From the moment he got off the train from Washington, Lamont, known to and highly respected by reporters, was tailed by them. Fortunately the ship was a few hours late. Lamont hired a tugboat and sailed out into the harbor unseen under cover of darkness. When the liner at last hove into view, he went aboard, found the Folsom ladies, and spirited them ashore and into a waiting carriage, which sped them to the Old Gilsey House on Fifth Avenue without being spotted. Lamont then returned to Washington after sending a prearranged wire to the anxious President: "Arrived safe. All in good hands." At that point—it was now 10 P.M.—the White House announced the coming wedding.

All next day the Old Gilsey House was mobbed by reporters and the just plain curious, held at bay by a platoon of policemen. Frances declined to give any interviews. When she went out to shop or just to get some air, she wore dark veils, used the service entrance, and rode in a closed carriage. Through it all she had a smile and a wave for the news reporters and gawkers, managing to win them over without saying a word or allowing anyone to speak on her behalf.

Cleveland arrived in the city the following evening to review the Brooklyn and Manhattan Memorial Day parades. Before heading to the home of Navy Secretary Whitney, where he was to spend the night, he made a brief stop at the Old Gilsey House to enjoy his first meeting with Frances since the previous September. It may have been then that he told her, in one of his most quoted remarks, "Poor girl, you never had any courting like other girls."[58]

After reviewing the Brooklyn parade next morning, Cleveland returned to Manhattan to review the second parade. As the 22nd Regimental Band reached the reviewing stand at Madison Square playing standard martial airs, it broke into the Mendelssohn Wedding March; another band played "He's Going to Marry Yum-Yum," from a recently opened Gilbert & Sullivan hit *The Mikado*; yet a third gave out with a popular sentimental ballad of the day, "Come Where My Love Lies Dreaming." The crowds lining both sides of the street loved it. Two blocks down Fifth Avenue from the reviewing stand the bride-to-be stepped out onto the second-floor balcony of the New York apartment of Postmaster General and Mrs. Vilas and waved her handkerchief. Seeing it flutter in the wind, the groom-to-be bowed gallantly in her direction and tipped his bowler. The crowds went wild.

Early in the morning of Wednesday, June 2—her wedding day—Frances and her mother arrived from New York in a private railroad car. On reaching the White House, she tripped gaily up the steps and through the great entrance "like a radiant vision of young springtime [and] from that instant every man and woman . . . was a devoted slave, and remained such." Cleveland greeted his bride briefly (there was no kiss) and, ever the workaholic, returned to his desk. Moments later, Vilas phoned to ask Lamont if the President had time to sign some documents. Said Cleveland: "Yes, I will sign—but tell him to get those documents here as quick as the good Lord will let him!"[59]

The twenty-nine guests arrived at six-thirty that evening, having to run a gauntlet of onlookers swarming all over the lawns and peering through open windows. At the stroke of seven, all the clocks in the White House began to chime, joined by church bells throughout the city. As Captain John Philip Sousa led his Marine Band in the Mendelssohn Wedding March, the bridal couple—there were no attendants—descended the grand staircase and entered the Blue Room, which was ablaze with a profusion of plants and flowers.[60] The Rev. Byron Sunderland read the Presbyterian vows, from which, at the groom's insistence, the word "obey" was deleted. (This was said to be his way of obviating snide remarks about robbing the cradle.) The bridal couple then led their guests into the East Room, where they promenaded for half an hour, greeting and chatting up each person individually. Contrary to the custom of the times, there was no display of wedding gifts except for the diamond necklace the President gave his bride. Everyone then moved to the State Dining Room for a formal dinner; dominating the table was a giant three-masted ship made of flowers and christened the *Hymen*.

The newlyweds disappeared after dinner, reappeared in street clothes, and left the White House via the Blue Room. Anticipating the massive crowds outside, estimated in the thousands, Cleveland had a pathway leading up to the south portico enclosed in tent canvas all the way down to where the waiting coach stood. Soon after nine that night, the Clevelands left on a special two-car train for Deer Park, a popular cottage resort in the mountains of western Maryland near the headwaters of the Potomac, for a six-day honeymoon.

Hopes of evading reporters proved futile; some thirty of them followed in a special train, though the hotel refused to rent them rooms or cottages out of consideration for the bridal couple. ("We arrived this morning at four o'clock," Cleveland wrote to Lamont. "There are a number of newspaper men here and I can see a group of them sitting on a bridge which marks one of the limits [imposed by the hotel], waiting for some move to be made which will furnish an incident.")

During the entire honeymoon the reporters, kept at a distance by special detectives who refused to let them remain stationary anywhere on the grounds, scrutinized the Clevelands constantly, training their spyglasses and binoculars on the cottage's bedroom windows and observing the pair unabashedly when they tried to enjoy breakfast on the porch of their cottage. Some went to the extreme of lifting the covers from dishes sent from the hotel dining room, to see what the newlyweds would be having for dinner. (Today's exotic journalistic ritual of harvesting celebrity garbage pails had not yet come into vogue among the fourth estate.) When they went for walks in the woods, or for carriage rides to enjoy the stunning view of the Blue Ridge Mountains, the reporters were always in hot pursuit, the most daring among them popping out from behind bushes and trees to ask the kind of fatuous questions we have come to expect from the media on the White House beat.

To Cleveland their "sniggering desire to make copy out of a sacred personal experience" was indefensible. Condemning them in a particularly vitriolic letter to the *New York Evening Post*, he later wrote: "They have used the enormous power of the modern newspaper to perpetuate and disseminate a colossal impertinence, and have done it, not as professional gossips and tattlers, but as the guides and instructors of the public in conduct and morals. And they have done it, not to a private citizen, but to the President of the United States, thereby lifting their offense into the gaze of the whole world, and doing their utmost to make American journalism contemptible in the estimation of people of good breeding everywhere." Small wonder that at a dinner in his honor at Harvard a few months later, when Cleveland saw reporters staring at Frances he interrupted his prepared remarks to exclaim in an aside: "O, those ghouls of the press!"[61]

Cleveland's negative feelings toward reporters were magnified by their evident inability to get enough copy on his wife. Even a brief vacation their first summer together was ruined because she was "continually watched and lied about, and I won't subject my wife to that treatment."[62] To their credit, the reporters did not lie about her. Like their readers, they adored Frances; she could do no wrong in their eyes. Not till Jacqueline Kennedy would a First Lady be so written about with such admiration and adulation.

The media's obsession with Frances Cleveland inadvertently precipitated something of a revolution in women's fashion. It seems that a few reporters were sitting around one day bemoaning the lack of anything going on at the White House momentous enough to share with their readers. Said one in desperation, "Can't we send a society item?" Said another, "Yes—if you've got one. I don't see a line in sight now." "Then let's manufacture one," suggested the first reporter, adding excitedly after a moment's thought: "I've got it! Let's say Mrs. Cleveland's decided to abolish the bustle." "Brilliant!" cried another. After some hectic scribbling they came up with a story that went out on the wires to the effect that the trend-setting First Lady had abandoned wearing bustles. When Frances saw the story she was at a loss how to react. It hardly seemed worth denying; however, to appear in public in a bustle would require explanations. Deciding on what seemed most expeditious, she ordered a gown without a bustle. Soon the bustle went the way of the chastity belt![63]

The constant attention to his wife prompted Cleveland to fear for her safety. Because of easy access to the White House, not only by reporters but curious onlookers as well, he decided they would reside there only during the social season, which lasted from December through March, and spend the rest of the time (to "escape this cursed grind") at Oak View, a twenty-year-old nondescript house he bought on twenty-three acres near the present-day Washington Cathedral and converted at considerable expense into a picturesque Queen Anne villa. (The press called it Red Top because of its newly painted roof, and Red Top it became in the public's mind.)

Protecting his wife from news reporters was only one of the reasons Cleveland bought it. From the day he moved into the White House he hated its fishbowl ambience; only eight rooms on the west end of the second floor, the family quarters, offered any privacy. Frances shared those feelings from the day of her own arrival there. Oak View was for the two an ideal alternative. Here she indulged her love of animals: the grounds were home to a colorful menagerie of ducks, foxes, kittens, quail, even white rats. Cleveland, who fancied himself a gentleman farmer, liked to chart the progress and performance of the productive stock, cows and chickens. Both Clevelands were dog lovers: in residence were a dachshund, a beagle, a St. Bernard, and, Frances's favorite, a French poodle she taught to understand commands in the language of its ancestors.

Oak View was kept staffed and open even when the Clevelands were at the White House; they liked to come out during the season, whether for a weekend or overnight, or merely to entertain close friends at tea. Like all vacation homes they would occupy, Oak View was barred to the press. When Massachusetts governor William E. Russell, a close friend who visited there on occasion, was once asked by the editor of *New England Magazine* to supply a photograph of the interior, he had to report that none existed: "Mr. Cleveland was very particular that no photographs should be taken of his family or of the interior of his home, and his wishes were observed by all who came there."[64]

Frances accepted without demur her husband's principle that a woman "should not bother her head about political parties and public questions," but "should be content to rule in the domain of the house." Yet, she succeeded in bringing him in contact with "people and ideas he had never considered before [and made] his relations easier with congressmen who had been offended when, as they felt, he was unreasonable about political concessions."[65] Another feat was to transform Cleveland's attitude toward formal dinner parties and balls, which Frances enjoyed and he loathed. She convinced him that such events would work to his political advantage, and they did. He soon found himself anticipating them—and watching his wife captivate with beauty and charm not only the most hard-bitten observers but his political adversaries as well.

Perhaps the most winsome words in this context were those of railroad magnate Chauncey M. Depew, the Republican leader, in a remark to Lamont: "My only regret about [the 1888 election] is that it will be so much harder for us to win against both Mr. *and* Mrs. Cleveland." The wife of yet another Republican fat cat admitted to feeling "dreadfully guilty, as if she were conspiring to increase" the President's popularity because she so openly admired his wife. And then there was the comment by one particularly rabid anti-Cleveland Republican: "I detest him so much that I don't even think his wife is beautiful!" "No more brilliant and affable lady than Mrs. Cleveland has ever graced the portals of this old mansion," said Irwin "Ike" Hoover, Chief Usher at the White House. "Her very presence threw an air of beauty on the entire surroundings, whatever the occasion or the company." The staff, to whom she gave thoughtful birthday and

Christmas gifts, adored her, not only for the gifts but for her concern for their physical and spiritual welfare, in addition to her consideration of them as functioning human beings instead of merely as servants. To the egalitarian Cleveland it was a source of great pride that his beloved Frank never compromised her sense of social commitment.[66]

Though not active in the suffragist movement, Frances Cleveland supported the idea of gender equality. Shortly after inaugurating a series of Saturday-afternoon White House receptions for working women, she was asked by a group of influential social arbiters to halt them. Their objection: about half the attendees were "clerks from the department stores and others—a great rabble of shop-girls. And of course a White House afternoon is not intended for them." Frances was incensed. "Indeed! And if I should hold the little receptions other than Saturday, they couldn't attend, because they have to work all other afternoons. Is that it?" "That's it exactly." Frances issued orders that nothing was to be scheduled for her that might interfere with the Saturday receptions "so long as there were any store clerks, or other self-supporting women and girls who wished to come to the White House."[67]

For Cleveland, there was a limit to how much the women of America had a right to expect from the one they looked upon as their White House intercessor. When some New York ladies sought permission to organize a "Frances Cleveland Influence Club," Cleveland vetoed the idea summarily. Another source of irritation for Cleveland was the commercial exploitation his wife was subjected to. When it was learned that she played the piano, manufacturers bombarded her with requests that she accept their instruments as gifts—in return for permission to advertise her use of them. Cleveland's "NO!" bounced off the White House walls. Gifts of value such as shares of stock in a mining company were returned without comment. Offers by sewing machine manufacturers to give "private previews" of their latest products in return for Frances's endorsement were denied out of hand.[68]

It was bad enough, to Cleveland's way of thinking, that press and public alike seized upon every bit of trivia about his wife, and that her photographs were being sold by the tens of thousands. But when advertisers brazenly took to using her name and picture on soaps, perfumes, liver pills, candies, ashtrays, even ladies' underwear without her permission, he was furious. One magazine claimed that the First Lady's peaches-and-cream complexion derived from her daily use of a brand of arsenic pills put out by its leading advertiser. The claim stimulated a flood of indignant letters to the White House taking Frances to task for commercializing her position. She was totally ignorant of the product; and anyway, as she had it made known publicly, her peaches-and-cream complexion derived exclusively from the daily use of soap and water.

Cleveland now asked Congress to legislate that anyone who employed "the likeness or representation of any female living or dead" related to the President without written consent be found "guilty of high misdemeanor" under penalty of a large fine and possible imprisonment. The bill failed to pass, the manufacturers stepped up their "Frankie" ads, and Cleveland could do little but vent his spleen, as he did in a blistering letter to one merchant: "An advertisement recently published by you in the *Albany Evening Journal* introduces the name of Mrs. Cleveland in a most indecent way. I suppose we must always have among us dirty and disreputable fellows; but I shall be surprised if you find such advertising profitable among the residents of so respectable a city as Albany."[69]

For Grover, his Frank could do no wrong. As when a friend asked him to go fishing on the next Sunday, and she announced in no uncertain terms: "No one goes out of this house on Sunday!" Or the time when, after she kept him waiting for a drive they had planned, the President threw down his coat and gloves irritably and roared that he would not go. Frances at last arrived and said merrily, "I am ready now." He quietly picked up his garments and off they rode. The two enjoyed a remarkably happy marriage despite—or perhaps because of—its May-December element. Many years later, near the close of their life together, Frances would tell him, "You know how dearly I love you. You do not mind me saying it over, any day . . . so I repeat it and repeat it."[70]

He knew. And he did not mind hearing it over and over again. Especially when dealing with problems that enraged a large segment of the public and earned him harsh denunciation—such as when he went head to head with those who were manipulating the whole program of veterans' pensions to commit arguably the most shameless defilement of the United States Treasury in the nation's history.

26

Taking on the corrupt Veterans Bureau

We must go back to the fifth-century-B.C. fratricidal hatred between Athens and Sparta for a parallel to the animosity between the North and the South in nineteenth-century America. Like their ancient Greek counterparts, the Americans did not suspend mutual ill will when the fighting stopped and the rebuilding was begun. Two decades after war's end, many in the South continued to mourn their "Lost Cause" with an intensity equaled only by the abhorrence with which many in the North looked down on the "Johnny Rebs."

Cleveland in his Inaugural Address expressed the desire that the American people "cheerfully and honestly abandon all sectional prejudice and distrust [and] work out harmoniously the achievements of our national destiny."[71] He led the way by distributing patronage in the former secessionist states so that the younger, forward-thinking men succeeded the older, as yet unreconstructed element—the so-called Bourbons, who vowed over mint juleps what has come down as a humorous tag line but at the time continued to reverberate meaningfully: "The South shall riiiise again!"

In a study based on firsthand observation, journalist Charles Dudley Warner described how Cleveland's policy of reunification was meeting with greater success than even Cleveland himself dared hope: "Immense satisfaction was felt at [his] election . . . , and elation of triumph in the belief that now the party which had been largely a nonparticipant in Federal affairs would have a large share and weight in the Administration. With this went, however, a new feeling of responsibility, of a stake in the country, that manifested itself at once in attachment to the Union as a common possession of all sections."[72]

Economic and social forces, not political ones, were contributing most to national unity. A new South was being born that was concerned more with the pursuit of business than the pursuit of a resolution to the questions that had caused the war in the first place. ("The South, having had its bellyful of blood, has gotten a taste of money, and is too busy trying to make more to quarrel with anybody.")[73] Birmingham's skyline was barely discernible in the haze of smoke belching up from a forest of steel mills. Atlanta, razed by the Union army, was now a rabbit warren of factories, well launched on its way to becoming the great railroad hub and distribution trade center it remains to this day. A major new industry, cottonseed, was rising phoenixlike from the ashes of King Cotton. (Some 600,000 tons were processed into oil in 1885 alone.) In the five years 1882–1886, while the population of the South increased only 16 percent, its wealth increased by more than 40 percent.[74]

But there was a fly in the ointment. Two flies, actually. Two powerful groups on both sides of the Mason-Dixon Line were tacitly bent upon keeping alive traditional sectional animosities in order to serve their own devious ends. These were the politicians who hoped to transmute those animosities into votes, and the newspaper owners who hoped to transmute the votes into revenue and influence. In Easter week of 1886, proof that the old rancors were alive and well became intensified when the aged Jefferson Davis emerged from Belvoir, his Mississippi estate, to lay the cornerstone of a Confederate monument before wildly cheering Montgomery crowds, and then repeated himself in Atlanta before an equally receptive audience. Throughout the region the editor of South Carolina's most influential paper was being hailed for calling the Civil War "a holy war of defense." In the North, it was another story. All this activity was construed as a sign that the South was awaiting the moment "to strike for lost empire and revenge." In Albany an indignant crowd vowed, "We'll hang Jeff Davis to a sour apple tree!"[75]

Cleveland managed to deal with these lingering sectional antagonisms so as not to let them derail his program of national reunification. This was owing to an idiosyncratic virtue which in other men was a fault: a congenital capacity for ignoring adverse criticism. Examples: He wished to go fishing on Memorial Day, so he went fishing. He adamantly refused to alter his schedule despite a plea that he visit Lincoln's tomb at Springfield while on his western tour; he even refused to make a speech while visiting Gettysburg. (He felt that Lincoln, whose memory he worshiped, had already said there for all time what needed saying.) And he accepted with equanimity being assailed in the North when in a letter commemorating the unveiling of a statue to Confederate hero Albert Sidney Johnson he said every American ought to take pride in that general's "nobility of character."[76]

About the only thing the North and South managed to agree on was the President's unwillingness to buy into their respective prejudices. To Cleveland, these prejudices were "contemptuous," and he insisted on braving them with forthright honesty, regardless of which side's ox was being gored. It was this honesty, exposing as it did so much that was selfish and, yes, downright absurd, about sectional hostility, that served the country well when Cleveland now defied an attempt by an alliance of unprincipled congressmen and unscrupulous citizens to drain the federal Treasury in quest of fraudulent pension benefits for Union veterans—under the shibboleths Patriotism and National Honor.

Because Grover Cleveland was the first Democrat to occupy the White House since the Civil War, it was easy for Republicans to interpret his unwillingness to approve dishonest pensions for Union vets as confirmation of his empathy for the South's "Lost Cause"—especially since he had bought his way out of serving in the war. But Cleveland saw in the pension system, as it was then being run, not only an unconscionable assault on the nation's purse but an affront to common decency and, for him the most heinous flaw, an insult to all those veterans and survivors of veterans whose pensions were honestly come by. Unlike his five predecessors, he would not tolerate perpetuation of this national scandal, mindful though he was that he was subjecting himself to denunciation not only by Republicans but by fellow Democrats as well.

It is a mathematical truism that any government disbursement under an equitable veterans' pension plan peaks within a decade, at the most two, of the war's ending. That is the point at which the number of legitimate pensioners begins to decrease through mortality. In 1866, there were 126,722 Civil War pensioners drawing a yearly total of about $13.5 million from the Treasury. Seven years later, 238,411 were drawing some $29 million annually. The number of pensions, which should have been *reduced* through natural attrition, had, in fact, more than *doubled,* thanks to vested interests. These included the veterans themselves, who could feed not only their own votes to hungry politicians but the votes of their kinfolk; the politicians, who eyed those votes Cassius-like; a multitude of deceitful claims agents and pension attorneys; and local merchants who anticipated the added infusion of money into the community that must soon cross their counters.

Encouraging them every step of the way was the Grand Army of the Republic. Composed of Union army and navy veterans, mostly Republican, the GAR was now at its peak membership of 400,000.[77] As conceived in 1862, the pension system was meant to compensate ex-servicemen whose injuries or ailments derived directly from wartime service; provision was also made for their widows, orphans, and dependent parents. In 1873, when the total number reached its apogee, the rolls began a slow decline. Through the exertions of the highly politicized GAR, that decline was halted precipitately six years later by one of the most preposterous pieces of legislation ever to get through Congress.

Called the Arrears of Pensions Act, it allowed a successful claimant to recover retroactively the amount he would have been entitled to if the pension had been granted when the disability occurred. Dishonest agents were now encouraged to seek out veterans in whose behalf they might present a new claim. Old soldiers whose wounds had long since healed now conveniently "discovered" (or had discovered for them) that their injuries had been "much more serious than initially diagnosed." Men who had suffered an attack of fever while on active duty became "convinced" the fever was in fact the root cause of every ill they had suffered since separation from the service. In addition, thousands of legitimately rejected claims were now revived and pushed through.

Prior to passage of this legislation, new claims averaged some nineteen thousand *yearly*. After passage, they averaged more than ten thousand *monthly*.

When Cleveland entered office, there were 345,125 pensioners drawing more than $65.5 million a year—a nearly 500 percent increase over two decades, a period during which the numbers should have gone in the opposite direction. This represented the single largest annual Treasury disbursement except for interest on the national debt. At least a quarter of the claims were patently ridiculous, and the number was increasing steadily.[78] In on the scam were thousands of "invalids" in fact robust and able-bodied or receiving pensions for ailments incurred in civilian life that not even a quack physician could possibly categorize as war-related. Countless were the "dependent relatives" in fact fiscally independent, and "widows" long remarried. Innumerable were the charlatans who pretended to be, and received checks made out to, legitimate pensioners long dead.

The success of the deceitful claimants was attributable to faults inherent in the system. Disability was determined by the pensioner's unfitness to perform manual labor, without regard to mental capacity or private income (let alone willingness). Evidence on which these pensions were granted was, by and large, proof furnished by comrades and neighbors biased in their favor. Often the examining physician was only too glad to help a friend and, at the same time, bring more money into the community—and into his own pocket.[79] Cleveland not only hoped to stop this appalling drain of public funds, he hoped to spare the war's genuine heroes dishonor imposed by these rapacious schemers. He insisted that all pension benefits go to those—and only those—who had genuinely suffered in the service of their country, be it North or South. "It is fully as important," he said in his first Annual Message to Congress, "that the rolls should be cleansed of all those who by fraud have secured a place therein, as that meritorious claims should be speedily examined and adjusted."

Compounding the problem, a new procedure had come into vogue that was meeting with great success. Decisions by the Pension Bureau were disregarded and the bogus claims taken directly to Congress in the form of private pension bills. The idea was foolproof: rare was the politician who would dare resist a claimant, lest he come off in the eyes of his constituents as unpatriotic. The Pension Bureau considered all claims equitably, interpreting the laws in a liberal yet impartial spirit. Congress had now set itself up as a rival court, and was reversing countless decisions made by that tribunal.

That Congress would enact special pension bills without consideration (and without merit) was to Cleveland an outrage. He suggested reliance on the Pension Bureau. Congress ignored the suggestion. Claims came in quicker than they could be scheduled for debate. In one day alone Cleveland received for his signature no fewer than 240 of these special bills—of which 198 authorized payment on claims previously rejected, with good cause, by the bureau. Indicative of the flood of shady bills, Congress set aside Friday evenings exclusively for acting on them. The Senate in a single day passed 400. In one six-month period, 4,127, a scant few of them legitimate, were introduced in the House, and an even larger number in the Senate.[80] If allotted but ten minutes each for consideration, they would consume four months of Congress's time. The demand on the President's time was likewise considerable, as he insisted on personally researching every claim. This did not keep him from tending to other pressing matters. It just kept him up later into the wee hours of the morning.

Cleveland's way of dealing with the three of every four he rejected was to return them with brief, often sarcastic, at times indignant messages. In one, he noted that the "injury complained of existed prior to . . . enlistment." Another he disallowed after learning that the name of the petitioner in question "is not borne upon any of the rolls of the regiment he alleges he was on his way to join" when allegedly injured. On another, he decided, "If the wounds were received as described, there is certainly no necessary connection between them and death fourteen years afterwards from 'neuralgia of the heart.' " In yet another, he wrote: "It is stated that about five years ago, while the claimant was gathering dandelions . . . his leg broke . . . [but] it is not evident that the fracture had anything to do with . . . military service." And in still another he summed up his exasperation: "We are dealing with pensions, and not with gratuities!"

Let us pause here to examine a handful of the more absurd claims, not so much for the comic relief they might offer—this was no laughing matter—as for an appreciation of the extent to which so many unprincipled claimants and an accommodating Congress were prepared to bilk the Treasury under the pretext of one's having served honorably under the flag.

Take the case of Cuthbert Stone, voted a pension for a disability incurred during his "long and faithful service" in the army. War Department records revealed that Stone enlisted October 25, 1861, and was reported as a deserter from December 31 of that year until November 1864; in January 1865, he was mustered out with his company, with no evidence of disability. Stone filed no claim until 1881—for having allegedly contracted a disability in the winter of 1863. He subsequently changed the date, claiming that the disease was contracted "while he was being carried from place to place as a prisoner, having been tried by court martial in 1862 for desertion, and sentenced to imprisonment until the expiration of his term of enlistment." Although Stone admitted to having spent most of his time in army service as a deserter (for which he was imprisoned) he was voted a pension in recognition of his "long and faithful service and high character." Cleveland, in vetoing the bill, held that "the allowance of this claim would, in my opinion, be a travesty upon our whole scheme of pensions, and an insult to every decent veteran soldier."

Then there was William Bishop, who hired himself out as a substitute in March 1865 and was mustered out little over a month later, having spent half his army career hospitalized with measles. In vetoing Bishop's pension bill, Cleveland wrote, with characteristic irony, "This is the military record of a man who remained in the army one month and seventeen days, having entered it as a substitute at a time when high bounties were paid. Fifteen years after this brilliant service and this terrific encounter with measles claimant discovered that his attack of the measles had some relation to his army enrollment, and that this disease had 'settled in his eyes, also affecting his spinal column.' This claim was rejected by the Pension Bureau, and I have no doubt of the correctness of its determination."

Cleveland ended another veto message with the belief "that if the veterans of the war knew all that was going on in the way of granting pensions by private bills, they would be more disgusted than any other class of our citizens." Among the other innovative claimants Cleveland turned down:

—a veteran who admitted that after being inducted "at home" he set out on horseback intending to complete his enlistment, but while en route his horse fell on his left ankle, which Congress believed entitled him to a cripple's pension;

—the widow of a veteran killed by a fall from a ladder in 1881 who traced his demise to a slight flesh wound in the calf incurred while in service sixteen years prior;

—a Kentucky police officer who sought a pension for the death of his son ten months after he deserted from the army (a similar claim was made by a Pennsylvania family whose breadwinner drowned in a canal six miles from home—while in the act of deserting);

—an Illinois vet who sought a pension for injuries received at his home twenty-three years earlier by the explosion of a Fourth of July cannon;

—the widow of a captain who passed on in 1883 from cerebral apoplexy, which she swore resulted from a hernia her hero contracted while on active duty twenty years earlier.

And then there was the rather creative vet who claimed to be suffering an eye disease that was a result of diarrhea brought on by army rations!

The ever chivalrous Cleveland exercised admirable restraint when it came to denying inventive claims by the fairer sex. When Congress voted one Mary A. Van Etten a special pension because her husband, whose service record was allegedly the stuff of which legends are made, drowned in 1875, Cleveland, after a scrupulous examination of the facts, wrote in his veto message:

> It is claimed that in an effort to drive across that bay in a buggy with his young son the buggy was overturned and both were drowned. The application for pension was based upon the theory that during his military service the deceased soldier contracted rheumatism, which so interfered with his ability to save himself by swimming that his death may be fairly traced to a disability incurred in the service . . . He was mustered out in 1863, and though he lived twelve years thereafter, it does not appear that he ever applied for a pension; and, though he was drowned in 1875, his widow apparently did not connect his military service with his death until ten years [later]. It seems to me that there is such an entire absence of direct and tangible evidence that the death of this soldier resulted from an incident of his service that the granting of a pension upon such a theory is not justified.

Occasionally, even the petition by a member of the fairer sex raised Cleveland's bile beyond the bounds of social acceptability. So it was with that of Mrs. Sallie Ann Bradley from Clinton County, Ohio. According to Sallie Ann's claim, her husband, T. J., and their four sons, Robert, John, Carey, and James, served both honorably and heroically with the Union army; she further claimed that two of the sons fell in battle, the third had his arm torn off by a shell, and the fourth lost an eye while on active duty. Her petition stated that T. J. began his active duty with the Ohio 24th and then transferred to the Ohio 18th, to be wounded in the Battle of Nashville. As a civilian (again, this is from the claim presented to Congress), T. J. endured a sorrowful, hand-to-mouth existence, drawing a mere $4 monthly, until 1880 when, laid low by battle wounds that refused to heal, he gave up the ghost. Whereupon his devastated widow, broken by sorrow and sickness and the ravages of destitution, was compelled to live out her declining years in the Clinton County Infirmary because her two surviving boys were too incapacitated by *their* war wounds to earn enough to help her out. Having thus suffered the destruction of her family in defense of the Union, Congress decided in Sallie Ann Bradley's behalf, she surely merited the $8 a month that she sought.

When Cleveland vetoed the bill after investigating the facts he was roundly cursed to hell and back for denying a pension to a pathetic woman who had given so much for her country. Though he had all the facts to sustain his decision, he refused to defend himself. To do so, he believed, was beneath the dignity of his office. The *Clinton County Democrat* conducted its own investigation, and on July 29, 1886, shared with its readers the true facts as gleaned from the tragic widow's neighbors, and from an inspection of what remained of her shattered family:

T. J. Bradley had been nowhere near the Battle of Nashville; he had "choked to death on a piece of beef when gorging himself while on a drunken spree, and, therefore, did not go to camp on the other shore [i.e., to his grave] when worn out with wounds and old age. So much for the old man." Sons John and James, supposedly dead in battle, were very much alive; in fact, all four Bradley boys came home from the war with their body parts intact. Robert died of yellow fever in Memphis several years after the war, and Carey committed suicide while on a drunken toot. As for "the eye and arm story," John—a shoemaker by trade and Democratic postmaster of Bentonville, Ohio—had indeed lost an eye, but from a nail flying into it while he was repairing a boot. James was indeed shot in the arm at Nashville, but it was not torn off by a shell. Mrs. Bradley was not now—nor had she ever been—an inmate of the Clinton County Infirmary, "and her boys are not unable to support her by reason of disabilities produced from wounds received in the army." But Sallie Ann was apparently not one to take no for an answer. The *Democrat* learned that the Senate had twice rejected bills to pension her. (Since the Republicans, who previously controlled the Senate, were an easy touch when it came to these phony claims, it is probable they turned her down solely because of son John's Democratic affiliation.)

The GAR's reaction to Cleveland's handling of the bogus pension claims was predictable. Encouraged by the Republicans, it branded him a shirker who had avoided participation in the war that saved the Union and condemned his soul to everlasting damnation. Such nonsense only deflected the public's attention from the true facts of his own war on fraudulent claimants. The GAR chose to disregard the moral and ethical implications of the pension scam, focusing instead on the notion that even a justified attack on a member was a threat to its very survival—especially if the attack was by a Democratic Commander in Chief.

Congress's behavior in all this was no less deplorable. One member even demanded legislated pensions for all Union veterans on the ground that each had come out of the war weaker than when he went into it! (Was he implying Confederate soldiers came out stronger?) The *New York Tribune* typified the attitude of the Republican press's antagonistic wing by denouncing Cleveland for "sending the destitute, aged mothers of soldiers to the poorhouse" so that the Democrats "may gain a reputation for economy." Former President Hayes, a Union veteran, weighed in with his opinion that Cleveland's policy was "penny-pinching."

Neither the GAR, the opposition papers, nor, for that matter, Hayes saw fit to note that Cleveland saw merit in many of the pension bills; that he signed more than twice as many as he vetoed, and far more than any previous President signed. Besides the Democratic newspapers, Cleveland did have the support of many influential Republican and Independent ones, all of which tried to impress upon their readers that his fight was for a great moral principle, and not merely to spare the Treasury extraneous appropriations.

Since so many of the pension claims he vetoed were revived during the Harrison administration, did Cleveland actually put the skids on the whole evil practice, as has been argued? Definitely so, when we consider that the number of audacious swindles fell off appreciably after he had appealed to public opinion—and to the consciences of those relatively few congressmen who happened to be blessed with one. Furthermore, he blocked a piece of pension legislation that was far more dangerous than it was absurd: the Blair bill of 1887.

Popularly known as the dependent pensions bill, it called for the government to give from $6 to $12 a month to any man who had served a minimum of ninety days in any American war. The bill passed the House on January 17, 1887, and the Senate ten days later, with the Republicans supporting it almost unanimously in both chambers. This set off one of the greatest dins of public disapprobation ever to assault Congressional ears. The *Chicago Tribune* warned it would "put a serpent of temptation at the ear of every veteran" to swindle the Treasury; to the *Washington Post* it was "one of the most reckless specimens of legislation ever presented in Congress"; the *New York World* pointed out that the pensions expenditures of the United States, now running at more than $76 million a year, represented the interest on a national debt of $2 billion (something the nation would not reach until well into the next century). General Edward S. Bragg of Wisconsin, whose pithy reason for supporting Cleveland in 1884 has been recorded, termed Blair "a bill to pension the rubbish of the United States, and to revive the business of claim agent in Washington."

Predictably, the GAR labored relentlessly in the bill's behalf; prominent among its catalog of specious arguments was the melancholy revelation that it had (allegedly) unearthed seven thousand veterans residing in poorhouses. The GAR did promise, though, with a straight face, that its ten thousand posts nationwide would guarantee that only those veterans worthy of the pension received it. Congressman John Alexander Logan, a founder and three-term GAR president, went on record as wanting the measure to cost more; he offered an amendment raising the minimum pension rate.

Cleveland responded with an anticipated veto, accompanied by a long trenchant message denouncing the bill for sanctioning fraud by inducing honest men to quit work in favor of living on the public dole. The "race after the pensions offered by this bill," he posited, "would not only stimulate weakness and pretended incapacity for labor, but would be a further premium on mendacity and dishonesty." Going on to review the entire pensions benefit scandal to date, he seized the opportunity to lecture Congress—and, by inference, the GAR—on how much two decades of this kind of chicanery had cost the nation in dollars and cents urgently needed to finance other, more worthy programs. Such was his obsession with detail, he was able to report the exact amount doled out for pensions from 1861 to date: $808,624,811.51.[81] The message did the trick. The veto was sustained. There would be no further attempt to enact a dependent pensions bill during either of his two presidencies.

27

"Calm scorn for sectional outbursts"

Having been beaten back on the pension issue, the Republicans, encouraged by the GAR lobby, thirsted for revenge. Ironically the means for slaking that thirst was handed them by Cleveland on a metaphorical silver platter. And though he quickly did an about-face that should have satisfied them, they continued to overwhelm him with a deluge of vituperation no President since Andrew Johnson had been forced to endure.

It started, innocently enough, with a memorandum from General Richard Drum to Secretary of War Endicott. Dated April 30, 1887, it called to Endicott's attention that there were now stored in the War Department a number of Union flags captured in battle but recovered on the fall of the Confederacy and sent there for safekeeping, along with a number of Confederate flags "which the fortunes of war placed in our hands during the late Civil War." Drum, a Republican and active in the GAR, suggested as "a graceful act" that the flags be returned to the respective states. The idea was in keeping with the growing practice among Union and Confederate veterans to hold joint commemorations on former battlefields. Endicott returned Drum's memo with the annotation: "Approved by the President." Adverse reaction came from two groups: those who decided Cleveland had erred egregiously, and those who decided he had offended egregiously.

Included in the first group were northern politicians who, like their southern analogues, chose to overlook that the order covered *all* captured standards, Union and Confederate alike. The governors of Wisconsin and Nebraska sent vigorous protests. The governor of Kansas wrote Cleveland that this action was "an insult to the heroic dead and an outrage on their living comrades." One Nebraska senator cited international legal precedent in opposing the return of captured flags. A Connecticut colleague wrote the President that he was "deeply saddened" and urged that flags taken from "our misguided brothers and wicked conspirators" be burned; if returned to the southern states, he warned, they would be revered as more than simply "mementoes of misapplied valor."

The second group of protesters included the anti-Cleveland press and a sympathetic legion of demagogic hypocrites. One major daily ran headlines like "The Old Slave Whip Cracking Again," "Now Pay the Rebel Debt," and "Slapping the Veterans in the Face," to dismiss the battle standards as "mementoes of as foul a crime as any in human history." Ohio governor J. B. Foraker advised the White House, "The people of this State are shocked and indignant beyond anything I can express," and warned, "No rebel flags will be surrendered while I am governor." Grabbing the most headlines, however, was Lucius Fairchild of Wisconsin, national commander of the GAR, who was presiding over a Grand Army national encampment at the time: "May God palsy the hand that wrote that order! May God palsy the brain that conceived it, and may God palsy the tongue that dictated it!"[82]

After careful consideration of the facts, Cleveland realized he had acted too impetuously in endorsing the Drum memo. In his eagerness to accelerate the healing process, he had exceeded the limits of his constitutional authority: the flags were national property, and thus not subject to executive order. Six weeks after receiving the Drum memo, he requested of Endicott that no further steps be taken in the matter, except to examine and inventory the flags and adopt proper measures for their preservation. Any directions as to the final disposition of them should originate with Congress.

There the controversy should have ended. But those determined to undermine Cleveland by perpetuating sectional animosities wouldn't give up. From all points of the compass came a deluge of abusive letters condemning the President as a "viper," "traitor," "skulker," "contemptible politician," "hater of Union veterans," "oppressor of the widow and the fatherless," "unworthy to breathe the air of heaven," ad nauseum. A number of more responsible newspapers pointed out what Cleveland had been saying all along: the GAR rank-and-file were, for the most part, decent, patriotic men who were being manipulated by their leaders. The thesis was well put by one northern paper: "Little by little, such political brawlers as Fairchild . . . crawled into responsible leadership" and poisoned the minds of worthy veterans to the extent that the very mention of President Cleveland's name drove them into fits of unwarranted resentment.[83]

Of the many prominent men, northern and southern alike, who were determined that the Fairchilds and the Forakers not further inflame sectional hostility, none spoke with more common sense, more eloquence, and more generosity than Governor Fitzhugh Lee of Virginia, Robert E.'s nephew. The idea of returning the flags did not originate with southern soldiers, he pointed out. While they would have "accepted again their banners bathed in the blood of brave comrades," veterans of the Confederacy recognized that flags taken in battle are the property of the victors, and were content to let them remain in their charge. As it happens, some northern flags had already been returned. However, he maintained, the country

> should not again be agitated by pieces of bunting that mean nothing now. The South is part and parcel of the Union today, and means to do her part toward increasing the prosperity and maintaining the peace of the republic, whether the flags rot in Washington or are restored to their former custodians. If any man hauls down the American flag shoot him on the spot, but don't let us get into trouble because another flag exchanged its resting place.[84]

In the spirit of Lee's statement a joint reunion was held at Gettysburg on the Fourth of July between a brigade of Philadelphia veterans and some visiting ex-Confederates who'd fought under the legendary George Edward Pickett. When it seemed that rational judgment would carry the day, the hatemongers, a highly vocal minority, eagerly scanned the horizon in search of yet another issue with which to halt their rapidly declining strength and influence at Cleveland's expense. They hoped that issue would be his cancellation of a proposed visit to the GAR Encampment scheduled for St. Louis in September.

This was the first time that the annual encampment, an event of national importance, was to be held in any southern or border-state city, and it was felt only fitting that the President attend. He accepted the invitation tendered by the mayor of St. Louis, David Fields, and was elated when the GAR executive committee officially invited him and resolutions to that effect were passed in local posts nationwide. Ignored was the carping by a clique who opposed his attendance on the grounds that to them the President was, and always would be, the draft-dodging archenemy of Union veterans.

Others announced plans to insult him to his face if he came; still others threatened physical violence. At an Army of West Virginia reunion in late August at Wheeling, many of the participants halted at a banner over the line of march that said "God Bless our President, Commander-in-Chief of our Army and Navy," and refusing to pass beneath it, folded their flags and marched around it, trailing their colors in the dirt.[85]

Anxious to know just what effect his appearing at the St. Louis encampment might evoke, Cleveland asked Fields to take a reading of public sentiment. Fields reported back that while the members with whom he'd met "desire to have you attend," they did express "a fear lest your presence will deter many posts from coming." He found "a growing sentiment among the local GAR" that the President decline the invitation. In order that he might do so gracefully, he was invited to the annual Fair and Veiled Prophet pageant to be held the week after the encampment.

Cleveland was in a quandary. To go to St. Louis under threat of insult and even bodily harm was unthinkable. But not to go was cowardly. Better to appear cowardly, he decided, than to subject the President of the United States to indignity. Reluctantly, he retracted his acceptance: "I might, if I alone were concerned, submit to the insult to which it is quite openly asserted I would be helplessly subjected if present at the encampment; but I should bear with me there the people's highest office, the dignity of which I must protect."[86]

The letter, which Fields made public, effectively ended all attempts by the hatemongers to embarrass the President. It was the GAR that suffered a public embarrassment, for failing to repudiate the contemptuous remarks of some of its leaders. There now followed a national flood of denunciatory newspaper editorials and a demand that sectional rivalries be buried once and for all time. Later in the year, Cleveland got in what proved to be the last word. When made public, the following letter won him ever more recruits in his battle against the further perpetuation of that sad legacy of the Civil War:

> No one can deny that the Grand Army of the Republic has been played upon by demagogues for partisan purposes, and has yielded to insidious blandishments to such an extent that it is regarded by many [as] an organization which has wandered a long way from its original design. . . . Such a sentiment not only

> exists, but will grow and spread unless *within* that organization something is done to prove that its objects are not partisan, unjust, and selfish.[87]

When the nation geared up for the 1888 presidential election campaign, sectionalism was moribund, because of the passing of time and the playing out of inexorable economic and social forces. But not to be overlooked was Cleveland's pivotal contribution: his "calm scorn for sectional outbursts, and his calm exposure of the pensions grabs and other selfish schemes lurking behind the carefully-manufactured attacks on the South."[88]

28
A triumphant tour

Cleveland had traveled little beyond Washington since taking office: to Indianapolis for a speech; to New York City for President Grant's funeral and Albany for President Arthur's; occasional hunting trips in the Adirondacks; a handful of "quickies" for speeches in the Northeast—that was about the extent of it. Three of those brief excursions are worthy of mention: to Philadelphia, for the Constitution centennial, when he delivered three speeches appropriate to the occasion in a single day; to New York City, to accept for the nation from France Frederic Bartholdi's *Liberty Enlightening the World*—the Statue of Liberty—whose lamp, he proclaimed, would "illumine the way to man's enfranchisement"; and to Harvard University eleven days later in connection with its 250th anniversary. (At Harvard, Cleveland refused to accept an honorary degree, his "disinclination" based upon "a feeling which I cannot stifle and which I hope may be humored without any suspicion of lack of appreciation or churlishness," Cleveland told a friend. The "feeling" was that university degrees should be earned, not distributed as gifts.)[89]

In the fall of 1887, Cleveland wrote asking Wilson Bissell to join him and Frances on a three-week journey to the West and South, an area he had always wanted to see. Never having been west of the Mississippi, he felt the time had now come to take a break from the pressures of work. The trip was to be "solely a social affair . . . no political tour." Also going along were two other close friends, Dan Lamont and Dr. Joseph Bryan. Cleveland personally oversaw all arrangements. Visits were planned to eighteen states, with stops lasting from a few hours to a day in the large cities, and layovers in the major metropolises of Chicago, St. Louis, and Atlanta. He insisted that "we are to have a family party with every freedom from restraint which that implies. . . ." The idea was to enjoy "an every-day-kind-of-visit-to-the-people. . . . Think of this. We shall see a wondrous country."[90]

The party left Washington on September 20 in a special train that included, in addition to baggage and supply cars, a parlor car for relaxation, a sleeping car for the Clevelands' guests, and, for the Clevelands themselves, George M. Pullman's private car, refurbished and redecorated, containing a large stateroom, dining salon and parlor combined, library, and private kitchen, presided over by "an accomplished cook." All expenses, including those of his guests, were paid for by Cleveland out of personal funds.

He demanded the schedule be strictly adhered to. All the host cities had planned a full program of public receptions—parades, balls, banquets, parades, even fireworks displays. Should the train pass through large towns, during daylight hours, it was to be slowed down to allow not Grover Cleveland but "the President" to be seen on the rear platform. In major cities, the Clevelands were to be driven about in an open carriage, so that they might be seen in the shortest time by the most people. ("He has become convinced by recent experience, that if there can be any gratification to any considerable number of people to look at the Chief Magistrate, that curiosity can be better satisfied by a drive through a crowd than it can be by compelling the crowd to accumulate about a platform," reported one paper.)[91]

The trip far exceeded Cleveland's greatest expectations. Most Americans did not share the politicians' antagonism toward their President. Reporters were surprised by the affection that greeted him at all stops. Typical was Richmond, Indiana, where the train halted five minutes to take on water and "a half acre of solid humanity awaited the train." The President shook every hand that reached up to where he stood on his car platform. During a four-minute stop outside New Lisbon, Wisconsin, three thousand people grabbed frantically to shake his hand. In the cities, the enthusiasm bordered on mass hysteria. At St. Louis, where "the enthusiasm over Mr. Cleveland's presence [surpassed] description," he was accorded a reception "that can never be effaced from his memory. Big and little, old and young, white and black, Republicans and Democrats, honored him. It was one tremendous welcome from 7 o'clock in the morning until midnight." In Milwaukee, where Cleveland was only the second Chief Executive to visit (Hayes had been there nine years previously), buildings on both sides of every major street were draped with bunting. Even the Republicans of Milwaukee had "a very kindly feeling for President Cleveland, and they entered heartily into the preparations for his reception. In fact, they were rather more active than the Democrats, and really deserve the credit for the successful results."[92]

Cleveland's speeches throughout the entire trip—he seemed to make one at the drop of the hat he always wore in public—were usually overblown and loaded with platitudinous compliments to audience and city in equal measure. The people loved it; he was invariably interrupted with shouts of "Cleveland is the man!" and "Hurrah for President Cleveland!" Though he stayed away from politics, people seized the opportunity to make a political statement: "Veto the pension grabbers!" This was particularly so in the South, where people were footing the bill for pensions that went almost exclusively to Union army veterans. Cleveland loved it.

Of all his public remarks, the most charming, most remembered were those in which he shared with the people his feelings for Frances. At an early-morning water stop outside Columbus, he greeted a crowd of about a hundred from the observation car with a hearty "Good morning." Someone yelled, "We would like to see your wife." "That is impossible now," replied the President, "she has a hard day's task before her, and is resting." "Well, we are right glad to see you, Sir," said another. "I thank you for that," rejoined the President, "but I expect you would prefer to see Mrs. Cleveland."

Perhaps so. The *New York Times* reported, "The public reception to Mrs. Cleveland was the most significant effort of the kind ever witnessed in Milwaukee." The *Ohio State Journal*, reflecting the consensus of editorial opinion, declared that the city of Cleveland "had seen at least 10,000 men here as well fitted to be President as he was, but . . . almost nobody was so well fitted to be a President's wife as Mrs. Cleveland."[93] In St. Paul, where Frances had attended school for a short time, her husband brought down the house when he noted Frances had, when a young girl, "dwelt among you and went to school. She has grown up and is my wife. If anyone thinks a President ought not to mention things of this sort in public, I hope he or she does not live in St. Paul, for I don't want to shock anybody when I thank the good people of this city because they neither married nor spoiled my wife; and when I tell them that I had much rather have her than the presidency."[94]

After a brief fishing interlude in Madison, Wisconsin, as guests of Postmaster General and Mrs. Vilas, who were vacationing at their home there and now joined the party for the return trip to Washington, the Clevelands moved into the South. Memphis was crowded with more than 100,000 people come to see them from Mississippi, Tennessee, Alabama, Arkansas, and Texas. In Atlanta, the churches were opened up to some 7,000 out-of-towners unable to find overnight accommodations. The southern phase of the journey was not without its dangerous moments and its sad moments. In Alabama, fire broke out on a trestle bridge just as the pilot train was crossing, but the crew managed to extinguish it before damage could be done, and the presidential train continued safely. At Memphis, after being formally welcomed to the city by chancery court judge H. T. Ellett, Cleveland was about five minutes into his prepared remarks when the judge dropped dead.

And then there were the silly moments, one of which outraged Cleveland (Frances prevailed upon him to let it go). It seems that as the two were being shown about the St. Louis Fair Grounds during the Veiled Prophet pageant—but the *New York Times* account tells it so much better:

A VERY EXPENSIVE PANCAKE

> ST. LOUIS, OCTOBER 18. Annie Knox, with one or two aliases, the woman who surprised 10,000 people at the Fair Grounds on the day of the President's visit by throwing a pancake at Mrs. Cleveland, was tried in the police court this morning. The evidence showed that Mrs. Knox was manipulating pancakes in a booth,

and as the President's carriage passed she suddenly threw a very large buttered pancake at Mrs. Cleveland, with such precision that it landed in her lap. She was heard to say: "You can't get as good a one as that at the Mayor's house." When arrested she said she just wanted to show Mrs. Cleveland what a St. Louis pancake was like. She testified when placed on the stand that the pancake was so hot that she could not hold it, and in throwing it away it somehow got into Mrs. Cleveland's lap. She was fined $50 and costs.

At the Atlanta hotel where the Clevelands were staying, "a ferocious personage" was halted by a sentry outside the sleeping President's room and said in a tone of voice apparently intended to be overheard: "I wish you would inform Mr. Cleveland that if Georgians are to be barred out from shaking hands with the President of the United States by sabers at his chamber, by——, Sir, he had better go back to Washington! Jeff Davis will be here next week, and there'll be no sabers between him and the gentlemen of Georgia!" The man was later judged to be "momentarily irresponsible." The President "never heard a thing."[95]

Cause of the outburst was Cleveland's decision ten days before in Madison to abandon the practice of shaking every hand thrust at him. ("Much dissatisfaction is expressed because the President and Mrs. Cleveland did not shake hands at the afternoon reception. They only acknowledged the greetings with smiles and bows as the people filed through the Capitol.") The reason was simply that their hands were achingly sore. Frances had collapsed in a swoon the day before while in Chicago from "the terrible crush of people at the station, coupled with the fatigue of the ordeal at St. Louis." She had by then "borne the ordeal" since leaving Washington "of shaking hands with 15,000 or 20,000 people." Both Clevelands would continue the practice of shaking hands at official receptions. But then, they would never again be subjected to such a heavy concentration of it as on their western and southern journey. Arriving back at Washington three weeks after starting out, Cleveland told the White House press corps, "Now that it is over, I am glad to be able to say that the unvarying warmth of the welcome extended to me fully assured me of the sincerity of the cordial language of the invitaions."[96]

29

Though disappointed, not discouraged

Cleveland could look back with pride and satisfaction on a number of achievements as he approached his last full year in office. Conspicuous among them were the Interstate Commerce Act (1887), which was passed in response to the many discriminatory railroad practices then in vogue and established the nation's first regulatory agency; and the Hatch Act (1887), which provided federal subsidies for agricultural experiment stations. These, plus his overturning of the Tenure of Office Act, passage of the Dawes Severalty ("Indian Emancipation") Act, his successes in the areas of labor, patronage, and pension reform, even relatively lesser attainments like legislation that provided for the commissioning of United States Military Academy graduates as second lieutenants—all bespoke the proficiency of a man believed by so many to be lacking in the leadership capacity we demand but do not always get in our Chief Executives.

Through it all, Cleveland revealed a willingness to condemn a hostile position while defending his own, regardless of the hue and cry it aroused, if he knew in his heart that he was acting in the best interests of his constituency—the American people. He did not particularly relish going into battle, but never balked when obliged to. As he prepared his third Annual Message to Congress, there loomed yet another such battle—one that divided the nation along class lines, just as the currency issue divided the nation across sectional lines.

Cleveland was a staunch advocate of low import duties, a position the Democrats had held, despite opposition from many within their own ranks, since passage, in the Polk era, of the Walker Act, which reduced the rates on many incoming goods. For the first two years of his administration, though, what attention Cleveland paid to the ongoing controversy between low tariff reductionism and high tariff protectionism was minimal. He had not publicly allied himself with the tariff reformers, who were among his primary supporters. Many of them wondered if he even knew anything about the issue. He knew that high import duties not only resulted in unacceptable favoritism to the protected industries but, worse, imposed an unfair tax burden on the working-class consumer. (Import taxes were the single greatest source of funding to run the federal government. On any given import, a higher tariff meant an increased cost to the consumer—and, by extension, an added burden to those in the low-income ranges.) Tariff reductionists took heart.

By 1880, low-duty advocates had become so well politicized that James Garfield would probably have lost the election he barely won if his Democratic opponent, Winfield Hancock, had attacked existing schedules, which even many Republicans conceded were too high, instead of evading the issue entirely—on the advice of Democratic protectionists. In November 1885, encouraged by Cleveland's election, the reductionists organized the National Tariff Reform League. With such slogans as "protectionism is the jugglery of the devil!" and "a paternal government is an infernal government!" the league soon became a potent political force.

From the time of his election, Cleveland was subjected to intense pressure by the reductionist lobby: letters, books, magazine articles, even one-on-one confrontations. He was made aware of the "shameful" surplus revenue in the Treasury caused by protectionism. Higher levies on imported goods affected adversely the majority of the people and led to a proportionate loss in their purchasing power. Too, a Treasury surplus was a natural temptation for Congress to pass excessive, if not superfluous, spending programs. Here, then, was a situation that could be as unhealthy for the national economy as a revenue deficiency.

Cleveland was impressed by the reformers' arguments, as he was with those advanced by Treasury Secretary Manning. Though in the vanguard of the tariff reform movement, Manning feared moving too rapidly, lest industry suffer and the Democratic party—whose ranks included a powerful protectionist faction dating back to Andrew Jackson—be driven into schism. Cleveland devoted a scant few lines to the issue in his first State of the Union Message, but what he said was meaningful: equity demanded that in tariff revision "industries and interests [well represented in Democratic ranks] which have been encouraged by such law, and in which our citizens have large investments, should not be ruthlessly injured or destroyed."

The leader of the forty protectionist Democrats in Congress,

Samuel J. Randall of Pennsylvania, did not represent a few wealthy manufacturing concerns, as did so many of his colleagues. His electoral district was made up of the laboring class, but his constituency was the entire state, whose profusion of steel mills, mines, and oil refineries depended entirely on a vigorous American market—and on the protection ensured by high import taxes on pertinent raw materials from abroad. Two weeks before Cleveland's inauguration, Randall wrote warning him of the possible danger faced by the party unless he included a few protectionists in his cabinet. Cleveland refused.

The end of Cleveland's first year in office saw the Democrats seriously, perhaps irrevocably, divided on the issue. Adding to the party's woes, even were reform to pass the Democratic-controlled House it would be defeated in the Republican-controlled Senate. Despite pressure from the low-tariff lobby, Cleveland hesitated to come out for downward revision. Nine months into the first year of his administration, however, while insisting that care be taken to avoid impairing established industries while at the same time protecting the interests of labor, he suggested that "within this limitation a certain reduction should be made" in customs revenue.

In the meantime Manning conducted a personal investigation of the United States Customs Service and discovered that the current tariff laws were "a chaos rather than a system." Then he gave Cleveland a sorely needed crash course on the subject. The tariff laws, like the laws on banking and currency, were a legacy of the Civil War. Not only had high war duties been maintained throughout the long postwar era of falling prices, they had even been increased. This despite confirmation by the Arthur administration that an alarming number of the high rates were detrimental to the very interests they were meant to protect, and that a cutback in duties would pave the way for prosperity.

Both parties had admitted as much in their 1884 campaign platforms. But neither party made a practical move toward reform. The rank and file of both parties agreed on one point: the existing schedules were a blight on large segments of American industry and a distinct threat to the nation's fiscal vitality. Few Democrats denied that the ball was now in their court. They were the party in power; if they did not honor their campaign commitment to effect tariff reform, they deserved to be thrown out of power.

On April 12, 1886, a bill drawn by House Ways and Means Committee chairman William R. Morrison of Illinois, the Democrats' Congressional point man in the low-tariff fight, was reported out. It called for putting many articles (e.g., salt, wool, lumber, hemp, and flax) on the duty-free list; replacing specific levies on woolen textiles with reduced ad valorem duties; and cutting rates on a number of products, including three that directly affected Randall's constituency: steel rails, pig iron, and window glass. At first blush it would seem that while the reductionists hoped to propitiate the powerful Randall, undercutting his state's major contributions to the American market with cheaper imports was hardly the way to do it. But a higher purpose lay behind the bill: Morrison hoped its appeal, especially to protectionist western farming interests whose constituents stood to benefit by lowered duties on these goods, would draw off enough of the forty House votes Randall controlled to, if not break, then at least neutralize his power when the low-tariff faction tackled the whole tariff issue head-on.

Cleveland lobbied personally for the Morrison bill, summoning doubtful congressmen to the White House to tell them "that in his opinion the good of the party demands action on the tariff." He failed to make "a single convert," though all who listened to him "admit that he has been very much in earnest." It seemed "this kind of missionary effort does not seem to be in his line."[97] Whether because Cleveland lacked a missionary's talent for persuasion or because Randall had not been properly reckoned with (presupposing he could be reckoned with at all), the Morrison bill suffered a crushing defeat when the Pennsylvanian moved that the House consider it as a committee of the whole. For Cleveland it was a humiliating snub when so many from his own party voted against consideration.

To show how protectionist Democrats were prepared to deal with the problem, Randall introduced a bill calling for lower rates on some items and higher rates on others (specifically, those inimical to Pennsylvania industries). The bill did not stand a chance, and Randall knew it. He simply wanted it on record that it reflected a "true interpretation of the Democratic platform." With Congress in summer adjournment, the tariff question was held in abeyance as the nation prepared for the 1886 Congressional elections.

The reformers now launched an all-out, do-or-die effort to force the issue by convincing state parties to nominate only reductionist candidates. Despite lavish sums with which the various industrial lobbies set out to defeat them, the reformers met with success in heavily populated Massachusetts and Connecticut. And in Pennsylvania, that hotbed of Democratic protectionism, Randall was faced with a formidable challenge to his Congressional clout, his first in twelve terms, by banker/industrialist William L. Scott, a close Cleveland political ally. Scott, whose appetite for politics had been whetted when he was a page in the House during the Polk years, had almost decided not to seek reelection when he was prevailed upon to do so—and to lead the anti-Randall revolt—by a petition from fifteen hundred low-tariff *Republicans* in his district.

Most attention was focused, however, on the President's home state, where the major newspapers supported low tariffs. Here Manning's people pulled out all stops. Their resolve to subsume party considerations in the greater interest of lower tariffs was demonstrated when the New York Democracy supported a reform Republican—successfully—against a Randallite Democrat.

Cleveland looked on with barely suppressed glee as the tariff assumed pride of place among issues in many Republican state conventions beyond the Mississippi, particularly in the Northwest, where the GOP was faced with an internecine revolt by the farmers fed up with being overly taxed for the benefit of the eastern industrialists. Iowa Republicans included in their platform a plank insisting duty schedules be revised downward. The Nebraska platform demanded that such a revision be effected as soon as possible, and that the duties not only be simplified but that they be put below Civil War levels. Indiana and Minnesota Republicans followed suit.

None of this helped in the larger picture, though. The better-financed Republican protectionists east of the Mississippi joined forces with the Randallite wing of the Democratic Party to win over the electorate. The high-tariff coalition scored a number of successes in the Midwest, notably Ohio and Illinois; but their greatest success—and the Democrats' greatest rout—was in Connecticut, where they gained control of not only the Republican party but the Democratic as well. Almost all Democratic candidates for the state nominating convention who opposed high rates were defeated, and incumbent reductionists were denied renomination.

At this point, Cleveland suffered severe political embarrassment when the controversial behavior of his Attorney General three years previously suddenly became a campaign issue. While in the Senate, Garland had been given $500,000 worth of shares in, and named attorney for, a new company called Pan-Electric. Pan-Electric had neither capital nor credit, its sole asset being a telephone patent that was worthless unless the Bell patent should be declared invalid. When Cleveland appointed him, Garland was asked by Pan-Electric to institute a government suit to test the validity of the Bell patent. He declined, and properly so, since he still held those gifted shares.

While Garland was home for a vacation it was announced that the Solicitor General would initiate the suit. This evoked a public outcry exacerbated by the revelation that Garland's stock holdings made up a tenth of the company's total. Asked by Cleveland for an explanation, Garland said the Solicitor General had acted without his knowledge. Cleveland ordered that the suit not be pursued pending a decision by Interior Secretary Lamar, to whom he referred the matter. Just as the 1886 Congressional campaign was heating up, Lamar decided to go ahead with the suit. This led to yet another outcry from the public, as the suit was scheduled to be prosecuted by Garland's Department of Justice. If it succeeded in breaking the Bell patent priority, he would realize a financial windfall.

Now that it had become a campaign issue, the House began hearings. Denying that the stock was a gift, Garland claimed it as remuneration for an assessment he had paid while helping to organize the company and swore he had never considered using his official influence in its behalf. The majority on the investigating committee returned a report of exoneration (the minority issued a separate report of sharp censure). Convinced that Garland had not acted improperly, Cleveland refused to consider dismissing him. But he doubtless would not have refused Garland's resignation, which should have been tendered.

The outcome of the 1886 elections, which offered the first test of public opinion on Cleveland's presidency, was inconclusive. In the House, the Democratic majority was cut from 184 to 160, resulting in a mere majority of eight over the Republicans, while in the Senate the Republican margin was cut from eight to two. Though it seemed the tariff reformers had suffered a potentially fatal setback with the defeat of their leader in the House, Morrison, and many of his allies, final figures showed otherwise. They won surprising victories in some states, the protectionists suffered surprising losses in others. In the New York delegation alone, all the Democrats besides one Republican were now pledged to lowering duties. All agreed that with a little more effort, and a few conciliatory changes, the election's outcome might have been different. Efforts to resuscitate the Morrison resolution failed despite Cleveland's personal appeal for passage and his threat to call a special session of the incoming 50th Congress to be devoted exclusively to both the tariff and silver issues.

Though disappointed, Cleveland was not discouraged. At the beginning of the year he had made it known he would not use the influence of his office on any legislation, at midyear he had summoned disobedient congressmen to his office for a dressing-down, and at year's end he had resorted to threats of an extra session. None of these approaches had worked. Now he'd have to come up with yet another. . . .

30

The Great Tariff Battle of 1888

The 49th Congress became history on March 3, 1887, without having dealt with a Treasury surplus that posed a threat to the nation's fiscal health. Two factors had led to a steady increase in government income far in excess of its needs—decades of high tariff fees, and immense sums being withdrawn from circulation and warehoused in federal vaults. To prevent direct contraction of the currency, which can be analogized to reducing the pressure in a boiler that has signaled it is about to explode, the administration increased purchases of outstanding bonds, buying $50 million worth in fiscal 1886 and $125 million worth in fiscal 1887. This proved no more than a temporary expedient. In his 1886 Annual Message to Congress, Cleveland cautioned that the nation had a choice between leaving most of the surplus "hoarded in the Treasury when it should be in [the people's] hands" and using it to fund lavish expenditures, "with all the corrupting national demoralization which follows in its train."[98]

As Cleveland tried to impress upon the Congress, this was a Hobson's choice. The tariff was the primary source of the nation's tax revenues, and must continue to be so—but not to the degree that it imperiled the nation's economic well-being. Most import duties were little lower than their wartime high, and on some articles far higher. What was needed—and posthaste—was a careful revision downward. Manning suggested remedial steps, verging on the radical. Before ill health forced him to resign in February 1887, he proposed two ways Congress might deal with the surplus revenue: attack the tariff (an "incompetent and brutal scheme of revenue") through the legislative process; or if Congress refused to go this route—which seemed increasingly likely—have the Treasury use the surplus to retire all the greenbacks in circulation, which now totaled some $346,681,000.

Only once since greenbacks were introduced during the Lincoln era as a wartime measure had a Treasury Secretary suggested retiring them. That was just after the war, and Congress rejected the idea on the grounds that doing so could spur a contraction of the currency. Foreseeing no such danger now, Manning proposed that the Treasury be allowed to redeem every canceled greenback with its equivalent in metal coinage, thereby keeping the volume of currency at its preredemption level. One persuasive objection to this bold but practical plan was that its adoption could well diminish the popular demand for tariff reduction. Manning considered this an academic argument. He also considered academic the argument that greenbacks were regarded as inviolable by the people nationwide, and that any attempts to retire them, especially in the West, might well fail. Manning was determined that Congress see it had no option but to deal with the surplus revenue. And that was one option the Congress—fairly salivating collectively on how they could pork-barrel that surplus—was averse to exercising.

In the waning days of the 49th Congress, Abram Hewitt suggested yet another remedy: allow the Treasury to anticipate any interest on United States bonds that might exceed 3 percent per annum; that is, to make advance payment to holders of 4- and 4.5-percent bonds.[99] This and Manning's proposals were greeted with a thundering silence. In the meantime the predicament was rapidly approaching flash point. Throughout the summer, state conventions gearing up for the 1888 presidential campaign agitated for revision and reduction. Cleveland feared, and rightly so, that this would be a replay of previous campaigns: pledges would be made to "do something about the surplus"—and conveniently forgotten.

Before leaving on his western trip he decided that an undaunted assault against protectionism was required—and that he must personally lead it. As a first step, he convened the Democratic leadership at his suburban Washington home over a September weekend to launch a series of meetings aimed at achieving party consensus and unity. It was agreed that some tariff reductions were absolutely imperative, that all loyal party men should be made aware of this, and that House Speaker Carlisle should initiate requisite legislation. The most important immediate result of these so-called Oak View Conferences was that the President's vigorous leadership raised expectations throughout the party.

Hailing his determination to present a unified front in Congress, the *New York Herald* editorialized (September 16, 1887) that while his behavior during January 1886 had "engendered a painful lukewarmness where only enthusiastic cooperation should exist," he was now exhibiting an aptitude for true statesmanship. The Oak View Conferences, the *Herald* was confident, would "create a better feeling everywhere, and prepare the party for an attack upon some important problems during the next session of Congress." Were he successful in this aggressive course of action the Democrats would have "a thoroughly live issue to go to the country with [in next year's presidential election], and one which will compare so favorably with the petty sectional hatred and the wretched and disgusting . . . business of the Republicans that they will present an invincible front." The American people wanted "big ideas," the *Herald* went on; and the party which "sees the whole continent and fits its policy to the magnificence of the opportunity is the only party worthy of the times in which we now live."

By the time he returned from his western tour, Cleveland had decided on the most radical course imaginable: he would devote his entire 1887 Annual Message to an unequivocal demand for tariff revision. While laboring over the message he was subjected to an endless barrage by reductionists and protectionists alike. Regardless of which line he took, let alone to what degree, he must alienate large segments of the electorate. He heard them all out—and was influenced by none. To one adviser who insisted that the President's best chance for alienating the least number of people lay in keeping to the middle ground, he replied, "I would stultify myself if I failed to let the message go forward from any fear that it might affect my election." To another he said, "What is the use of being elected or re-elected, unless you stand for something?"[100]

Dispatched to the Congress on December 6, the message began by calling attention to the current financial emergency, "which imperatively demands immediate and careful consideration." Total annual revenues largely exceeded the sum necessary to meet government operating expenses. Various proposals to eradicate the surplus were either impractical or unwise. (One, a highly touted scheme to deposit the federal surplus in banks throughout the country, was "exceedingly objectionable in principle" as it incurred the danger of "fostering an unnatural reliance in private business upon public funds.") There were two elements he refused to compromise on. The first involved federal taxation. In fiscal 1886–87 the government took in $103 million more than it required. Of the total receipts ($336 million), $217,286,893 came from customs taxes, the balance from internal revenue taxes. The Democratic party's high-tariff faction had urged that a tax reduction be achieved in part by cutting down the internal revenue receipts on whiskey and tobacco. Cleveland insisted that the tariff—and only the tariff—must be the source of the entire reduction. The second compromise he refused to consider was to decrease luxury taxes but leave at current levels duties which protected American manufacturers: "The taxation of luxuries presents no features of hardship, but the necessaries of life used and consumed by all the people, the duty upon which adds to the cost of living in every home, should be greatly cheapened."

Cleveland then got to the crux of the problem. Under existing tariff laws ("the vicious, inequitable, and illogical source of unnecessary taxation"), protection had been raised to a preposterous extreme. Having been continued on many articles long past necessity, it constituted the imposition of unjust burdens on the poor. Example: taxes on such "necessaries" as coffee, sugar, and clothing cost the ill-paid laborer and hard-pressed farmer almost as much as these goods cost men of great wealth. We "rejoice in American skill and ingenuity, in American energy and enterprise," Cleveland observed. Yet—and here the tone became mocking—whenever the tariff issue was raised, it suited the purposes of protectionists to call even the most domestic manufacturers "infant industries" still needing "the highest and greatest degree of favor and fostering care that can be wrung from Federal legislation."

Turning next to a theme he said could not be overstated, Cleveland pointed out that of the more than four thousand imports subject to duty, few competed with domestic manufacture; many were "hardly worth attention as subjects of revenue." An abundant reduction could be effected in the aggregate by adding them to the free list. Our "progress towards a wise conclusion" would not be improved by dwelling upon the theories of protectionism and free trade. This savored too much of "bandying epithets." What confronted the nation was a *condition* (emphasis in the original) and not a theory. Relief from this condition might "involve a slight reduction of the advantages which we award our home productions, but the entire withdrawal of such advantages should not be contemplated." The question of free trade was "absolutely irrelevant," while the "persistent claim made in certain quarters that all the efforts to relieve the people from unjust and unnecessary taxation are schemes of the so-called free traders is mischievous and far removed from any consideration for the public good." Cleveland concluded:

> The simple and plain duty which we owe the people is to reduce the taxation to the necessary expenses of an economical operation of the Government and to restore to the business of the country the money which we hold in the Treasury through the perversion of governmental powers. These things can and should be done with safety to all our industries, without danger to the opportunity for remunerative labor which our workingmen need, and with benefit to them and all our people by cheapening their means of subsistence and increasing the measure of their comforts.[101]

Among the country's leading papers and periodicals, great admiration was expressed even by those ever ready to attack Cleveland on issues. The *Philadelphia Press* offered "a thousand thanks to President Cleveland for the bold, manly, and unequivocal avowal of his extreme free trade purposes!" Said the *Boston Journal*: "We do not approve the President's recommendations, but we may frankly say that we like the tone of his message." The *New York Commercial Advertiser* predicted that the "concise, able, and manfully candid message will have a decisive weight in the future of parties and of legislation." *The Nation* pronounced the message "the most courageous document that has been sent from the Executive Mansion since the close of the Civil War." Said the *New York Evening Post*: "This message . . . makes the revenue question the paramount and controlling one in American politics." The protectionist press, on the other hand, was bitter, at times downright insulting. "Free-trade; cant, and humbug" insisted the *Chicago Journal*, while the *Commercial Gazette* decided that Cleveland was little more than an "ignoramus, dolt, simpleton, idiot—[a] firebug in public finance."[102] Cleveland's tariff message was a masterful act of statesmanship, and it drew the public to his side just as what came to be known as the Great Tariff Battle of 1888 was getting under way.

The first shot was fired by Cleveland's 1884 opponent, James Gillespie Blaine. Visiting in Paris at the time, he gave an interview to the *New York Herald* on December 8 that made the front page of just about every major American paper. Its gist: if *he* were President (and the interview suggested he was entering the lists once again) he would maintain the high tariff, repeal the internal revenue tax on tobacco immediately (giving millions of Americans a Christmas present of cheaper cigars), and earmark the whiskey taxes, which he would hold at their present levels, to fortify all major Atlantic seaboard cities. Here Blaine appealed shrewdly to no less than four major interest groups: the high-tariff lobby, lovers of cheap tobacco, the anti-British (primarily Irish) immigrants, and proponents of a strong coastal defense.

The interview was a brilliant one, and Blaine proved anew his great popularity with the powerful high-tariff arm of his party. The minority arm was another matter. The *Chicago Tribune* reflected the consensus of this thinking when it criticized Blaine for cynically offering the hard-pressed western farmers, to whom high tariffs were particularly burdensome, cheaper smokes and "chaws" while refusing to allow much-needed tax reductions on such necessities as imported clothing, lumber, and tableware. At the same time, the paper reminded the Republicans of their 1884 campaign pledge "to correct the inequalities of the tariff and to reduce the surplus" and cautioned that such a pledge could not be breached "without disloyalty to Republicanism." "The monopoly trusts and rings which have combined to capture the Republican party," added the *Tribune*, had "undertaken a bigger contract than they can reasonably hope to carry out." Eastern newspapers amplified the warning: not only was it politically imprudent for the Republicans to maintain an inflexible protectionist posture, it was downright indefensible.

The most eagerly sought reaction to Cleveland's message was Samuel Randall's. When it came, on the heels of the Blaine interview, its tone surprised no one. The House point man for Democratic protectionists had previously made known his belief that the party might effect a compromise on high duties. Saying he would now fight for one, Randall predicted the new Congress would reduce the revenues by at least $60 million—but not as Cleveland proposed. "A large part of the reduction will be in the repeal of internal taxes, which the President does not seem to favor—and a large reduction will also be made in the rate of duty on imports." Federal taxes, he posited, would be cut on tobacco, licenses, and fruit distillates. Other duties would be lowered and the free list enlarged, but this would be done "without the least injury to any of our established and useful industries, and without lowering in the least the remuneration now awarded to labor."[103]

Reductionists dismissed Randall's words as the "predictions" of an irksome minority member in the twilight of his career; one, in the bargain, whose input had not been solicited at the Oak View Conferences (for which he never forgave Cleveland). However, his approach found particular favor with many influential Democratic newspapers in heavily populated, heavily industrialized Pennsylvania, Ohio, and sections of New England. Joining his roll of admirers were newspapers in the South, where, in consequence of the region's having not joined in the Industrial Revolution until after the war and thus having not caught up with the North, protectionism was deemed the only acceptable course. But Cleveland was convinced that tolerating Randallism was insupportable. Endorsed by party leaders, to whom it was crucial that all Democrats unite behind tariff reform, he let it be known that anyone who followed the Pennsylvanian need not expect to receive any patronage or political favor. This led even Randall's closest allies to repudiate him and line up behind the President.

Meanwhile, as the politicians reacted to Cleveland's tariff message, public opinion, like the biblical voice of the turtle, was being heard in the land. The leading eastern newspapers dispatched correspondents to interview businessmen, workingmen, and farmers with the rapidity and avidity that their spiritual heirs of our own time solicit the insight of stock market manipulators, libidinous rock stars, and other such icons. Predictably, manufacturers dependent on homemade materials were apoplectic at the idea of lower duties, while importers favored Cleveland's approach. The latter group, though, were unable to decide upon which goods should come in at a lower rate and which left alone; likewise the laborers and farmers, whose position on the issue depended on how each was affected personally.[104]

Cleveland insisted his tariff message be followed immediately with legislation for new schedules. He settled on Roger Q. Mills, chairman of the Ways and Means Committee, to lead the fight in the House. The committee reported out a tentative bill which eliminated those points too radical even for Cleveland and the Democratic leadership. Rate alterations were moderate, some lower than the average 7 percent reduction; some—chiefly on raw materials—were even lower. Many articles, most of which affected people on the lower socioeconomic stratum—e.g., salt, lumber, copper ore, tin plate, hemp, flax, jute, and, most important of all, raw wool and finished wool goods—were to come in free. Heavy cuts were made on finished iron and steel (though iron ore and pig iron were dealt with cautiously). As a package the bill embraced most of Cleveland's wishes, though it appeared to be extravagantly sectional in approach, with cuts on some articles favoring one area, some favoring another. Cried the critics, this was not bona fide reform; this was reform sullied by self-indulgent local concerns.

Justified or not (and they probably were), their cries were all but ignored when, on April 17, Mills moved that the House go into committee of the whole to deal with the bill. Though no one ever accused Mills of being Daniel Webster redivivus, his arguments, which consumed some two hours, were exceptionally effective. In the post–Civil War era, he pointed out, taxes which adversely affected the rich man's pocketbook were repealed, while those adversely affecting the poor man's net income were retained. While the postwar nation was still saddled by a debt in the range of $2 billion, he then reminded those colleagues whose knowledge of recent history was remiss, Congress "made haste to roll all the burden of taxation off the shoulders of the wealthy and lay them upon the shoulders of the toilers." Still, the fundamental evil of the existing tariff schedule did not lie in unfair taxation, he wanted it made clear, but rather in its devastation of our own export values. More than 75 percent of the nation's exports were agricultural products—mainly cotton, followed by wheat, pork, beef, and dairy products, in particular butter, cheese, and lard. But the high duties we imposed on imports were inhibiting the reception of these goods in foreign markets.

Then, in a scornful passage that brought down the House, Mills denied the protectionists' boast that high tariffs inevitably led to high wages: "They say, as a matter of course, if you increase the value of the domestic product the manufacturer is able to pay higher wages. Unquestionably he is, but does he do it? No. Mr. Jay Gould, with his immense income from his railroad property, is able to pay his boot-black $500 a day, but does he do it. Oh, no, he pays the market price of the street. He gets his boots blacked and pays his nickel like a little man."[105]

The so-called Great Tariff Debate climaxed on May 19 with two days of oratorical fireworks by the best speakers on both sides of the aisle. (The Republican fight was led by Ohio congressman and future President William McKinley.) The Mills bill passed the House by a narrow margin of 162 to 149, the nays of four recalcitrant Democrats being more than offset by the yeas of three Republicans and three Independents. Among those observing the action from the Distinguished Visitors Gallery was the President's Lady, who rushed off to report the outcome to her impatiently waiting husband.

As anticipated, the Republican-controlled Senate blocked the bill. Still, Cleveland had scored a major victory: he had won his party over to supporting low import duties, in the process making the whole tariff question the central issue of the upcoming presidential campaign. Of equal consequence, he had— But here let us consider the reaction of Edwin Godkin, one of the original Mugwumps. The vote on the Mills bill, he wrote, would serve as

> the historical record of the transformation of the Democratic party which President Cleveland has accomplished. There could be no more forcible illustration of the value of civic courage to a nation than has been afforded by him since December last. At that time his tariff-reform message, by its boldness and utter disregard of political expediency, filled his own party with consternation and his opponents with delight. But the step, having once been taken, could not be retraced. . . .

Slowly but surely the Democratic leaders have pulled themselves up to the President's advanced position; and after less than eight months of argument and agitation the vote is taken which shows that the party is practically a unit behind the first leader which it has had for a quarter of a century.[106]

PART V

1888–1889

31

The election was Cleveland's to lose

Cleveland's renomination for the presidency was a foregone conclusion. There were, of course, those disgruntled party factions—the Randallite protectionists and, leading the band, Tammany Hall—that abhorred him, and the many party regulars who thought him too headstrong, too intractable. Still, all, including a reluctant Tammany Hall, had to admit that the Democrats could not recapture the White House without him. Even many mainline Republicans openly conceded that Cleveland was proving to be an exemplary Chief Executive. Earlier in the year at a dinner in his honor, Theodore Roosevelt said, "I come now to Mr. Cleveland's Administration. I give him the credit for all the good he has done." The remark elicited a loud burst of applause. George Curtis, speaking for the Independents, said Cleveland was not only "better than his party," he was "stronger than his party."

His adversaries knew that in Cleveland they had a formidable opponent. In hopes of knocking him out of the race, they made political hay of preposterous, totally groundless rumors then making the rounds to the effect that he habitually beat his wife. It was said that once while in a drunken stupor he physically threw her out of the White House in the middle of the night at the height of a blizzard. He was also accused of being verbally and physically abusive to his mother-in-law.[1]

Cleveland ignored these whoppers, believing that dignifying them with a response would only increase their circulation. They increased anyway. Frances got a letter from a Mrs. Maggie Nicodemus of Worcester, Massachusetts, advising that the city was "in a state of agitation over an item which appeared in one of the daily papers." She asked the First Lady to comment, "as I wish to convince some friends with whom I conversed today, that the whole thing is a falsehood." And just what was the item that had reduced Worcester to a state of agitation? A reputable local Baptist clergyman was spreading tales, gleaned while attending a church convocation in Washington, of all that presidential brutality. Frances wrote in reply, "I can only say in answer to your letter that every statement made by [the clergyman] is basely false, and I pity the man of his calling who has been made the tool to give circulation to such wicked and heartless lies. I can wish the women of our country no greater blessing than that their homes and lives may be as happy, and their husbands may be as kind, attentive, considerate, and affectionate as mine."[2]

Denials notwithstanding, the gossip continued. Republican newspapers disavowed any part in the whole business. "The country knows that the Republican press has not circulated any of these vile stories or discussed the subject," wrote one incensed editor—adding that without exception, the stories were originated by Democrats. Furthermore, "the very worst talk of all originated among Democrats who were active and prominent in the headquarters of the National Democratic Committee of New York." No one seriously believed that the stories originated within the New York Democracy. Many, though, did believe they originated within the precincts of Tammany Hall. Had not the anti-Cleveland sachems whooped it up when "boomlets" were launched for former congressman Randall and Governor Hill by factions anxious to see Cleveland go down as a one-term President?

To suggest Randall as a possibility was simply a feeble swipe at the President over the tariff issue. Hill was another matter. He was determined to replace Cleveland in the White House. Though he did not command the support to achieve that goal at this point in time, he did command enough support to damage Cleveland, having won over many of the old Tilden Democrats, and, as he saw it, reunite their divided party under his aegis. Manning advised it would be suicidal for the New York delegation to go to the 1888 nominating convention split on the Cleveland renomination "and then have him crowded down [their] throat by other delegations." Southern and western states, detesting New York on principle (and Tammany in particular), would support Cleveland, being "only too glad to force us into line."[3] It took a while for Hill and his followers to accept Manning's logic, but accept it they did, albeit with ill grace.

On the Republican side, the frame of mind in which the party planned for their 1888 nominating convention can best be described as pessimistic. Cleveland's strong appeal to the electorate was beyond question, as was the sad fact that the party had no issue upon which to build a viable campaign. Trashing the South would be like flogging a dead horse. So, too, the economy; the country was riding an unexpected crest of prosperity. To touch the only other urgent issues—currency and tariff—would be like touching fire, though they were prepared to do just that, should the Democrats, as now seemed probable, raise them. As the Republican elders saw it, about all they had going for them was that James Gillespie Blaine would once again bear their standard. And the party rank and file did not share the elders' enthusiasm for "the Continental Liar from the State of Maine."

Admittedly, Blaine had the support (and financial backing) of the nation's manufacturers because of his high-tariff stance, and of the Irish voters for reasons already noted. But Republican opposition to Blaine was coalescing in the West around a rump group of pragmatists convinced that their only chance to beat the incumbent lay in a candidate who stood for sound currency (i.e., maintaining the gold standard) and a more flexible approach to the tariff. Despite their efforts, though, party leaders did not consider seriously the idea of removing Blaine from the lists.[4]

Then, in early February, like the proverbial bolt from the blue, Blaine removed himself. Writing from Italy, where he was traveling, to Republican National Committee chairman B. J. Jones, the Plumed Knight insisted his name not be put into nomination, for "considerations entirely personal to myself." Two weeks later, in conversation with an American newsman in Florence, he elaborated. The letter to Jones was "the result of much deliberation and careful thought." He believed he had "no right to be a candidate again"; any man who had been his party's candidate and had been defeated, Blaine insisted, owed it to his party not to be a candidate a second time. Besides, he "could not go through the burden and fatigue of another Presidential canvass—such a one as the canvass of the last campaign."

The statement was an amalgam of truth and half-truth. Blaine had no objection to a loser's seeking another chance, especially if he was the loser. But he was a clinical hypochondriac (a fact not known outside his immediate family circle). While en route to Italy he had caught a chill standing on the rear platform of his train without an overcoat, and on reaching Milan had taken to his bed. According to what his Italian doctor subsequently told the *New York Sun*, the chill had left Blaine in an unfathomable state of depression when he wrote the Jones letter and gave the *World* interview.

The party hierarchy refused to accept Blaine's decision, convinced that he was their only hope for turning out Cleveland and, in the process, recapturing the House of Representatives. They took heart in the letter's ambiguity: he may have declined to run, but he'd said nothing about declining a draft. Again Blaine poured a cold—and this time convincing—douche on their hopes, making his refusal categorical in a letter from Paris to Whitelaw Reid: "Assuming that the Presidential nomination could by any possible chance be offered to me," he wrote coyly, "I could not accept it without leaving . . . the impression that I had not been free from indirection, and therefore I could not accept it at all."[5]

The strongest contender for the nomination now seemed to be Senator John Sherman of Ohio. A brother of popular war hero General William Tecumseh Sherman, and one of the leading political figures of the day, Sherman was a diehard free-silver advocate. Most of the Blaine people detested him, for a variety of reasons: he was their man's chief rival; he was too severe and aloof to arouse the passions of the electorate; and, a major consideration here, he did not come from a critical state. Ohio could be taken for granted. (Seven Presidents, all Republican, came from Ohio: Grant, Hayes, Garfield, Benjamin Harrison, McKinley, Taft, and Harding.) Not so the pivotal states of New York and Indiana. It was from either of the two, party strategists decided, that their candidate must come.

The New Yorker with most delegate appeal was Chauncey Depew. But his lack of appeal to voters was a major problem. Though he was brilliant, engaging, and one of the great orators of the day, Depew's controversial record as a railroad attorney militated against him. The last thing the Republicans needed was to remind the voters of the Little Rock & Fort Smith mess that had so hurt them in 1884, which Depew's association with the New York Central would guarantee.

Turning to Indiana, the party's headhunters found a pair of qualified candidates in Benjamin Harrison and Walter Quintin Gresham. Both had served with distinction in the Civil War; both were prominent lawyers and politicians. Gresham seemed more politically attractive. Postmaster General and then Treasury Secretary under Arthur and now a federal judge, he strongly advocated civil service reform, a moderate reduction in the tariff, and an objective approach to the ongoing economic and social turmoil. But these were the very qualities that made him unacceptable to the party's all-powerful Blaine wing. With Gresham heading the ticket, it was feared, and with good reason, that the nation's protectionist manufacturers would, at the very least, sit out the election, and at the very worst, support Cleveland out of sheer meanness.

That left the genealogically attractive but personally off-putting Benjamin Harrison. Grandson of the ninth President and great-grandson and namesake of a signer of the Constitution, Harrison was said to be so taciturn when introduced to people that it was not generally known English was his first language. Even close friends derided his frigidity. It was claimed that he bestowed a favor in so frigid a fashion he once turned a friend into a foe for life; that his handshake was compared to a wilted petunia; and that when a visitor was refused an audience with him by a secretary who insisted, "I'm sorry, sir, but the President cannot be seen," the visitor exclaimed: "Can't be seen? My God! Has he got as small as *that?*"[6]

A man of abundant intelligence (though one had to probe deeply for evidence), Harrison was an apostle of high tariff. Accordingly, he foresaw no problem with the party platform, in particular the plank which pledged the Republicans to "favor the entire repeal of internal taxes, rather than the surrender of any part of our protective system." Hoping to carry that other critical state, the convention chose as Harrison's running mate Levi Parsons Morton, one of New York's most successful bankers, former congressman, former diplomat, and future governor. (Morton could have had the vice presidential nomination with Garfield in 1880—and thus become President instead of Arthur—but declined because he preferred to remain in the Senate.)

The election was not Harrison's to win but Cleveland's to lose. And Cleveland did precisely that. It must be underscored, however, that the fault was less his than his party's, as suggested by the fact that he won more popular votes than Harrison.

32

A disastrous campaign

Cleveland's renomination at St. Louis was effected despite efforts by the Tammany-led Hill forces to paint him in the eyes of the large Irish constituency throughout the Northeast as a "British tool" in the employ of "Ireland's cruel enemy to aid her work of enslavement." A number of influential newspapers in the major states—primarily New York, the Democrats' must-win state—were subsidized to create a demand for Hill's candidacy. Cleveland could not "quite keep my temper when I learn of the mean and low attempts which are made by underhand means to endanger the results to which I am devoted."[7]

When the New York party met to pick its delegation to the national convention, Cleveland orchestrated from behind the scenes the successful beating-back of the Hill forces. With his people in firm control, the convention adopted a "frank commendation" of the Cleveland administration, "as a guide to those of his friends who should become members of the platform committee." Stressing that "all the pledges and assurances" made at the 1884 national convention "have been fully kept and realized," it added that the "allegiance and adherence" to the principles proclaimed by the state convention for the 1887 Congressional campaign "are hereby again declared." These included "that the people should not be unnecessarily taxed under a pretext of Governmental necessity; that in promotion of the public welfare and in the interest of American labor and the healthful condition of our established industries and enterprises, taxation for the mere purpose of unfairly benefitting the few at the expense of the many, is a perversion of governmental power; and that a large surplus in the National Treasury drawn by vicious taxation from the channels of trade is a dangerous and indefensible abuse."

The "frank commendation" (written by Cleveland) went on to

note the President's "wise guidance and administration of public affairs"; that on his watch "our system of government has been restored to the honest simplicity impressed upon it by its founders"; and that

> integrity and ability have been substituted for artifice and incapacity in public places; the Civil Service has been purified, elevated and improved; economies have been inaugurated, useless offices have been abolished and business methods have been introduced in the management of governmental affairs; millions of acres of the public domain have been wrested from the grasp of foreign and domestic speculators and returned to settlers seeking homes; the waste and corrupt misuse of funds appropriated for the rebuilding of our navy have been exposed and corrected and the scandals arising therefrom no longer offend the moral sense of the people; thousands of names of deserving [Mexican War] veterans have been added to the pension rolls; the rights of every citizen have been maintained at home and abroad; sectional hate has been discouraged and friendly relations among all our people have been promoted.[8]

The proposed platform was accepted unanimously, as was Cleveland's request that the convention send to St. Louis a delegation irrevocably committed to his reelection.

The most remarkable aspect of the St. Louis convention was its choice of a running mate. It was, in a word, calamitous.

Governor Allen Thurman of Ohio was the party's most admired, most beloved elder statesmen; none could match him for ability, integrity, or experience; and he did, after all, come from a populous, needed-to-win state. On that basis alone, his being the unanimous choice was understandable. Not understandable, though, was why the Democrats picked a septuagenarian whose health was a matter of grave concern to his physicians and whose antithetical views on currency and tariff reform were a matter of grave concern to the party's standard-bearer. It's safe to assume that Cleveland's agreeing to Thurman on the ticket was wanting in enthusiasm.

Just as Cleveland's men settled Governor Hill's hash at the New York State nominating convention, so did they settle the hash of those delegates who brought to St. Louis ideas for a campaign platform that did not jibe with the President's own. After the intraparty animosity that typifies any platform debate—in itself an academic exercise, given the speed with which most component planks of any platform are relegated to the figurative woodpile long before the electoral college has met to certify the winner—the delegates reaffirmed the 1884 platform and endorsed Cleveland's great tariff speech of the previous December.

Not because of arrogance but because of political awareness, Cleveland awaited the news of his renomination with a spectacular lack of apprehension. When Lamont sought him out with the telegram of confirmation from St. Louis, he found the President in the White House library examining textbooks for use by Indian children on federal reservations. Cleveland glanced at the telegram and then turned back to the books. A few days later, as was his habit, he shared his feelings in a letter to Wilson Bissell.

He foresaw the coming campaign as a "very quiet" one. He "sometimes" thought that "perhaps more enthusiasm would have been created if somebody else had been nominated" after the "lively scrimmage at Saint Louis." Still, he meant to be "as good a candidate as I can," and after the people had their say on Election Day he'd "be content and doubly so in case of success because my reluctance to again take on the burden has been fully considered, discounted, and dismissed, and because I am sure in being a candidate again I am but answering the demands of public and political duty." The letter concluded with an admixture of uxorial warmth, dismissal of his enemies' calumny, and a willingness to accept that things—especially presidential elections—often do not work out as envisioned: "My wife sits by me and bids me send you her affectionate regards. I tell you, Bissell, I am sure of one thing. I have in her something better than the presidency for life—although the Republican party and papers do say I beat and abuse her. I absolutely long to be able to live with her as other people do with their wives. Well! Perhaps I can after the 4th of March."[9]

Our nation's history has been punctuated by critical issues of a divisive nature that were decided in the polling place but should have been resolved in the Congress. The ferocious give-and-take of a political campaign, where chances for compromise are impeded by the actuality of aroused passions, is hardly the most appropriate forum for dealing with portentous problems, two of which come readily to mind: the slavery question of 1860 and, sixty years later, the question of joining the League of Nations. Instead of subjecting such factious profound issues to formal deliberation in a setting of comparatively calm reflection, we allow them to become caught up in the contentious bitterness of a quadrennial political circus. Whereupon the contesting parties, eager to attack, and simultaneously pushed into extreme positions, tend to repudiate the reasonable attitudes they would doubtless favor in a more placid setting.

Worse yet, the victorious side will all too often convert into national policy, even legislation, the imprudent convictions it embraced in the heat of electoral battle. It can be argued compellingly that under a parliamentary system of government in 1860, with no presidential election constitutionally mandated, the nation might conceivably have resolved the issues of slavery and states' rights by means more civilized than fratricidal bloodletting, and that without the bitter election of 1920 the United States might have, with moderate reservations, joined the League.

So, too, returning to the Cleveland era, might the tariff issue have been equitably settled—and not been allowed to achieve the unacceptably high level of protectionism it did during the Harrison administration—had its fate been reserved exclusively for judgment by the voters' legislative representatives instead of by the voters themselves in 1888. The Republicans must have realized this when they planned to, if at all possible, overlook the issue as they set out to recapture the White House.

It is wrong to assume, as do many historians, that Cleveland's stand on the tariff doomed his second bid for the presidency, and that the Republicans used it as added justification to pass the egregiously protectionist McKinley Act two years later. Since the campaign yielded no national consensus on tariff policy, two realities contradict those historians: Cleveland received a majority of the popular vote, and his loss in the electoral college was owing to a set of factors totally unrelated to the tariff question. First of these was campaign organization; the second, campaign strategy.

With unlimited funds, courtesy of the wealthy manufacturers, and the support of powerful interest groups like the GAR because of Cleveland's stance on the pension issue, the Harrison camp inundated the landscape with a flood of circulars and speeches intended to panic the voter into fearing the horrors of mass unemployment, economic depression, and death by starvation on a scale not experienced by mankind since the Flood, were any downward revision of the excise schedules to be considered. (So much money was raised to ensure Harrison's election—close to $4 million, a phenomenal sum for the times—the 1888 race was known as the "Boodle Campaign.") It was imperative that the Democrats enlighten the voters on what the opposition hoped they did not realize: Cleveland did not object to tariffs—only to tariffs far in excess of the government's needs.

But the Democrats were not inspired by imperatives. Indeed, considering their choice for the two top campaign posts, they may have been inspired by an urge to self-destruct. Named as national chairman was William H. Barnum of Connecticut; named to chair the executive committee was Calvin S. Brice of Ohio. The two shared an interest in tariff reform that was equidistant between tepid and gelid. Barnum, who stood to be affected negatively by the importation of duty-free raw materials (he owned large iron ore tracts in Michigan), made no secret of his protectionist sympathies. He had labored to trash the tariff-reform movement in his state; it was even rumored in the months preceding the St. Louis convention that he secretly advocated denying Cleveland the renomination. As for Brice, also from the world of big business, he was known to be considerably less than rhapsodic about Cleveland's ideas on reform in general and on tariff reform in particular.

Part of the blame for so absurd a choice of managers, particularly of Brice, attaches to Cleveland himself. He acted on the advice of Thurman and Senator Arthur Pue Gorman, who had successfully managed his 1884 campaign (and would stab Cleveland in the back over the tariff in his second presidency). An ally of Brice in a few railroad ventures, Thurman, like Gorman, advocated Brice as a charming moderate who would help invalidate the high-tariff lobby's unfounded charge that the Democrats were prepared to settle for nothing less than an across-the-board free trade policy on all imports. As for Barnum, Cleveland found him quite resistible. But since the party chairmanship was a position from which he could not have been removed without some difficulty, Cleveland chose not to make it an issue. Besides, the all-important New York State campaign was in hands both loyal and capable, including those, in Erie County, of his closest friend and most ardent booster, Wilson Bissell.

Within days of the nomination, many in the Cleveland camp urged that the Democrats forgo the tradition among all parties to delay active campaigning until the shank of the summer. Eugene Chamberlain, Manning's successor at the *Albany Argus*, begged that the party "begin at once to educate the voters," and, toward that end, buy abundant space in the labor press and penny-dreadfuls that were the daily fare of the working class, and circularize the country. Cleveland's advisers urged that he run an aggressive canvass. Cleveland agreed. But the men running his campaign did not, and he refused to interfere with their strategy. Some strategy! Not only did they feel it unnecessary to propagandize tariff reform, they did not feel the need to jump the gun. Instead, they opted to run an old-fashioned campaign and leave it to the Republicans to (they hoped) commit tactical errors, which they might then exploit.

The Republicans were determined there be no tactical errors, like those that helped do Blaine in four years before. This time out, they were paradigms of efficiency and sagacity. They were also paradigms of chicanery and deceit. The national chairman was Matthew S. Quay of Pennsylvania, a pro-big-business graduate of and apologist for that state's Cameron machine, considered the nation's most iniquitous political finishing school. The campaign treasurer was W. W. Dudley, an incompetent Indiana attorney who had elevated bribery to a fine art. Both men were experts at "frying the fat" (the phrase is Quay's): getting the party's fat cats to contribute more than was really needed. Not only individuals but such well-financed groups as the Protective Tariff League (of which Thurman was one of the organizers), which enjoyed the support of the "One Thousand Defenders of American Industries," gave until—

We dare not say "until it hurt." Pain was not a consideration if it meant saving the country from what they perceived was the depravity of low tariffs. What might have been painful, though, was the knowledge of where most of their campaign contributions wound up. Quay's predilection for misplacing finance records rendered moot the questions of just precisely how much fat he and his associates actually fried, how much went into the campaign, and how much went south. In the light of their success on Election Day, it is doubtful that even one of those Thousand Defenders spent so much as five minutes in pursuit of answers.

Before the appearance of the first autumn leaves, warnings reached Cleveland that his campaign was not going too well. As luck would have it, he was at the moment on a collision course with Canada and Great Britain.

33

First confrontation with a foreign power

America's militarists of the period shared with many of her industrialists the belief that it was the nation's inherent right to colonize the continent westward and southward to its geographical limits, and then push ever westward across the waters. Cleveland refused to share this belief. Unlike his predecessors—notably Polk, Grant, and Arthur—to whom this so-called Manifest Destiny was not a doctrine conceived by man but a dictum conceived by God, Cleveland considered it every bit as odious as imperialism and misguided nationalism. Corollary to his repugnance at the idea of the United States as a predatory state was Cleveland's determination that we never get caught up in conflict with any foreign state unless attacked or otherwise provoked. His foreign policy was a cautious one: any excuse that might invoke the threat of foreign adventure must be arrested in its incipient stage.

This is not to suggest Cleveland would back down in the face of peril to America's vested interests or moral authority, whether within the Western Hemisphere, as defined by the Monroe Doctrine, or anyplace else in the world. As will be seen when we come to his second presidency, he held his ground in Venezuela, though it brought the United States and Great Britain closer to war than at any time since 1812. So it was now with Canada, when the nation wound up on a collision course not only with our neighbor to the north but with her mother country across the seas. Cleveland rued the whole business. But the gauntlet was thrown down, and as President he was obliged to pick it up.

New England's fish-packing industry was among the world's most lucrative. Every year some fifteen thousand fishermen set out from

Maine and Massachusetts ports in more than five hundred boats, averaging 80 to 125 tons, to harvest the waters of the North Atlantic. Most were hired hands whose "wages" were a share in the proceeds from half the catch; the other half went to the boat's owners, many of them corporations, who provided all the gear. By the 1871 Treaty of Washington between the United States and Great Britain, which supplanted a treaty dating back to 1818, these fishermen were guaranteed valuable rights while in Canadian waters that covered inshore fishing, bait purchase, and transshipment of cargoes. Two years before Cleveland took office, Congress abrogated the treaty effective July 1, 1885, in part because of long-standing resentment over the exorbitant compensation for those inshore rights, in part to halt the guaranteed free admission of Canadian fish into the American market.

The situation became volatile when Canadian warships began arresting American fishermen and confiscating their boats. Cleveland and Secretary of State Bayard realized that Canada was within her rights, consonant with a meticulous interpretation of the 1818 treaty now governing the fisheries issue in default of the abrogated 1871 agreement. They managed to negotiate a provisional extension of that pact, but for no more than six months. Cleveland's anxiety to resolve the issue was informed by three objectives: to persuade Canada to look more kindly on Americans fishing in their waters; to conclude a treaty that would settle the issue once and for all time; and—should reason and negotiation fail, and retaliation against Canada become the only alternative—to base such retaliation not on a sectional basis but on a national basis, since Cleveland saw the problem as one for all Americans, not exclusively New Englanders. Canada made known she was not averse to negotiating a new treaty, and in the interim was prepared to conform with Cleveland's first objective. Even the British, as an interested third party, adopted a conciliatory approach. It was Cleveland's third objective that created the biggest problem. And the problem was homegrown:

Senate Republicans, led by those from New England, vowed to defeat any agreement that failed to secure tariff protection for American-caught fish. Also, they were adamant that any American retaliation must include the antecedent precondition that it benefit the New England region. While the motive was not stated openly, the Republicans also hoped the fisheries problem would reap the ancillary benefit of energizing traditional Irish-American and Yankee prejudices toward Great Britain, to the administration's political disadvantage. All this in the midst of a presidential election.

As the 1887 fishing season opened, Secretary of State Bayard urged that British Prime Minister Salisbury prevail upon the Canadians to halt the boarding and seizure of our schooners by their navy, as was becoming all too common. At the same time, Bayard posed the threat of "embittered rivalries staining [the U.S.–Canadian] long frontier with the hues of hostility." Salisbury got the Canadians to agree to London's negotiating on her behalf, and at his insistence, Canadian warships halted their anti-American activities pending outcome of negotiations. The 1887 fishing season concluded without major incident.[10]

Having thus bought time and calmed the roiling North Atlantic waters, Cleveland pushed for a new treaty—and came smack up against a stone wall of Republican resistance. The Senate Foreign Relations Committee led the move to block the President's treaty-making powers. Hoar of Massachusetts carried the absurdity a step further by moving that it be "the judgment of the Senate that under present circumstances no negotiation should be undertaken with Great Britain in regards to existing difficulties with her province of Canada which has for its object the reduction, change, or abolition of any of our present duties on imports."[11] Seeing this as a brazen attempt to obstruct his constitutionally defined role as President, Cleveland arranged with Salisbury that a six-man joint commission convene in Washington to draft a new treaty. Under terms of a treaty drafted in mid-February 1888, the contesting nations were granted mutually acceptable advantages.

Meanwhile, Cleveland concerned himself with retaliation for Canada's abusive treatment of the American fishermen. It was not a matter of inflicting retroactive punishment. He felt that legal precedent must be established to deal with such contingencies for the benefit of future Presidents. New Englanders in Congress, supported by their protectionist confreres, demanded as the only acceptable retaliation a total ban on Canadian ships and Canadian-caught fish in American ports. Cleveland reacted to the proposal with uncharacteristic rage. He saw this as a Republican scheme to give New England shipowners a monopoly on the American fish market. From a legal point of view, he insisted, any nonintercourse of a retaliatory nature must be across the board, applicable to railroads as well as ships.

Resorting to sectional measures was as improper as catering to special interest groups on any issue affecting the American people as a single entity. Any retaliation must be implemented "not to protect solely any particular interest, however meritorious or valuable, but to maintain the national honor and thus protect all our people."[12]

The Democratic-controlled House voted Cleveland the retaliatory legislation he wanted, giving him discretionary powers to close American ports to Canadian vessels, suspend the transporting of Canadian merchandise in bond across American territory, and halt the movement of all Canadian railroads in the United States. Similar legislation was introduced in the Senate, authorizing the President to suspend passage of all "engines, goods, or vessels" to or from Canada. Despite Republican misgivings, the House-Senate compromise produced a watered-down plan which Cleveland signed with reluctance—and with no intention of ever putting it into effect so long as current conditions prevailed.

The treaty went to the Senate for ratification just as the 1888 presidential campaign was getting under way. Expectations for fair treatment by the Republican majority were unrealistic. (One senator told the British envoy, "We cannot allow the Democrats to take credit for settling so important a dispute.") The Foreign Relations Committee voted out an adverse report, and the Republican members outdid each other in attacking Canada and England. Blaine, home from Europe to assist in the campaign, grabbed headlines with his considered opinion that the treaty was "a complete abandonment of the whole fishing interests of the United States."

A Democratic attempt to postpone the vote until after the campaign failed. On August 21, just when Cleveland was being advised that his chances for reelection were becoming cause for apprehension, the treaty was rejected by 27 yeas to 30 nays. In practical terms, this was not a disaster. Great Britain, hoping, like Cleveland, that a mutually acceptable treaty would eventually be worked out, was anxious to defuse the issue. Besides, a *modus vivendi* adjunctive to the treaty, giving the United States most of its advantages, remained in effect.

Cleveland counterattacked two days later—and pulled off perhaps the greatest coup of his first presidency:

In a message to Congress reviving his demand for sweeping retaliation, he called for "immediate legislative action conferring upon the

Executive the power to suspend by proclamation the operation of all laws and regulations permitting the transit of goods, wares, and merchandise in bond across or over the territory of the United States to or from Canada."[13]

It was a brilliant stroke and a staggering one, and it left the Republican leaders, in the words of one observer, "completely dazed." Ostensibly aimed at Canada, it was really aimed at the Senate, which had talked with great bravado of a mock retaliation that would actually enrich New England fishing interests. Now the President, matching their bluster and then some, was saying, in effect, "You want retaliation, I'll give you retaliation!" As Cleveland had counted on, reaction in the states contiguous to Canada was compounded in equal doses of horror, chagrin, rage—and fear. Maine coastal merchants were horrified at the probable loss of their highly lucrative winter transshipment trade with Canada. New England railways foresaw disaster if they were unable to haul Canadian freight. Upper New York ports foresaw destruction of their enormous import trade in Canadian goods. In Detroit, the merchants predicted total ruin. From all round the forty-eight states, investors in border and Canadian railroads added their voices to the din of protest.

The House quickly enacted appropriate legislation, and what Cleveland counted on now came to pass. In the Senate the once blustering, now deflated Republicans, realizing that the nation's economy, New England's in particular, was perilously close to being devastated, had no alternative but to table their own retaliatory proposals without further public comment. (What they chose to say in private, though, can well be imagined.) Their *bête noire* in the White House had finessed them, and humiliatingly. By adhering to a typically evenhanded and forthright path, he not only resolved a potentially explosive situation, he scored a great tactical triumph by insisting that any retaliation must be adopted on a national scale and not to benefit special interest groups. In doing so, he forced the Republicans to come to terms with the consequences of having acted irresponsibly in rejecting the treaty.

Lost in all the tumult was the fact that by his handling of the Canadian fisheries issue, as by his handling of the Tenure of Office Act, Cleveland reaffirmed the prerogatives of his office and restored the constitutionally mandated system of checks and balances between the executive, the judicial, and the legislative branches that, in the post-

Jacksonian period, had come perilously close to being thrown out of whack. Like the Tenure of Office Act, the fisheries issue was a constitutional crisis Cleveland resolved brilliantly, to the everlasting gratitude of all those who followed in his presidential footsteps.

An unexpected dividend for Cleveland was the approbation—easily translated into votes—he won from the Irish-Americans. They saw in his demand for retaliatory legislation a kick in the arse of the bloody Brits. Even the predominantly Irish Tammany sachems now saw him in a less hostile light, as did the nation's previously adversarial Irish-Catholic press, to judge by their adulatory editorials. Hundreds of wires poured in from prominent citizens of Gaelic lineage, Republican as well as Democratic, all variations on the theme "God bless you for your devotion to old Erin."

Unfortunately, most of this goodwill was soon lost (though illicitly filched probably better states the case) when the Republicans chose to interpret Cleveland's message to Congress as an electioneering ploy to win over the Irish vote in collaboration with, of all things, an unintentional assist from the Salisbury government. Enter now one George Osgoodby of Pomona, California, who set out to "prove it" and in the process perpetrated the single dirtiest trick in any presidential campaign prior to the Nixon-Agnew canvass of 1972.

Posing as a naturalized American of English birth named Murchison, Osgoodby wrote a letter to the British envoy to the United States, Sir Lionel Sackville-West, "confidentially" seeking his advice on how to vote in the coming election:

> I am unable to understand for whom I should cast my ballot, when, but one month ago, I was sure Mr. Cleveland was the man. If Cleveland was pursuing a new policy toward Canada, temporarily only and for the sake of obtaining popularity and the continuation of his office for four years more, but intends to cease his policy when his reelection in November is secured, and again favor England's interests, then I should have no further doubt, but go forward and vote for him. I know of no one better able to direct me, sir, and most respectfully ask your advice in the matter. . . . As you know whether Mr. Cleveland's policy is temporary only and whether he will, as soon as he secures another four years in the presidency, suspend it for one of friendship and free trade, I apply to you privately and confi-

dentially for information which shall in turn be treated as entirely secret.

Whether Sackville-West fell into the trap or leaped in is unascertainable and unimportant. He told Osgoodby the Democrats knew what any party in an American election knew: favoring Her Majesty's Government was bound to cost them votes. Still, he felt Cleveland to be the best choice, for after the election he would be "reasonable." The Democratic party was "still desirous of maintaining friendly relations with Great Britain, and still desirous of settling all questions with Canada which have been, unfortunately, reopened since the rejection by the Republican majority in the Senate and by the President's message to which you allude." Therefore, he declared, all allowances must be made "for the political situation as regards the presidential election thus created." Though "impossible to predict the course" Cleveland might pursue "in the matter of retaliation should he be elected," there was "every reason to believe [he would] manifest a spirit of conciliation" in dealing with the fisheries question.

Osgoodby turned the letter (dated September 13 and marked "Private") over to the Republican campaign, which shrewdly decided to sit on it until October 24—two weeks before Election Day. When it was made public, Republican newspapers joined with all the nation's Catholic and pro-Irish journals in an orgy of Cleveland-bashing. They seized upon it as a basis for appealing to the Irish vote, arguing that Cleveland put British interests above those of his own country's loyal Hibernian sons. Democratic and pro-Cleveland Republican newspapers demanded Sackville-West's recall.[14] When Salisbury refused to recall Sackville-West, an outraged Cleveland revoked his credentials and ordered him to leave the country.

Such action was justified. More than accusing the President of having resorted to rank hypocrisy in an attempt to delude the voters, Sackville-West had interfered in American domestic affairs by advising "Murchison" (and thus all other English-born American citizens) whom to vote for. Not even the Republicans could deny Cleveland was right to boot him out; any diplomat who committed such an impropriety deserved no better.

Cleveland was unable to undue the letter's damage. Most of the Irish-Americans who had decided to support him now rushed to rejoin the Harrison fold, encouraged by compelling orators like Sherman and Blaine. Sherman brought Anglophobic audiences to their feet with his charge that the administration had *always* been pro-British. Blaine convinced them that Cleveland's entire policy—especially tariff reduction—was patently pro-British and inimical to the best interests of all Irish-Americans.[15]

34

"The other party had the most votes"

Among the many causes for Cleveland's defeat besides dismal campaign organization, the Republicans' superiority at propagandizing their cause, and the Sackville-West incident, one deserves our attention here, if only to remind us how politically foolish, and potentially self-destructive, Cleveland could be when, as was his custom, he refused to use his office to influence his party.

David Hill, who succeeded Cleveland as New York governor in 1884 and was elected in his own right two years later, had given the state's large bloc of independent voters ample reason to distrust as well as detest him. Due to the shifty, unscrupulous Hill's involvement in a number of scandals, they were outraged he would dare seek reelection. They felt he was not only unfit to govern New York State, he was unfit to govern any of its wards. Hill and his Tammany pals felt otherwise. And they gave not a damn who knew it.

With the hour approaching for the Democrats to make their 1888 gubernatorial nomination, intraparty opposition took on foreboding undertones. As a last resort, a delegation of anti-Tammany party leaders, fearing Hill's success could cost Cleveland the critical support he needed in New York, rushed to the White House. Knowing that he made it a cardinal rule never to interfere in local politics, but hoping it was a rule he might bend under the circumstances, they pleaded that he openly dictate the party's choice for governor. "To these overtures," wrote one New York paper after verifying what had been a highly confidential discussion, "Mr. Cleveland replied that under no circumstances would he interfere with the party management of the State. True to his principles, as in all things, the President kept his hands off."[16]

Could Cleveland have stopped Hill if he had put his hands on? That's arguable. But he would have at least distanced himself from Hill, and that would have redounded to his advantage not only in pivotal New York but throughout the Northeast, where mainline Democratic voters particularly detested Hill and Tammany. When the state party convened on September 22 in Buffalo, though mention of his name set off a deafening cacophony of boos and hisses while mention of Cleveland's provoked prolonged applause, Hill won the nomination.

To give the whole sordid business a gloss of party harmony, Hill magnanimously endorsed the national campaign platform, subordinating his own views on all issues to Cleveland's. Also, while stumping the state in his own behalf he loyally stumped for the President as well. That was the good news. The bad news was that Hill was a slick willie, with a curious aptitude for attracting two voters for every one he repulsed. This worked to Cleveland's disadvantage: those voters Hill turned on would not necessarily support the President, while the ones Hill turned off were sure to vote for Harrison out of malice.

As the Cleveland campaign stumbled along, Hill engendered opposition that was to jeopardize not only his own chances but the President's. He now came under pressure to endorse Hill and thus court the backing of his powerful Tammany machine. He adamantly refused. Brice, pleading for such an endorsement, vowed that the New York State Brewers Association would deliver 25,000 votes to him if he did so. Cleveland held his ground. "But Governor Hill is as much a Democratic nominee as you are yourself!" argued Brice. To which a now irate Cleveland shouted: "I don't care a damn if he is—each tub must stand on its own bottom!"[17]

While it can never be known precisely how much Hill harmed Cleveland in the campaign, the damage had to have been considerable, as it cost him the votes of three powerful blocs: the independents, many of whom returned to the Republican fold; the Prohibitionists, to whom Hill's ties with the liquor interests was a sin of the first magnitude; and, perhaps most significant of all, the political machine men, a crafty crew who played a rather Machiavellian game: should Cleveland carry New York while the Republican candidate defeated Hill, Hill's career would, of course, go down the political drain; should Cleveland lose and Hill win, they would be credited with having backed a rising star instead of a setting one.

As the campaign passed the halfway mark, Cleveland was getting warnings from close friends that he was losing the battle. Wilson Bissell complained of Brice's appalling leadership and lack of commitment, adding that while all their men "pretended" to be working hard "there seemed a sort of amateurish air, and I gained the impression that they have washed fully as much as they will hang out." Typical was the comment by a prominent congressman who was "disgusted and made heartily sick by the apathy and indolence manifest" at Democratic headquarters.[18]

Cleveland moved to shore up the campaign through letters of advice and admonition to Brice and Barnum. More would have been accomplished had he made a few trenchant speeches—if not on the stump, then at least through press interviews. But Cleveland allowed as how he was preoccupied with Congress (which remained in session until October 20 over tariff legislation) and insisted, moreover, that his cabinet remain off the campaign trail and hard by their desks. No one was buying this, as it was a universally accepted article of Clevelandian faith that making speeches was beneath the dignity of his high office. The people simply must take him on his record.

Compounding the problem, the party lacked speakers capable of attracting nationwide attention, as the Republicans had in Blaine, Sherman, and, of course, Harrison, who delivered some eighty highly effective speeches from the front porch of his Indianapolis home. He may have been frigid and unapproachable, but as a stemwinder he had few peers. Cleveland, who knew his limitations on the stump, took the rather ingenuous attitude that any campaign should be "one of information and organization." Every citizen "should be regarded as a thoughtful, responsible voter" and furnished with the means for "examining the issues involved in the pending canvass for himself."[19] The task of furnishing those means he would leave to others, in particular his running mate, Allen Thurman.

Thurman's proficiency on the stump was both pathetic and embarrassing. His worst performance came in early September before twenty thousand New York loyalists. Aged, debilitated, and not too happy to be the star attraction at Madison Square Garden ("God knows that I would rather be at home with my dear old wife than in any office in the world"), Thurman began: "I have heard it said since I was nominated for the Vice Presidency of the United States that Allen G. Thurman is an old, weak, broken-down man. I don't know what to reply to this. It seems to me, though, that I am not quite as well as I ought to be, and I am in no condition to speak to an immense audience like this tonight. I want to speak. But I am too unwell—" At that point, his face having suddenly become ashen, Thurman turned away from the horrified audience and had to be practically carried to his chair. (It was later given out that he was suffering from acute gastroenteritis.)

Thurman's sad showing made no more difference to Cleveland's chances than any other factor. If the proof the Democrats came up with concerning Republican bribes by men close to Harrison in Indiana and New York did not help them, and it did not, nothing could have helped. It was in such a frame of mind that Cleveland awaited the returns in the White House library with his wife and a few close friends. Earlier in the day, perhaps yelling ouch! before being pinched, he'd written to an old friend that he'd welcome a return to public life: "You know how I feel in the matter and how great will be the *Personal* [emphasis in the original] compensations of defeat. I am very sure that any desire I may have for success rests upon the conviction that the triumph of my party at this time means the good and the prosperity of the country. You see, I am in a good mood to receive the returns whatever they may be."[20]

At midnight Navy Secretary Whitney came in from the mansion's telegraph room to announce, "Well, it's all up." In New York City, Republicans (and a few Tammany Democrats) paraded up and down the streets singing gleefully,

Down in the cornfield,
Hear the mournful sound;
All the Democrats are weeping—
Grover's in the cold, cold ground.

The final tally showed Cleveland winning the popular vote by a plurality of 100,476, according to one computation, and 115,534 according to another,[21] while in the electoral college Harrison, having captured the key states of Indiana and New York, which Cleveland had won by narrow margins in 1884, got 233 votes to his 168. This was not the first time in our history that a slight shift in the distribution of the popular plurality would alter the outcome. Nor would it be the last. Asked by reporters to what he ascribed his defeat, Cleveland flashed a smile and said: "It was mainly because the other party had the most votes."[22]

That seemed as good a reason as any.

A few days later he said in a press interview, "It is better to be defeated battling for an honest principle than to win by a cowardly subterfuge. Some of my friends say we ought to have gone before the country on the clean administration we have given. I differ with them. We were defeated, it is true, but the principles of tariff reform will surely win in the end."[23]

From the vantage point of history, it is impossible to quarrel with the spin put on Cleveland's defeat by his greatest biographer, Allan Nevins. If in addition to presenting his tariff message a year or even six months earlier—so that by election time its sound logic would have informed public opinion—Cleveland and his aides had organized a more energetic campaign and chosen a superior manager to the apathetic Brice, the result might have turned out differently. True, the country might have been spared such dreadful endowments by the Harrison administration as the McKinley Tariff, the Dependent Pensions Act, and the Sherman Silver-Purchase Act. Still, Cleveland's 1888 defeat was truly a blessing in disguise:

> A portentous storm was steadily brewing in the [American] West. The clouds were piling higher and higher, but the tempest was not to burst until the years 1893–96. When it did burst a statesman was needed in the White House—not a Harrison, not a McKinley, but a leader of unyielding courage and rocklike principle. The country could well do without Cleveland in the next four years in order to have his strength and bravery available in the fearful crisis that was coming.[24]

35

Trouble in Samoa

Cleveland could look back on a job well done. He had succeeded where many Presidents have failed in successfully realizing the goals he established when taking office. But he refused to dwell upon this in his fourth State of the Union Message, a month after his defeat. He believed there was nothing to be gained in stating the obvious; rather, he believed it was more important to address the appalling consequences of the class division in force a century after the nation's birth.

Our cities, he told Congress, had become "abiding-places of wealth and luxury"; our industries were yielding "fortunes never dreamed of" by the Founding Fathers; our businessmen were "madly striving in the race for riches, and immense aggregations of capital outrun the imagination in the magnitude of their undertakings." While we could take justifiable pride in our nation's growth, closer scrutiny revealed "the wealth and luxury of our cities mingled with poverty and wretchedness and unremunerative toil." The fortunes amassed by our business leaders were "no longer the sole reward of sturdy industry and enlightened foresight," but resulted "from the discriminating favor of the government . . . largely built upon undue exactions from the masses" of the American people. The chasm between management and labor was "constantly widening"; ours was evolving into a two-class society—"the very rich and powerful [and] the toiling poor." While the rich could boast of the great achievements of aggregate capital, the average citizen was "struggling far in the rear [or being] trampled to death beneath an iron heel." The long-suffering farmers were in revolt against "the impoverishment of rural sections." Large corporations, which should have been "carefully restrained creatures of the law and the servants of the people," were rapidly "becoming the people's masters."

Warming to a theme that had not yet been resolved but would be facing him on his return to the presidency four years later, Cleveland noted that "instead of limiting the tribute drawn from our citizens to the necessities of its economical administration, the government persists in exacting, from the substance of the people, millions which, unapplied and useless, lie dormant in its treasury. This flagrant injustice, and this breach of faith and obligation, add to extortion the danger attending the diversion of the currency of the country from the legitimate channels of business." Under the same tariff laws by which these results were effected, he insisted, the government allowed many millions more to be added to the cost of living, "and to be taken from our consumers, which unreasonably swell the profits of a small, but

Rev. Richard Falley Cleveland, President Cleveland's father. *Photo courtesy of the New Jersey Division of Parks and Forestry, State Park Service, Grover Cleveland State Historic Site.*

Ann Neal Cleveland, President Cleveland's mother. *Photo courtesy of the New Jersey Division of Parks and Forestry, State Park Service, Grover Cleveland State Historic Site.*

Grover Cleveland's birthplace in Caldwell, New Jersey as it appeared circa 1902–08. *Photo courtesy of the New Jersey Division of Parks and Forestry, State Park Service, Grover Cleveland State Historic Site. Photo restoration by Al J. Fraza.*

The Cleveland house in Fayetteville, New York, where young Grover Cleveland spent the happiest ten years of his childhood. *Photo courtesy of the New Jersey Division of Parks and Forestry, State Park Service, Grover Cleveland State Historic Site.*

Fayetteville Academy, down the road from the Cleveland parsonage in that town, which Grover and his brothers attended as children. *Photo courtesy of the New Jersey Division of Parks and Forestry, State Park Service, Grover Cleveland State Historic Site.*

Institute for the Blind, 34th Street, New York City where Cleveland worked as an assistant teacher, 1853–54, after the death of his father precluded his plans to attend college.

Grover Cleveland as mayor of Buffalo in 1882; within two years he would serve as governor of New York State and be elected President of the United States. *Photo courtesy of the Buffalo and Erie Historical Society.*

Cleveland (l.) and seven of his eight siblings, unidentified, taken around 1872, when he was just beginning his political career in Buffalo, New York. *Photo courtesy of the New Jersey Division of Parks and Forestry, State Park Service, Grover Cleveland State Historic Site. Photo restoration by Al J. Fraza.*

Wilson S. "Shan" Bissell, Cleveland's closest friend and favorite epistolary correspondent; he served as Post-master General in the second Cleveland presidency. *Photo courtesy of the New Jersey Division of Parks and Forestry, State Park Service, Grover Cleveland State Historic Site.*

Samuel Tiden, leader of the New York Democratic Party, who "okayed" Cleveland's selection as the party's presidential nominee in 1884. It was Tilden who lost the White House to Rutherford B. Hayes in an election that remains one of the nation's most controversial. *Photo courtesy of the New Jersey Division of Parks and Forestry, State Park Service, Grover Cleveland State Historic Site.*

Daniel Manning, shown here around 1885, the Democratic politician who was instrumental in Cleveland's becoming President, and who served him capably as Secretary of the Treasury and closest advisor. *Photo courtesy of the New Jersey Division of Parks and Forestry, State Park Service, Grover Cleveland State Historic Site. Photo restoration by Al J. Fraza.*

James Gillespie Blaine, "the Constitutional Liar from the State of Maine," shown around the time he contested Cleveland in one of the dirtiest presidential campaigns in American history. *Photo restoration by Al J. Fraza.*

This anti-Blaine cartoon, which appeared in Puck on June 4, 1884, during his run for the presidency against Cleveland, came to be known as "the Tattooed Man." *Photo restoration by Al J. Fraza.*

This cartoon from The Judge (September 27, 1884) labeled "Grover the Good" reflected the popular doggerel of the day in which the Republicans, alluding to his alleged illegitimate son, cried, "Ma, Ma, Where's my Pa?" to which the Democrats replied after Cleveland's election to the presidency, "He's gone to the White House! Ha! Ha! Ha!" *Photo restoration by Al J. Fraza.*

Rose Elizabeth Cleveland, the President's intellectual spinster sister who was his official hostess prior to his marriage. *Photo courtesy of the New Jersey Division of Parks and Forestry, State Park Service, Grover Cleveland State Historic Site.*

Titled "At His Post," this cartoon by the pro-Cleveland Thomas Nast (*Harper's Weekly,* July 3, 1886) depicts the President guarding the U.S. Treasury from the outrageous fraudulent pension claims by Civil War veterans and their survivors. *Photo courtesy of the New Jersey Division of Parks and Forestry, State Park Service, Grover Cleveland State Historic Site. Photo restoration by Al J. Fraza.*

ABOVE: Frances Folsom Cleveland shown here a year before she and the President left the White House following his second administration and retired to Princeton, New Jersey. *Photo courtesy of the New Jersey Division of Parks and Forestry, State Park Service, Grover Cleveland State Historic Site. Photo restoration by Al J. Fraza.*

RIGHT: Frances Folsom, Cleveland's ward who became his bride, shown here in her wedding gown. *Photo courtesy of the New Jersey Division of Parks and Forestry, State Park Service, Grover Cleveland State Historic Site. Photo restoration by Al J. Fraza.*

"The President's Wedding" from a *Harper's Weekly* illustration. It was the first presidential wedding ever to take place at the White House. *Photo courtesy of the New Jersey Division of Parks and Forestry, State Park Service, Grover Cleveland State Historic Site. Photo restoration by Al J. Fraza.*

Souvenir card of Cleveland and the First Lady, whom he insisted be known as "the President's Wife," and the White House, known at the time as "the President's Mansion." *Photo restoration by Al J. Fraza.*

Adlai E. Stevenson, Cleveland's second Vice President. The two were not close, mainly because of the their divergent views on the bimetallism issue. *Photo courtesy of the New Jersey Division of Parks and Forestry, State Park Service, Grover Cleveland State Historic Site.*

Cleveland's second cabinet, 1896. Prominent among them were Daniel Lamont (far left), who started as Cleveland's private secretary and was one of his closest advisors; and, next to him, the acerbic Richard Olney, who served Cleveland as both Attorney General and the Secretary of State. Not shown is Vice President Adlai Stevenson, from whom Cleveland kept a respectable distance, as the two were poles apart on the issue of bimetallism. *Photo courtesy of the New Jersey Division of Parks and Forestry, State Park Service, Grover Cleveland State Historic Site. Photo restoration by Al J. Fraza.*

Frances Folsom Cleveland and the Cleveland's first child, Ruth, in 1892; Ruth, for whom the candy bar "Baby Ruth" is named, was the only one of the five Cleveland children not to survive childhood. *Photo courtesy of the New Jersey Division of Parks and Forestry, State Park Service, Grover Cleveland State Historic Site. Photo restoration by Al J. Fraza.*

Esther Cleveland, the Cleveland's second child, and the first to be born to a President in the White House (September 9, 1893). *Photo courtesy of the New Jersey Division of Parks and Forestry, State Park Service, Grover Cleveland State Historic Site. Photo restoration by Al J. Fraza.*

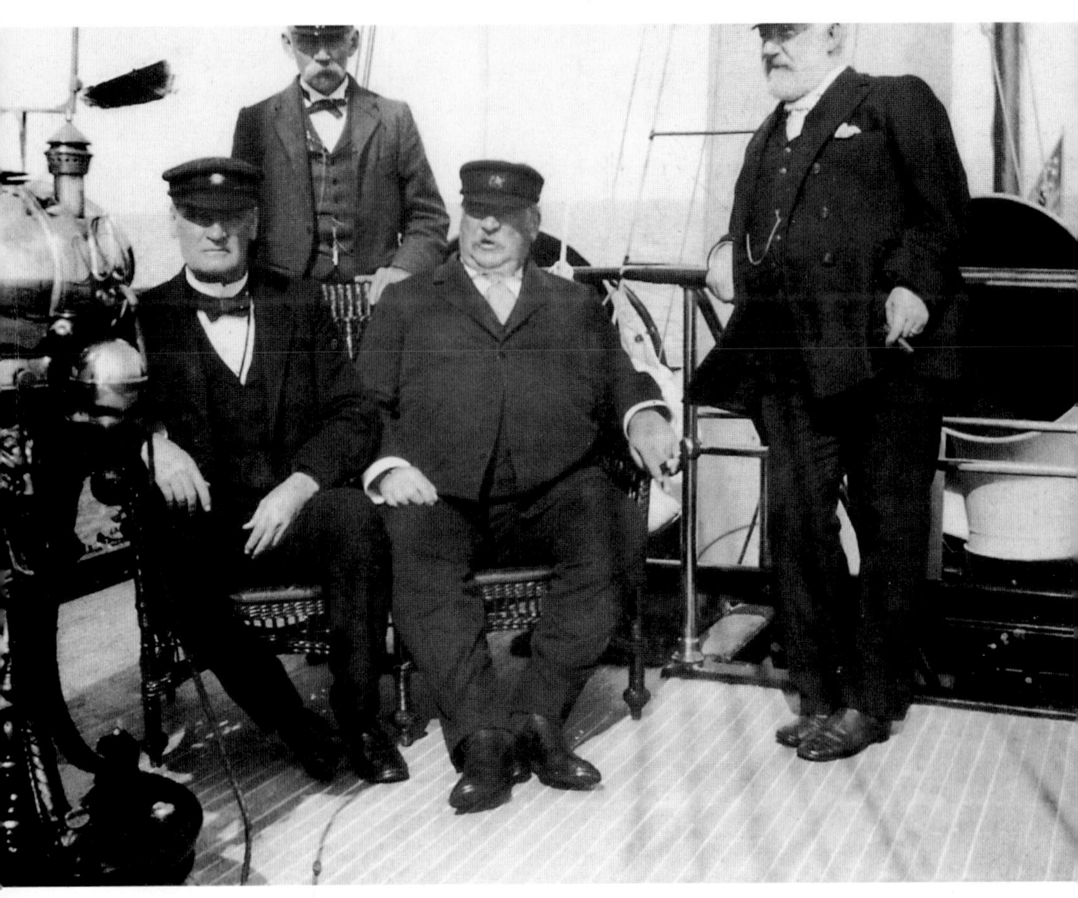

Taken toward the close of his second presidency, this rare photo shows Cleveland aboard the yacht *Oneida* owned by his close friend industrialist Elias C. Benedict (standing holding the cigar); it was on this yacht that Cleveland's secret cancer surgery was performed out on Long Island Sound. Also shown are two of Cleveland's closest political allies, William L. Wilson (standing rear) and J.G. Carlisle (seated left). *Photo courtesy of the New Jersey Division of Parks and Forestry, State Park Service, Grover Cleveland State Historic Site. Photo restoration by Al J. Fraza.*

Dr. Joseph D. Bryant, Cleveland's personal physician and duck-hunting companion, shown here in 1914; it was Bryant who organized the team that operated on Cleveland for cancer of the mouth—and who was probably most responsible for keeping it a secret for almost a quarter of a century. *Photo courtesy of the New Jersey Division of Parks and Forestry, State Park Service, Grover Cleveland State Historic Site. Photo restoration by Al J. Fraza.*

William Jennings Bryan, the pro-silver orator who became Cleveland's bitterest political foe; shown here in 1896, by which time he was succeeding in wresting control of the Democratic Party from Cleveland. *Photo restoration by Al J. Fraza.*

Cleveland's successor, William McKinley, being administered the oath of office on March 4, 1897 by Chief Justice Melville W. Fuller, named to the Supreme Court by Cleveland. *Photo courtesy of the New Jersey Division of Parks and Forestry, State Park Service, Grover Cleveland State Historic Site. Photo restoration by Al J. Fraza.*

Westland, the Cleveland's home at Princeton, where the President died on June 24, 1908. *Photo courtesy of the New Jersey Division of Parks and Forestry, State Park Service, Grover Cleveland State Historic Site. Photo restoration by Al J. Fraza.*

Rare photo of Cleveland and President Theodore Roosevelt, with whom he had an on-again, off-again political relationship dating back to Cleveland's governorship of New York, when Roosevelt was a leader in the state legislature. Shown here at the 1903 World's Exposition when Cleveland was in retirement at Princeton. *Photo courtesy of the New Jersey Division of Parks and Forestry, State Park Service, Grover Cleveland State Historic Site. Photo restoration by Al J. Fraza.*

Cleveland at his favorite sport, duck hunting, with his favorite gun, "Old Death and Destruction," on South Island, South Carolina, a year before his death. *Photo restoration by Al J. Fraza.*

The last known photo of Grover Cleveland, taken for the *New York Herald* on March 5, 1908, three months before his death. *Photo courtesy of the New Jersey Division of Parks and Forestry, State Park Service, Grover Cleveland State Historic Site. Photo restoration by Al J. Fraza.*

powerful minority." The people still must, of course, be taxed for the support of their government through the tariff. But to the extent that the majority were "inordinately burdened beyond any useful purpose and for the benefit of a favored few," the government, "under pretext of an exercise of its taxing power, enters gratuitously into partnership with these favorites, to their advantage, and to the injury of a vast majority of our people." Surely this, Cleveland maintained, was "not equality before the law."

No other President before (or since) had spoken so radically on the disparity between the haves and the have-nots. But then perhaps no other President was as prepared, *in extremis,* to see the imposition of stringent curbs upon wealth. "Communism is a hateful thing and a menace to peace and organized government," said Cleveland in peroration; "but the communism of combined wealth and capital, the outgrowth of overweening cupidity and selfishness, which insidiously undermines the justice and integrity of free institutions, is not less dangerous than the communism of oppressed poverty and toil, which, exasperated by injustice and discontent, attacks with wild disorder the citadel of rule."[25]

Cleveland's last months in office were clouded by an international crisis involving the South Pacific island kingdom of Samoa that started long before he entered the White House and was now threatening to degenerate into a shooting war with Germany.

Compared to his contemporaneous world leaders, Cleveland's achievements in foreign affairs were, overall, insignificant. Still, what he achieved by taking a resolute stand against imperialism—by the British in Venezuela and the Americans in Hawaii (both to be dealt with in Part VII, covering Cleveland's second presidency), and now by the Germans in Samoa—was considerable. In an age when powerful nations found it morally acceptable to disregard the autonomy of, if not ride roughshod over, powerless ones, Grover Cleveland pursued a policy both admirable and innovative: "I do not believe that nations any more than individuals can safely violate the rules of honesty and fair dealing."[26] He may at times have failed, as he did in Hawaii. Still, he initiated the American ideal of giving rather than grabbing in our conduct with weaker countries. "We have a moral right to expect that no change of native rule shall extinguish the independence of the islands." So wrote Secretary of State Bayard in 1888, at the height of the Samoan dispute. As he would with Hawaii, with Samoa Cleveland stood tall in his defense of a helpless sovereign people.

American presence in the Samoan Islands dates to 1872, when one of the paramount chiefs granted the United States permanent rights to the harbor of Pago Pago on the island of Tutuila. American merchant seamen were by then visiting regularly in search of trade and temporary safe haven. Two years later the Samoans adopted their first constitution, encouraged by A. B. Steinberger, one of those Caucasian vagabonds who materialized on the beaches of Polynesia from time to time during the nineteenth century in hopes of transforming an edenic island into a private sandbox. Modeled on the American Constitution, the Samoan one differed radically in the area of representative government: the premier was all but supreme and omnipotent. Steinberger, an American citizen, was named premier. (The fact that he did not figure in the momentous events of fourteen years later suggests that by then he had either passed on to greener island pastures or had simply passed on.)

When it became evident that American missionaries were pushing the Samoans toward annexation by the United States, German and English nationals who also regularly visited the islands demanded, and received, concessions. This led first to friction among the Westerners, all of whom shared in the rather lucrative Samoan trade, then to a surfeit of agreements, not only with the local government but among each other. All the treaties shared two features: they were secret, and they disregarded the well-being of the Samoans. Rivalries among the three powers soon escalated to the degree that open conflict international in scope lay in the island nation's foreseeable future.

In the summer of 1878, the Grant administration, hoping to finesse the competition, concluded an advantageous treaty with the Samoans that was even more advantageous to the United States. It opened the main port of Pago Pago to American commerce duty-free, and granted extraterritoriality, which guaranteed the right of resident and visiting Americans to be judged "according to the laws of their [own] country." The march toward conflict over Samoa between the Western powers was reduced to an amble when the United States, Britain, and Germany agreed to respect native sovereignty under the traditional Polynesian system of government: an assembly of chiefs, led by a head chief—in this case, Malietoa—in whom was invested the title and dignity "King of Samoa."

Five years later, in keeping with Bismarck's strategy to match the British presence in the Pacific, Germany secretly imposed a new treaty that threatened Samoan independence. Malietoa accepted it only under threat from the German consul general, Herr von Brandeis, backed up by a small flotilla anchored offshore. When Malietoa wrote in protest to the German emperor (the letter was ignored), the Germans covertly inspired a Samoan faction led by a perfidious chief, Tamasese, to rebel against the popular king. In January 1885, charging the natives with failing to honor the treaty obligations, Brandeis seized Apia and the Mulinuu peninsula, seat of the Samoan government. There matters stood when Cleveland took office six weeks later.

Malietoa, citing the 1878 treaty, appealed to the American consul general for "the protection of the United States, until existing difficulties are settled." Without consulting his superiors at the State Department, Consul General Greenebaum granted the protection, over the vigorous objections of his German and British colleagues. Cleveland realized that simply vetting Greenebaum's action would not resolve what problems might arise from a German takeover. He prevailed upon Great Britain and Germany to join with the United States in a conference intended to select "a competent and acceptable Chief" to rule the islands under a joint protectorate of the three powers, conditional to a mutual pledge that none of the signatories annex the islands nor establish a separate protectorate. Cleveland's idea of tripartite control was not to make permanent any form of foreign control over Samoa, which would have contravened America's traditional policy of avoiding foreign alliances, but to "insure stable government in which native interests shall be under autonomous native control."

Germany had an idea of her own. Retaining her hold on Apia, she openly recommended all details of the Samoan issue be left to the tripartite conference to settle—while secretly encouraging Samoan nationals, whose loyalty Bismarck's representative purchased, to agitate for the kingdom's absorption as a German colony.

Between July 1886 and February 1887, agents sent out to Samoa by the three governments gathered information in preparation for the upcoming conference. The German agent reported that the Samoans favored a German protectorate. This was denied by the British agent.

The American agent documented Germany's long history of intrigue in the area and confirmed that the British agent supported Cleveland's plan to establish an autonomous native government. Meanwhile, Cleveland learned that the Bismarck government was secretly distributing arms and instigating a pro-German uprising to be led by their puppet "King," Tamasese.

At Cleveland's insistence, Secretary of State Bayard advised Bismarck's envoy to Washington, Von Alvensleben, that the United States was aware of German carryings-on at Samoa and expressed the hope that "the just and benevolent plan of cooperation by the three powers will not be allowed to be impeded by any such inconsistent and maleficent action as has been so reported." He added a veiled threat: the United States would "promptly check such action." Von Alvensleben denied his government's knowledge of any pro-German native uprising. Had he been asked, he would also have denied what soon became obvious: Germany's agreement to the conference was but an exercise at masking her determination to have Samoa, one way or the other.

The conference got under way at Washington in June 1887, and it blew up in Cleveland's face. The British abruptly reversed themselves by supporting Germany's "suggestion" that the proposed tripartite protectorate be but a prelude, not to eventual self-determination by the Samoans but to eventual annexation "by an interested party." It was assumed that the "interested party" would not be Great Britain, which already enjoyed an extensive presence in the Pacific, but Germany, which was emerging as a colonizing power in the area. The British flip-flop was baffling—until what Britain knew in confidence soon became common knowledge:

Bismarck had placed "an uncommonly strong fleet" in South Pacific waters which, ship for ship and man for man, surpassed the English forces in the region. The British, who preferred to assimilate the islands of Polynesia through diplomacy rather than through battle, knew of and dreaded Bismarck's colonial policy in the region, which was to subdue a defenseless people by sending in a heavily armed and manned flotilla when a schooner or two whose crew carried truncheons might easily do the trick. Having come to terms with the Iron Chancellor's ambitions in the Western Pacific, Britain concluded a formal agreement with Germany calling for both parties to respect each other's sphere of influence in the area and "not to make any acquisition of territory, nor to establish protectorates, nor to oppose the operations of the other, in the sphere of action respectively assigned to it."[27]

The tripartite conference had opened with the understanding that, pending its deliberations, Samoa should remain *in status quo.* There it remained when the conference ended a few weeks later without having agreed on much more than the size of the table and the fine Washington weather. Cleveland realized there was little he could do but wait for the second German boot to fall. It fell a few weeks later, when Alvensleben told Bayard his government found it "necessary" to declare war on King Malietoa. Bismarck was confident, and rightly, that England would tacitly accept this and the United States would do nothing.[28]

Germany overthrew Malietoa, forcing him into exile, and enthroned its puppet, Tamasese. Early in October, on advice from Greenebaum that resident Americans were in danger, President Cleveland ordered the U.S.S. *Adams* to Apia from its station in the Hawaiian Islands. Its arrival in Samoan waters was greeted by four German warships anchored in the harbor. Playing Richelieu to King Tamasese's Louis XIII was Bismarck's envoy, Herr Brandeis (self-styled "Chief Leader of the Government"). The general discontent he provoked among the natives led Maraafa, the chief of Atua, to launch a revolt against the puppet government. When he proved victorious three weeks later, the White House immediately recognized him as "King of Samoa by the will of the people."

Cleveland knew Germany would settle for nothing less than annexation. Determined that this not happen, he ordered a flotilla of warships to Apia. Next, he sent a message to Congress outlining his efforts to protect American interests in the Pacific. A few weeks later, he prepared a second message in which he denounced Bismarck in terms that few Presidents had ever used against the head of a foreign state. But on due consideration, he decided not to send it. This was just as well. Had he done so, it would almost surely have led to a break in relations between the United States and Germany. And since German-Americans were a large and powerful voting block, such a break was the last thing the administration needed in light of the approaching election.

President-elect Harrison suspected that war with Germany had moved from the back burner of possibility to the front burner of probability. His first act on taking office was to dispatch three warships to Apia, where Germany already had four and England one. But the Samoan situation was resolved, if not by divine intervention then certainly by a force of nature that could be defined as such. On March 16, as the Germans and Americans were awaiting instructions from their respective home governments on whether to start a shooting war, Apia was suddenly struck by a powerful hurricane that sank both flotillas (but spared the lone British ship). "Thus, with the duration of a single day," said Robert Louis Stevenson, who witnessed the event, "the sword arm of each of the two angry powers was broken; their formidable ships reduced to junk; their disciplined hundreds to a horde of castaways."[29]

A pleasant distraction for Cleveland from the irritation over Bismarck's South Seas adventure was a chance to make the most important appointment of his presidency: the eighth Chief Justice of the United States. Morrison R. Waite, named to the court by Grant, had died the previous March after a fourteen-year tenure.

Unlike some other Presidents, Cleveland refused to use the Court as a dumping ground for political cronies. ("I won't appoint a man to be Chief Justice of the United States who might be picked up in the street some morning!")[30] His choice was fifty-five-year-old Melville W. Fuller. The two had met only a year before, when Fuller impressed Cleveland with his legal mind, extensive scholarship, blameless character, and cultural refinement.

Born in Maine, long a resident of Chicago, where he built an outstanding reputation before the Illinois bar, Fuller's lack of general public recognition led the *Philadelphia Press* to call him the most obscure man ever appointed to head the Court. The worst that could be said about him was that he wrote an elegy on the death of Grant that gave new meaning to the term "wretched verse." Senate Republicans vowed to defeat the nomination, not because of the man's judicial talents but because a Democratic President had made it.

Fuller won confirmation, and went on to justify his selection. A strict constructionist on the powers of the government, he resisted all attempts to regulate corporations severely or impair property rights. Though not a confirmed reactionary, he opposed constitutional innovation. All this, plus the high esteem and personal affection in which Fuller was held by colleagues, was a matter of personal satisfaction to Cleveland. Fuller's appointment to the high court was a laudable one—which is more than can be said for some made by a number of successive Presidents down to our own time who have sent to the Court men so ill suited for the position that the very act of nominating them would seem to constitute criminal intent.

36

"We are coming back just four years from today"

Cleveland eagerly anticipated his retirement. As he wrote to Wilson Bissell, "You cannot imagine the relief which has come to me with the termination of my official term. There is a good deal yet which seems to result from the presidency and the kindness of people in a social way which keeps me in remembrance of Washington life, but I feel that I am fast taking the place which I desire to reach—the place of a respectable private citizen." (Cleveland often claimed that he always felt like a "prisoner" in the White House—though it must be admitted that the claim was made after his second presidency.) He did not, though, want his efforts over the past four years to be forgotten. From the moment he lost the election he set about rallying his loyalists. "Temporary defeat brings no discouragement," he wrote to the Massachusetts Tariff Reform Association; it only

> proves the stubbornness of the forces of combined selfishness, and discloses how the people have been led astray and how great is the necessity of redoubled efforts . . . In the track of reform are often found the dead hopes of pioneers and the despair of those who fall in the march. But there will be neither despair nor dead hopes in the path of tariff reform, nor shall its pioneers fail to reach the heights. Holding fast to their faith and rejecting every alluring overture and every deceptive compromise which would betray their sacred trust, they themselves shall regain and restore the patrimony of their countrymen, freed from the trespass of grasping encroachment.[31]

To other organizations he wrote in like vein, stressing the need to systematically educate the people on the tariff issue. Jurist William Butler Hornblower has left an account of his call to pay his respects to the defeated President.

> I was asked into his private reception room, and found him sitting at his desk alone. After a few words of greeting he spoke of his tariff message, which seemed to be on his mind. He said: "My friends all advised me not to send it in. They told me that it would hurt the party; that without it, I was sure to be re-elected, but if I sent in that message to Congress, it would in all probabilities defeat me; that I could wait till after election and then raise the tariff issue. I felt, however, that this would not be fair to the country; the situation as it existed was to my mind intolerable and immediate action was necessary. Besides, I did not wish to be re-elected without having the people understand just where I stood on the tariff question and then spring the question on them after my re-election."
>
> He paused a moment and then added, as if speaking to himself:
>
> "Perhaps I made a mistake from the party standpoint; but damn it, it was right," and he brought his fist down on his desk. "I have at least that satisfaction."
>
> "Yes," I said, "Mr. President, it was right, and I want to say to you, that not only was it right, but that the young men of the country are with you and four years from now, we mean to put you back in the White House."[32]

Facing the Clevelands was the task of disposing of the myriad personal gifts received from around the country. Those of intrinsic value were returned. What remained was an awesome and diverse collection. Included were baby pictures by the thousands of both the Clevelands' namesakes, countless babies' first teeth and first shoes, and innumerable "Grover" and "Frances" dolls of every shape and size, all sent because it was known that Cleveland loved children (though he and Frances had yet to begin a family). There were many gallons of patent medicines and various lotions, good luck charms (loads of rabbit feet), beds and bedding, table covers and napery. For Grover the smoker and sportsman, there were boxes of cigars, dozens of fishing rods and a profusion of gear (sinkers, hooks, flies, reels, creels), and a small arsenal of guns. From those to whom Grover and Frances were

America's sweethearts came a plethora of execrable holograph manuscripts, including one, reflecting the author's ignorance of or disregard for historical plausibility, which hailed "the Caesar of all the world" and "his fair, modern Helen." From all points of the compass came such exotica as "a piece of gold dug up in Michigan" (along with a request that the President wire an offer for the land from which it came); a rusty horseshoe marked "please accept" and a silver-plated shoe said to be from the hoof of the legendary racehorse Nancy Hanks; a tankard of "mad dog medicine" ("a remedy for internal fever, it is Plesen to Drink no bad tast"); "a Panel painted in soil subject being roses" (with the suggestion "You might feel like sending me $100 and we will be quits"); a suit of robes ("such as are worn by the High Priests of the Mormon Church"); a bust of President Garfield sculpted from soap; a well-filled flask from which Daniel Webster once swilled.

At Oak View, the benefactions were of a more animate nature. Except for the "two baby foxes," which were simply given their freedom by opening the back gate, most of the donated livestock had already been disposed of, along with those purchased by the Clevelands. (A pair of white rats managed to beget three generations before their banishment en masse when a descendant bit Frances's finger, and an Angora kitten was deprived of all nine of its lives at one clip after taking an ill-advised dive over a banister.) One admirer sent a fine Irish setter, but Cleveland sent it back with a note that, as President, he had little time for hunting, and to keep him "would not be fair to the dog." From a sporting acquaintance came a flock of quail, which Cleveland intended to keep for the rest of their natural lives as a pleasurable recollection of the many hours of bird-hunting that complemented his happy childhood. He built a pen large enough so that the quail could exercise their wings, lest they lose the ability to aviate. Unfortunately, the mesh of the wire selected for the pen was also large. As the birds were released into their new habitat they escaped into their natural milieu, much to the carpenter's horror—and the President's amusement. (Oak View itself was sold, at a $100,000 profit. The land is today Washington's exclusive Cleveland Park residential area.)

The last few weeks were devoted to a final round of official entertaining, among the events a formal reception honoring the Supreme Court and a dinner party for the Harrison family. The night before the Clevelands left the White House, crowds surged back and forth before the mansion singing "Grover's in the cold, cold ground." Both Clevelands accepted it with good humor, especially Grover, who in addition to anticipating the freedom that awaited him, refused to consider his loss a defeat. "It is not proper to speak of it either as my victory or my defeat," he told a news reporter. "It was a contest between two great parties battling for the supremacy of certain well-defined principles. One party has won and the other has lost—that is all there is to it."[33]

Whether Frances shared her husband's interpretation of the presidency as a form of modified penal servitude is open to speculation. Her attitude may be divined from an incident that occurred on Inauguration Day after the President had gone off to accompany his successor to the Capitol for the formal transfer of power, and she was bidding goodbye to the servants. "Now, Jerry," she told Jerry Smith, the head butler, "I want you to take good care of all the furniture and ornaments in the house, for I want to find everything just as it is now when we come back again."

"Come back again?" asked Smith, wondering if the First Lady had either forgotten this was her last day in residence or had taken leave of her senses.

"Yes. We are coming back just four years from today."[34]

PART VI

1889—1893

37
In retirement

The fifty-two-year-old Cleveland was now faced with having to decide where to make his home. With the Republicans back in power, Washington held no attraction for him; and he would not return to Buffalo ("the place I hate above all others"). After deliberating a number of lucrative offers, he accepted an invitation to join the prestigious New York City law firm of Bangs, Stetson, Tracy, and MacVeigh, headed by Francis Lynde Stetson, a close friend and adviser. (Stetson, one of the nation's leading corporation lawyers, was financier J. Pierpont Morgan's attorney; Tracy was Morgan's brother-in-law.)

The Clevelands took a suite at the fashionable Victoria Hotel until they could find a house to their liking. To Vilas he wrote of being "pelted by real estate men" and of his and Frances's being swamped by "a surfeit" of social attention since leaving Washington. The letter's true interest lies in how Cleveland, with characteristic humor, touched upon one aspect of the American presidency that is debated to this day: "And still the question, 'What shall be done with our ex-Presidents?' is not laid at rest; I sometimes think [Henry] Watterson's solution of it, 'Take them out and shoot them,' is worthy of attention."[1]

That September, following his annual fishing trip in the Adirondacks, Cleveland rented a house at 816 Madison Avenue near Sixty-eighth Street, over which the faithful Sinclair presided as butler-valet. Pride of place among its appointments went to a striking life-size bust of Frances on a black pedestal. The two led a subdued social life, seeing only close friends and avoiding formal dinners out of regard for Cleveland's abhorrence of postprandial speeches (his own or anyone else's). Political and business associates were discouraged from calling, but were always welcome in his office. Close friends who were always welcome in his home included utilities tycoon Elias C. Benedict; Cleveland's Treasury Secretary, Charles Fairchild; journalist Richard Watson Gilder; famed comic actor Joseph Jefferson; lawyer and diplomat Oscar Straus; and Brooklyn mayor Alfred C. Chapin.

Cleveland's position with Bangs, Stetson was "of counsel." He was not a partner and did not share in the firm's profits, but, like all the partners, he contributed a tenth of his legal fees to office expenses. This entitled him to one of the best suite of offices and use of the law library and clerical and support staff. As in Buffalo, he was often asked to referee a complicated case in which he was not involved; thus was validated his reputation as a man who could bring to a dispute not only impartiality but, in addition, the perspicacity and masterful comprehension of the law the cases demanded. The firm had taken Cleveland on because he was an excellent attorney, not because he was an ex-President.

He did his work entirely in the office—Cleveland did not believe in bringing his work home—and, a habit from his Buffalo days, wrote his own briefs and correspondence in longhand. Too, he did not call on the clerks for service, preferring to do his own legal research. He was fondly remembered in later years by all those junior to him as an exceptionally considerate man who never raised his voice or talked down to them. Of the partners, he was closest to Stetson; the two would spend long hours discussing politics. We may assume that during these discussions Stetson encouraged his friend not to dismiss out of hand the idea of another run for the White House.

As his own boss, Cleveland was free to take on as many or as few cases as he pleased. Though frequently called into consultation with the partners (on occasion he'd write a brief for them), he seldom appeared in court. No longer was he willing to sit up all night memorizing a next day's summation. He wanted to be free to enjoy his home, his marriage, his friends, and the pursuit of a leisure he had not known since childhood. He especially enjoyed walking to his office, which was downtown in the Wall Street area, all or part of the way from home, weather permitting (in inclement weather he rode the public horse tram); it was the only physical exercise the very non-physical Cleveland indulged in.

Cleveland arranged his work so that he and Frances were free to be away from the city until mid-September at the earliest. In their first post–White House summer they rented a cottage near the Richard Watson Gilders on Cape Cod's Buzzards Bay, an inlet of the Atlantic. For the following summer they rented a larger house, and then bought Gray Gables, a two-story clapboard structure overlooking the bay from Mountain Point on acreage that was almost primeval. Virgin woods surrounded the multiangled house on three sides; the fourth side gave onto the bay's placid waters, where Cleveland loved to fish from his own catboat, often in the company of Jefferson and his son Charles, to whom he took an avuncular affection. Adding to Gray Gables' charm was the lack of a railroad station, which rendered the house approachable only from the sea or by a six-mile carriage drive. Other friends besides the Jeffersons and the Benedicts who summered in the area included railway magnate John M. Forbes (one of the original Mugwumps), book publisher William W. Appleton, and Boston attorney Richard Olney (he would hold two major posts in the second Cleveland cabinet). Often, friends of long standing like Bissell and Lamont were urged to come with their wives for an extended visit. Before going to the Cape for the summer or returning to New York for the winter—sometimes both in the same season—the Clevelands would stop at the Saranac Inn in the Adirondacks for a few weeks of quiet fishing, often joined by a friend or two, often just by themselves. Cleveland brought along his favorite rifle, which he named Death and Destruction, if he felt like a little hunting. After some time, fishing became his exclusive recreation of choice, and Death and Destruction was retired to the attic.

At Buzzards Bay, Cleveland cultivated the locals, especially the fishermen, when he found they were prepared to treat him as just another summer resident and not as a world figure. The gentlest side of his nature was reserved for the neighborhood children; he was often spotted repairing their toys, or whittling a weather vane or a reel for one of them. Long after passing into their own adulthood these youngsters liked to recall how the ex-President endeared himself by a willingness to enter into their world without patronizing them or talking beyond their comprehension as they discussed anything from local gossip to life's vagaries to current events of world significance. Cleveland himself would recall these summers as among the happiest days of his life.

It was expected that as an ex-president, Cleveland would travel wide and far. But the idea of travel for recreation or educational purposes had no appeal. (In later years, he admitted having wished to meet Bismarck and Salisbury; "he admired them for the same rugged individualism he admired in himself.")[2] The farthest he ranged during this period was to Boston, Philadelphia, Ohio, Rhode Island, and Michigan, and then only when invited to address select audiences. Otherwise, his appearances were limited to the New York area, and were for the most part nonpolitical. One such journey was to Buffalo, where Cleveland was invited to address both the Buffalo Democratic Club and the German Young Men's Association, the latter then celebrating its golden anniversary. After renewing old friendships and acquaintances and being wined and dined by the city fathers, and seeing his speeches described in the press as "powerful," and being heard "with breathless attention," Cleveland felt he could once again think less unkindly of the city where he began his political career.[3]

38

"I should like to know what pledge I have broken"

The political resurrection of Grover Cleveland was initiated at the first general assembly of the Democratic Society of Pennsylvania, where chairman Chauncey Black acclaimed him as a "champion of the masses" and "challenger of the classes . . . cut down by venal treachery . . . and overwhelmed by the tide of monopoly's corruption." Black then brought the assemblage to its feet with the ringing words "We are for tariff reform. From the high ground to which our great captain led us last year, we will not retreat one inch!"[4]

Cleveland was loath to play any political role throughout his first year of retirement—even that of nominal party leader or elder statesman. He limited his speaking to public issues, feeling that it ill befitted an ex-President to speak with the authority derived from that office on topics of public concern.[5] Addressing the New York Circulating Library, he insisted there be "no mistake about one thing: duty and inclination dictate that I should, as much as possible, assume a modest position, free from any imputation of arrogating to myself special influence or control. There is a great deal in this which might be amplified, but which I hope will occur to you without amplification."[6]

This may come off as the characteristic gibberish of some street-corner pseudo-evangelical charlatan. But deliberately abstruse Clevelandian comments such as these often proved, on closer scrutiny, to be more than merely a five-finger exercise in grandiloquence.

The demand among Cleveland Democrats that he consider a third run for the presidency was predicated on four beliefs: having won a plurality in the popular vote in '88, he deserved another chance; the party was in danger of being taken over by its basest elements; the Harrison administration was rapidly evolving into a disaster that must not be permitted to recur; and Grover Cleveland was the only Democrat who stood any chance of recapturing the White House. They vowed to keep Cleveland before the public, with a view to his renomination in 1892. "I am in a miserable condition," he wrote a friend, "a private citizen without political ambition, trying to do private work and yet pulled and hauled and importuned daily and hourly to do things in a public and semi-public way which are hard and distasteful to me. . . . To refuse, as I am obliged to, the many requests presented to me is . . . wearing and as perplexing."[7] He may not have been especially keen about seeking another presidency; whether he was especially keen about refusing another nomination was something else. According to Gilder, he was beginning to think more and more about public issues—and about his recent position at the epicenter of those issues.

Never one to sell the American people short, Grover Cleveland had faith in the public to do the right thing; and he never tired of reminding friends and colleagues that whenever he had taken a direction he believed was the only correct one, even though it might ravage his popularity, he was pleasantly surprised by the public approval his action evoked. Occasionally, he would voice indignation over having been misrepresented—often by his Mugwump allies. ("They say I have gone back on every civil service pledge. I should like to know what pledge I have broken!") While he thought the reformers to be at times hypercritical, he never lost faith in the collective intelligence of the electorate.

According to Gilder, Cleveland always insisted "that if right political policies were simply and clearly put before the American people, they would generally make a wise and honest decision. He was sometimes discouraged; but I do not think he was ever fundamentally shaken in his belief." Reviewing his first term. Cleveland offered neither excuses nor apologies. "No man can lay down the trust which he has held in behalf of a generous and confiding people, and feel that at all times he has met in the best possible way the requirements of his trust; but he is not derelict in duty, if he has conscientiously devoted his efforts and his judgments to the people's service." Cleveland insisted he had discharged the responsibilities of his office faithfully, no matter how disagreeable they were deemed by many. He had "neither faltered before duty, quailed before threats, nor fallen captive to the enervating whisper—the politician's Lorelei—'This will be popular.' "[8]

By the end of the year—we are still in 1889—with the hopes of his loyalists for a political comeback quickly assuming a dynamic of its own, Cleveland began to move slowly but inexorably away from his fixed position. On December 12, he addressed the subject of ballot reform before the Merchants' Association of Boston. Though it's extremely unlikely he intended it as such, this speech, which won him the admiration of even such staunch Republicans as industrialist Andrew Carnegie, was the opening gun in the campaign for Cleveland's third nomination. Adjuring one and all to practice political honesty in the purest sense of the term, he concluded with the conviction that

> good men have no cause for discouragement. Though there are dangers which threaten our welfare and safety, the virtue and patriotism of the American people are not lost. . . . Thus will they discharge the sacred trust committed to their keeping; thus will they still proudly present to the world proof of the value of free institutions; thus will they demonstrate the strength and perpetuity of a government by the people; thus will they establish American patriotism throughout the length and breadth of our land; and thus will they preserve for them-

> selves and for posterity their God-given inheritance of freedom and justice and peace and happiness.[9]

Later that week, at a reception given by the American Copyright League for some 250 of the nation's major literary figures, though Cleveland was not present the mere mention of his name "was greeted with such prolonged and vigorous cheering that it seemed almost to put a slight by contrast on the guest and on the orators of the day; it was tribute, in fact, such as no other American could count on from such an audience."[10]

Still, Cleveland had his doubts. A few weeks later, George Parker raised the idea of a renomination. "Why should I have any desire or purpose of returning to the presidency?" Cleveland asked.

> It involves a responsibility almost beyond human strength for a man who brings conscience to the discharge of his duties. Besides, I feel somehow that I made a creditable showing during my first term, all things considered, and I might lose whatever of character and reputation are already gained in it. I do not want the office, and, above all, I do not feel that I can take the risk involved in a second term after the intervention of one by another man and an opposing party. It would be necessary for me to start new again, and I do not feel equal to it.[11]

One must assess those doubts judiciously. Despite his negative opinion of ex-Presidents who speak "with the authority derived from that office on topics of public concern," Cleveland now showed he was prepared to do just that. What provoked him to speak out was Harrison's sorry record to date, which he attributed in large part to the several disparate predatory interest groups who had seized control of the Republican party and were now proving too powerful for its leader. These included the GAR, in a successful quest of even more outrageous pension benefits; the manufacturers, to whom keeping import duties excessively high was a sacred cause; the silver interests, intent upon disposing of the fruits of their mines, even if it meant debasing the nation's currency; the investment interests that would benefit most by such overseas ventures as the impending illegal theft of Hawaiian sovereignty; and the many members of the so-called Billion-Dollar Congress who believed the most effective way to reduce the Treasury surplus was to pork-barrel it away on superfluous or redundant projects.

Cleveland's opinions about Harrison were mixed. He deplored his attitude on the tariff and silver questions and could not forgive his having allowed the Treasury surplus, a public legacy, to be squandered by extravagant, let alone unnecessary, appropriations. But he praised highly Harrison's judicial appointments, believing (as do historians) that no President excelled him in naming to the federal judiciary the best men available. ("I cannot see how he does it; I thought I realized the importance of the federal courts, resisting mere party pressure and giving to my appointments the most zealous care, but I must confess that Harrison has beaten me.")[12]

When the McKinley Tariff Act became law a month before the 1890 elections, Cleveland was swamped with appeals to urge that voters return a Democratic Congress. He was also urged to support the reformers in their fight to dislodge the unscrupulous Tammany-run government of New York mayor Hugh J. Grant and have done with Grand Sachem Richard Croker. But Cleveland was reluctant to rush in where he believed ex-Presidents should fear to tread—especially in New York State. Still, to judge by his response to a plea from Dan Lamont that he at least meet informally with a group of prominent Tammany men hoping to explore some avenue of accommodation, he seemed willing—if not quite ready—to compromise that reluctance.

The inclination was "growing on me, daily, to permit things other than politics to claim the greatest share of my attention," he wrote Lamont from Saranac Lake, where he and Frances were spending a few days before returning to New York for the winter. If he had his way, "and regarded personal considerations exclusively," he would put a stop "to the mention of my name in connection with any political office." Along with his "personal repugnance to the atmosphere of politics in their present phase," he was "nearly convinced" that his renomination for the presidency would result in party defeat. He saw "no use in mincing matters." Governor Hill and his Tammany confederates "would never permit me to carry the State of New York." The letter concluded in rather ambiguous words that have to be read at least twice, if one is to extract their full flavor:

> But with all this, I am far from believing that I have a right to set up my own judgment and wishes against those of personal and

> political friends, and if an interview such as you suggest would in their opinion be useful to our cause I ought to be willing to consider the subject.[13]

Later that week, Cleveland gave an interview to the *Albany Argus* in which he was found to be still very much in the vanguard of the struggle for tariff reform, ballot reform, civil service reform, and all other reforms meant to alleviate "the positive distress daily threatening our people's homes under the operation of a new and iniquitous tariff law" in addition to other "reckless enactments which stifle the results of the people's suffrage." The *Argus*'s conclusion that the Democrats "knew no discouragement in 1888 [and] will not waver nor falter in 1890," in tandem with Cleveland's failure to challenge this conclusion, was enough to convince supporters that he would not turn them down if asked to head the 1892 ticket.[14]

If Cleveland can be equated with a man waiting for an epiphany to set him on the path he wished to take—and he can—such an epiphany came in the guise of the 1890 Congressional elections. Popular denunciation of the McKinley Tariff gave Democrats overwhelming control of the House. (Not a total surprise, since the party in the White House has always invariably taken a beating in off-year, i.e., Congressional, elections.) Pleased as Cleveland was by the election of 235 Democrats and the retention of but eighty-six seats by the opposition, what pleased him most was the significant discontent the tariff engendered throughout the land, giving new meaning to the term "excessive protectionism."

Traveling to Columbus, Ohio, in November 1890 to address a birthday banquet for his 1888 running mate, Allan Thurman, Cleveland denounced the act—and its author—in one of his most belligerent (and populist) speeches. Contemptuously dismissing one Ohio legislator's well-publicized words about "the demand for cheaper coats" and "a cheaper man or woman under the coats" as insulting to America's multitudinous working class, Cleveland found "no fault with the accumulation of wealth" and was "glad to see energy and enterprise receive their fair reward." But, he argued, when "men in high places of trust, charged with the responsibility of making and executing our laws, not only condemn but flippantly deride cheapness and economy within the homes of our people, and when the expenditures of the government are reckless and wasteful, we may be sure that something is wrong with us, and that a condition exists which calls for a vigorous and resentful defense of Americanism, by every man worthy to be called an American citizen."[15]

Just after the turn of the year, before the annual Jackson Day Dinner of the Philadelphia Young Men's Democratic Association, Cleveland gave perhaps the greatest speech of his entire public career. Titled "The Principles of True Democracy," it raised the possibility of his renomination to inevitability in the thinking of his partisans. He began, in one magnificent sentence, with a definition of true democracy that is as relevant today as it was on the day it was delivered. True democracy implies

> equal and exact justice to all men, peace, commerce, and honest friendship with all nations—entangling alliance with none; the support of the State governments in all their rights; the preservation of the general government in its whole constitutional vigor; a jealous care of the right of election by the people; absolute acquiescence in the decisions of the majority; the supremacy of the civil over the military authority; economy in the public expenses; the honest payment of our debts and sacred preservation of the public faith; the encouragement of agriculture, and commerce as its handmaid, and freedom of religion, freedom of the press, and freedom of the present.

These, he argued from the historical perspective, had generally been complied with by the Democratic party and disregarded by the Republicans, which party he described as now listening "for the footsteps of that death which destroys parties false to their trust." Then, in what amounted to establishing the grounds for the coming presidential campaign—and here he was speaking not as his party's potential candidate but as its conscience—he defined the objectives of a truly patriotic presidency, its political stripe notwithstanding, in words that resonate to this day:

> It is right that every man should enjoy the result of his labor to the fullest extent consistent with his membership in civilized community. It is right that our government should be but the instrument of the people's will, and that its cost should be lim-

> ited within the lines of strict economy. It is right that the influence of the government should be known in every humble home as the guardian of frugal comfort and content, and a defense against unjust exactions, and the unearned tribute persistently coveted by the selfish and designing. It is right that efficiency and honesty in public service should not be sacrificed to partisan greed; and it is right that the suffrage of our people should be pure and free.

"We should remember," he concluded, proposing the party of Jackson as the only one dedicated to fulfilling these objectives,

> that the way of right and justice should be followed as a matter of duty and regardless of immediate success. Above all things let us not for a moment forget that grave responsibilities await the party which the people trust; and let us look for guidance to the principles of true Democracy, which are enduring because they are right, and invincible because they are just.[16]

39

The Silver Letter

In November 1889, delegates representing thirty states pledged to bimetallism—the use of gold and silver interchangeably as coin of the realm—met at St. Louis to demand that Congress allow unlimited minting of silver coinage as legal tender for all debts. When Congress, now embracing six new states in the Northwest, all of them silverite (Montana, Idaho, Washington, the Dakotas, and Wyoming), met in December, it passed, after much heated discussion between the two chambers, the Sherman Silver Purchase Act. Designed to supplant the 1878 Bland-Allison Act, this one went further. It authorized the government to purchase almost twice as much silver (4.5 million ounces a month), thereby adding substantially to the amount already in circulation.

Cleveland found particularly alarming the support given the bill in the South, the traditional Democratic stronghold. His alarm reached cosmic proportions when Democratic conventions in twenty-one states soon went on record as supporting unlimited silver coinage. As the Harrison presidency passed its midway point and one Democratic leader after another declared for this position, rumors began to fly that the ex-President himself was ready to support such a "soft-money" policy. The rumors were believed to be the work of eastern Republicans who, motivated in part by fears about Harrison's chances for reelection, hoped to embarrass Cleveland, to them the only man capable of replacing their man in the White House. Their reasoning: Cleveland's silence on a supposed "conversion" to free silver would give credence to the rumors. If he spoke out against bimetallism he would divide the Democrats and, his enemies prayed, ruin his chances for the nomination.[17] Thus was the stage set for one of the most dauntless acts of Grover Cleveland's public career.

In January 1891, the Senate, with the support of all but one Democrat, passed a free coinage bill. The now incensed Cleveland was warned by his advisers that speaking out publicly against silver would mean destruction of his political future. His response: "I am supposed to be a leader in my party. If any word of mine can check these dangerous fallacies, it is my duty to give that word, whatever the cost may be."[18] He gave that word a month later in response to an invitation from the New York Reform Club to address a meeting called by the city's business leaders to voice their opposition to free-silver coinage.

Regretting his inability to attend, Cleveland called the proposed adoption of the measure now pending in Congress for unlimited coinage "the greatest peril" for the nation and warned:

> If we have developed an unexpected capacity for the assimilation of a largely increased volume of this currency, and even if we have demonstrated the usefulness of such an increase, these conditions fall far short of insuring us against disaster if, in the present situation, we enter upon the dangerous and reckless experiment of free, unlimited, and independent silver coinage.[19]

This Silver Letter, as it came to be known, was given wide circulation. Western and southern newspapers fairly buried its author in an editorial outpouring of rage. In the more conservative East, Cleveland was extolled for his wisdom and lauded for his courage. ("It matters not whether such a man be of one party or another. It is enough that he is an American statesman to whom the welfare of the country is greater, more important, than self.")[20]

Still, despair was the order of the day among Cleveland loyalists, while elation at what was seen as his political death was the order of the day among his antagonists. Voicing the fear of the Clevelandites—certainly not because of his stand on free silver per se, but because they saw his stand as suicidal for the party as well as for himself—Dan Lamont implored Cleveland to send a countervailing letter to the Ohio Democratic convention in July "setting the silver position aside as one on which neither party is united." He suggested Cleveland might "perhaps state your opposition briefly to the ultra silver proposition and then take in the tariff question as the issue on which the parties divide, and give them something on that that could be used as a campaign leaflet. . . . Some such letter," Lamont felt, "would set the party back on the tariff question and away from the silver issue."[21] Cleveland was as unmoved by Lamont's plea as by the furor the letter aroused.

Denunciations of Cleveland over the Silver Letter were still coming in from all directions when he and Frances left for their summer home on Cape Cod to pursue the quiet bucolic life he so loved and which to him was both so relaxing and so invigorating. "How little and frivolous all this seems to me!" he wrote a friend regarding the uproar. "Not because I do not realize the importance of everything in the remotest way connected with the great office of President but because they appear to be indices of the meanness and malice of men and politicians."[22]

The tumult caused by the Silver Letter soon declined into quiescence, as did the entire silver issue. It was almost as if both major political parties had tacitly agreed to lay aside a volatile issue they knew must be confronted head-on, but which neither had any desire to confront at a time when the American people were gearing up for a presidential election. The unlimited coinage bill went down in the House. The silverites were satisfied (at least for the time being) with what the Sherman Act had won them: the government's purchase of 4.5 million ounces of silver monthly. It would absorb just about the entire output of the western mines. The silver issue would prove to be a minimal factor in the 1892 campaign, much to the relief of all concerned. Only *after* the election would it take center stage as a legislative casus belli.

On the Democratic side, a major factor in the 1892 campaign was David Hill's attempt, in collusion with Tammany, to wrest control of the party, now that they controlled its New York State branch. Not only was the governor's ambition to push Cleveland aside for the presidential nomination beyond doubt, it was feasible. In Hill's corner were the free-silver and protectionist Democrats in the East and the South. Cleveland's chances for again being the party's standard-bearer were no less viable, however. Rank-and-file Democrats nationwide loved him, hated Hill, and were united in the belief that a man who had twice won a plurality of the popular vote deserved a third chance.

A year earlier, following an extended lecture tour, Henry Watterson told Cleveland he had been traveling much around the country, "and among Democrats, have heard no other name than yours seriously considered." There was "no doubt" Cleveland was "stronger today than ever before." However, Watterson warned, while Hill was "out of the question—not to be thought of for a moment," he might "so muddy the stream as to put you at a disadvantage." He urged that Cleveland rally his friends. "The man never lived who can afford, in the long run, to stand wholly aloof and alone," he added sententiously.[23]

Cleveland, who surely needed no one to warn him of Hill's intentions, looked on with repugnance as he persuaded the Tammany-controlled state legislature to elect him to the United States Senate, which Hill viewed as his stepping-stone to the White House. His first move was to announce that he would not resign as governor. Serving out one's gubernatorial term while sitting in Congress may not have been moral or ethical, but at the time it was legal. Since Hill refused to heed the advice of many, including his own people, to give up the office, it was only to be expected that he would not give a damn about public opinion. And that was best summed up by one of his state's (and the nation's) most influential newspapers: "We do not hesitate to say that no other man in public life today would be guilty of such misconduct and continue to hold up his head."[24]

On October 8, 1891, at a mass meeting of the New York State

Democracy, Cleveland was prevailed upon, for sake of party unity, to introduce Hill and other party bigwigs. Hailing Democratic gains in Congress and various statehouses in the 1890 elections, he warned it was "evident that if our opponents are permitted to choose the line of battle they will avoid all national issues." Then reiterating his stand on tariff reform, Cleveland ended with a call to arms that led those present (Hill and his gang excepted) to decide he just might be the man to lead them in the coming battle. The fifty-four-year-old ex-President was in a joyous mood throughout the meeting. Five days earlier, Frances had given birth to their first child, Ruth, in whose honor the Curtiss Candy Company would later name the still popular Baby Ruth candy bar.

While Cleveland was busy basking in the joys of fatherhood, Hill was busy touring the West and South in quest of pro-silver and protectionist delegates to the 1892 nominating convention. Though Cleveland had not yet entered the fray he was moving inexorably in that direction. He feared that Hill's nomination—now a distinct possibility—would doom the doctrines of sound money, low tariff, and civil service reform.

Then came Hill's speech to his ever growing band of disciples at Elmira, New York, on December 4. Taking as his theme "The Issues for 1892," he called for a return to the tariff of 1883 (whereas Cleveland wanted an entirely new tariff) and insisted upon the continuation of silver coinage (which Cleveland wanted ended entirely). Hill on this occasion also attacked Cleveland as a man who would commit the country to "gold monometallism," which to silverites was a crime to be equated with child molestation.

The Elmira speech came on the same day that Cleveland wrote to Bissell of his disgust with "Hill's performances" to date, and his conviction that with Hill the Democratic party was "either rushing to overwhelming defeat or the people are heedless of everything political that may happen. Was it for this," he asked rhetorically, "that we braved temporary defeat in order that we might stand on principle? And what becomes of all our fine promises to the people?" Eight days later, after studying the published text of the Elmira speech and fearing the worst, Cleveland signaled his willingness to contest Hill for the nomination. "I have every possible desire," he again wrote Bissell, "to see our party succeed on decent honest lines, and have a strong disinclination to being exhibited at the tail end of a procession which means the betrayal of the principles we profess and the deception of the people."

Bissell all but tripped all over himself in his eagerness to share the letter with other Clevelandites. It was what they had been waiting three years to hear.

40

"The people are not dead but sleeping"

As election year approached, a group of leading eastern capitalists, appalled by Harrison's support of the McKinley Tariff Act and Sherman Silver Act, convinced that Harrisonian Republicanism was hostile to their interests (and to the long-range stability of the country) and apprehensive of what was now emerging as the Populist-driven "western revolt" by proponents of free-silver coinage and an end to all tariffs, concluded that Grover Cleveland was the only statesman around whom they could rally; and that, moreover, he was the only electable Democrat. Not only were these men powerful in their own right, they represented powerful interests.

Commanding the fealty of the leading bankers was Charles Fairchild, Cleveland's first-term Treasury Secretary. His Navy Secretary, William Whitney, had behind him a considerable part of the Wall Street establishment. The brothers Straus, Oscar and Isidor, represented the powerful mercantile interests. And a number of the principal railroad men were prepared to take their cue from Henry Villard, the German-born journalist and railway financier who was an honest and honorable version—indeed, a mirror image—of Jay Gould.

Villard sought to assure the hesitant Democratic leadership in Congress that Cleveland could take the nomination from Hill and go on to defeat Harrison. The assurance was met "with smiles" that would have been whoops of joy, had it been known that Hill's candidacy was to prove, in Allan Nevins's felicitous words, "a mere rocket, brilliant and alarming for a moment but fading into blackness so suddenly that men rubbed their eyes to see it gone."[25]

Hill was pursuing a five-point strategy to win the nomination:

recruit the support of free-silver Democrats in Congress, rally support among dissident southern Democrats, capture the New York delegation to the nominating convention, make a concerted effort to secure delegates in populous neighboring New Jersey and New England, and try to nail down the western silverites. It was a clever scheme. But, as is so often the case with clever schemes, it was too clever by half.

The signs looked promising. In the Senate, Hill bonded with Calvin S. Brice, Cleveland's 1888 campaign manager, and Arthur Pue Gorman, another veteran of the 1888 campaign, who had turned against Cleveland over the tariff issue; played a major behind-the-scenes role in electing Charles Crisp, a leading Democratic silverite, as Speaker of the House; and was largely responsible for naming William Springer of Illinois, a man of protectionist leanings, to head the all-powerful Ways and Means Committee and Richard P. Bland, leader of the free-silver movement in Congress and in the Democratic party, to head the also powerful Committee on Banking. He then undertook an extended vote-getting junket of the South, on which he demonstrated that his battle for the nomination was more than a chimerical quest. Wherever he spoke he was hailed by wildly cheering crowds; this was particularly so in the region's major state, Georgia, where Hill promised the poor that as President he would guarantee soft money, low prices, affordable mortgages—in sum, an end to all hardships that informed their lives.

An indication of the problems the well-organized Hill faction posed for Cleveland was described by Justice Lamar, his first-term Interior Secretary. In Georgia, Alabama, Virginia, and Mississippi, he wrote Cleveland, there was now a "skillfully planned movement organized by able, adroit, and ambitious men" whose intention it was to secure in their respective states delegates to the Chicago convention pledged to Hill, "by the same methods that had been employed in [Cleveland's] own State."[26] Those "same methods" were an audacious stratagem Hill's forces pulled off before he left on his southern tour, a stratagem that even the politically astute Lamar could not see would prove to be Hill's undoing:

The Democratic National Committee had set the nominating convention for June 21 at Chicago. Edward Murphy, the wealthy Troy, New York, brewer and party state chairman and Hill confederate, called a state convention for February 22 at Albany to pick a slate of delegates who would go to Chicago bound to Hill. It was the first time in twenty years that a state convention was to be held earlier than April 20, and Murphy's purpose in breaking with party tradition was evident. Politicians from the cities and urban areas allied with Hill would be caucusing to select delegates at a time when snow-choked roads inhibited participation in the selection process by small-town anti-Hill workingmen and farmers. Such a move by the country's largest state convention would—or so Murphy hoped—impress the other states and thereby catalyze a Hill "boom."

Party regulars were enraged. Almost every Democratic and Independent newspaper echoed the *New York World*: "An act of midwinter folly; illogical, unfair, undemocratic and unwise." From Lamar came word that the South, where Cleveland was still popular, had been aroused to "an insuperable repugnance" by the whole idea. Nationwide, fear was expressed in Democratic circles that if the idea of such a "Snap Convention," as the Albany parley became known, caught on, the Chicago convention would be just an assembly of manipulated politicians and not a truly representative body. At a mass meeting on February 11, New York's pro-Cleveland forces called on the state committee to cancel the Albany meeting. When the call went ignored, they formulated plans for a convention of "anti-snappers" at Syracuse in May.

The pro-Hill forces insisted that the entire New York delegation, bound by the unit rule, go to Chicago committed to their man. This set off an orgy of celebrations by Hill's supporters nationwide. It also led the pro-Hill *Atlanta Constitution* to predict his nomination on an early ballot. Henry Watterson, who had urged Cleveland to take Hill on, now wrote that "Mr. Cleveland is no longer a possibility" and that his nomination would be for the Democrat party an act of "deliberate suicide." He suggested that Democrats nationwide emulate New York, "setting Mr. Cleveland aside and advancing Mr. Hill to the party leadership."[27]

Massachusetts governor William Russell, leader of the sound-money forces in New England, rushed to the New Jersey resort of Lakewood, where Cleveland maintained a getaway cottage. Fearing, as did so many loyalists, that Cleveland was about to withdraw from contention, Russell had come with assurances that the majority of Democrats were unwavering in their allegiance. He could have, as they say, stayed home. Far from considering a withdrawal, Cleveland was more determined than ever to vanquish Hill, for the country's sake as well as his own.

On the same day the Snap Convention was coming to order in Albany, Cleveland was at the University of Michigan in Ann Arbor, where he had been invited to give the Washington's Birthday address. Speaking characteristically from memory, Cleveland held forth on Washington's exalted place in the nation's pantheon and as American youth's quintessential role model. Then—quite probably for the first time in his public career, presumably for emphasis—he read from his manuscript these eloquent lines:

> Interest yourselves in public affairs as a duty of citizenship; but do not surrender your faith to those who discredit and debase politics by scoffing at sentiment and principle, and whose political activity consists in attempts to gain popular support by cunning devices and shrewd manipulation.
>
> You will find plenty of those who will smile at your profession of faith, and tell you that truth and virtue and honesty and goodness were well enough in the old days when Washington lived, but are not suited to the present size and development of our country and the progress we have made in the art of political management.
>
> Be steadfast. The strong and sturdy oak still needs the support of its native earth, and, as it grows in size and spreading branches, its roots must strike deeper in the soil which warmed and fed its first tender sprout. You will be told that the people have no longer any desire for the things you profess. Be not deceived.
>
> The people are not dead but sleeping. They will awaken in good time, and scourge the money-changers from their sacred temple.[28]

With publication of the entire speech in all the major papers, the deafening outburst of approval that greeted Cleveland's remarks, both for their inherent philosophy and their transparent allusion to what was going on back at Albany, reverberated throughout the land.

Two months later, in one of his most eloquent letters, Cleveland shared with Lamar his "inmost thoughts," confessing to having "passed through much that is trying and perplexing to me" of late. He had to admit that the office of President had not, for him personally, "a single allurement. I shrink from everything which another canvass and its result involve." He knew "the dark depth that yawns at the foot of another defeat." He would gladly avoid both, were he to "consult alone my comfort, my peace, or my desire." His "discomfort" arose from "a sense of duty to honest people and devoted friends" and the knowledge that forces were at work "which certainly mean the complete turning back of the hands on the dial of Democracy and the destruction of party hopes." Was he "the instrument through which Democratic principles can be saved, whether party supremacy immediately awaits us or not?" he demanded. Were "folly" to defeat the party, ought he be "called upon to place myself under the falling timbers?" (This consideration, Cleveland admitted, smacked "of care for myself which perhaps ought to be discarded.")

Then moving from the valley of despair toward the mountain of determination, Cleveland declared himself "obedient to the cause of the country and of my party." Whatever the election's outcome, none could say he "refused to serve in time of peril or abandoned those whom I have been instrumental in calling to the field where is waged the battle of Democratic principle." However, he was not convinced that the nomination was his for the asking. He knew he could "easily be disposed of, either by the selection of a candidate more available, or by the adoption of a campaign policy on the financial question which I am not willing to further." He promised, "If I am given my discharge I shall thank God most fervently" and "be a happy helper" to whoever the party nominated.

But would the party carry the day, if the Democratic protectionists and silverites failed to see the folly of their ways? If not, Cleveland lamented, he would "sadly await the announcement of a party defeat which will be predetermined." Should "our southern friends" contribute to that defeat by their support for Hill, he warned, they would be "left alone with their free coinage heresy. The West is slipping away from their side. The danger is that another idea, and a charge of heedlessness for the public safety on the financial question will do service in the place of the memories of the civil war." Cleveland ended the letter on a note of profound trepidation in light of Hill's strength in the South: "As one who loves his country, and believes that her interest is bound up in democratic supremacy, I am most uncomfortable and unhappy in the fear that the South will not see until too late the danger of their marriage at all."[29]

Cleveland was roused from this, his darkest moment in the campaign, when it became apparent that Hill's Albany stunt had hurt him around the country. Joseph Pulitzer's *World,* which came out early for Hill but was now appalled by his campaign tactics, dismissed the whole ploy with the contemptuous remark that the presidential election would not be confined to the Empire State, and that the other forty-three states would participate. This energized Cleveland's New York partisans to raise money and stage a mammoth convention at Syracuse which chose its own delegation to Chicago. They knew there was no chance of its being seated. Their purpose was to show the country how pervasive the anti-Hill sentiment was in his own state.

Even before the Syracuse convention got under way, Hill's expectations for a nationwide boom went the metonymous way of all flesh. At the second state convention, Rhode Island's, his faction's efforts failed to prevent selection of a delegation pledged to Cleveland. Led by Governor Russell, the Massachusetts Democrats called for an early convention in order to influence the other states; it not only selected a slate committed to Cleveland, it passed a string of resolutions endorsing his candidacy. The worst news for Hill came out of Georgia, where Cleveland's forces turned back a powerful coalition of pro-Hill silverites and protectionists led by House Speaker Crisp. When Hill learned that his strongest southern state was sending a slate of delegates to Chicago bound to Cleveland, he knew his chances for securing the nomination were fading.

The Democrats convened at Chicago two weeks after the Republicans renominated Harrison on the first ballot at Minneapolis. Harrison was not the convention's unanimous choice. He was particularly disliked in New York, a dislike that became magnified with the addition of Whitelaw Reid to the ticket. Reid, editor-publisher of the *New York Tribune,* was hated by New York machine Republicans for his part in helping Garfield dump the Grant Stalwarts. A zealous Blaine supporter in '84, Reid detested Cleveland but supported a number of his major second-term policies.[30]

Cleveland was nominated on the first ballot. As soon as his name was put into nomination the delegates chanted:

Grover! Grover!
Four more years of Grover!
In he comes,
Out they go,
Then we'll be in clover!

As anticipated, the western and southern Democrats noisily opposed Grover's stand on the currency, while his own state's delegation, packed with Tammany men, grabbed every opportunity to transform the floor into a guerrilla-theater show of hostility. The details need not detain us. It is enough to say that Cleveland's was a narrow victory, but a victory nevertheless. Of the total available votes (909½), he won a mere 10⅓ more than the 607 required for nomination. Hill, who led the remaining pack of ten, received 114. Farther back in the field was Adlai E. Stevenson, Assistant Postmaster General in the first Cleveland administration. Though he won only 16⅔ votes for the first spot on the ticket, he was the convention favorite for the second spot. The Cleveland people preferred Isaac P. Gary of Indiana, but Stevenson was a soft-money man; it was hoped he would help the party among the western silverites in general and in Illinois in particular. Faced with possible Democratic defections in the South and the Hill faction's schemes in New York, it was crucial that Cleveland carry heavily populated Illinois and increase his following in the Midwest.

The convention's biggest battle was in the platform committee over the tariff. When it led to an open floor fight, Cleveland's forces won by a healthy majority, 564 to 342. Promising a lower tariff, the platform denounced protectionism as fraud and robbery, called the McKinley Act "the culminating atrocity of class legislation," and deftly straddled the divisive currency question by coming out in favor of bimetallism, but under such conditions as would maintain the parity of the two metals. (The Clevelandites really had no intention to compromise their advocacy of monometallism. But they did have every intention to win this election.) Other planks included supporting antitrust laws, condemning czarist Russia's oppression of its Jews and Lutherans and expressing empathy for home rule in Ireland, advocating the improvement of inland waterways, a transisthmian canal in Central America, federal aid to education, and statehood for Arizona and New Mexico. But it was the tariff issue that dominated the platform.

41

Cleveland in his most truculent mood

This time out, Cleveland wisely signed on as campaign director his former Navy Secretary, William C. Whitney, one of the leading political strategists of the day. The campaign got off to a fractious start. With Hill sulking Achilles-like in his tent, his Tammany myrmidons threatened to forgo the election and join him. Whitney had successfully defended Richard Croker, Tammany's Grand Sachem, against a charge of murder. Feeling an obligation to Whitney, Croker promised to bring party boss Murphy and the other sachems into line. The promise was undeliverable. Hill and Murphy felt no obligation to anyone but themselves and each other. In August, Whitney sent Cleveland, then summering at Buzzard Bay, the draft of a conciliatory letter that he wished to send to Murphy over the candidate's signature.

Cleveland refused. His reaction to the idea can be gauged in the following letter to Wilson Bissell, as close an adviser as he was a friend, which began by repeating "an old story which you have doubtless heard":

> A frontiersman had occasion to leave his cabin and his wife and children for a number of days and nights. When he returned he found that his house had been burned and the mutilated and charred remains of his family were scattered about the ground. He leaned upon his gun in silence for a moment, and then remarked with earnestness: "Well, I'll be damned, if this ain't *too* ridiculous!"

Cleveland "felt like saying just that" after reading in the previous day's paper that New York's Tammanyite lieutenant governor, William F. Sheehan, was to chair the campaign state committee. There was between the two an enmity dating from their Buffalo days when Cleveland made his acceptance of the mayoral nomination contingent upon Sheehan's brother, John C., being denied renomination for the number two spot on the ticket. The two had only recently patched up their friendship. But it was a friendship of political convenience—the kind of friendship that never made many demands upon Cleveland. His condition was "not improved" by Whitney's request. "I'll see the whole outfit to the Devil before I'll do it. . . . I expect to see Whitney on Monday. I am glad it is not today, for I don't believe I could hold myself in."[31]

It would seem at first glance that in opposing Whitney's overtures to the Hill camp Cleveland was being politically unreasonable. In fact he was being politically cunning. Many in his camp feared that courting Tammany would provoke antagonism among the Independents and, even worse, among conservative Democrats—not only in New York but nationwide. But Whitney was determined. Did the candidate forget that the loss of New York had cost him the 1888 election? Was it not wise to go that extra mile to keep so pivotal a state in line this time around? Whether currying favor with Hill would jeopardize the Democrats nationwide was moot. After all, Whitney pointed out, not *everyone* beyond the Hudson River despised the man. Not moot, though, was the need to carry New York. "Murphy has the votes," he wrote Cleveland on August 22.[32]

A few days later, with Cleveland not having budged, Whitney insisted he was making "perhaps a fatal" error; unless the Tammany-controlled New York Democracy was reconciled, "you cannot carry this State." Cleveland's response: if strenuous efforts were made in the West, he could lose New York and still win by carrying Illinois and Wisconsin. Whitney refused to accept this argument. He kept after Cleveland until, in a meeting at Gray Gables on September 3, Cleveland acquiesced. But only to a point, as he wrote a close adviser. He would meet with the opposition with all the agreeability he could muster—but "would not pledge myself to do their bidding in case of success."[33]

A few days later, Cleveland went to New York City and directly to the Hotel Victoria, where by prearrangement he met with Judge D-Cady Herrick of Albany, an old friend and adviser. Cleveland was in his most truculent mood, telling Herrick that while he had been coerced into soliciting the state committee for its support, he could never accept such support at the expense of those in the state who had stood by him. Herrick argued that the Murphy machine should be recognized and assured him it could be neutralized. His argument: the state committee had many bright men who could be given appointments abroad, while others could be given posts in Washington, where Cleveland could keep an eye on them. Also, Cleveland could appoint allies to federal offices throughout New York. In six months, his faction would have control of the state organization, and Murphy's muscle would be but a matter of historical record. At that point—

But let Robert McElroy, who learned what took place directly from the survivors of that famous Victoria Hotel Dinner of Reconciliation, tell it in his words:

> Mr. Whitney came in, accompanied by [Don M.] Dickinson [a close Cleveland adviser who had replaced Vilas as Postmaster General when Vilas replaced Lamar at Interior], and among them they persuaded Mr. Cleveland to meet the Tammany chiefs, Murphy, Croker, and Sheehan. . . . Judge Herrick was urged to be present also, but declined, feeling that he was *persona non grata* to Tammany. But Mr. Cleveland proved conciliatory only in the going. When the dinner was ended, and the hour for discussion had arrived, he turned to the expectant machine men and said:
>
> "Well, gentlemen, what do you want?"
>
> "We want pledges from you," replied Mr. Sheehan. "We want to know what you are going to do if you are elected. We want you to give us promises that will satisfy us that the organization will be properly recognized if you become President again."
>
> Mr. Cleveland doubled up his huge fist and smote the table.
>
> "Gentlemen," he said, speaking slowly and with almost painful distinctness, "I will not go into the White House pledged to you or to any one else. I will make no secret promises. I'll be damned if I will!"
>
> Again the big fist whacked the table.
>
> "What are you going to do then?" inquired Mr. Sheehan cynically.
>
> "I'll tell you what I'm going to do," said Mr. Cleveland as he rose to his feet.
>
> "I intend to address a letter to the public in which I shall withdraw from the ticket. I intend to explain my situation and to report what you have said to me here. I will tell the voters of the country that I cannot give any secret pledges, and that unless I do you will not support the Democratic ticket. I will tell

the voters that I do not want to stand in the way of a Democratic victory. That is what I shall do. Then, gentlemen, you can pick out a candidate to suit you, and if he is a proper man and the candidate of the party I will vote for him."

There was a pause.

"But I'll tell you one thing, Mr. Sheehan," added Mr. Cleveland, as he turned to the now breathless Lieutenant-Governor, "in my opinion public indignation will show you and your organization out of sight before the end of the week."

Mr. Croker leaped to his feet at this point, exclaiming: "This must stop, Mr. Sheehan; I agree with Mr. Cleveland. He cannot make any pledges and it is not right to ask for them."

Thus did Mr. Whitney's policy of conciliation conciliate by conquering, and Grover Cleveland again faced the election of a free man.[34]

42

The most decisive victory since Lincoln's reelection

While the '84 campaign was the dirtiest on record, the '92 campaign was the cleanest. And the quietest, and most mannerly. There was no personal abuse of the candidates; rallies and torchlight parades were kept to a minimum. The pressure was on Harrison. He must not only defend his record, he must explain to the people why their money had been so lavishly spent so unnecessarily in so many areas by the Billion Dollar Congress. Cleveland, conversely, had nothing to defend. Moreover, the public remembered how he had delivered on his '84 campaign promise to effect reform, and campaigned in '88 against the high tariff—which Harrison had raised even higher. Saddled with a miserable record, Harrison was further saddled with a bloody labor war for which he was not responsible but for which he had to accept accountability by virtue of its breaking out on his watch.

On June 29, workers belonging to the Amalgamated Association of Iron and Steel Workers, the nation's most powerful trade union, struck the Carnegie Steel Company at Homestead, Pennsylvania, to protest a proposed wage cut. Management responded with a lockout.

Two days later, on orders of plant manager Henry Clay Frick (Carnegie was at the time spending the summer in his native Scotland), a squad of strikebreakers arrived to open the plant. To protect them—and the plant itself—from the strikers whose jobs these so-called scabs would be taking, Frick brought in a force of three hundred Pinkerton men recruited from as far away as New York and Chicago. Each was told he would be paid $15 a week. None was told exactly what he would be doing to earn it.[35]

As a barge bore them up the Monongahela River to the plant on July 6, they were met by a hail of gunfire from the strikers behind barricades protected by plates of pig iron and iron; a mob of five thousand sympathizers shouted encouragement while running for cover. Sharpshooters sprayed "Frick's private army," as the Pinkerton men were referred to scathingly in the press, while the "army" fired in return from under cover of the barge's thick walls. Two small cannon were now brought up by the workers, who pumped machine oil into the water in a vain attempt to set the barge afire, while sympathizers flung sticks of dynamite from the riverbank. The battle ended only with the surrender of the Pinkerton men. They were allowed to come ashore and march away from the site—now littered with ten slain and more than sixty wounded. Though it began as a struggle over wages, with hours and working conditions ancillary factors, the Homestead Strike was ultimately a struggle for supremacy. Having successfully introduced the principle of collective bargaining, the Amalgamated had won what the workers considered a satisfactory wage scale, whereas Frick was out to destroy the union—at Carnegie's insistence.[36]

Public opinion disapproved of strikers resorting to violence and supported the use of eight thousand militia to protect the Homestead plant when it broke the strike with nonunion labor. (The strike, which was officially ended on November 20, led to a weakening of unionism in the steel industry that lasted until the 1930s. But, as will be seen when we come to Cleveland's second presidency, unionism in the rail industry was still to be heard from.) But public opinion also deplored the hiring of strikebreakers and was highly sympathetic to the principle of collective bargaining. Few could deny the claim by union leaders that not only the employees but the public as well had explicit rights in the policies of the far-flung Carnegie empire, since Carnegie, like so many industrialists, had amassed their great fortunes behind the walls of protectionism. The Democrats, for their part, did not find it too difficult to propose the high tariff embodied in the McKinley Act as one of the root causes of the tragedy at Homestead.[37]

In accepting the nomination, Cleveland referred acrimoniously to the events at Homestead as "the tender mercy the workingman receives from those made selfish and sordid by unjust governmental favoritism" and spoke of the hardships the nation's laborers were forced to endure under "the exactions wrung from them to build up and increase the fortunes of those for whose benefit" special subsidies were mandated by law. When anarchist Alexander Berkman tried to assassinate Frick, much of the Republican press accused Cleveland of inciting the deed, with the rather flimsy argument that the Democrats were openly more sympathetic to the strikers than were the Republicans.

In a desperate attempt at damage control, Harrison's running mate, Reid, appealed to Carnegie for continued recognition of the union at Homestead. Carnegie was receptive to the idea at first, but then did an abrupt about-face and cabled Frick that "probably the proposition is not worthy of consideration."[38] Since Carnegie was a great admirer of Cleveland, it would take no leap of the imagination to suspect that in denying Reid's plea he was doing his bit toward sabotaging the Harrison campaign. Here we have one of those secondary but interesting historical happenings that are fun to speculate about but impossible to prove either way.

(Adding to Harrison's problems was a new wave of labor unrest in the South and West, the most consequential occurring at Coeur d'Alene, Idaho, where a consortium of eastern owners of a rich silver mine had been cutting wages steadily. In July, the well-armed miners seized the mine and threw out the nonunion men brought in to replace them. Harrison crushed the strike by sending in federal troops. He repeated himself a month later, after several thousand state militia were unable to break a switchmen's strike in the Buffalo rail yards. American labor and their sympathizers were now prepared to vent their ire by voting Harrison out of office.)

Cleveland made no public campaign appearance of note. Added to his well-known unwillingness to canvass in his own behalf was the periodic agony brought on by the gout. ("I am more lame than 'I wish I was.' ") Dr. Bryant, visiting him in July, found his patient "grunting as you know full well, suffering from an excess of medicine rather than the lack of it." Cleveland was one of those who "always believes that if a little will do some good, a bottle full must be of great advantage indeed."[39] He spent most of the campaign summer at his Cape Cod home, enjoying his infant daughter. ("Ruth lives her sweet little life in the midst of it all as unconsciously as though it were not history.") In late August, at the urging of Whitney, he came to New York and made himself available for a few days.

What his supporters now noticed for the first time was a strong desire to win, a great—and welcome—departure from his at times passive mood in the 1888 campaign. He personally wrote countless letters to party leaders throughout the country urging them on to even greater effort, as in this one to Senator Daniel W. Voorhees of Indiana: "I am extremely anxious to be elected. I want to carry Indiana. I do not for a moment suppose I can do this without your help. I hope that you will give the ticket the benefit of your experience and familiarity with Indiana politics."[40] Voorhees, a free-silver Democrat who had come out for Cleveland, was among a number of like-minded men—including quite a few Republicans—to whom Cleveland was the only man with the courage to lead the nation as signs abounded that dangerous times were looming.

This feeling was not confined to politicians; it was prevalent in intellectual circles as well. At Amherst College, epicenter of New England Republicanism, all but ten of the school's thirty-three tenured professors signed a testimonial hailing Cleveland's "courage, his constancy, his public spirit, his studious neglect of his merely personal interests where they conflict with the calls of public duty." They lauded his tariff message, his pension vetoes, and his Silver Letter as "conspicuous instances of disregarding personal considerations for the public good." And they urged "all our fellow citizens to give Mr. Cleveland their hearty support."[41] There were many prominent Republicans who did not have to be urged, among them Walter Gresham, who had contested Harrison for the 1888 nomination and who would play a leading role in the second Cleveland presidency.

Harrison withdrew from active campaigning when his wife fell ill with the tuberculosis that would carry her off just two weeks before Election Day. Cleveland followed suit out of courtesy—not that he'd been all that active to begin with.[42] Down to its very last day it seemed as if the election could go either way, mainly because the waters were muddied by the third-party Populists. Silverite Democrats in five states the party had written off over the currency issue—Idaho, Kansas, Colorado, North Dakota, and Wyoming—did not nominate electors but, instead, supported the Populists, who also had the Republicans' support in the South. Still, as the results started coming in, it was obvious that a Cleveland landslide was in the making.

There was no surprise when it became known that New Jersey, Connecticut, and Indiana had gone for Cleveland. But that he carried Illinois, Wisconsin, and California was stunning. These were thought to be safe states for Harrison, so much so that the Democrats had written them off, along with the five already mentioned. (In solidly Republican Ohio, the shift of a mere 750 votes would have given the entire state to Cleveland.) Cleveland swept the electoral college, winning 277 to Harrison's 145. As for the Hill threat in New York, Cleveland won enough votes in the electoral college that he did not need to carry the state—which, in fact, went for him solidly. Cleveland had scored the most decisive victory since Lincoln's reelection in 1864 on a bipartisan ticket.[43]

Worth recording here are the comments of the next Democrat to succeed Cleveland in the White House. Said Woodrow Wilson, at the time a Princeton professor: "Signs are not wanting that the Republican party is going to pieces and signs are fairly abundant that the Democratic party is rapidly being made over by . . . the extraordinary man who is now President."[44] But perhaps the prize for the best assessment of Cleveland's stunning comeback goes to a leading Republican on Capitol Hill. Looking back from the vantage point of sixteen years, he described it as "God's mercy to this country that Grover Cleveland, and not Harrison, was elected President."[45]

PART VII

1893–1896

43

"The people got exactly what they wished"

Cleveland's second administration began on a note of felicity and warmth between President and public that seemed to mock the chill of Inauguration Day. A severe rainstorm the night before had brought with it a cold front that dumped an inch of sleet on the streets by the time the public began to gather at the Capitol. The pavement was wet and treacherous, and because of the storm and the biting winds, the streets and buildings could not be decorated as planned. Authorities wanted to move the ceremonies indoors, but Cleveland insisted they be held on the Capitol's east portico, as planned. People had come from all over the country, he said; they were entitled to witness the event.

A great roar went up from the crowd when the Cleveland party appeared; an even greater reception was accorded his wife, "whose appearance had moved the great throng to vociferous applause."[1] People who had not seen Cleveland during the past four years were quick to note his thinning, almost white hair and pale tight skin sagging around the eyes and in the cheeks. Still, he moved with confidence. They did notice a tendency to touch frequently the walrus mustache that drooped over his lower lip; but it was assumed, and correctly so, that he did this only to be sure it looked neat at all times.

Taking as its keynote the need "to constantly watch for every symptom of insidious infirmity that threatens our national vigor," Cleveland's second Inaugural Address was a reiteration of past speeches before Congress. This was not because he was deficient in new ideas, but because he wanted to remind the people of the docket started eight years previously that he was determined to complete. Nothing was more vital to our supremacy as a sovereign state, he emphasized, "and to the beneficent purposes of our Government than a sound and stable currency," adding: "The danger of depreciation in the purchasing power of the wages paid to toil should furnish the strongest incentive to prompt and conservative precaution."

Next, he addressed the topic that four years earlier had led to his defeat at the polls: "protection for protection's sake." In electing an exponent of low tariff over an incumbent who favored high levies, he claimed, the voters were demanding that Congress ("the people's servants") root out and destroy "the brood of kindred evils which are the unwholesome progeny of paternalism." Paramount among these evils was the granting of millions in unjustified veterans' pensions (the Harrison administration had revived the practice).

He then recapitulated a catalog of Clevelandian themes: "public expenditures should be limited by public necessity"; "waste of public money is a crime against the citizen"; "frugality among the people is the best guaranty of a contented and strong support of free institutions"; "misappropriation of public funds is avoided when appointments to office, instead of being the rewards of partisan activity, are awarded to those whose efficiency promises a fair return of work for the compensation paid to them"; business and industrial "aggregations and combinations frequently constitute conspiracies against the interests of the people, and in all their phases they are unnatural and opposed to our American sense of fairness"; the Indians "as the nation's wards . . . should be promptly defended against the cupidity of designing men and shielded from every influence or temptation that retards their advancement." He vowed to seek a sweeping tariff reform at the earliest possible moment, not bend to the plea of those powerful Democrats who demanded he "do something for silver," and refuse to trim sails on pension and civil service reform.[2]

The Republican *New York Times*, reflecting the opinion of the majority of the nation's most respected newspapers, lauded the speech as being "so absolutely pervaded with the sanity of statesmanship, so free from the taint of partisan politics, so far above the infected atmosphere of demagogy." It commended "this calm sanity that pierces through all the confusion and mist that are raised by conflict of opinion and of passion." And it extolled Cleveland's contention that government taxes should go to support only the government's proper roles on a basis of rational economy, and "not for the profit or advantage of private interests." The editorial then expounded upon an idea that is so often overlooked, one germane to our own generation as it was to Cleveland's:

> [T]he great body, probably more than three-fourths of the voters of each of the great political parties, go to the polls with very little independent or intelligent idea of what they are voting for, guided almost wholly by party associations. But these masses balance each other, and between them stand the voters who vote their convictions, who have a fairly clear notion of the consequences of their action, and who are determined in it by their knowledge of the parties and of the candidates and of what may be expected from them.

It was this class to whom Cleveland's

> character, his conception of duty, the principles to which he is devoted, the measures by which he desires to see these principles applied, are well known. They voted for him because of these, and his eminent success is due, not only to his courage and candor and fidelity, but to the appreciation of these qualities among the voters who do their own thinking. If he is strong in a remarkable degree, it is in the enlightened confidence and respect of the voters who really shape the course of politics in the Republic.

The *Times* concluded, in what essentially was a valedictory four years before the fact:

> Mr. Cleveland will do his work and pass again into private life. But the qualities of the American people that have enabled him

to do that work so far, and will enable him to go on with it, will remain, strengthened by his career, and available for the support of other leaders who shall equally deserve it.

As Cleveland was being driven back to the White House, he was greeted with cheers from one end of Pennsylvania Avenue to the other. On every stand set up for the Inaugural Parade, "men and women joined in the applause, and from the crowds upon the sidewalk there was continued cheering, which sounded like volley firing from down a long line." When the now effervescent Cleveland stepped onto the reviewing stand, "[h]is appearance started the cheering again. And once more the President was given a most hearty reception. He lifted his hat, as he was obliged to do many times in the afternoon."[3]

The parade, indeed, the entire day, was all the more festive for Cleveland in that he saw his election as a vindication both of his first-term policies and of his '88 defeat; above all was the confidence he felt the people shared that he would set things to right. By the time he and Frances arrived at the Inaugural Ball at the Pension Building, he was positively euphoric. For them both, it had been a long day. They arrived at nine-thirty, but "about an hour later . . . made their adieus and finally turned their faces homeward after what has undoubtedly proved a day of utmost intense and prolonged excitement."

It remained for the *New York Times* to put the events of March 4, 1893, in their proper perspective. Cleveland had "a very firm purpose to hold his party to its duty as well as to perform his own," the paper editorialized next day. But it was well worth remembering that, "powerful as is Mr. Cleveland's personality and efficient as his leadership has been, the remarkable career that he has already had, and that to which he is now called under such unusual conditions, would have been closed to him had he not found adequate support among the voters." This was all the more significant because the high position he now held in the public life of the American Union "has been conferred on him with the utmost deliberation, and after his character and his purposes and even his definite policy were thoroughly known to the country."

His 1884 election, the *Times* wrote in peroration, was owing to "a peculiar combination of circumstances, and especially to the fatuous choice by the Republicans of a candidate [Blaine] who was sure to be rejected by a very large and influential class of those who had previously acted with that party." But there was no such fortuitous element in the 1892 election. The issues presented to the public were very distinct and the choice was made impartially and intelligently. Grover Cleveland was in November 1892 what he'd been known to be in 1884, and it was because of that knowledge by the voters that he was returned to the White House: "The people got exactly what they wished, and knew exactly what they were getting."

Though the Harrisons had done little in the way of redecorating, they had initiated a number of welcome innovations. Electricity came in 1891—though Mrs. Harrison was so frightened by it she refused to touch the switches. Too, a number of bathrooms were installed in the upstairs family quarters; during their first residency, the Clevelands had only one. A third modernization was the upgrade in communications; where in 1885 there was but one telephone, there was now a switchboard with a full-time operator. (Also commendable was Mrs. Harrison's war against the army of rats whose hold on the mansion over the years was so pervasive—and so brazen—they practically took their meals with the tenants *sans souci.* Though a platoon of exterminators attacked the pantries and kitchens with a fervor reminiscent of Hercules' assault upon the Augean Stables, on a scale of one to ten their success would rate no more than, say, a seven. Soon after the Clevelands moved back in, a servant reported that while making his rounds one day he discovered that "a great rat had forced his way into the cage, had just killed the poor little canary and was going to have a great feast on him, when I arrived in time to make for him. He burst through the door and made his escape.")[4]

Day-to-day running of the domestic establishment was again in the hands of the capable Sinclair; in his capacity as White House Steward he oversaw the family's personal servants, which numbered a mere seven, including Ruth's nurse. Special attention was given by the public to the First Child. In good weather she was taken out to play on the south lawn, to the delight of tourists. When they began to secrete themselves in the shrubbery to steal a quick embrace, her mother ordered the gates locked. Since fashions of the day allowed a pregnant woman to hide her condition almost till delivery day, and neither of the Clevelands felt it necessary to advertise the impending event, it came as a surprise to the nation when on September 9, 1893, Frances gave birth to her second child, Esther—the first, and to date only, child of a President born in the White House.

44
Divisive issues

Grover Cleveland's election victory positioned him to be the strongest President since the Civil War. His party had not only carried the doubtful states of New York, New Jersey, Connecticut, and Indiana but the Republican strongholds of Illinois, Wisconsin, and California as well. Most of the influential papers nationwide had supported him, as had the eastern financial establishment. Of greater significance, for the first time since 1856 the President's party would control both houses of Congress.

A sound prognosis was illusory, however. Cleveland needed a unified party behind him to deal with the nation's problems. And the Democrats were bitterly—one may say unalterably—divided over the tariff and currency issues. Only through conciliation might he maintain the party harmony without which his presidency must fail. It is a verity of American politics that no man can successfully lead the nation who cannot lead his party. Principle and party are irrevocably entwined, in the sense that legislative endorsement of even the most creditable principles is conditional upon the support of a unified party. This was something that Cleveland failed—or was unable—to appreciate. Faced with so divided a nation, as was the case in 1893—hard money vs. soft money, tariff protectionism vs. reductionism, labor vs. capital—the prospect for successful leadership is contingent upon the Chief Executive following one of three paths. He can seek to represent all the people by doing little or nothing, and thus be a weak leader. He can pursue a policy of compromise on the potentially divisive issues, and help to unify the country. Or he can be uncompromising on major issues, and escalate the divisiveness of both party and country.

Cleveland followed the third path, and therein lay much of the misery that pervaded his second presidency. Though invariably the right ones morally, his decisions rarely reflected a national consensus. It almost seemed that he was determined to prove how forceful and how principled he could be, instead of how unifying. Compromising on issues—or at least suggesting a willingness to do so—might have gone a distance toward making his intransigence a tad more palatable. But compromise was to Cleveland an alien concept. So was even creating the illusion of compromise, which might have helped.[5]

Many of the troubles Cleveland faced arose from economic and social forces that were operating when he returned to office—forces over which he had little or no control. As America entered the 1890s it was in the midst of an industrial and business expansion that redounded beneficially to the nation as a whole, though not to all citizens. Two decades of postwar expansion had favored the financial, commercial, and industrial interests, making the underprivileged increasingly dependent upon them. Money moved tropismatically toward the relative few instead of into a more universal circulation. An inevitable repercussion was the rapid separation of the nation along class lines.

There was more. For twenty-five years after Appomattox the prejudices and emotional issues fostered by the well-intentioned but disastrously executed Reconstruction tended to overshadow, if not obscure, the problems of a nation transforming itself from a basically agrarian economy into a basically industrialized one. By the time Grover Cleveland returned to the White House the transformation had passed the point of no return. The nation envisioned by Jefferson was being transmuted into the nation envisioned by his chief foe Hamilton, and problems inherent in a revolutionized economic life were now the alpha and omega of political thought. The great land boom of the 1880s in what we know today as the Midwest precipitated a massive economic deflation. In Kansas alone, between 1887 and 1893, more than eleven thousand farms went into foreclosure while over three-quarters of the land in fifteen counties went into the hands of mortgage companies. This condition was replicated in varying degrees throughout other agricultural regions. Farmers in the South, for example, were devastated by a declining market and overproduction, while mortgage indebtedness grew in direct inverse ratio.

The general economic discontentment was aggravated by a suspicion that somehow the nation's institutions were not geared to the workings of a democracy as promised by its Founding Fathers. Debtors from all walks of life felt justifiably threatened by the scarcity of money and inflation and the often draconian behavior of their creditors. To this was added the conviction among the native laboring class that their earning capacity—ergo their livelihood—was imperiled by immigrants pouring into the country in unprecedented numbers. Small businesses were endangered by unfair practices of the railroads and larger industrial trusts: regulation was proving to be ineffectual, as was antitrust legislation. Labor agitation became so prevalent that in one year alone, 1890, there were more strikes than in any other year in the nation's history.

Those most vocal about the failings of a "democratic" America were in the West and South, where the people were predominantly agrarian and debtor, and commercial enterprises were mostly of the small competitive variety we know as "mom and pop" stores. Merchants, along with the farmers who were their clientele, found themselves at the mercy of economic conditions they could hardly understand. They saw themselves as—and in effect were—hostages to the vagaries of the eastern credit markets and railroad barons. It was to them incomprehensible why a downturn in commodity prices in, say, New York or Chicago should cause a hardworking farmer in, say, Nebraska to lose his land. Nor could they fathom why the fate of an entire region was contingent upon the railroads, whose rate schedules made it more costly to ship goods of manufacture or fruits of the land to, say, Chicago from, say, the Dakotas than from, say, New England.

In their mind, exorbitantly inflated costs and excessively deflated prices were to be blamed exclusively, not on the reality of industrial capitalism—a worldwide economic network controlled by an impersonal market system—but on those within the system with whom they had immediate contact: mortgage lenders who charged usurious interest rates, railroads which charged rapacious transportation fees, and, above all, merchants who charged unconscionably high prices for machinery and equipment. These were, in turn, identified with the eastern capitalists, who instead of producing wealth manipulated money to the disadvantage of those compelled to create goods under intolerable conditions, with little or no promise of decent recompense. Furthermore, to the farmers the low prices their crops now fetched were directly attributable to the shortage of circulating currency—a shortage they believed to be the result of predatory policies of Wall Street bankers, whom they accused of exploiting the nation's wealth to serve their own selfish interests.

To the preponderance of America's citizenry—the have-nots—it was axiomatic that powerful eastern interests had controlled both major political parties since the Civil War. While, as we have seen, the Cleveland Democrats were in the vanguard of much needed reform—in the economy, in governmental operation, in the civil service, in tariff reduction—they were, like the rest of the party's leaders, conservatives.[6] It must be said, though, that instead of empathizing with the nation's have-nots, the conservative "haves" held to the view—simplistic at best, fallacious at worst—that complex socioeconomic tribulations were motivated by questions of morality. According to this thinking, it was accepted almost as Holy Writ that moral virtue led to material success, immorality led to poverty; that those capable of surmounting society's adversities succeeded in life while those incapable of doing so failed; that healthy competition led to a healthy national growth; and that attempts to contain or repress private initiative were antithetic to social good and contravened nature's laws.

Just as today's conservatives cannot legislate immorality out of existence (a reality the more hidebound among them refuse to accept), yesterday's conservatives could not theorize social unrest out of existence. During this period of economic disorder, whose victims were unwilling to differentiate between Republicans and Democrats—probably because they were unable to—discontent with the established parties led to the birth of the Populist party. Its constituents, predominantly from the West, believed survival depended upon popular control of the nation's finance, land, and transportation. Included in their demands, which they hoped to achieve through the ballot, were many that in time became the law of the land (albeit through the efforts of the two major parties). Among them: a graduated income tax, a pliant currency system controlled by the government and not by the banks, the eight-hour workday, direct election of United States senators, women's suffrage, and the referendum.

The Populists also demanded the free and unlimited coinage of silver, a demand elucidated by William Jennings Bryan, who would succeed Cleveland as leader of the Democratic party. We will deal in due course with that succession. But for now, let us return to the White House of the honorable, well-intentioned, incorruptible twenty-second—now twenty-fourth—President of the United States, and attempt to fathom why a man who brought to Washington such a plethora of goodwill and racked up a record of truly estimable achievements left Washington four years later one of the most despised of all American Presidents.

45

"I cannot get the men I want to help me"

Financial storm clouds were looming on the horizon. The 1890 failure of Baring Brothers in England and the collapse of Australia's banking institutions had worldwide repercussions. At first they affected the United States only tangentially. Though prosperity had returned, it was on unsteady footing. Cleveland was able to appreciate, as did men with acuity in matters fiscal, what hazards the Sherman Silver Purchase Act presented in this immediate period of international economic instability. He resolved to build a strong cabinet of men who shared not only his apprehensions but his determination to face them head-on.

"I am dreadfully perplexed and bothered," he wrote a friend. "I cannot get the men I want to help me."[7] Among them was Thomas Bayard, whom Cleveland wanted to again head the State Department. Bayard preferred to be, and was appointed, our envoy to Great Britain. Another rejection came from Charles Fairchild, whom Cleveland wanted again at Treasury; he preferred to remain in private life. Still another to decline a post was George Gray, a former Delaware attorney general, whom Cleveland wanted for Justice. Gray was reluctant to leave the Senate, but this was just as well: the President would soon be in need of every Democrat in that chamber whose sympathies he could muster. Despite these and other turndowns, and though it took until late in February to accomplish the task, Cleveland managed to organize a cabinet that was, by and large, the equal of his first. Where it differed was in the surprise some of the appointments generated.

Preeminent among these was that of Walter Q. Gresham to be Secretary of State. The sixty-one-year-old Gresham, a lifelong Republican, had served as President Arthur's Postmaster General (1883) and Secretary of the Treasury (1884). Having headed the more enlightened opposition to the old-guard faction in the '84 and '88 presidential campaigns, he broke with the party over its high-tariff policy and supported Cleveland in 1892 against Harrison, his fellow Hoosier and political rival of long standing. Cleveland stuck by the appointment even though it outraged many in his party. A man of sound judgment, excellent intentions, and lofty ideals, Gresham shared Cleveland's ideas when it came to shaping foreign policy. Unfortunately, he could not translate them into success, in part because of poor health (he was to die his second year in office) and his want of tact in dealing with the Congressional Democratic leadership.

For Treasury, Cleveland prevailed upon former Speaker of the House John Griffin Carlisle, who had moved on to the Senate. Among Carlisle's strengths were an expertise in the areas of finance and taxation, a keen intellect, and the friendship and respect of many important politicians, especially in Congress, where his influence would be imperative for the administration.

To head Justice, Cleveland selected Richard Olney, a Boston attorney who had built a successful practice marked by a profound knowledge of the law and a tenacity in applying it. Olney was so little known outside Massachusetts—his public career had been limited to a few terms as a selectman in West Roxbury and one term in the state legislature—he placed on no one's list of suggested names solicited by Cleveland from leading Democrats. Liberal Democrats were angered by the appointment, deploring Olney's record as a corporation lawyer; the post of Attorney-General, they argued, demanded a more independent-thinking man if the antitrust laws were to be enforced. But Cleveland was confident Olney was the right man for the job. That his confidence was misplaced became manifest when he shifted Olney to another post midway through the presidency.[8]

For Postmaster General and Secretary of War, Cleveland chose two old friends, Wilson Bissell and Daniel Lamont. Though neither had ever held important public office, both proved that nepotism can often work to the public's advantage. This was particularly true of Bissell, who selected the best-qualified men for his subordinates and did away with many ineffective innovations of Chester Arthur's PG, John Wanamaker, who introduced methods more suitable to his family's great department store. As for Lamont, Cleveland had hoped he would again become his private secretary. But "the Colonel," who had added to his political acumen a talent for making a fortune in New York financial circles (where most post–Civil War fortunes were conceived and given birth), considered a secretary's position infra dig. Since his duties with the War Department were fairly light—the American army during this period was one of the least significant, least engaged on the planet—Lamont was free to again double as Cleveland's deft political adviser and "assistant President."

Cleveland's most obscure appointment, and most controversial, was Hoke Smith as Interior Secretary. Editor/publisher of the *Atlanta Journal,* Smith led the fight in Georgia against both the Populists and the pernicious influence of the pro-Hill forces. To Cleveland's foes—notably the Hill people—this smacked of hypocrisy: the President was using a cabinet post to reward a political hack; so much for that promise to staff the executive branch only with qualified men, regardless of past political favors. In fact, Cleveland chose Smith for his strong advocacy of tariff reform, sound money, and a demand for vigilance against private exploitation of government lands, the national forests, and the Indians. He intuited that Smith would be the most capable Secretary since the department's creation. This proved to be the case.

Hoke Smith represented the new South. The other southerner to join the cabinet, Navy Secretary Hilary Abner Herbert, represented the old South. A native of North Carolina and veteran of the Confederate army, he left the House of Representatives, where he had represented Alabama for eight terms, to accept the appointment. Herbert was one of the most competent men ever to head the navy, overcoming Congressional opposition to an expanded navy, which he saw as the nation's first priority, now that the United States was a two-ocean power.

For Secretary of Agriculture, Cleveland made an especially propitious choice in Julius Sterling Morton, a popular and influential agriculturist, politician, and newspaper editor. A "sound money" man despite his popularity in "soft money" Nebraska, Morton first attracted Cleveland's attention when he withstood efforts by that state's free-silver Democrats to effect an alliance with the Populists.

The administration was faced with a veritable plethora of major problems, among them the nation's worst depression in twenty years, a major labor confrontation that would earn Cleveland the enmity of

America's workingmen, a political insurrection in his own party, and, on a most personal level, life-threatening cancer surgery. Most immediate was the problem that started just five days after his inaugural when Cleveland sought to rectify one of the most ignominious episodes of nineteenth-century colonial history: the illegal acquisition of a sovereign nation by a handful of missionaries.

46

"I am ashamed of the whole affair"

In his eight years as President, Grover Cleveland pursued a foreign policy that opposed overseas entanglements in general and imperialist tendencies in particular. On those few occasions when he acted against another nation, he did so from a sense of either obligation or honor, never from a sense of militaristic adventure. Just as he stood up for the Samoan Islands against Germany because he opposed the conquest of a lesser state by a greater one, so did he stand up for the Hawaiian Islands against his own nation. He could have let the annexation of Hawaii move inexorably to its inevitable culmination. But he opted for confrontation, which he hated, as it was to him the only way a weak and defenseless people might retain their independence. It was not the idea of annexation that Grover Cleveland opposed, but the idea of annexation as a pretext for illicit territorial acquisition.

The theft of Hawaiian independence with the sanction of the Harrison administration constitutes one of the most heinous incidents in our nation's history; indeed, so heinous that chroniclers of foreign policy during the Cleveland/Harrison/McKinley years play down its worst aspects and pretend the whole thing never happened the way it actually did: a handful of second-generation American missionaries and sugar planters deposed the rightful monarch and stole her nation's sovereignty in contravention of both American foreign policy and American morality.

American involvement in the Hawaiian Islands began in 1820 with the arrival of a small band of New England Congregationalist missionaries. Like the seamen off the whaling and merchant ships who preceded them, they came uninvited; unlike those others, they came to convert, not exploit. It was left to their sons and grandsons to show how man will do just about anything in the name of Christianity except practice it. Their positive achievements cannot be denied. They created from the spoken language a written one and then taught the people to read and write, and exerted a great moral influence by helping the Polynesians curb the excesses of those visiting seamen off the whalers, merchant ships, and naval vessels of the various world powers, mostly American, who introduced into the islands the syphilis, measles, tuberculosis, typhoid, smallpox, mumps, and alcoholism that would halve the native population in a generation and reduce it by *80 percent* by century's end.

Given Hawaii's geographical importance—it lay astride the great east-west Pacific trade routes, at the center of the whaling industry, and boasted natural harbors and resources—it was inevitable she eventually come under the suzerainty of one of the world powers. As merchants and planters who were heirs of those first missionaries insinuated their way into the kingdom's political and economic power structures, eventual annexation to their fathers' native land became a goal. A powerful coalition of mostly American native-born *haoles* (people of foreign extraction), sons of and grandsons of those earliest missionaries and known as the Reform party, managed to gain virtual control of the Hawaiian legislature and judiciary. In 1887, these Reformers carried out a bloodless émeute that imposed upon King Kalakaua a constitution of their own creation.

Under this new charter—which its authors decided need not be submitted to the people for ratification—cabinet ministers, whose approval was required for all royal acts, could not be dismissed without consent of the legislature, which also could override any royal veto. Suffrage was restricted to men with large incomes or property holdings (effectively disenfranchising the overwhelming preponderance of natives) and was extended to all Caucasian aliens resident in Hawaii at least three years *including men who were not—nor had plans to become—naturalized.* By the time Cleveland left office in 1889, the Reformers—now known as the Annexationists—had so metastasized Hawaii's body politic that few men doubted her days of independence were numbered.

Hawaii's annexation by the United States was no crime, in Cleveland's opinion—so long as it was the free choice of the Hawaiian people. In fact, he had supported the sentiments of his first Secretary of State, Bayard, who saw it as the obvious course to "wait quietly and patiently, and let the islands fill up with American planters and American industries, until they should be wholly identified in business interests and political sympathies with the United States. It [is] simply a matter of waiting until the apple should ripen and fall."[9]

But the Harrison administration did not wish to wait. Secretary of State James Gillespie Blaine, a leading advocate of overseas expansion, was a close friend and benefactor of the new U.S. Minister to Hawaii, John S. Stevens. From the moment of his arrival at Honolulu, Stevens bombarded the State Department with letters and secret memos, and the mainland Republican press with letters and editorials, to the effect that the islands' "ultimate possession by the United States [was] of the utmost importance" to American commerce in the Pacific. "Shall Americans sleep while others are awake to take from them these natural advantages?" Stevens asked rhetorically. "Time and tide wait neither for men nor nations."[10]

Indicative of how disproportionate an influence the American *haoles* exerted in Hawaii, when Cleveland returned to the White House there were two thousand American residents in the entire kingdom, of which only 637 were registered voters. Small wonder that Lorrin Thurston, a Honolulu-born son of missionaries and the chief orchestrator of the overthrow, told Blaine of his "strenuous doubts" that annexation would ever pass, "were it put to the electorate here at Honolulu." What the Annexationists needed desperately was a catalytic event. It was Kalakaua's sister and successor, Queen Liliuokalani, just two years on the throne, who provided that catalyst by attempting to replace the hated Reformer constitution with a new charter more attuned to the needs of her people.

The legislature was the designated body for such change, but with their influence in that body, the Annexationists could block all attempts to effect it. Liliuokalani saw as the only rightful recourse promulgating the change herself. The new charter, which she wrote, was intended to return legislative control to the people in the sense that the American people "control" their Congress through the ballot and the right of recall. Property qualifications by which the Reformers had disenfranchised indigent natives were rescinded, and residents wanting to vote had to become naturalized citizens (a step many had refused to take because they wanted to retain their American citizenship). This would have disenfranchised over a quarter of the current voters. But that one-fourth were noncitizens, who owned over nine-tenths of the private property in the kingdom.

Also often overlooked by chroniclers of the Hawaiian Revolution: the proposed changes did not deprive the resident foreigners of any rights or privileges granted by the 1887 charter. In fact, Liliuokalani wanted them to remain in the islands, intermarry with the natives if they wished (her husband was from Boston), and, if they so desired, become citizens. Hawaii's chief justice, an American named Arthur Judd, later tried to excuse the unconscionable part he and his fellow *haoles* played in deposing Liliuokalani on the grounds that "[t]he new Constitution would have made it impossible for white men to live here." In fact, under the old constitution it had become impossible for *natives* "to live here."

The usurpation began on Saturday, January 14, 1893, when the queen, having prorogued the legislature and announced she would proclaim her constitution, was forced to back down by her cabinet ministers, whom the Annexationists had cowed into withdrawing their support. She promised her people to promulgate the charter at some future date. Interpreting her promise as a threat, Thurston led a group of Annexationists in organizing a thirteen-man Committee of Public Safety. The committee's first order of business was to bond with Stevens and the equally supportive G. C. Wiltse, commander of the American warship *Boston*, in harbor as part of President Harrison's program of maintaining a squadron in Hawaiian waters "to protect American interests."

Liliuokalani's government sought to defuse the situation by compromise. This should have ended the crisis. But the committee did not want it ended. Around four o'clock that afternoon, they sent word to Stevens that the public safety was menaced and concluded: "We are unable to protect ourselves without aid, and therefore pray for the protection of the United States forces." An hour later, some 160 marines in full battle gear, accompanied by medics and two artillery pieces, came ashore from the *Boston*. Though Stevens was to insist otherwise, American armed forces had invaded a friendly sovereign state without provocation.

Bolstered by the marines' presence, the Committee of Public Safety set up a provisional government; to give it a sense of legality, they convinced Supreme Court Justice Sanford Dole, the popular and respected son of missionaries, to take the presidency. Between one and two o'clock the following afternoon, when city life all but came to a complete halt and most people, including government workers, returned to their homes for lunch, the usurpers made their way to Government House, where the government had neglected to post a guard and just a few easily intimidated clerks were on duty. There they proclaimed the deposition of the queen, dissolution of the Hawaiian monarchy, and establishment of a provisional government "to exist until terms of union with the United States has been negotiated and agreed upon." Within the hour, pursuant to prior agreement, Stevens recognized this new government "in the name of the United States." This despite the fact that he was not only acting without the consent of his superiors (cable connections between the islands and the American mainland were still a few years away), he was "recognizing" a government that was neither *de facto* nor *de jure.*

Had Liliuokalani been able to deal with the insurgents alone, the Dole government would have been out of business within the hour. But she was unable to withstand the power of the United States, as personified in Stevens and Wiltse (and those marines). She could, however, or so she believed, trust to American justice. That night, she surrendered conditional until such time as the facts could be ascertained by Washington.

Told by Dole that his commissioners would be leaving next day by charter steamer to present its case for annexation, Liliuokalani requested, and was refused, permission to send her own agents on the same ship. By the time they got to Washington, Dole's people and Blaine had negotiated an annexation treaty, which President Harrison rushed over to the Senate on February 15, with a request for immediate ratification. With Harrison's presidency drawing to a close and the Senate reluctant to act on the pending treaty, friend and foe alike of annexation openly speculated on what Cleveland would do when he returned to office.

Five days after doing so, he withdrew the treaty from the Senate "for the purpose of reexamination." Next, determined to have all the facts, he sent former congressman James H. Blount to the islands for a personal investigation on his behalf. Not only was this move hailed in the Democratic press, where prevailing sentiment opposed annexation, but also in the pro-annexationist Republican press—where it was assumed that Cleveland had withdrawn the treaty simply to preclude Harrison's getting all the credit for acquiring Hawaii! Blount, they reasoned, would gather his facts, the Democrats would tidy up the treaty, and it would then be resubmitted and promptly ratified.

Blount's first actions on arriving at Honolulu were to order the *Boston*'s marines, who were performing police duty for the provisional government, back to their ship, and the new government's flag lowered and the Hawaiian flag again raised. After personally reviewing all pertinent State Department documents, including Stevens's confidential correspondence with Blaine, Cleveland was not surprised by Blount's report, of which the most pertinent statement was: "The American Minister and the revolutionary leaders had determined on a new addition to the United States and had agreed on the part each was to act to the very end."[11]

Cleveland decided that the great injustice done the Hawaiians must be righted, but was not sure how to go about it. Secretary of State Gresham said that anything short of restoring the legitimate government "will not, I respectfully submit, satisfy the demands of justice." Gresham's high moral path, Cleveland agreed, was commendable. But realities had to be considered: the government, now a few months in power, had armed itself, and could only be removed by force. But that would be an act of war, beyond Cleveland's power to initiate unilaterally; and it was doubted that both Congress and public opinion would let him resort to armed intervention. Albert S. Willis, who replaced Stevens, was ordered to try reconciliation. Dole refused to dissolve the provisional government, and Liliuokalani refused to grant amnesty, insisting she would settle for nothing less than the immediate return of her throne. On December 4, in response to a public outcry on the American mainland that he "do something about Hawaii," Cleveland announced he was seeking to "undo the wrong that had been done by those representing us and to restore, as far as practicable, the status existing at the time of our forcible intervention."

Two weeks later, in a Special Message to Congress on the Hawaiian Question, he reiterated that it was our government's custom "to do justice in all things without regard to the strength or weakness of those with whom it deals" and warned that the United States, being one of the world's—and history's—most enlightened nations, would do its citizens "gross injustice if it applied to its international relations any other than a high standard of honor and morality." Accordingly, "if a feeble but friendly state is in danger of being robbed of its independence and its sovereignty by a misuse of the name and power of the United States, the United States can not fail to vindicate its honor and its sense of justice by an earnest effort to make all possible reparation." In commending the problem "to the extended powers and wide discretion of the Congress," he gave assurance that he would be "much gratified to cooperate in any legislative plan which may be devised" for its solution "consistent with American honor, integrity, and morality."[12]

Cleveland's moral arguments were persuasive. But so far as Congress was concerned, arguments in support of "Manifest Destiny" were even more persuasive. The House of Representatives condemned the overthrow and refused to sanction annexation as matters now stood—but was unwilling to attempt a restoration of the deposed queen by force. The Senate, on the other hand, took the attitude that the United States should stay out of Hawaiian affairs and insist that all other nations follow suit. This amounted to letting annexation await a more convenient season. That time came in the wake of the Spanish-American War, which broke out on April 25, 1898. Following Dewey's historic victory at Manila Bay, President McKinley remarked, "We need Hawaii just as much and a good deal more than we did California. It is Manifest Destiny." Two months later he signed a hastily enacted joint resolution of both houses annexing the islands, and on August 12, the same flag Cleveland had ordered hauled down was raised again in token of American sovereignty. "Hawaii is ours," a saddened Cleveland wrote to Richard Olney on July 8, 1898, as the last act of this drama was being played out. "As I look back upon the first steps in this miserable business, I am ashamed of the whole affair."

It must be said that Cleveland subjected the Executive Branch to the humiliation of having to ask the Legislative Branch to assume the lead in resolving a foreign relations impasse (though it can be argued persuasively that he had little choice in the matter). Regardless, he deserves to be praised, not damned. He may not have foreseen all the implications of his approach, but he did foresee its hopelessness, and that it would subject him to condemnation. Yet, he persevered, motivated not by a concern for what was politically correct, but for what was *morally* correct. Moreover, at a time when small nations were becoming the prey of great ones, and the United States had fallen victim to the stigma of colonialism, he insisted that the country he had once again been called upon to lead must fulfill the noblest commitment to morality and altruism.

47

Arguably his finest moment

In attempting to restore Hawaii's sovereignty, Grover Cleveland showed himself to be a man of courage. In successfully having the Sherman Silver Purchase Act repealed, he showed himself to be a statesman of courage. It was arguably his finest moment, the Mount Everest of a public career punctuated by many high achievements.

The Sherman Act of 1890, a boon to the western silver-mining states, committed the government to a yearly purchase of 54 million ounces of the metal (the region's estimated total output) at market value, against which Treasury ("Sherman") notes were issued, redeemable in either silver or gold. Most people, of course, redeemed theirs in gold. This inflated the currency by about $50 million yearly. Compounding the situation, the flow of gold into the Treasury from customs practically ceased as the world powers scrambled either to get their hands on more of the precious metal or hold on to what they already had. With the world now on the gold standard, no nation wanted to be caught with any appreciable amount of silver. Not only must America's own depleted and steadily diminishing gold reserve meet all domestic legal obligations, it must satisfy her international obligations. By the close of 1891, faced with a deficit trade balance and the world's gold supply at a premium, what the Treasury was enduring was not so much a dangerous outflow of gold as an absolute hemorrhage.

When Cleveland retired from office in 1889, he turned over to Harrison a cash balance of $281 million, of which $196,689,614 was in gold. Such was the scope of reckless spending that marked the Harrison years, when Cleveland returned to the White House he received from Harrison but $112,450,577, only $103,500,000 of it in gold. (It would have been below the legally allowable minimum of $100 million, but Harrison got several millions from New York bankers in exchange for greenbacks during the closing weeks of his presidency, as a means of securing the gold reserve—until he was safely out of office and no longer accountable.) Cleveland had every right to fear what could well befall the nation, given the international economic distress that derived in large measure from the erratic fiscal practices of the preceding twenty-five years and the Baring Bank failure. To suppose that the United States might avoid being unfavorably affected by that economic distress was to suppose that a child with an underdeveloped immune system might frolic among a gang of moppets with nasty head colds and come away with nothing more deleterious than a passing sneeze or two.

From the time of his reelection, Cleveland had been under pressure—from trusted and knowledgeable advisers, influential financiers, and Tammany alike—to repeal the Sherman Act and thus put an immediate end to the silver heresy, which they saw as the major cause of the nation's fiscal ill health. Henry Villard stated the case succinctly: a financial panic was coming. Either Cleveland must act at once or his administration would he held responsible and his policies doomed to failure.[13]

Cleveland authorized an announcement to be made that immediately on taking office, he would insist that Congress deal specifically with the Sherman Act; to underscore that its repeal was imperative, notice would be served on all Democrats in Congress that no appointments or political patronage benefiting them would be considered until they had complied. Just as the announcement was to be released to the press, Cleveland abruptly changed his mind: he would make no such announcement before taking office. The decision was based on three factors. First, a repugnance to having it appear he was yielding to Wall Street pressure being whipped up by the eastern press. Second, the advice of close advisers that he hold off and let the new Congress deal with the issue when it met in the fall, lest he seem to be exerting undue pressure and thus set the Executive Branch and Legislative Branch on a potentially fatal collision course. Third, and perhaps most overriding, his belief that the time was not yet ripe for repeal—which Cleveland believed *could succeed only if public sentiment in its favor were allowed to develop.*

Ten days before inauguration the Philadelphia & Reading Railroad, with debts topping $125 million, went into bankruptcy. Economists saw this as an indicator of events to come. To stem the drain on the Treasury, immediately on taking office Cleveland moved fast to augment gold reserves without having to issue bonds (something the Harrison administration had suggested but which would have been about as effective at this point in time as reattaching a severed limb with a Band-Aid). He had Treasury Secretary Carlisle request that banks in various major cities exchange part of their gold coin for other forms of currency held by the government. In three weeks the Treasury reserve was up to $107 million. Within days it began to drop as the gold drain continued; on April 22, it fell below the legally permissible $100 million floor for the first time.

Two days earlier, Carlisle had announced the Treasury would pay demands on the federal government in gold "as long as it has gold lawfully available for the purpose." This raised widespread trepidation that the new administration would soon begin redeeming notes in silver. Legally, this was allowable, though it would have been analogous to taking the nation off the gold standard. As protests flew in from every direction, Cleveland emphasized that gold payments would be maintained. Leading those who expressed profound relief was Andrew Carnegie: Cleveland "saved this country from panic and entire confusion in its industrial interests."[14]

Carnegie's relief was short-lived. Within two weeks, the stock market fell off, rallied feebly, and then collapsed. The great Panic of 1893 was under way.[15] Within the month, a quarter of the nation's railroads had collapsed, representing $2.5 billion of capital and over forty thousand miles of track. By the middle of August, upward of two million people, nearly 15 percent of the nation's industrial labor force, would be unemployed. Labor leader Samuel Gompers estimated the figure would reach 20 percent by year's end.[16]

To dramatize their plight and demand government relief, a Massillon, Ohio, utopian reformer named Jacob Coxey called for a march on the nation's capital by the unemployed. Coxey's first recruit was a California Theosophist named Carl Browne, who believed that when people died their souls and bodies went into separate pools from which new humans were fashioned. (Browne also maintained that he and Jesus Christ bore a remarkable resemblance, though he did admit to the certainty that Jesus, unlike himself, did not wear fringed buckskins, silver-dollar buttons, and a splendiferous beard that parted down the middle and reached out in all directions, giving its wearer the appearance of a con man who peddled Kickapoo joy juice to ingenuous Indians.) The two announced they would start from Massillon on Easter Sunday with twenty thousand marchers and reach Washington on May Day. (May Day, which probably began as a spring fertility festival in antiquity, had been designated in 1889 by the Second Socialist International as the holy day of organized labor.)

Editorials denouncing the whole business as "revolutionary"—hence dangerous—raised public interest in and encouraged more recruits for the Army of the Commonwealth of Christ, to give Coxey's Army its preferred name. News reporters were sent to cover the army, which now included colorful recruits like Dr. Cyclone Kirkland, who claimed he could forecast hurricanes through astrology; a black minstrel, Professor C. B. Freeman, self-styled "the loudest singer in the world"; a gnomic creature introducing himself as "The Great Unknown" who was a bona fide traveling snake oil salesman; and "Professor" J. J. Thayer, who led the "Commonwealth of Christ Brass Band."[17] Scores of men riding the rails hobo-style, driving wagons, or traveling by shank's mare materialized at Massillon. An hour before noon on Easter Sunday, a column of four hundred, headed by Coxey and Browne astride horses, set out. Riding behind in a wagon was Coxey's wife and newborn babe, Legal Tender; their son Jesse sported a blue-and-gray uniform to symbolize the unity of North and South in the struggle for social justice.

Despite the expectations of press and hecklers alike, the army did not disintegrate for want of recruits, let alone provisions. On the contrary. As it moved eastward, thousands joined in. At each stop the travelers were met by sympathetic citizen groups who plied them with farm produce, meat, bread, even packaged goods. At Pittsburgh, where labor troubles were a way of life, the tumultuous welcome committee included union marchers, parents with their children, and Socialists. Cleveland approved his Attorney General's orders that Secret Service operatives trail the vagabond army, but at no time did he consider it any threat to the nation's safety. In the meantime, other "armies" had sprung up throughout the West and Northwest and were fast converging on the nation's capital.

On April 28, the Coxeyites reached Washington in a mood of euphoria and a state of depletion. Though their reception was compounded of hostility and ridicule, this did not deter Browne, who broke through police lines, intending to force his way into the halls of

Congress. He was promptly clubbed to the ground. Meanwhile, Coxey, having reached the steps of the Capitol, was about to read aloud his "Address of Protest" when he was arrested and charged with walking on the grass. Police then scattered the "troops," and Coxey's Army and the movement it had spawned quickly came to an inglorious end.

As the economic situation worsened, Cleveland was inundated with calls from his advisers, telegrams from brokers and bankers, and newspaper editorials calling for a special session of Congress to face the crisis head-on. Joining in the chorus, chambers of commerce throughout the land voted resolutions demanding such action. As Cleveland had hoped would happen, the public was slowly coming around. Economic hardships brought on by the panic and publicized by Coxey's Army had spread rapidly westward, where silver sentiment was most prevalent, and the resolve there to fight repeal was being shaken. During May and June, refusal by New York banks to rediscount notes of western and southern commercial institutions forced many of them to go under. This gave the nation's agricultural sections a bitter taste of the misery being felt elsewhere. As one major paper editorialized biblically, the western states had "sown the wind in the silver-purchase law; now they must reap the whirlwind." Those states sustained a severe blow when it was learned that India, the last major holdout, had demonetized silver. The metal was no longer welcome on the world market. Mines in the Mountain States shut down by the score; in Colorado alone, unemployment rose by thirty thousand and half its industries closed down.[18]

On August 1, savings banks announced that sixty days' notice would be required from depositors wishing to withdraw funds. New York banks refused to cash any checks except for small amounts. A total of 642 banks failed, an incredible number for a nation of 66 million people. Many brokerage houses went under, mines and factories closed, unemployment rose in ratio to the rapidly growing money deficit, and a currency famine set in as people hoarded not only gold but silver and greenbacks as well. Particularly hard hit were the farmers: out West, the Pillsbury flour mills were reduced to buying wheat with scrip; down South, cotton crops could not be sold because of the unavailability of money.

Meanwhile, Cleveland issued a call on July 1 for Congress, which had adjourned on June 30 for the summer, to reconvene in special session on August 7 for the express purpose of repealing the Sherman Silver Purchase Act—unconditionally. The lack of confidence in and fears regarding the economic situation, he said, had caused great losses. Unemployment was rampant, the industrialists and financiers were in a state of high anxiety and even higher uncertainty, the masses had succumbed to desperation—and in some cases, actual starvation. Rescinding the silver purchase clauses was crucial to the nation's fiscal health, if not its fiscal sanity.

Lost in the clamor was the fact that while Cleveland opposed free coinage of silver, he never objected to use of the metal as currency. What he feared, and fought vehemently, was the substitution of a silver basis of value for the established gold standard. The Sherman law had done precious little to allay his fears. As President he was responsible for what was rapidly becoming the impossible task of keeping the two metals at parity. The government must be prepared to pay a gold dollar whenever a Treasury note, which represented only a deposit of about sixty cents' worth of silver, was presented with a demand for redemption in gold. And with the price of silver having fallen to seventy-seven cents an ounce, it was senseless to believe, as the western mining interests argued, that the continued monthly purchase of 4.5 million ounces might increase the metal's value.

Reaction to the demand for the special session was predictable. In the East, support for Cleveland was near-universal: newspapers and business leaders regardless of party affiliation demanded repeal, the sooner the better. In the West, it was generally agreed that the steadily worsening state of the nation's economy justified such a session; in once-hostile areas the feeling ranged between wavering on the repeal issue and out-and-out support. But it was also the near-universal assumption in the silver-producing western states that the metal must not be abandoned. For allies, they could count on the South, where, with opinion divided between the small farmers who opposed repeal and the planters and merchants who urged it, its representatives vowed to fight any legislation that failed to expand the currency.[19]

The choice of August 7 as the date for Congress to reconvene was dictated by Cleveland's personal physician. On the rough draft of Cleveland's message dated June 30 is a note in Lamont's hand: "Written the day the President left Washington on account of illness. . . . The operation was the next day."[20]

48
A twenty-five-year secret

There is, of course, never a "good" time to undergo cancer surgery, be the candidate pauper or prince. For Cleveland, and for the country, the timing could not have been worse. News of the President's life-threatening condition could have further trashed an already battered economy. And waiting in the wings was a Vice President who favored free-silver coinage; a Stevenson succession could have had a fatal effect on not only the cause of repeal but on the nation's economic recovery as well. A total news blackout was clamped on Cleveland's illness. With the exception of a few close advisers and friends like Dan Lamont and Elias Benedict and, of course, the surgical team, all sworn to absolute secrecy, the public—including the cabinet—was not made aware of the facts until a quarter of a century after the event, when Dr. W. W. Keen, one of the attending surgeons, revealed the story in *The Saturday Evening Post.*[21]

What follows is based upon the Keen account.

On April 27, Cleveland attended the International Columbian Naval Review along the Hudson in New York City, held in conjunction with the opening of the Columbian Exposition (1893 World's Fair) in Chicago, which Cleveland attended on May 1. While returning to Washington two days later he experienced some pain on the roof of his mouth, on the left ("my cigar-chewing") side. On May 5, he detected a "rough spot" in the area, but said nothing. Over the next few weeks the pain increased. On June 18, he agreed to an examination by the White House physician, Dr. R. M. O'Reilly. O'Reilly discovered an ulcer "as large as a quarter of a dollar, extending from the molar teeth to within one-third of an inch of the middle line and encroaching slightly on the soft palate, and some diseased bone." A biopsy specimen sent (anonymously) to both U.S. Army pathologists and Dr. William H. Welch of Johns Hopkins revealed it to be a malignancy.

Cleveland's close friend Dr. Joseph D. Bryant, a noted New York surgeon, confirmed the diagnosis. "What do you think it is?" asked Cleveland, showing no apparent concern. Replied Bryant, "Were it in my mouth, I would have it removed at once." Cleveland agreed, but according to Bryant he insisted that under no circumstances would he consent "to a time and place that would not give the best opportunity of avoiding disclosure, and even a suspicion that anything of significance had happened to him. The strong desire to avoid notoriety . . . was dwarfed by the fear he had of the effect on the public of a knowledge of his affliction, and on the financial questions of the time. . . . Had the seriousness of the operation on Mr. Cleveland become known . . . and before his evident good health put to rest the fears of the community and emboldened the sound-money men in Congress, the [Panic of 1893] would have become a rout."

Assuming complete charge of the case, Bryant would not accept responsibility for any delay beyond mid-July if the growth progressed, as was common in such cases. Cleveland set the first day of July as the earliest possible date. Bryant set August 7 as the earliest he could safely return to Washington; and this was presupposing that the cancer had not metastasized and there were no postsurgical complications—in itself a heady presupposition. Lamont was informed of the situation and ordered to plan accordingly. To assure optimum secrecy, it was arranged that the surgery would take place at sea aboard Elias Benedict's yacht *Oneida.*

Bryant assembled a surgical team that included his assistant, Dr. John F. Erdmann; Dr. Keen, one of the nation's leading surgeons, to assist; Dr. E. G. Janeway, a general physician, to administer the anesthesia and monitor the patient; and Dr. Ferdinand Hasbrouck, a dental surgeon. The *Oneida*'s salon was stripped bare and converted into a surgical theater. The crew was told that the President, whom they knew from previous cruises, would be having major dental work while aboard, and that the fresh sea air, elaborate surgical ambience, and team of skilled doctors were necessary against the chance of blood poisoning or any other complication setting in, given the patient's importance to the nation. No suspicions were aroused, not even on the part of the yacht's steward, who was to don a surgical gown and gauze and function as an orderly during the operation.

On the afternoon of June 30, Cleveland slipped out of the White House with Dr. Bryant and Lamont and boarded the private railway car of a friend, which was attached to the four-twenty northbound train. Frances, then seven months pregnant with Esther, had already left for their Cape Cod summer home with Ruth and her nurse. The press was not told the President would be away from Washington but was told the First Lady would. Should word of his having left the city get out, reporters were to be told he had joined his family for a brief rest. (This was the story given to the White House staff and cabinet officers.)

At New York, Cleveland and Dr. Bryant went to the Battery (Lamont went directly to his New York City home) and were ferried out to the *Oneida*, where the surgical crew had already assembled. If he was spotted by anyone and word got around that he was aboard, the public was to be told the President was going to his summer home by sea. This would have held up; Cleveland was known to have logged upward of fifty thousand miles as Benedict's guest. To assure his patient the most perfect possible night's sleep Bryant insisted upon, the yacht lay at anchor in the tranquil waters of the East River's Bellevue Bay—which was overlooked by Bellevue Hospital. The doctors were ordered to keep out of sight, in order to avoid possible recognition by Bellevue personnel. That evening Cleveland sat on the rear deck (out of view of the hospital) smoking one of his customary cigars and chatting with his doctors till nearly midnight. He enjoyed a good night's sleep, without the need of medication.

Next morning there was a leisurely breakfast, in which the party was joined by Lamont and Benedict. Dr. Janeway examined the patient and was satisfied with his findings: little if any arteriosclerosis, pulse within normal limits for a man of his girth, kidneys within normal range. Throughout the morning his mouth was repeatedly irrigated and disinfected. Shortly before noon he was brought to the salon and propped up in a chair that had been lashed to the mast.

What Bryant and Keen most feared was the possible effect of ether on the President. He was fifty-six and extremely corpulent, with a short, thick neck: a perfect candidate for an apoplectic stroke, which could have been brought on by the radical procedure he was now to undergo. It was decided to begin the surgery under nitrous oxide, in the administration of which Dr. Hasbrouck was an authority. Warned by Hasbrouck that he doubted the patient could be kept anesthetized with this so-called "laughing gas" long enough to complete the surgery, Bryant said that when it became absolutely necessary, they would go to ether—and pray!

The *Oneida* backed slowly into the East River on the noon tide and out through Hell Gate onto a mercifully placid Long Island Sound. Benedict and Lamont kept themselves very much in evidence on deck, so that it would appear from shore as well as from passing yachts that the *Oneida,* known for its connection with the President, was simply out on its owner's Fourth of July pleasure cruise. While waiting for the patient to be prepped, Dr. Bryant anxiously told the captain, "If you hit a rock, hit it good and hard, so that we'll all go to the bottom!"[22]

By the use of a cheek retractor, the hour-long operation was performed entirely within Cleveland's mouth. This obviated an external incision; he would be left with a perfectly normal appearance (which helped to keep the surgery a secret for all those years). After Dr. Hasbrouck extracted the patient's two left upper bicuspid teeth, Dr. Bryant, maneuvering what resembled an electric carving knife, removed the entire left upper jaw from the first bicuspid to just beyond the last molar, taking care not to penetrate the orbital palate containing the eye socket unless the cancer had spread to the area. Fortunately, it hadn't.

At that point, midway through the surgery, Dr. Hasbrouck said the nitrous gas would soon be wearing off and the patient would awaken. Dr. O'Reilly administered ether, all offered a brief prayer, and Dr. Bryant resumed. Exposure of the patient's antrum—the large hollow cavity in the upper jaw—revealed a gelatinous mass (later confirmed to be a sarcoma); this was excised, along with as many wild fringe cells as possible. Bleeding was kept to a minimum, thanks to the extravagant use of ice packs, manual pressure, and cauterizing; in all, only six ounces ("a tumblerful") was lost and it was necessary to ligate only one blood vessel.

The operation was concluded at 1:55 P.M. when the large cavity was packed with gauze to arrest any postoperative blood seepage, and the patient, his temperature and pulse mercifully normal, was returned to his cabin. An hour later he came to, in understandable pain; one-sixth of a grain of morphine was administered hypodermically, and he went back to sleep. This was the only narcotic he was given during the entire ordeal. When Cleveland again came around, Bryant and the others took turns reading to him to help pass the time. Next day, he was able to get out of bed and move about briefly as the *Oneida* cruised off the coast at reduced speed. He was not told of the only untoward incident of the entire voyage—one that led a few weeks later to arguably the greatest instance of stonewalling in pre-Watergate American presidential history.

It seems that Dr. Hasbrouck had insisted on being put ashore as soon as the operation was completed. This was vetoed, out of fear that going into harbor might compromise the secret; also, and potentially life-threatening for the patient, was the possibility of the yacht hitting a rough current while docking, which could bring on a hemorrhage, even a stroke. Hasbrouck became irate, claiming his work was finished; besides, he was already two days late to assist in surgery on another very important patient. It was decided to put him ashore at New London.

By July 3, the patient was up and about all day, enjoying the curative sea breezes. Next day, the surgical team, except for Dr. Bryant, was put ashore at Sag Harbor, Long Island, and the *Oneida* set a course for Buzzards Bay, arriving at Gray Gables late the following afternoon. Cleveland walked unassisted—and unnoticed—up the private dock and into the arms of his relieved wife. He was immediately bedded down for the night. Lamont, meanwhile, headed for an unused barn on the estate to deal with a mob of irate reporters who had converged from all over. For five days there had been no word on the President's whereabouts, except that he had left Washington and joined the *Oneida* in New York City. And now with the yacht having docked but no sign of its most illustrious passenger, answers were demanded.

Lamont "confessed" that the President had been treated for two ulcerated teeth and a recurrence of pedal rheumatism, a chronic condition; his doctors had decided to treat him at sea, because of the curative salt air; he was now reuniting with his wife, and would then retire for the night. This seemed to satisfy the reporters. Next morning they went after Lamont again, on learning Vice President Stevenson had heard the President's health was critical and was leaving at once for Cape Cod to investigate personally. Lamont finessed that move by telling them the President was doing fine, the Vice President was not expected at Gray Gables, and, as a matter of fact, he had not been invited. Stevenson took the hint and stayed away.

By the second week in July, Dr. Bryant, having stayed on, was able to take Cleveland out to fish from a rowboat. Bryant's purpose was threefold: the sea air would be therapeutic, the patient's spirits would soar, and the sight of the President enjoying himself at his favorite sport would convince reporters that the Lamont cover story was legitimate. A few days later, Dr. Kasson Gibson, a noted New York orthodontist, came to fashion a plug of vulcanized rubber for the gaping hole in Cleveland's jaw. Cleveland now began work on his message to Congress, but the going was difficult.

On the 17th, Dr. Bryant decided another procedure was indicated to ascertain that all the diseased tissue had been removed and the prosthetic device was not aggravating the wound. Again, Drs. Keen, Janeway, and Erdmann secretly boarded the *Oneida* at New York City. The *Oneida* picked up Cleveland and Bryant at Gray Gables and put out to sea. All suspicious tissue was removed and the entire surface cauterized. The procedure was brief, and Cleveland was returned to Gray Gables, where he recovered quickly.

A few days later, Cleveland received his Attorney General, Olney, whose assistance Lamont had solicited to help write the coinage-repeal message to Congress. Like all his fellow cabinet officers except Lamont, Olney was ignorant of the true extent of Cleveland's medical problems, having bought Lamont's ulcerated-teeth-and-rheumatism tale. He would later recall that Cleveland "had changed a good deal in appearance, and lost a good deal of flesh, and his mouth was so stuffed with antiseptic wads that he could hardly articulate. The first utterance that I understood was something like this: 'My God, Olney, they nearly killed me.' He did not talk much, was very much depressed, and at the same time acted, and I believe felt, as if he did not expect to recover."[23] Cleveland's spirits began to rise as he worked on the speech. (A comparison of Olney's draft with the message as finally sent to Congress shows that the body of the argument is clearly the President's own work, and proves that despite his physical discomfiture and depressed state, he was determined to continue composing his own state papers.)

Cleveland insisted on returning to Washington not later than August 5, as he wanted at least a day or two to buttonhole influential House Democrats prior to Congress's reconvening. This he did, returning to Gray Gables on the 11th to continue his recuperation. He returned to Washington on the 30th, at which time Dr. Bryant pronounced him "All healed."

The entire cover-up was almost blown just as the repeal battle in Congress was being waged. The *Philadelphia Press* in its August 29 edition published a three-column piece from its New York correspondent, "Holland," alleging the true facts of the "Cleveland case": a team of surgeons (all properly identified) had performed radical oral surgery (properly detailed) on the President aboard Elias Benedict's yacht *Oneida* the day after his call was issued for Congress to reconvene. The leak was traced to Dr. Hasbrouck. When he was finally allowed to leave the *Oneida,* it was to assist a pompous society doctor named Leander P. Jones. To account for his lateness, Hasbrouck explained what he had been doing. Jones, indignant at not having been consulted on the President's case, tipped off his friend "Holland," who rushed to interview Hasbrouck. Persuaded that the story was public knowledge and rather proud of his role in it, Hasbrouck filled in the details.

The story was received by the press with incredulity—but quickly led to outright dismissal when those closest to the action told "the real facts." Lamont reiterated the molars-and-rheumatism story, and Dr. Bryant, according to his assistant, Dr. Erdmann, lied more in this regard than in all the rest of his life put together. As for Hasbrouck, he was portrayed as a nasty prevaricator who had been called in for a routine extraction—and dismissed for almost botching it.[24] L. Clarke Davis sent an open letter from Cape Cod to the press saying the story "has a real basis of a toothache"; if it had any other, "Mr. Cleveland's closest friends do not know it." Davis—who in fact was telling the truth as he and most of the others around Cleveland believed it to be—added: "I have seen the President at intervals since he first came to Buzzards Bay this summer, passing hours and days in his company and in the boat fishing with him. I passed all of last Monday with him, fishing, and I have never seen him in better health—never stronger, physically or mentally, and I consider him, in both respects the healthiest man I know."[25]

The stonewalling by Cleveland's men (and that of his friends, like Davis, who didn't know they were in fact doing just that) worked. The story was pooh-poohed by the media, "Holland" was characterized as a scandal-mongering embarrassment to honest journalism, and the President, whose facial features betrayed no evidence of "alleged" surgery, appeared to all observers like the Cleveland of old when he spoke before a Pan-American Congress in Washington a few days later. Not even his enemies tried to exploit what was now accepted as a phony yarn!

49

"I know there is a God, but I do not know his purposes"

Congress reconvened on August 7 and next day received the President's message. Noting that while tariff reform had "lost nothing of its immediate and permanent importance," Cleveland believed that the nation's dire financial condition "should at once and before all other subjects be considered by your honorable body." Then it got to the business at hand, beginning in a good news/bad news mode. The nation's "unfortunate financial plight [was] not the result of untoward conditions related to our natural resources." Neither was it "traceable to any of the afflictions which frequently check national growth and prosperity." In fact, crops were "plenteous," the nation could expect an abundance of "remunerative production and manufacture," and investments and business enterprise seemed secure.

But "suddenly financial distrust and fear [had] sprung up on every side"—a condition "principally chargeable" to the Sherman silver-purchase legislation. In the three years since its passage the government had bought more than $147 million worth of silver, with many of the notes used in its purchase being paid in gold, and there now loomed the threat of an entire substitution of the Treasury's gold supply with the cheaper metal—which, stating the obvious, was not acceptable as a medium for settlement of the nation's international obligations. Were the United States not to join the rest of the world on the gold standard, both our international posture as a recognizable world power and our very existence as a viable trading nation would be irremediably compromised. The American people, Cleveland insisted, were "entitled to a sound and stable currency, and to money recognized as such on every exchange and in every market of the world." Their government had "no right to injure them by financial experiments opposed to the policy and practice of other civilized states." The bottom line: Congress's only course was to repeal the Sherman Act.[26]

The House debate began on the 11th, the same day Cleveland returned to Gray Gables to continue his recuperation, and raged for two weeks, with both sides firing their best oratorical artillery.

Crowded visitors' galleries and packed benches of hastily scribbling news reporters braved the stifling August heat to witness this epic battle that pit the West and most of the South against the East in one of the most dramatic confrontations seen on Capitol Hill since Secession. High point of the debate was the speech by William Jennings Bryan, leader of the silverites. His dramatic stance, complemented by a handsome face, square jaw, and ringing tones, suggested how Demosthenes must have come across to the ancient Greeks. For three hours he mesmerized an audience that included passersby who rushed in from the lobbies, senators who came on the run from their chamber, and a press gallery full to overflowing.

Bryan's remarks were notable more for their delivery than for their content as he reiterated in thundering tones the salmagundi of familiar soft-money themes. There was not enough gold or silver upon which to base exclusively the world's supply of specie. To drive either metal out of circulation must result in a contraction of the currency; demonetizing silver had already led to such a contraction, which had resulted in increasing the value of gold. This in turn increased the burden of fixed debts, at the same time reducing the price of commodities produced by the debtor class. If the United States would only be courageous, it could preserve the parity of gold and silver at the old ratio of 16:1. What was now required was not an annulment of silver coinage, but an avowal of national purpose—something, Bryan added with heavy irony, that would offset the machinations of the capitalist classes and their creditors.

The House was moved by Bryan's rhetoric, though not by his reasoning. When the vote was taken on the 20th, the Wilson repeal passed 239 to 108.

Pleased as Cleveland was over the outcome, it was premature to break out the champagne. The repeal measure must now go to the Senate for consideration. There, for two months, the opposing forces went at each other in an admixture of partisanship, vituperation, and outright character assassination. The long, at times violent struggle reminded the nation anew of the constitutionally mandated anomaly that a small state like pro-silver Nevada, with a population of less than 46,000, had the same voting power in the Senate as a major state like anti-silver New York, with a population of close to six million. Having returned to Washington, Cleveland could observe the debate from close at hand. Except to hope for the best, that was *all* he could do.

Midway through the Senate debate a filibuster by the silver forces, which they were prepared to continue indefinitely, if need be, induced a sense of despair among the opposition. (Cloture as a parliamentary device was not then an option.) Even Cleveland, in a letter to Don Dickinson, admitted to being "very much depressed . . . looking full in the face a loss of popular trust in the Democrat party which means its relegation to the rear again for many years if not its disruption." But he was not about to give up. "[T]he fight will continue until no further fight can be made."

Three days later he wrote Richard Gilder, "I know there is a God, but I do not know his purposes, nor when their results will appear. I know the clouds will roll away, but I do not know who, before that time, will be drowned in their floods." To L. Clarke Davis he confessed he was "growing very tired physically," adding that if he did not believe in God he "should be sick at heart." He wondered if "the good people of the Country will see before it is too late the danger that threatens, not only their financial well-being, but the very foundations upon which their institutions rest." He admitted to sometimes feeling "very despondent and very much deserted. I believe in the people so fully, and things are often so forlorn here, that I want to feel and hear my fellow Countrymen all the time. Are they still about [i.e., standing with] me? I think so often of Martin Luther's 'Here I stand—God help me.' "[27]

Cleveland's despair gave way to wrath on Saturday the 21st, when thirty-seven of the Senate's forty-four Democrats sent a letter to Daniel Vorhees, chairman of the Senate Finance Committee, who was leading the fight for repeal, urging an end to the fight by compromise. Their plan: extend the purchase clauses of the Sherman Act to July 1, 1894; coin the seigniorage of all bullion in the Treasury up to that date; and issue no more notes of a smaller denomination than $10.[28] (Seigniorage is the profit or revenue realized when bullion is purchased at a price less than the value stamped on the metal at its time of coinage.) Even more heinous to Cleveland, the *Washington Post* said that he had abandoned his determination to settle for nothing less than unconditional repeal and was now amenable to the proposed compromise. The *Post* even suggested he bow to the inevitable, on the theory that half a loaf is better than no bread at all, adding that even Carlisle and the rest of the cabinet now favored such a course.

When the cabinet met to deal with the Vorhees letter, Cleveland banged the table with a fist—his customary expression of profound rage—and swore he would not yield an inch. Carlisle quickly wrote a press release avowing that the President "adhered" to the position that the Sherman silver law "should be unconstitutionally repealed." Furthermore, it was "not true that Secretary Carlisle is, or has been, in favor of the compromise which was subscribed to by a number of the Senators on Saturday. He and the other members of the Cabinet are opposed to the measure."[29]

The wave of public sentiment engendered by the statement, and the implication that Cleveland would fight for repeal on his terms even if it meant holding the Congress hostage, triggered collapse of the opposition. On October 30, repeal passed by a vote of 48 to 37. Two days later, by a vote of 194 to 94, the House accepted the Senate version, and the Sherman Silver Purchase Act—and the Great Silver Debate of 1893 it precipitated—became history.

While there is no gainsaying the part played by his men in the trenches, led by Wilson in the House and Vorhees in the Senate, and the efforts of the many newspapers in constantly applying editorial pressure in behalf of repeal, it was generally agreed, in the words of the *New York Times* (November 1, 1893), that "[p]raise is due first to the Administration of Grover Cleveland, which has stood like a rock for unconditional appeal." The *Times* predicted that in treating with the 1893 crisis, history would record "that at that moment, as often before, between the lasting interests of the nation and the cowardice of some, the craft of others, in his own party, the sole barrier was the enlightened conscience and the iron firmness of Mr. Cleveland." Writing retrospectively in *The Atlantic Monthly* when Cleveland left the White House in 1897, Woodrow Wilson said:

> It was the President's victory that the law was at last repealed, and everyone knew it. . . . Until he came on the stage, both parties had dallied and coquetted with the advocates of silver. Now [the] silver men were forced to separate themselves and look their situation in the face, choose which party they should plan to bring under their will and policy, if they could, and no longer camp in the tents of both. Such a stroke settled what the course of Congressional politics should be throughout the four years

of Mr. Cleveland's term, and made it certain that at the end of that term he should either have won his party to himself or lost it altogether.

Sadly, as will be seen, Cleveland fulfilled the second alternative of the Wilson prophecy. For now, it is enough to say that as a result of the silver battle, Cleveland and Bryan emerged as mutually antipathetic leaders of opposing Democratic factions. The rising chief apostle of free silver had been a loyal Cleveland man in '84 and '88, but opposed his '92 nomination, claiming that he "was completely dominated by the banking influence in New York City." While it is true that these interests contributed largely to Cleveland's campaign and election, Bryan's allegation that he sold out to Wall Street to regain the White House is not to be seriously entertained. Imputing to Cleveland such unseemly motives was habitual; so too his consistent refusal to respond in kind. While acknowledging that Bryan and the other silver advocates could be loyal Americans, he emphatically denied they could be real Democrats, having rejected the hard-money policy he had established for the party. The breach among the Democrats over the silver issue helped pave the way for the Republicans to regain a hold on the White House for sixteen years, a hold that would have lasted yet another twenty years if Theodore Roosevelt's vendetta against his handpicked successor, Taft, had not resulted in Wilson's election.

Could Cleveland have foreseen the ultimate result of his stance on hard money versus soft money? And would he have been more flexible on silver coinage if he had? Based on our knowledge of the man and his record, we can assume he would have taken the same track he followed: unconditional repeal. Grover Cleveland was a rarity among politicians, certainly among American Presidents, in that he was more concerned with the economic exigencies of the moment than with the political exigencies of the future. He realized that in allying with the hard-money Republicans he was cutting across his own party lines, thus creating a temporary coalition that imperiled not only his party's discipline but its solidarity as well. He had to suspect—and if he didn't, the professionals would have made sure he did—that his currency ideas would alienate him from so many Democrats, possibly the majority, who were prepared to read him out of the party over the silver issue. But he refused to consider the consequences. The only consequences Cleveland considered were the dangers faced by the nation deriving from the continued debasement of its currency. As President, he felt obliged to terminate that peril.

50

The single most humiliating failure

"My pollertics, like my religion, [are] of a exceedin accomodatin character," wrote the nineteenth-century American wit Artemus Ward. Cleveland would have spared himself incalculable misery if *his* "pollertics" had been more "accomodatin." Nowhere is this more evident than in his attempt to resolve the very issue that won him reelection and became the linchpin of his second presidency. Traveling to the funeral of former President Hayes at Freemont, Ohio, in January 1893, while President-elect ("He was coming to see me," he told Frances, "but he is dead now, and I will go to him"), Cleveland was asked by a reporter if there was to be a tariff revision. "What were we elected for?" he demanded rhetorically. "What were we elected for?"[30]

The 1892 Democratic campaign platform denounced protectionism as fraudulent and the McKinley Tariff as "the culminating atrocity of class legislation" that brought not prosperity but hard times. "If public officers are really the servants of the people," Cleveland told Congress in a pre-inaugural letter, then any failure to give the relief so long awaited would be "sheer recreancy. Nothing should intervene to distract our attention or disturb our effort until this reform is accomplished."[31] Only the need to raise revenue justified the imposition of tariffs at all, he insisted. And current schedules were bringing in more revenue than was required to run the government. Lowering rates would result in less costly necessities, regular employment, a wider market, a settled prosperity. He was sure sufficient revenue could be realized under a new tariff schedule allowing duty-free import of raw materials for American manufacture and lower rates on finished goods.

Repeal of the Sherman Silver Purchase Act was the high point of Cleveland's second administration. His attempt to repeal the McKinley Tariff Act was the low point. It was, in fact, the single most humiliating failure of his entire political career—a failure to which Cleveland himself made a contribution of epic proportions.

As soon as it repealed Sherman, the House, which had to stay in special session while awaiting Senate action on the measure, took up the tariff. Cleveland's point man in Congress, Ways and Means Committee chairman William L. Wilson, began holding daily hearings. Working fast, under Cleveland's prodding, so fast, in fact, that the five Republicans on the committee were treated as if they hadn't bothered to show up for the proceedings, Wilson ended hearings abruptly on September 20 so that he would have a bill ready when Congress convened in regular session. That bill, bearing his name, was introduced on December 19 and pushed along with the speed usually reserved for such legislation as authorizing a hefty raise in Congressional salaries.

Andrew Carnegie, speaking for the business and industrial interests, hoped that the President would "not subject the tariff issue to radical surgery."[32] The Wilson tariff bill, which Cleveland in fact coauthored, would hardly qualify as radical surgery. It was, actually, rather conservative: not totally free-trade, but a step in that direction. Important raw materials like lumber, coal, iron, and wool were placed on the free list, besides sugar, both raw and refined. But only moderate reductions were called for on such manufactured goods as linens, woolens, and cottons, to give domestic manufacturers a competitive edge. Cleveland claimed, and justifiably so, that the bill dealt with the tariff "consistently and as thoroughly as existing conditions permit."

As anticipated, the protectionist press, to use one of our own generation's more colorful clichés, went ballistic. The *New York Tribune* equated the bill with hauling down and spitting upon the American flag, while the *Philadelphia Public Ledger* ululated that it would revolutionize our entire economic system in the most pernicious way imaginable. The radical free-trade press was equally critical; Watterson's *Louisville Courier-Journal*, for one, condemned the measure as "feeble and inadequate."[33]

There was something in the proposed schedule to offend just about every sectional interest. Farmers were infuriated over the free-wool clause: it would reduce profits from their flocks. Mine owners were infuriated over the idea of iron ore being placed on the free list.

The idea of duty-free refined sugar was a grievous blow to the sugar trust, which had been given a subsidy by the McKinley Tariff and wanted retention of the duty on refined sugar, while admitting raw sugar duty-free for processing in its mills.

Wilson held a tight rein as amendments came flying in from all directions. Of the few that succeeded, one stood out in bold relief: inclusion of an income tax provision, added under pressure from the western states. Cleveland had earlier approved a modest tax on corporations, but opposed a tax on personal income as politically counterproductive. Besides, he was concerned that the question of its constitutionality might distract from and thus delay action on the bill. Prodded by Wilson, Cleveland agreed to "a small tax upon incomes derived from certain corporate investments as a necessary corrective to temporary deficiencies." Such an amendment, he reasoned, should assure support from the agrarian states when the bill came to a vote, and acceptable adjustments could be made when it went to the Senate.

What chances the protectionists thought they had of defeating reform in the House were dashed when Richard Croker instructed the Tammany-controlled New York Congressional delegation to back the President. On February 1, 1894, the House voted, after a ringing oration by Wilson that ended with an eloquent appeal for party unity: "This is a roll of freedom, and in the name of honor and in the name of freedom, I summon every Democratic member of the House to inscribe his name upon it."[34] Enough members inscribed their name to pass the measure by a vote of 204 to 140. (The balance of the members were either absent or abstained in order to avoid the record. Most of the eighteen dissenting Democrats were from heavily populated states. The party's Cassandras took proper note.) So busy were the reductionists in congratulating themselves they almost forgot that the Senate had yet to act. And it was there Cleveland was to learn a hypothesis that later generations would come to know as Murphy's Law: if anything can possibly go wrong, it will.

Though the Democrats controlled the Senate, the margin was slender: forty-four Democrats, thirty-eight Republicans, three Populists, and three vacancies. The Populists invariably voted with the Democrats, increasing the margin; but on this issue they parted company.

The Wilson bill, as they saw it, had not gone far enough. The Populists wanted duties slashed on all manufactured imports, on the theory that doing so would best stimulate foreign demand for American agricultural products in which their states led the nation.[35]

As the debate was about to get under way, it was reported that at least six party regulars opposed Cleveland. This proved to be a low estimate. So low, in fact, that what ensued was not so much a formal debate as a self-destructive horror show. The four from West Virginia and Alabama opposed removing duties on free coal and iron ore. Both gentlemen from Louisiana opposed any measure failing to impose a heavy duty on sugar. The Democrats from New Jersey, Ohio, and Pennsylvania had their own reasons for opposing some of the bill's clauses, based on respective state interests. Opposition by the westerners was, of course, identical to that expressed by their colleagues in the House. Despite instructions from Tammany to back the President, David Hill refused to support any bill containing an income tax clause.[36]

Leading the Democratic insurgents—Cleveland referred to them contemptuously as "obstructionists"—was Maryland's Arthur Pue Gorman, a former ally, in whose honor the Senate version of the Wilson bill was called. He believed the party was wrong to push for tariff reform while the country was in the midst of an economic depression; that he was an avowed protectionist, Gorman swore, was beside the point. Compounding Cleveland's predicament, a number of Democrats allowed their personal feelings to becloud their beliefs on the question. When John Tyler Morgan, who fought him fiercely both on the silver purchase and Hawaiian annexation issues, declared, "I hate the ground that man walks on," many colleagues murmured that the gentleman from Alabama should *not* speak only for himself. In the front ranks of the Cleveland-bashers were the spoilsmen who hated him for his refusal to cut them in on patronage, and those to whom the President was not to be forgiven for refusing to put their special interests above the nation's. Because he had by now disbursed just about all of his patronage capital in bringing fractious senators into line on the currency battle, threats that he might try this tactic in the tariff battle were dismissed out of hand.

Cleveland's feelings about the Senate at this point in time are suggested by a joke then making the rounds of Washington.

It seems that one night he was roused from a deep sleep by Frances whispering frantically, "Wake up, Grover, wake up! There are robbers in the house."

Replied Grover: "I think you are mistaken, my dear. There are no robbers in the House—but there are lots in the Senate!"

A less apocryphal indication of Cleveland's state of mind is reflected in remarks to a friend: "I still believe that right will win, but I do not now believe that all who loudly proclaimed their desire for better things were in earnest. At any rate, not a few of them are doing excellent service in the cause of the worst possible political methods, and are aiding in bringing about the worst and most dangerous political situation. . . ."[37]

Even before debate on the Gorman measure got under way, the Senate's belligerence toward Cleveland was magnified by one of its most savage confrontations with any President over a Supreme Court nomination. When Justice Samuel Blatchford died in the summer of 1893, Cleveland nominated as his successor William Butler Hornblower, a highly respected New York attorney. It was said Hornblower had but one enemy, his state's senior senator, David Hill. If so, that one was enough. Two years before, a Hill crony, Isaac H. Maynard, as state deputy attorney general, had filched public records to destroy an election return from Dutchess County, assuring the Democrats control of the state senate. Hornblower was appointed to a committee named by the state bar association to investigate. It found Maynard guilty of "one of the gravest [transgressions] known to the law." When Maynard later sought election to the state's highest court, the New York Court of Appeals (the electorate had already rejected him once before), he lost by a decisive plurality. Hill saw this as a crushing rebuke not only to Maynard but to himself. When Hornblower came up for confirmation, Hill spitefully corralled enough senators to defeat it.

The nomination doubtless would have succeeded if only Cleveland had been willing to lobby a number of high-tariff senators who thought Hornblower was a creditable candidate. Even several western Democrats would have honored a personal request by the President to support Hornblower despite their split with him over silver coinage. Judiciary Committee chairman Pugh of Alabama was justifiably incensed that he had not been consulted by the President either before or after the nomination went to the Senate. But, as Hornblower later wrote, "It was characteristic of Mr. Cleveland not only to disdain the arts of conciliation but also to ignore the personal elements in the political world."[38]

Hornblower's (and Cleveland's) defeat was interpreted by the press and public alike as a tacit challenge to Cleveland from Hill not to nominate for the Supreme Court any man who had opposed his friend Maynard simply because he had perpetrated a heinous felony that would have bought jail time for someone less politically connected. Others who voted against the nomination sent a tacit message of their own: henceforth, in submitting a candidate for the High Court, the President must respect the traditional Rule of Senatorial Courtesy.

The Independents, more loyal to Cleveland than his own party, urged that he meet Hill's challenge with defiance. He did just that. Hill let it be known he would support the nomination of Rufus W. Peckham, of the New York Court of Appeals. Cleveland knew Peckham well from his Albany days; he had vowed to "get you down to Washington yet, Rufus." His nomination would have resolved the issue and put a capable man on the bench. But Cleveland refused on principle to cut a deal with Hill. He nominated Wheeler H. Peckham, Rufus's brother, instead!

Surely Cleveland knew that Wheeler Peckham had played an even more significant part than Hornblower in blocking Hill's attempt to elevate Maynard to New York's highest court; that as president of the bar association it was he who appointed the committee that investigated Maynard, of which he was an *ex officio* member; and that he had campaigned vigorously against the nomination and election to the Senate of Hill, whom he abhorred.

If Cleveland thought he could shame Hill into backing down, he was carrying naiveté to Himalayan heights. Hill told the press Peckham was a man of many prejudices, and, what is more, was totally lacking in any judicial experience or temperament. This was all rubbish, of course. But it led many to doubt Cleveland's ability—or willingness—to select only the best-qualified men for the Supreme Court.

Next, to enlist the support of Republican senators Lodge and Hoar of Massachusetts, who had voted for Hornblower's nomination, Hill made a secret deal by which he agreed to furnish enough votes on the Democratic side to defeat an enemy of theirs for a foreign service post. Hill then schemed with southern and western Democrats who favored Peckham but resented Cleveland over the silver coinage repeal.[39] Few of them had any use for Hill; like the Republicans, they just wanted to stick it to the President. The Peckham confirmation failed by ten votes. (Hornblower's had failed by six.)

At Carl Schurz's suggestion, Cleveland nominated Frederic Coudert, convinced he would be confirmed despite his having served on the committee that investigated Maynard. But before Hill could raise a proper fuss, Coudert declined to accept, for business reasons. At this point, Cleveland caved in. He named Edward D. White of Louisiana, one of his most vocal opponents on the tariff issue. Senate confirmation was unanimous.

Did Cleveland err, had he in fact taken temporary leave of his senses, in settling for White? Not at all. He realized that a prolonged nomination fight could exacerbate the damage to his relations with Congress created by the currency fight. Also, he hoped that naming White to the Court would weaken the high-tariff bloc. Where Cleveland erred was in mishandling the Hornblower nomination, following it up with one he had to have known would never fly. How different it might have been if he "had only allowed us from the beginning to go to Senators and mollify them," remarked Secretary of State Gresham; "how much better it would have been!"[40]

A year and a half later, when Justice Howell Jackson died, Cleveland again wanted to nominate Hornblower. But Hornblower removed himself from consideration, as did (again) Coudert, Cleveland's backup choice. He next named Rufus W. Peckham, and to assure himself that Hill would not use this as an excuse to stage another intraparty ruckus, wrote him a tactful, almost obsequious letter: "Have you any desire as to the time of sending in the nomination? . . . I would be glad to have him [confirmed] very early if you could find it consistent and agreeable to pave the way for it."[41] Hill found it very consistent and agreeable. He had, it will be recalled, wanted Rufus Peckham on the Court in the first place! Beyond that, thanks to Hill's machinations and the President's mishandling of the high court nominations, the country bore witness to a victory for "Senatorial Courtesy"—and a humiliating rout for Grover Cleveland.

For five months the Senate did not so much debate the Gorman tariff reform bill as transform it into what one disgusted congressman called "a free-lunch counter" where each member could "walk up and help yourself." Amendment followed amendment, as every member sought to write his own or his state's special interests into the final product. The total rose to an incredible 634 when on July 3, the measure passed by a vote of 39 to 34. (There were twelve abstentions; the three vacancies had not yet been filled.) The duty-free raw material idea, which lay at the heart of Cleveland's plan, had been practically destroyed. Thus did the Senate approach the task of tariff revision, "not to subordinate personal desires and ambitions to the general good, but to subordinate the general good to personal desires and ambitions. In a spirit of live and let live, each Senator was allowed his slice, and as a result the Wilson Bill lost its character so shamelessly as to become almost unrecognizable."[42]

All that Cleveland could hope for now was that when the House (Wilson) and Senate (Gorman) versions went to the Committee on Conference the two chambers would, through compromise, fashion an acceptable piece of tariff reform legislation he and the country could live with. At his urging, the House conferees went on the attack. But there was no budging the Gorman faction. On July 18, with the public now disgusted, the Republicans now jubilant, and the Democrats now in complete disarray, Cleveland was told that the joint committee was unable to reach an acceptable compromise on the bill's final shape.

In hopes of setting off a firecracker under the obstructionists, he was persuaded by Wilson to make public a letter he had written the congressman before the Senate version passed. What was intended as a firecracker of the last resort turned out to be a bomb of the first magnitude. "Every true Democrat and every sincere reformer," he wrote, "knows that the bill in its present form and as it will be submitted to the [House-Senate] conference falls far short of the consummation for which we have long labored. . . . [O]ur abandonment of the cause of the principles upon which it rests mean party perfidy and party dishonor."[43]

Viewing the President's remarks as a vicious attack on the obstructionists's integrity as gentlemen and party loyalists, Gorman launched the most bellicose attack ever delivered on the Senate floor by a member against the leader of his own party. The letter was the fruit of deception and deceit, he bellowed. His Democrats had labored beyond the call of duty in their attempt to achieve an equitable tariff revision against an awesome bloc of Republican opposition. (Actually, a number of Republicans had supported some form of tariff reduction.) What is more, their amendments had been "as well known to [the President] as to me." While neither Cleveland nor his Treasury Secretary was "in love with all the provisions of these amendments, from no quarter, high or low, from the President through the Cabinet, or by any member of this body, was it ever suggested or intimated that there was any violation of Democratic principles!"

Unable to keep a reign on his emotions, Gorman stormed up and down the aisle as he denounced Cleveland, declaring himself unable to remain silent under so abhorrent an imputation of his and his colleagues' party loyalty as that contained in the letter to Wilson. He reminded the President, and the world, that what he dared call "obstructionists" were in fact honorable men—and honorable Democrats—who had fought for tariff reform when "cowards in high places dared not show their heads." Gorman ended by accusing Cleveland of "violating the spirit of the Constitution."[44]

Cleveland had meant the letter as a bid for party support at the expense of the obstructionists—and he succeeded. Democratic state conventions in Massachusetts, Florida, Indiana, and Iowa passed resolutions endorsing its sentiments. Public meetings for that purpose were held in Maryland (even though, or perhaps because, it was Gorman's home state). Eastern papers, led by the *Baltimore Sun* and *New York Herald,* lauded in extravagant terms the letter and its author. But all the public remonstrances it evoked against the high-duty crowd were for naught.

The letter's timing was simply terrible. Had he written it in February, when the Democrats first caucused, popular opinion might have had an influence on the legislators. Even in May or early June, when he learned the bill was in trouble, a dramatic appeal for public support might have worked. But coming after the Gorman faction inflicted their havoc, remonstrances had no effect. On August 16, with the joint-chamber conference hopelessly deadlocked, Wilson advised Cleveland that what they had now was the best they could hope for. Two days later the Wilson-Gorman Tariff Act went to a sorely disappointed President for his signature. Simply stated, it contained too much Gorman and not enough Wilson.[45]

There is no denying that Cleveland faced formidable odds in seeking tariff reform. But there is also no denying that if he had heeded the advice of those who urged that he deal with the tariff first, instead of giving priority to the silver issue, his ramming of the Sherman Act repeal through Congress would not have made him so many enemies in his own party at a time when he desperately needed every friend he could get. The fight over tariff reform bared three fatal flaws in Grover Cleveland's political persona: an ignorance of how to go for his opponents' Achilles' heel, an ignorance of the most advantageous moment to solicit public sentiment and use it as an efficacious weapon, and a sporadic political myopia.

Cleveland was in a quandary. Could he in all good conscience sign a bill he had so scathingly condemned? Conversely, could he veto it, thereby exposing his party to ridicule—and, worse, leaving open the probability that the McKinley Tariff would remain on the books? He wrestled with the decision for more than a month, during which he came down with an attack of malarial fever and went to Gray Gables to recuperate, returning to Washington on August 22. During that time he was blitzed with pleas from his friends and associates, led by Carlisle, that he sign. There was, of course, a third constitutional alternative, the pocket veto: hold the bill ten days and let it become law without his signature. This would preclude both the condemnation a veto might earn him and the embarrassment of a probable veto override, yet leave him on record as having opposed the measure. It was the course he took.

In a long letter to one of his champions in Congress, Cleveland defended his decision to let Wilson-Gorman become law without his signature. Despite "all its vicissitudes and all the bad treatment it received at the hands of pretended friends," it represented "a vast improvement to existing conditions." It would "certainly lighten many tariff burdens that now rest heavily upon the people." it was "not only a barrier against the return of mad protection," It was "a vantage ground from which must be waged further aggressive operations against protected monopoly and governmental favoritism." Then, in one of the several eloquent passages that set this letter apart among the bulk of his epistolary efforts over a lifetime, he said:

> I take my place with the rank and file of the Democratic party who believe in tariff reform and who know what it is, who refuse to accept the results embodied in this bill as the close of the war, who are not blinded to the fact that the livery of Democratic tar-

> iff reform has been stolen and worn in the service of Republican protection, and who have marked the places where the deadly blight of treason has blasted the counsels of the brave in their hour of might.

Going on to castigate "the trusts and combinations—the communism of pelf—whose machinations have prevented us from reaching the success we deserved, should not be forgotten nor forgiven," he closed with the solemn promise that tariff reform would not be settled "until it is honestly and fairly settled in the interest and to the benefit of a patient and long suffering people."[46]

Promises notwithstanding, the battle begun nine years previously was over for Cleveland, and not on his terms. And he knew it. The fight for an evenhanded corrective to the calamitous McKinley Tariff would not be raised again during his presidency. The nation was still subject to great distress emanating from the Panic of 1893, with business and industry dangerously close to depletion. And the weakened Democratic party was critically divided.

51

The Chicago Pullman Strike of '94

On the same day he wrote the letter to Wilson that so provoked the Democrats in Congress, Cleveland took the first step toward what was to provoke more controversy than any other event of his second term. This was his handling of the gravest clash between capital and labor the country had yet known—the great Chicago Pullman Strike of '94, which earned him more vilification by organized labor than suffered by any previous President. Overlooked by those, including the majority of historians, who persist in making of him one of labor's all-time paradigmatic antagonists, is that he was sensitive to and empathetic with the labor movement's plight and ambitions. But he would not let sensitivity and empathy stop him from ensuring the maintenance of law and order. Just as he refused to be branded a tool of the capitalist class, so did he refuse to court labor's vote if it meant acting against the best interests of the nation as a whole.

In acting as he did, Cleveland was not setting precedent. Court injunctions in labor disputes had been used by earlier Presidents, and federal troops had been called out previously to subdue violence by railroad strikers; President Hayes did so in 1877. But while Hayes waited until asked by the local authorities before dispatching troops, Cleveland did so before being asked, and despite pleas from local officials that he not do so.

There is ample justification for laying the lion's share of blame at the feet of Attorney General Richard Olney. Having with characteristic common sense decided to move decisively to end the quickly spreading strike, Cleveland was right to follow the advice of the man he had made the nation's chief law enforcement officer. Too, Cleveland was so preoccupied with the ongoing tariff battle in Congress he thought it prudent to leave all legal details in more capable hands. Unfortunately, the strategy Olney devised was short on candor, lacking in caution, and deficient in objectivity. Being a strict constitutionalist, Cleveland did not accept his Attorney General's counsel without demur. But accept it he did. And for that he cannot escape accountability. To his credit, Cleveland assumed complete blame. In his own account of the strike, *Presidential Problems,* he never once questions Olney's behavior in the crisis. But then, Monday-morning quarterbacking was not Cleveland's style.

The Pullman Palace Car Company, makers and operators of sleeping and parlor cars for most of the nation's railroads, provided a village in suburban Chicago for its more than four thousand employees and their families that featured red-brick cottages, well-paved streets, excellent sanitary arrangements, and beautiful parks and lakes. The company might have been entitled to the gratitude it expected from its employees but for the underlying discontent caused partly by George Pullman's attitude that he was benevolently bestowing gratis what in fact his employees were paying for—and paying for dearly. The rents charged in "Happy Pullman Town" were upward of 25 percent higher than comparable rents elsewhere in the Chicago area. If proof is wanted that Pullman was not quite the benefactor he considered himself, we have the word of no less a representative of corporate interests than Mark Hanna: "Oh, hell! Go and live in Pullman and find out how much [he] gets sellin' city water and gas ten percent higher to those poor folks."[47]

Hanna was not alone in his low opinion of Pullman. The *Chicago Times,* which supported the strike ("absolutely justifiable"), described him as a "cold-hearted, cold-blooded autocrat [who] wears no mask [and whose] character is reflected in his countenance. A pair of small piggish eyes gleam out from above puffed cheeks, and the glitter of avarice is plainly apparent from their depths." Other papers and journals were no less critical. *The North American Review* included Pullman in its list of patricians who did not fight for their country's liberties "but for its boodle; their octopus grip is extending over every branch of industry; a plutocracy which controls the price of the bread we eat, the price of the sugar that sweetens our cup, the price of the oil that lights our way, the price of the very coffins in which we are finally buried."[48]

Throughout the winter of 1893–94, Pullman reduced wages by 25 percent incrementally, maintaining that such a move was necessitated by the decline in business due to the ongoing Panic of '93. Yet the company was enjoying excellent financial health. Its undivided surplus profits totaled $25 million; in the previous year it had distributed over $2.5 million in dividends on a capital of $36 million. Later asked by federal investigators if he did not think it would have been wise to give his employees a fair living wage out of these funds, Pullman replied, "I do not. It would have amounted to a gift of money to these men; it was simply a matter of business."[49]

Employees pleaded for at least a reduction in their rents. They were refused, despite Pullman's knowledge that after paying them, the typical family was left with about seventy-six cents a day for food and clothing. In May, a committee representing the employees requested that either wages be raised or rents reduced. Pullman not only refused, he fired three of the petitioners. A few days later, five-sixths of the workers struck in protest. The company's response was to lay off the loyal one-sixth and close up shop.

The strike would have attracted little attention had it been localized. But two powerful national railway organizations were involved, one representing labor, the other management. Approximately four thousand of the workers belonged to the American Railway Union, a radical alliance founded a year before by men disgruntled with all existing railroad alliances. Its leader was Eugene V. Debs, arguably the most morally principled leader in the history of American trade unionism. Within the year membership totaled 150,000, in 465 locals. In early June, its national convention called for arbitration in the

Pullman dispute. When management rejected the idea, the ARU voted to boycott and strike against all Pullman cars, effective June 26.

Eight years before, the heads of twenty-four railroads that either centered or terminated in Chicago had organized the General Managers' Association. With twenty-four lines extending over some 41,000 miles of rails in the Midwest, its initial purpose was to coordinate their activities in various fields. At first the GMA paid little attention to labor. When the ARU issued its strike call, the GMA took Pullman's side. As the strike rapidly spread beyond Chicago, a federal inquiry concluded that capital was "determined to crush the strike rather than accept any peaceable solution through conciliation, arbitration or otherwise."[50]

Within days, twenty thousand men had walked out in Chicago, and an additional forty thousand farther west. Movement of the mails was blocked on the Southern Pacific lines in California, and similar complaints were coming in from other areas of the West. Cleveland directed Olney to wire all U.S. district attorneys in California to "see that the passage of regular trains carrying United States mails . . . is not obstructed" and to "procure warrants or any other available process from United States courts against any and all persons engaged in such obstructions."[51]

As June ebbed, the situation worsened; the Debs-led ARU boycott was proving effective. When efforts were made to move blocked trains, attendants quit in a body. On June 29, freight traffic in and out of Chicago was half paralyzed; next day it was almost at a standstill. Debs issued strict guidelines for all workers "against being a party to any violation of law—municipal, State or national—during the existing difficulties." Law and order must be respected, and any member who committed violence in any form "should be promptly arrested and punished, and we should be the first to apprehend the miscreant and bring him to justice." The strikers "must triumph as law-abiding citizens or not at all."

Debs had learned on reliable authority that "thugs and toughs have been employed to create trouble, so as to prejudice the public against our cause. The scoundrels should be made in every case to pay the full penalty of the law." The railroads, he reminded his men, had the right to hire replacements for the strikers: "Our men have the right to quit, but their right ends there. Other men have the right to take their places, whatever the propriety of so doing may be." All strikers must "keep away from railroad yards or rights of way, or other places where large crowds congregate [and] where there is any likelihood of being an outbreak." Debs ended his proclamation by urging that workers "[r]espect the law, conduct ourselves as becomes men, and our cause shall be crowned with success."[52]

Debs's hopes that the GMA might be defeated by an entirely peaceful strike were dashed on June 29 when a thousand strikers and supporters stopped the Chicago & Erie's New York Limited at Hammond, Indiana, and forced the crew to detach two Pullman cars. Next day, at Chicago, crowds temporarily delayed two express trains on the Illinois Central and Panhandle lines.

Who were those "thugs and toughs" that Debs claimed had been hired by the railway managers to make trouble? Twelve million people had come to Chicago for the Columbian Exposition. When it was over and the visitors went home, they left behind an army of 100,000 itinerant laborers, vagabonds, and lawless adventurers who had come to the fair and been left stranded there by the depression. By the winter of 1893–94 they were walking the streets in search of work, their hapless situation intensified by the devastated economy. Soup kitchens and other charity ventures by a concerned Chicago citizenry helped to relieve the misery; when winter set in, many of the homeless were allowed to sleep nights on the floors of City Hall. But such civic gestures, while noble, were ineffectual. Many of the unfortunates were willing to sell their services to the highest bidder—and labor could not match capital's bid.

By the beginning of July, most freight traffic into and out of the West was paralyzed, and mass demonstrations in and around Chicago raised real fear that it was but a matter of time before uncontrollable violence became the order of the day. The *Chicago Tribune* led the conservative press in scare headlines on the order of "Debs Is a Dictator"; "Mob Is in Control"; "Mob Bent on Ruin—Debs Strikers Begin Work on Destruction." The *Inter Ocean* kicked in with gems like "Unparalleled Scenes of Riot Terror and Pillage" and "Anarchy Is Rampant." The *Washington Post*, in a story datelined Chicago, acted responsibly in saying, "The situation tonight is more alarming than at any time since the trouble began," but then went on irresponsibly:

> War of the bloodiest kind in Chicago is imminent, and before tomorrow goes by the railroad lines and yards may be turned

> into battlefields strewn with hundreds of dead and wounded. Lawlessness of the most violent kind was the order of things today. . . . [A]narchists and socialist element made up largely of the unemployed, were preparing to blow up the south end of the federal building and take possession of the millions of money stored in the treasury vaults.

The *New York Times* urged that all workers who quit their jobs in sympathy for the strikers be declared "criminals," condemned Debs as a "lawbreaker at large, an enemy of the human race [who] should be jailed," and demanded that the actions "his bad teaching has engendered must be squelched." *Harper's Weekly* declared that in attempting to break the strike "the nation is fighting for its own existence." Until "the rebellion [is] suppressed all differences of opinion concerning its origin, or the merits of the parties to the dispute out of which it grew, [are] irrelevant to the issue of the hour, and must await the future."

While many clergymen expressed sympathy for the strikers and their aims, the Rev. Herrick Johnson of Chicago's Presbyterian Theological Seminary declared with an evident thirst for blood, preferably strikers' blood, "The time has come when forbearance has ceased to be a virtue. There must be some shooting, men must be killed, and then there will be an end to this defiance of law and destruction of property. Violence must be met by violence. The soldiers must use their guns. They must shoot to kill." Numerous otherwise responsible people agreed.[53]

Cleveland saw it as his constitutional obligation, complemented by applicable statutes, to guarantee the unobstructed movement of the mails and to maintain interstate commerce. Not so easily defined was the question of how much right the government had to interfere with the strikers. It could—and must—deal with them severely if they resorted to lawless obstruction. But what constituted lawless obstruction? The liberal view: nothing short of outright violence and rioting. The reactionary view: the mere act of inciting men to strike. Attorney General Olney took the reactionary view, which he now set about to impose upon the President.

Olney's attitude toward the strikers was rooted in a fervent prejudice against anyone who would deny property rights, particularly corporation rights. He was outraged that strikers would dare tie up the nation's transportation system; and being a man who could disown his favorite child simply for marrying a dentist he disliked, Olney was resolved to do more apropos his sense of outrage than merely express it. Though the strike did not affect traffic east of Chicago, it took no great leap of the imagination for him to prophesy the ripple effect on the rest of the nation unless federal action—if need be, of draconian magnitude—were taken at once. "It seemed clear," he later remarked, "that whatever was done should be done at Chicago because that was the center and headquarters of the strike and that, *if smashed there* [emphasis in the original], it would collapse everywhere else."[54]

Were the decision his alone, Olney would have sent federal troops into Chicago without waiting for action by the courts. But knowing Cleveland would act only in support of the appropriate judicial tribunals, he decided on a bold tripartite plan: have the courts issue an injunction against the strikers, have a federal judge and the chief marshal on the scene attest that the injunction could not be enforced, and then persuade Cleveland to send troops to the rescue of the courts.

As a first step, Olney appointed a special counsel to aid the U.S. attorney in Chicago. Under the circumstances, it was an extraordinary appointment. He asked the GMA to suggest a candidate, they suggested Edwin Walker, counsel for the Chicago, Milwaukee & St. Paul, and Olney named him two hours later.[55] Illinois governor John Altgeld objected strenuously to the appointment, since it suggested to the strikers that the government was siding with the railroad owners.

Despite Altgeld's guarantee that he was capable of handling the situation—he had not yet deemed it necessary to call out the militia—Cleveland responded to the owners' call for protection of their property by authorizing the swearing-in of 3,600 special deputies. Chosen, armed, and paid for by the GMA, they were essentially armed forces of the railroads operating under the authority of the federal government. Chicago's superintendent of police described them, for the most part, as a motley band of "worthless and drunken," "thugs, thieves, and exconvicts."[56] Their presence led to further outbreaks by strikers in the Chicago area.

On the last day of June, the superintendent of the Railway Mail Service at Chicago telegraphed his superiors at Washington that despite the horror stories running daily in the conservative press, "[no] mails have accumulated at Chicago so far. All regular mail trains are running nearly on time with a few slight exceptions." Nevertheless, Thomas E. Milchrist, the U.S. attorney for Chicago, wired Olney, "[v]iolent interference with transportation imminent," and requested that the federal marshal on the scene be told "to place special deputies upon all mail trains, with orders to protect the mails." Olney wired back, "[It seems] to me advisable not merely to rely on warrants against persons actually guilty of the offense of obstructing United States mails, but to go into a court of equity and secure restraining orders which shall have the effect of preventing any attempt to commit the offense. I feel that the true way of dealing with the matter is by a force which is overwhelming and prevents any attempt at resistance."[57] By that "force," Olney meant the United States Army. He was desperate to give Cleveland an excuse to intervene.

Though he opposed Olney's suggestion to dispatch troops without being so requested by Altgeld, Cleveland did go along on an injunction. Issued on July 2, it ordered Debs and all other persons involved "absolutely to desist and refrain from in any way or manner interfering with, hindering, obstructing, or stopping any of the business of any of the [involved] railroads as common carriers of passengers and freight between or among a number of States . . . and from in any way or manner interfering with, hindering, obstructing or stopping any trains carrying the mail." Once arrested, the strikers were subject to peremptory jailing, without trial.[58]

For the railway managers, the injunction could not have come soon enough. Just that day, movement of freight trains in and out of Chicago was almost at a standstill, and traffic was disrupted all over the Northwest. The grain trade was paralyzed. Chicago meat-packing houses had to close down, as livestock were being unloaded throughout the upper Mississippi Valley. Factories were shutting down for lack of coal, throwing thousands out of work. Hospitals were running short of ice. Governor Altgeld had to order state troops to Danville, Decatur, and Cairo to liberate trains of the Wabash, Chicago & Eastern Illinois and the Illinois Central lines. At Sacramento, California, a crowd of three thousand halted all railway traffic. In the Chicago area the strike seemed close to achieving its goals. Passenger trains were few and often came in hours late; suburban traffic was in chaos. "The railway managers were completely defeated," Debs later said of the situation just before the injunction was issued. "Their immediate resources were exhausted, their properties were paralyzed, and they were unable to operate their trains."[59]

As yet, there was no violence in Chicago. But in the small town of Blue Island midway between there and Joliet, a mob materialized along the Rock Island tracks—and unwittingly played into Olney's hand. When federal marshal Arnold appeared, escorted by 125 deputies, to read the injunction and order them to disband, the mob reacted by capsizing the railway cars and otherwise impeding traffic. A deputy was stabbed, and Arnold was rolled in the dirt (more to embarrass than harm him). He at once telegraphed Olney: "Have read the order of the court to the rioters here and they simply hoot at it. . . . We have had a desperate time here all day and our force is inadequate. In my judgment it is impossible to move trains without having the Fifteenth Infantry from Fort Sheridan moved here at once. There are 2,000 rioters here and more coming. Mail trains are in great danger."

In fact, the Blue Island strikers refrained from violence, no doubt because of it the presence of federal marshals and rumors, assumedly spread by the marshals, that federal troops were on the way. Calm also settled over Chicago. Mayor Hopkins later testified to having been assured by the officials of the different railroads "that they received the most efficient protection they had ever received during similar troubles."[60]

Olney was not happy. He wanted—he needed—a stronger demand for dispatching federal troops, hinting as much in a wire to Milchrist on July 3; he said that if it became necessary to send in troops, "they will be used promptly and decisively upon the justifying facts being certified to me. In such case, if practicable, let [special counsel] Walker and [Marshal] Arnold and [a] United States Judge join in statement as to the exigency."

Milchrist took the hint. Within the hour, Olney received a wire signed by Arnold and endorsed by Milchrist, Walker, and Judge P. S. Grosscup, expressing the belief that "no force less than the regular troops of the United States can procure the passage of the mail trains or enforce the orders of the Court." It was his "judgment" that they "should be here at the earliest possible moment. An emergency has arisen for their presence in the city."[61]

The dispatch reeks of deception and delusion. It speaks of a mob "in the city"—i.e., Chicago—when it in fact refers to the Blue Island disorders far from Chicago's city limits. Contradicting Mayor Hopkins's evaluation, it speaks of turbulence which while grave on July 2 had subsided by the next day, as later confirmed by the press and Chicago police and civic officials. It contends that only federal troops could restore order, even though state and local militiamen had proved effective at Cairo, Danville, and Decatur. And it suggests that men in other trades were quitting their jobs, which was not true, and makes the supposition that they would join the strike, which had no basis in fact.

Still, it was the certification of emergency Olney so eagerly wanted. He rushed at once to the White House, where the cabinet was meeting. Earlier that day, General Nelson Miles, commander of the Western Department, had counseled that federal troops *not* yet be dispatched. Gresham, a longtime Chicago resident, agreed, as did Lamont, who was already on record against intervention. But opposition in the cabinet evaporated after Olney burst in waving the Arnold telegram as if it were a winning lottery ticket. At Cleveland's insistence, Lamont went at once to the War Department (it was now three-thirty in the afternoon) and telegraphed orders from the President that troops stationed at Fort Sheridan be sent into Chicago.

Early next morning—as the United States celebrated its 118th birthday—troops composed of infantry, artillery, and cavalry deployed at three points: the Chicago stockyards, Grand Crossing, and Blue Island. Reporters calling at Olney's office that day noted his pleasure at this latest turn of events. He wanted them to know he had just wired Milchrist to convene a grand jury as soon as possible to indict Debs and his lieutenants. "We have been brought to the ragged edge of anarchy," he said in what may have been either a euphoric or manic state; "it is time to see whether the law is sufficiently strong to prevent this condition of affairs. If not, the sooner we know it the better, that it may be changed."[62]

Next day, Altgeld sent a long wire of protest. Had the facts been "correctly presented" to the President, he would not have sent in the troops; such action was "entirely unnecessary and, as it seems to me, unjustifiable." The State of Illinois was "able to take care of itself," local officials were fully "able to handle the situation." Some of the railroads were "paralyzed," the governor admitted, but "not by reason of obstructions, but because they cannot get men to operate their trains." There were, he conceded, "a few local disturbances, but nothing that seriously interfered with the administration of justice, or that could not be easily controlled by the local or state authorities." Asking for the army's "immediate withdrawal," Altgeld promised that should the situation at any time become so serious that his state militia could not check it, he would "promptly and freely ask for federal assistance."

Cleveland wired back that the troops were sent "in strict accordance with the Constitution and laws of the United States, upon the demand of the Postoffice Department that obstruction of the mails should be removed, and upon the representations of the judicial officers of the United States that the process of the federal courts could not be executed through the ordinary means, and upon competent proof that conspiracies existed against commerce between the States"—which were "clearly within the province of federal authority."

Altgeld replied immediately, reminding the President that he was not legally justified in sending in federal troops without their having been requested. Cleveland's response: he was "still persuaded" he had "neither transcended my authority nor duty in the emergency that confronts us," and until "active efforts" were undertaken by all local authorities "to restore obedience to law and to protect life and property," the troops would to remain.[63]

For the next few days, Cleveland barely left his desk, speaking often and at length with General Miles over a direct telephone wire set up between the White House and Chicago, as cabinet officers and army leaders involved in the crisis came and went until all hours of the morning.

The term "crisis" hardly overstates the case. Trains were forced to a halt by mobs, who now took to burning boxcars by the hundreds, smashing switches, and driving signalmen from their towers (though efforts were made not to interfere with passenger cars). In Chicago, six large buildings at the Exposition grounds were put to the torch. At the height of the disorders, sounds of pistol shots quickly transformed empty streets into rivers of rioters running amok. Also running amok, so to say, were rumors to the effect that elegant department stores and the homes of their millionaire patrons were about to be, or were in fact being, looted. "Mob Rule Supreme" and "Fired by the Mob:

Chicago at the Mercy of the Incendiary's Torch" typified the news headlines.

After a sporadic exchange of gunfire over two days between mob and military, both sides met in bloody collision. On July 6, General Miles wired Lamont at the War Department of lawlessness along the railway lines: hundreds of cars and buildings were afire, and transportation was being obstructed in various ways, including the cutting of telegraph lines. Army troops had dispersed mobs at Chicago and were moving along the Rock Island line to support a group of federal marshals making arrests for violation of the July 2 injunction. Thirteen of the twenty-three lines that centered on Chicago were entirely obstructed. The remaining ten were able to run only mail and passenger trains, many of which were stoned and fired upon by mobs as they moved in and out of Chicago. One engineer was killed, the first such casualty.

After positioning the troops already in Chicago and along some of the lines, Miles moved the balance of his command—eight companies of infantry, a battery of artillery, and one troop of cavalry—into bivouac in Lake Front Park, "ready for any emergency and to protect Government buildings and property." He informed Cleveland that his men had dispersed a mob firing freight cars near the stockyards, where all lines converged. Other troops had dispersed a mob that captured a mail train.[64]

While Miles was sending his latest dispatch, Governor Altgeld ordered state militia into the city, at the request of Mayor Hopkins; by sundown approximately five thousand were in position. Next morning, on the basis of the Miles dispatch, Cleveland proclaimed martial law in Chicago. All unlawful gatherings were ordered "to disperse and retire peaceably to their respective abodes on or before twelve o'clock noon" of the following day; there would be "no vacillation in the decisive treatment of the guilty."[65]

A day later, with the conflict by now having spread as far west as the Pacific Coast, south to the Mexican border, and north to the Canadian border, the President issued a second proclamation ordering "all good people at certain points and places within the States of North Dakota, Montana, Idaho, Washington, Wyoming, Colorado, and California, and the Territories of Utah and New Mexico, and especially along the lines of such railways traversing said States and

Territories as are military roads and post routes and are engaged in Interstate commerce and in carrying United States mails [to] retire peaceably to their respective abodes [by three o'clock the following afternoon]."[66]

On the following day, Debs and his lieutenants—the top leadership of the American Railway Union—were indicted and arrested on federal charges of obstructing the mails. This was followed quickly by the collapse of the strike and an end to disorder.

With few exceptions the nation's leading papers and journals commended Cleveland's deployment of the troops, as did most citizens (union men and their families and sympathizers excepted), to judge by the volume of letters and wires to the White House. A Senate resolution endorsing the President's "prompt and vigorous measures" was passed (July 11) with a great chorus of ayes from both sides of the aisle. But approval was not universal. Cleveland came under attack from two disparate groups—champions of labor and champions of states' rights.

As for the latter group, Altgeld's charge that the President had acted too precipitately on the basis of overly exaggerated reports and without first allowing Illinois authorities ample time to deal with the situation may be morally correct, but not legally so. The President was right to claim that the government need not await local requests to protect the mails and interstate commerce, which fall under federal purview. He was correct in asserting that he acted entirely within his legal and constitutional powers.

As for the champions of labor, their rancor over the President's behavior would play a pivotal role in William Jennings Bryan, "the Great Commoner," replacing Grover Cleveland as the Democratic party's titular head. At a mass meeting of ten thousand in New York City, reformer Henry George, speaking for a number of prominent like-minded citizens, criticized Cleveland respectfully but firmly: "I yield to nobody in my respect for the rights of property, yet I would rather see every locomotive in this land ditched, every car and every depot burned and every rail torn up, than to have them preserved by means of a federal standing army."[67]

For Cleveland, there was a painful personal aspect to labor's disapproval of his conduct. In discharging his responsibilities as he saw them (rather, as Olney made sure that he saw them), he was acting not only with characteristic scrupulousness but with characteristic courage. But Altgeld and Hopkins were not only the state's Democratic chiefs, they had labored more than anyone else to carry Illinois for him in 1892. By sending in the troops, Cleveland not only incurred their hostility, he hurt himself irreparably among the Illinois Democrats.

Cleveland's most partisan defenders believed that even men most sympathetic to the rights of labor must exonerate him on the grounds that he was led sadly astray by his Attorney General. In his way, Olney was as much the villain as Pullman, and arguably more so than Debs. Either Cleveland, who considered Olney his most capable cabinet officer, refused to believe he was also the most deceptive, or, as is more likely, he refused to assign accountability for having done what he felt the situation demanded of whoever was President at the time.

A commission he named to investigate the strike condemned the "selfish paternalism" of the Pullman Company, characterized the General Managers' Association as "an illustration of the persistent and shrewdly devised plan of corporations to override their limitations and usurp indirectly powers and rights not contemplated by their charters" and exonerated Debs and the other indicted officers of the ARU on the charge of provoking violence. The real culpability for the disorders, the report went on, "rests with the people themselves and with the government for not adequately controlling monopolies and corporations, and for failing to reasonably protect the rights of labor and redress its wrongs."

Loss to the railroads in property destroyed, hire of federal marshals, and incidental expenses was set at $685,300; loss of earnings to the lines was estimated at $4,673,000. The 3,100 Pullman workers lost $350,000 in wages, and 100,000 workers on the twenty-four railroads involved lost close to $1,390,000. Cost to the federal government brought the grand total to at least $10 million. Of the hundreds of men on both sides wounded in varying degrees, twelve were killed. Five hundred and fifteen men and women were arrested on charges of murder, arson, burglary, assault, intimidation, rioting, and lesser crimes, of whom seventy were indicted along with Debs. A federal grand jury found: "The conditions created at Pullman enabled the management at all times to assert with great vigor its assumed right to fix wages and rents absolutely, and to repress that sort of independence which leads to labor organizations and their attempts at mediation, arbitration, strikes, etc."

On December 10, Cleveland submitted the full report to Congress. Four days later, the Illinois Circuit Court, deciding that the facts did not exculpate the ARU leaders, sentenced Debs to six months in prison and his associates to three each, "for contempt of court." (The decision was based on the Sherman Antitrust Law, "to protect trade and commerce against unlawful restraint and monopolies.") Debs and the others appealed to the Supreme Court, arguing that the findings of the lower court did not constitute disobedience to the writs served upon them. The case was argued in March; a decision handed down two months later upheld the circuit court verdict and Cleveland's injunction: "The United States may remove everything put upon highways, natural or artificial, to obstruct the passage of interstate commerce, or the carrying of the mails."[68]

The temptation is overwhelming to wish Cleveland had waited at least a day or two before interfering in Chicago. If by then rioting had broken out, the state militia was not yet on the scene, and the federal marshal and his thousands of deputies were unable to clear the tracks, dispatching the troops without being requested to do so would have spared him much subsequent criticism and resentment. A special train was standing by at Fort Sheridan that could have put the troops into the city within two hours, so that no real danger would have been incurred by delay. Also, it can be argued persuasively that violence would not have even broken out but for the presence of the troops. (Here one is reminded of Benjamin Franklin's observation when informed of King George III's decision to send his redcoats to Boston: "If sent they will not find a rebellion—but they will create one.") But the fact remains that Cleveland was determined, as he himself put it, that "[if] it takes the entire army and navy of the United States to deliver a postal card in Chicago, that card will be delivered."

In fulfilling that determination, he self-inflicted a fatal political wound, and in the process condemned himself to an eternity of obloquy as one of organized labor's favorite foes. Despite what rebuke we can impute to Olney and Altgeld, it is Cleveland who must bear ultimate responsibility.

But then, one suspects that Cleveland himself felt the same.

52

"I am so depressed during these days"

Cleveland began his 1894 correspondence with a letter to Richard Gilder on January 4: "I am thinking these days that I have my full share of perplexities—indeed I am never without them—and I am also thinking that they can be met in but one way and that is by keeping the heart and conscience right and following their lead." Four months later he told Gilder, "In the sphere of public affairs I feel that I have my full share of trouble and perplexity but I have never lost hope and have never doubted that the end would compensate for all. The American people ought to have learned a valuable lesson. I don't know whether they have or not."

By year's end, Cleveland's "perplexity"—a word that appears frequently both in his private correspondence and public comments during this period—had given way to despondency. He had followed the lead of his heart and conscience, he reiterated; it was the only path he knew. But the American people, thanks in large measure to their elected leaders, had not learned any lesson, valuable or otherwise, that might have ameliorated the economic horrors confronting them. "I am so depressed during these days," he wrote Gilder the day after Christmas, 1894. "I am sure I never was more completely in the right path of duty than I am now and more sure I never did better public service than now; but it is depressing enough to have no encouragement from any quarter."[69] Even more perplexity and depression were to be his lot.

As the business decline that followed the Panic of '93 moved westward from the industrialized East it collided head-on with an agricultural decline that already had tenant sharecroppers and small farmers literally facing starvation. To their economic woes were added a medley of hardships natural in origin: a plague of chinch bugs and grasshoppers competed for the meager crops, and blizzards devastated emaciated subnormal cattle herds as neighbors were compelled to stand by powerless and watch each other's land and home go on the auction block. Numerous families dropped below the subsistence level as money became for them an extinct commodity. Acreage once fertile for planting crops was now fertile for an agrarian revolt—and the most powerful such movement the nation had ever seen was completing its gestation phase.

To call it a revolt is perhaps to misread its aims. Call it, rather, a crusade; a people's—populist—movement that saw men throughout the nonindustrialized regions west of the Mississippi and south of the Ohio arise to demand not only a redress of the wrongs that had ignited such a sorry state of affairs but changes that would lead to a new and equitable social order. Specifically, a fair-minded distribution of the wealth and equality, to be effected through a graduated income tax, popular election of senators, and curbing of the powerful industrial and commercial trusts.

Contributing to the overall situation as the second Cleveland presidency approached its midway point were external factors that frustrated attempts by demagogic westerners and right-wing easterners to simplify a problem which both factions conveniently, or perhaps self-servingly, refused to acknowledge was complex in scope. World food markets were glutted as a result of extended colonization by the major powers and rapid advances in transportation and agricultural machinery. Here at home, the American West had grown too rapidly for its own and the nation's good. The broad agricultural region from Minnesota and the Dakotas down to Oklahoma and Texas had been developed with awesome speed. Over the previous decade, total land under cultivation in the United States had increased by some 305 million acres, or more than 50 percent, as the number of farms rose from 4 million to 5.7 million. And these were the years when increasing competition from other countries was diminishing America's capacity to export the grains that were the region's largest cash crop.

An added predicament: as American farmers moved into the West they brought too little capital and even less caution. Having gone heavily into debt for land and equipment, they were now being squeezed out as prices were forced down through overproduction of major staples like grain, beef, and pork. At the beginning of 1890, almost four years before the panic, farm mortgages totaled 2.3 million, for an aggregate value of more than $2.2 billion. With rates running as high as 15 percent on top of unconscionable commissions for renewals, annual interest charges alone topped $200 million. Also, the farmer's property was not only tangible and easily assessed, it could not be taken as a tax deduction. Independent farm owners became renters overnight; in a number of states, especially Kansas, which like Nebraska suffered the added horror of drought, whole counties were in foreclosure. Farm prices were in free fall; a common sight was farmers dumping their grain into the street rather than accept the prices being offered by the elevator operators—prices which would not have covered the cost of moving the grain to market, let alone sowing and reaping it.

Adding to the average farmer's tribulations, which he shared with the average workingman, his portion of the national tax bite was excessive and unreasonable. Federal revenue was raised wholly by indirect taxes on articles of general consumption, with the tariff producing roughly two-thirds and internal revenue taxes the other third. Since rates were established equally without regard for one's capacity to pay (which would explain the demand by the lower classes for a more equitable personal income tax), the share paid by the farming and working classes was disproportionate to their income (as was, for that matter, the share paid by the monied class). In addition, partly because of the tariff and partly because of the great trusts, commodity prices did not fall commensurate with food prices. Clothing, farm implements, and household furnishings were maintained at a high level. Too, the railway trusts not only refused to abate charges, they actually raised rates on shipping grain from the Midwest's "breadbasket" to the Atlantic Coast. Intensifying the problem were three inherent defects in the nation's banking system: an inadequate concentration of banking reserves; a need for resilience in the issuance of banknotes; and a paucity of facilities adequate for expanding credit in periods of financial pressure through the rediscounting system, used by European banks of issue. These were defects the correction of which lay two decades in the future. Not until the first Wilson administration would a thoroughgoing currency reform be effected.

Cleveland saw as his most urgent priority maintaining the national credit by maintaining the gold standard. Resolution of the current economic crisis, he believed, and rightly, would follow as a matter of course. Much as he hoped to ease, if not eradicate, the farmers' plight, be it through subsidies, loans at reduced rates, or even bailouts—what we today call entitlements—he could not consider doing so at this time. Because of the spending excesses of the Harrison years and the calamitous effects of the Panic of '93, money was now unavailable but for the most important government needs.

Cleveland's having repealed the Sherman Act was proving to be less a victory than a truce—a truce which the great corpus of agrarian debtors saw as confirmation that he was the compliant whore, if not indeed the zealous paramour, of their capitalistic oppressors. Having earned the hostility of four groups, any one of which was capable of impeding his ability to govern—Congress, the silverites, the West, and the South—Cleveland must now face yet another misery, one that goes with the office: the tendency of the American public to impute accountability for major calamities besetting them to whoever is occupying the White House at the time.

Accordingly, Grover Cleveland was held personally responsible not only for the economic depression that had permeated the trans-Mississippi area but for the psychological depression that grew out of it. As invective rained down from all directions—most of it from the direction of his own party—he moved rapidly and decisively to stave off the nation's total financial collapse. The gold reserve was melting away. Combined attack by holders of the outstanding $450 million in paper specie ("Sherman" notes or silver certificates, and greenbacks) was creating havoc: when redeemed for gold coin, they had to be reissued by law, and could then be returned and redeemed for yet more gold. The Treasury was now vulnerable to an endless chain of redemption by which the gold reserve was being continuously depleted, bringing the government ever nearer to the point where payment in that metal, legally required, would have to be refused.

Compounding the dilemma was the increasing extent to which gold was being exported to settle trade or bond obligations. The total amount of gold in the country—the preponderance of it in banks and private hands—had fallen to below $600 million. It did not take a perspicacious economist, or even an imaginative storefront clairvoyant, to foresee the utter chaos that lay just beyond the fiscal horizon.

The only available means of replenishing the nation's gold reserve—on which, as heretofore noted, there was by law a floor of $100 million—was through issuance of government bonds, as authorized by Congress in the Resumption Act of 1875. While its primary purpose was to provide for the resumption of specie payment that had been suspended as a war measure in 1861, the act had an intolerable stipulation: the bonds need not be made payable in gold, only "payable in coin." To expect the public to purchase 5 percent ten-year bonds, 4.5 percent fifteen-year bonds, or 4 percent thirty-year bonds with such a stipulation was unrealistic, as the purchaser must risk redemption in the "coin" of depreciated silver, should the Treasury Department so order.[70]

Repealing the Sherman Act was the first step in Cleveland's monetary reform. As he now prepared to take the second step—a bond issue to secure the gold necessary to maintain the nation's reserve—the free-silver men of both parties prepared to obstruct him all the way.

Two factors had militated against any governmental bond issue in 1893, the first full year of Cleveland's second presidency: his fear that doing so would complicate his in-progress attempts to repeal the silver-purchase law, and his hope that Congress might enact better legislation governing such issues without White House prodding. Meanwhile, the gold reserve was being forced below the legally imposed $100 million limit as people hoarded the metal by funding their customs or internal revenue debts to the government in silver certificates. And because certificates presented for redemption at the Treasury had to be put back into circulation, the same notes did duty many times in sucking gold from the federal vaults. On the day the Sherman purchase repeal passed the Senate, the gold reserve stood at $84 million; on the last day of the year, it had dropped to $80 million; eighteen days into the new year, it would fall to $69 million. Clearly, drastic measures were demanded.

The Treasury Secretary was empowered to sell certain kinds of bonds to provide gold for the redemption of greenbacks. Shortly after the new administration came in, Carlisle had asked Congress for authority to float an issue at a lower interest rate and with an earlier redemption value than allowed by the 1875 law. Western legislators persuaded Congress to refuse, arguing that they had made enough concessions; if gold failed, they said, then let the Treasury use silver to redeem the silver certificates. As the government was compelled by law to maintain the two metals at parity, this would have meant forcing the country's finances onto a pure silver basis—an option Cleveland would not even consider. (It should be realized that the rest of the world was on the gold standard. The prospect of the United

States, already a debtor nation, even attempting to settle its foreign obligations in unacceptable silver specie was too horrendous to contemplate—a fact pointedly ignored by the silverites in Congress.)

As there was no direct income tax and the government lacked the power to issue money, the Treasury's only alternative to maintaining its reserve was to buy or borrow gold. And its ability to borrow depended on foreign confidence in the dollar—a confidence which at this point in time was abysmally low. When, around mid-January 1894, it was estimated that the Treasury gold deficit for the current fiscal year would reach $78 million, Cleveland lost his patience. At a cabinet meeting, he struck the table in exasperation and blurted out: "I believe in taking the bull by the horns and coming out with an issue of bonds!"[71] He ordered Carlisle to proceed at once with a sale, notice of which was circularized on January 17. The offering was for $50 million, in denominations of $50 and multiples thereof, redeemable in ten years at 4 percent interest. It won the support of the eastern press—and, it should go without saying, the condemnation of the western press.

At first the issue appeared doomed. Prospective buyers distrusted the clause about payment "in coin" at maturity, while leading bankers expressed doubt as to its legality under the 1875 act, and fear that future questions regarding use of the proceeds might affect the integrity of the bonds themselves. Silverites in the House rushed through a resolution that proceeds of the sale could not lawfully be used for current expenses, or for any other purpose than to maintain the gold reserve. Their intention was to induce popular misgivings about the bonds. Consequently, many of the submitted bids were immediately canceled. As the deadline neared, less than $5 million was subscribed. Cleveland ordered Carlisle to plead with the major New York bankers, whose patriotism he roused to the extent that they "effectively exerted themselves, barely in time to prevent a disastrous failure of the sale." (The bankers took the bonds at a price on which they later lost money.)[72]

The success of this first issue was minimal at best. Of the $58,661,000 realized, $24 million represented no actual gain: in order to obtain the gold to finance their subscriptions, some of the bidders withdrew it from the Treasury by presenting legal-tender notes! The drain on the gold reserve continued apace. It was obvious that before long another bond issue would be required. A month later, Cleveland

and Congress clashed over a bill introduced by Richard P. "Silver Dick" Bland, the Democratic champion of silver interests (and coauthor of the Bland-Allison Act) calling for the coining of silver seigniorage and other loose bullion in the Treasury. The Treasury had accumulated enough of this bullion to coin about $55,150,000 in silver dollars. The bill passed both houses in record time and was rushed over to the White House for Cleveland's signature.

It was not forthcoming. This despite assurances that the sum involved would not adversely affect the economy; that there were no legal impediments to its coinage; and, most meaningful, that signing the bill would allay western fears and benefit the entire nation's fiscal health. Even some Democratic newspapers which had supported repeal of Sherman advised that the President yield on Bland. Their reasoning: doing so would be a tolerable, albeit small, concession to the party's silverite faction after their defeat over the Sherman Act, and would in the process restore the unity urgently required by the shattered Democratic party. William Jennings Bryan said that while the Sherman repeal had divided the Democrats into two hostile, irreconcilable factions, the seigniorage bill presented the opportunity to reunite them.

Many of Cleveland's sound-money supporters urged him to veto. Others, led by Gresham, urged that he sign, asserting that the amount of silver involved would not further threaten the currency situation, whereas the rancor aroused by a veto would jeopardize his chance to secure needed Congressional authority for an effective bond issue. It was a valid argument. There already were in circulation over 382 million silver dollars, coined between 1878 and 1890, in addition to over $150 million in silver certificates, so that an added $55 million would not matter, whereas placating a hostile Congress certainly would. Still others urged that Cleveland sign the bill strictly in the interest of party unity, a notion that enraged him: he failed to see how sound-money men could expect to purchase party unity by advocating an increase in unsound money. (According to the *Springfield Republican* on March 30, 1894, "Never before has such pressure been brought to bear upon [the President] to overlook for once a matter of principle, affecting the whole country, in favor of party unity and success.") A group of western and southern Congressional Democrats insisted Cleveland sign the seigniorage bill, warning that unless he did so there was no hope the party would win a majority in the next Congress. One of them added the clincher that it would scarcely be possible for himself and several others present to be reelected in November.

As always, Cleveland was not prepared to yield on a question of principle, regardless of personal consequences. Declaring indignantly that the integrity of the nation's finances and the credit of the United States government were too important to be seen only in terms of party unity—*any* party's unity—he scathingly attacked those who "pandered to the delusions of the people and voted for all sorts of legislation in order to keep themselves in office." So far as he was concerned, "the credit of the government and the condition of the national finances were too important to be treated from that point of view, and that he had a decided contempt for anyone" who would dare solicit his support for such legislation for such a reason. One delegate emerged from the meeting in a state of utter stupefaction: "I never had a man talk like that to me in my life!"[73]

Four days later, Cleveland vetoed the Bland bill, arguing that its enactment would reflect a retrogression from the sound financial intentions of the Sherman repeal, and that nothing should be done that would doubtless inhibit the economic recovery which was by then slowly (perhaps too slowly) but surely getting under way. The rage of the pro-silver press was predictable; the *New Orleans Times-Democrat,* for one, foresaw the Democratic party as "booked for ruin." Still, Cleveland had taken the correct course. Despite claims by the silverites that the administration was seeing, if not in fact creating, a crisis where none existed, the outflow of gold from the Treasury, both in domestic redemption and in settlement of ongoing trade obligations in Europe, had been increasing quicker than in any previous period of the nation's history.

Cleveland's intent that his veto not be overridden—a definite possibility—led to one of his cleverest ploys, one that comprises an amusing albeit informative sidebar to the entire episode. The account comes from Sam Small, Washington reporter for the *Atlanta Constitution* and a close friend of House Speaker Charles Crisp, whose residence in the Metropolitan Hotel he shared when Congress was in session. On April 3, five days after the Cleveland veto, Crisp was summoned to the White House sometime after midnight. He insisted that Small accompany him, as he wanted a witness.

On being shown into the second-floor library, where Cleveland was at his desk, the Speaker was told: "Mr. Crisp, I sent for you because my veto message is coming up tomorrow. I understand a number of Democrats have filed applications to be heard in an attack on the veto and on me. That will be very damaging to the party. This is a vicious and hurtful bill; my motives in trying to destroy it have been entirely patriotic; if it is passed over my veto, or if any considerable demonstration is made in favor of it, that will inflict great injury on the nation."

"But how can I do anything, Mr. President?" asked Crisp.

Cleveland replied he had "counted noses" and was satisfied he could command a majority in the House "if the question is brought to an issue *immediately without further delay.*" His backers had selected a member "to move the previous question"—i.e., vote on the override—"instantly. We want you to recognize him. Debate will be cut off and the veto will be sustained."

Crisp was aghast. Some of the most influential Democrats had filed demands to be heard in support of an override. If discussion was cut off, they would be outraged, and would vent their anger on him. "Do you know what this means to me?" the Speaker demanded. "My people in Georgia are for silver; my political career will be ruined!"

Cleveland stared Crisp down. "Mr. Speaker," he roared, in the leonine manner he would evoke for such occasions, "what is your political future weighed in the balance against the fortunes of the country? Who are you and I compared with the welfare of the whole American people?"

"Well," said Crisp slowly, falling back under the attack, "if you put it that way—I'll consent."

Next afternoon when Bland arose on the House floor and called for three days of discussion, the Speaker summarily cut off debate (and a characteristically orotund oration which Bryan had prepared for the occasion) and the veto was sustained.[74]

First the Sherman Act repeal, then the first bond issue, now the Bland seigniorage repeal: disaffection for Cleveland by fellow Democrats was rapidly evolving into a profound hatred. In Congress, a group of bitterly anti-Cleveland Democrats organized themselves as "the Wild Horses," much to the delight of the perennially Cleveland-bashing Republicans. Typical of their behavior was the ferocious harangue on the House floor by Joseph C. Sibley of Pennsylvania. After accusing

Cleveland of acting like a despot, Sibley thundered, "We have reached a time when the government of this people requires more than a combination of brains, belly, and brass." In the upper chamber, John Morgan of Alabama took the Senate floor to shout: "I hate the ground the man walks on," adding that all Cleveland followers were "cuckoos."

Other conspicuous Cleveland-haters within his own party included Joseph Bailey, because the President had retaliated for the Texan's lack of support by denying him any federal patronage; and, for similar reasons, John R. McPherson of New Jersey and Francis Cockrell of Missouri. North Carolina's Zebulon B. Vance declared Cleveland "could not have carried a single electoral vote south of the Potomac" had his program been known to the electorate in 1892. David A. Wells, a leading tariff reformer since the Grant period, wanted it known he was "coming to cordially dislike Cleveland." And "Pitchfork Ben" Tillman, on the stump campaigning for the Senate, told his wildly cheering South Carolina constituents that "when Judas betrayed Christ, his heart was not blacker than this scoundrel Cleveland, in deceiving the Democracy. He is an old bag of beef and I am going to Washington with a pitchfork and prod him in his fat ribs."[75]

As the nation prepared for the 1894 Congressional elections there were several states in which Cleveland could not muster the support of even a single Democratic newspaper. Typical was the *Atlanta Constitution:* "The people have been taken in and done for. They have been made the victims of as corrupt a conspiracy as ever disgraced the world's political records. They have been sold out . . . by those whom they selected to protect their interests. To the dogs with such false and pretentious democracy!" Meanwhile, the Populists exploited the widespread resentment against Cleveland to push their crusade into high gear. Determined to broaden the split in Democratic ranks, they established new party newspapers and made new converts.[76]

The bleak economic picture alone would have made Democratic chances in November remote at best; with anti-Cleveland enmity sweeping the country, the party's likelihood of avoiding a total rout was exiguous in the extreme. When the results came in, they far exceeded what the President's enemies dared hope for and his friends dared fear. The old House membership of 219 Democrats and 127 Republicans gave way to 104 and 244, respectively; in twenty-four states, not a single Democrat was elected to that chamber, and in each of six others, only one Democrat was elected.

For the Republicans it was the greatest gain by any party in a midterm election in the nation's history until the Republican rout of exactly a century later. Not only did Cleveland find himself faced now with strong opposition in both the House and Senate, but given that most members from his own party were against him, his hopes for getting any required legislation through Congress ranged from the dubious to the despondent. (Results in the gubernatorial races were equally bleak for the President's party. Wisconsin, New York, and Illinois, which the Democrats had taken in 1892, were now lost to the Republicans, who even took the traditionally Democratic statehouses in West Virginia, Missouri, Maryland, and Delaware.)

Even had the results been otherwise, Cleveland would have been too preoccupied with the economy to indulge in delight. By Election Day, the need for a second bond issue was critical if the nation's credit was not to collapse.

53

The crisis rapidly approaches flash point

Cleveland's hope that proceeds from the first bond sale would give stability to the Treasury had turned out to be illusory. The continuing loss of revenue resulting from the depression, intensified by the continuing erosion of public confidence, proved it to have been little more than a stopgap measure. As the nation prepared to elect a new Congress, the Treasury's cash balance barely topped the legal minimum of $100 million; of this, less than $70 million was in gold. Delay in passing the Wilson-Gorman bill led to a drop in imports for the first half of the year (breaking all records in time of peace), while receipts under the revised tariff schedules were much less than forecast. In addition, gold was still being exported at a steady rate; $73.7 million was sent abroad in the twelve months ending November 30, 1894. This resulted not from a negative trade balance—the balance had in fact by now become favorable—but from anxieties among

European bankers that the United States faced imminent financial collapse; this in turn had a negative effect on the sale of American securities on the continent.

On November 14, 1894, with the gold reserve now down to $61 million, Treasury Secretary Carlisle issued a circular calling for bids on another $50 million in 5 percent ten-year bonds, the date for closing of bids to be ten days thence at high noon. Precautions were taken to prevent bidders from simply withdrawing gold at one Treasury window to pay for the bonds at another. Carlisle insisted that the banks refuse to aid customers in such transactions; to drive the point home, he threatened to publish the names of those banks which did.

Although close to five hundred bids were received, Carlisle awarded the entire issue to a single syndicate of bankers who promised a net yield to the Treasury of more than the aggregate of the other highest bids. Another important advantage in doing it this way: no gold would be drawn from the Treasury. All told, the government struck a fairly good bargain. Early in December the gold reserve rose to $111 million. (The syndicate did not do all that well; its efforts to dispose of the bonds were hampered by the ongoing depression, and in the end it actually lost money on the deal—though not a soul in the western states would believe it.)

Success was ephemeral. The first issue had sustained the Treasury for ten months. This second issue did so for only ten weeks. As the winter of 1894–95 set in, every city and town across the nation had its own horror stories of unemployment, misery, starvation. In financial circles, confidence was rapidly falling through the floor as the pro-silver majority in Congress persisted in their demands for free coinage, heavier greenback issues, and other palpably inflationary schemes. Bank failures continued at an alarming rate, as more and more people hoarded gold. By the middle of December, legal tenders were again being presented in large numbers at the Treasury for redemption, and a third bond issue was being spoken of as inevitable. A total of $31 million in gold left the Treasury by year's end, thus putting the reserve again far below the $100 million floor as the new year came in. "The Treasury was like a critical patient who, having received two hypodermic injections, lay at the point of collapse while his doctors frantically prepared a third."[77]

Gathered about the operating room—to continue the metaphor—stood the soft-money faction murmuring darkly that the second bond issue was indisputable proof that the President, in collusion with eastern gold interests, was irrevocably committed to the destruction of silver money. The silverites also littered the landscape with broadsides denouncing Cleveland and Carlisle as "traitors, Judases, tools of the bloated baronage of wealth, friends of financial bloodsuckers"—and these were the ones that could be printed in a public newspaper. They believed, with all the fervor of an impassioned evangelist conveniently misquoting Scripture, that if the government paid its debts in their favorite metal and allowed the country more "soft" (for which read cheap) currency, poverty and suffering would soon be problems of the past. Ancillary to this belief was their unalterable conviction that Cleveland and the eastern bankers were conspiring to use the gold dollar as a fiscal battering ram to push America's poor and laboring classes deeper into a quagmire of destitution.

In his 1894 annual message to Congress, Cleveland had pledged an undying fight to maintain the gold standard, allowing as how he was certain no one wished the government to go into default or off the gold standard—though here Cleveland was indulging in a bit of irony on a grand scale, knowing full well that the westerners were offering up daily invocations that the nation be forced to do just that.[78] Selling bonds was the most expedient means to raise the federal gold reserve, he said; but Congress was not helping matters by insisting that none be marketed except on the restrictive terms of the 1875 Resumption Act. "As long as no better authority for bond issues is allowed than at present exists," the President warned, "such authority will be utilized whenever and as often as it becomes necessary to maintain a sufficient gold reserve, and in abundant time to save the credit of our country." He did not warn the obvious: there was a natural limit to how many issues could be floated.[79]

In late January 1895, a feeling of panic escalated in banking circles when it was learned that $20 million in gold had been withdrawn from the Treasury in nine days alone. Carlisle had only recently sent to Congress a currency reform plan on which he had been working since taking office, but he tabled it as the result of a frantic letter to Cleveland from Isidor Straus. Visiting Wall Street, Straus found "a very grave feeling of apprehension, and talk of extraordinary heavy shipments of gold [abroad]." The Europeans, "thoroughly aroused as to our inability to continue on a gold basis," were "consequently selling their American investments as rapidly as the market will take them without inordinately depressing quotations. That naturally calls for heavy gold shipments [from America], which nothing but a restoration of confidence in the stability of our currency can arrest." Straus urged that Cleveland exert his influence toward legislation that would authorize the issue of gold bonds *and* retirement of greenbacks and Treasury notes, and allow national banks to issue currency up to the par value of the bonds.[80]

On the day he received the Straus letter, Cleveland received a "private and strictly confidential" report from the Treasury to the effect that the actual gold reserve was again down to $68 million and withdrawals were rapidly continuing despite the existence of a large currency surplus that in normal times would assure an ample reserve. But, the report warned, a large number of gold certificates were outstanding against the reserve, and so much of the reserve was in bullion that the government had only $22 million in gold coin for distribution among the Treasury itself and the nine subtreasuries. A sudden run on the subtreasury at New York, whose banks held around $20 million in gold certificates, would trigger disaster, causing the government to suspend specie payments—which it was obliged by law to honor. The report went on to urge that Congress immediately authorize Carlisle to buy enough gold to bring the reserve up to the $100 million mark and concluded with the suggestion, in effect a demand, that Congress legislate to ensure that henceforth all paper specie redeemed in gold "should not be reissued except in return for a deposit in gold coin of equal value."

During December 1894, when $58,538,500 in gold realized from the second bond sale was added to the Treasury reserve, nearly $32 million was withdrawn; the first month of the new year would see a further depletion totaling more than $45 million. By early February 1895, the Treasury was losing more than $2 million *daily*. At this rate, it would be only a matter of weeks before the government was in default on its gold obligations. Knowing that the result would be catastrophic, Cleveland sent a special message to Congress on January 28 concerning the "gravity and embarrassment of the situation," which he defined as "a lack of confidence, widespread and constantly increasing, in the continuing ability or disposition of the Government to pay its obligations in gold." The Treasury, he declared, was being "despoiled" of the gold obtained by bond sales "without canceling a single Government obligation, and solely for the benefit of those who find profit in shipping it abroad, or whose fears induce them to hoard it at home." There were on that day some half-billion dollars in outstanding government currency notes (i.e., in paper specie) for which gold could be demanded; and the law required, the President reminded Congress for the proverbial umpteenth time, that when redeemed in gold, the notes could be reissued—and redeemed for gold yet again, and again, and again. He asked that Congress authorize the Treasury to issue 3 percent long-term bonds, in small denominations, payable in gold, to be made the basis for issuing an equivalent amount of banknotes by those banks holding them; that the Treasury be authorized to redeem and cancel the paper species as fast as they came in, instead of allowing them to go out and come back in an endless destructive chain; and that the payment of all import duties be required in gold, so as to assure a constant flow into the Treasury.[81]

Legislation incorporating these recommendations was introduced in the House by William Springer of Illinois. The eastern press, both Republican and Democratic, commended the plan, and members from both parties throughout the region were urged by the business interests in their respective constituencies to vote its passage. But the western bimetallists were not concerned with relieving the Treasury's fiscal embarrassments, only with capitalizing on those embarrassments in order to legally flood the marketplace with the plentiful yield of their silver mines. They suggested gratuitously that the Treasury begin fulfilling its obligations in silver coin, of which there was an obvious surfeit. The Springer bill never had a chance. All that it accomplished was to show that not since Reconstruction had the nation been so divided by section and by sentiment on a single issue.[82]

With Congress unyielding on monetary reform, the specter of the nation being forced onto a silver standard, and the dollar threatening to decline in value to sixty cents, Cleveland had no choice but to hurriedly float a third bond issue with the express purpose of replenishing the government's gold supply, even though it must conform to the extremely unsatisfactory 1875 law. He and Carlisle preferred it be by public subscription, a tried and true way, but eastern financiers warned against this, given the lack of available time. The only alternative was to sell the bonds privately and hastily to some syndicate of financiers. That way, the gold would be delivered up front, and selling the bonds would be *their* problem. Financier August Belmont, sounding out European financial houses on the possibility of selling the bonds there, discovered a general disinclination to have anything to do with American securities.

The crisis was rapidly approaching flash point. On January 30, Assistant Treasury Secretary William Curtis, in New York to meet with bankers there, advised Cleveland that Wall Street was frightened and panicking, and the subtreasury was worried whether it could even keep up gold payments till the end of the week. Next day Curtis met with J. P. Morgan and Belmont, both of whom agreed that the critical state of the Treasury and grave public anxiety militated against any chance of obtaining gold by a public bond offering; though prospects for selling a loan in Europe were doubtful, negotiations should be attempted toward that end. Tentative agreement was reached between the government and a syndicate formed by the House of Morgan and Belmont (representing England's House of Rothschild) for a bond sale of $100 million, with the necessary gold to be brought from Europe.

Adherents of the gold standard were elated at the prospect. In one day, demands for the precious metal at the New York subtreasury fell off by more than $1 million. Nine million dollars in gold which had been placed aboard a Europe-bound steamer was actually retrieved and returned to the subtreasury during the night. Predictably, the silverites were in a rage at what they interpreted as "dark-lantern financiering" by the government and a "conspiracy" between Cleveland and Wall Street. Carlisle, still hesitant about a private sale, was dissatisfied when a second conference between Curtis, Morgan, and Belmont in New York resulted in more detailed terms: the bankers demanded bonds which would pay 3.75 percent to the syndicate, they would take only $50 million of them, and they would not promise to obtain more than half of the required gold in Europe. Carlisle wanted to sell $100 million in bonds, on more generous terms. He had no problem convincing the ever cautious Cleveland that they could effect a better bargain. On February 3, the Morgan-Belmont offer was rejected, in favor of a public issue.

Morgan and Belmont were certain that such a plan would fail, as most of the gold to buy the bonds would have to come from the Treasury, and the announcement of a public bond sale would have to be followed shortly by an announcement that the government was in default—arguments impossible to refute. Rushing to meet with Cleveland and Carlisle at the White House, they insisted that an immediate infusion of gold coin from Europe was the only way to avoid panic and disaster, and that such an emergency purchase need not interfere with yet another public bond flotation at a later time, when the financial situation had improved. Cleveland and Carlisle opposed closing with the two pending action on the Springer bill; its defeat was certain within a few days, but, as Carlisle later put it, "we had asked for the legislation, and we thought it was hardly respectful to Congress to undertake to negotiate a sale of bonds pending" the bill's imminent disposal.[83] Carlisle's rationale aside, awaiting action on the Springer bill was for the President a matter of practicality. Popular pressure demanded that the bond issue be a public offering. Should the Springer bill be defeated, he could then deal with the bankers yet suffer far less popular criticism. Morgan and Belmont agreed to return at week's end, by which time Springer would have been voted upon.

Events now moved rapidly to a climax. On February 7, to no one's astonishment, the Springer bill failed. Arriving at the White House next morning, Morgan found the President eager to cut the best possible deal for the government but, like Carlisle, still hesitant about abandoning a public issue. At one point during their talks, Cleveland received a phone call to the effect that there was now less than $9 million in gold coin in the New York subtreasury. The heavy silence that ensued was broken by Morgan's remark that he was aware of a large draft about to be presented for payment. "If that $10 million draft is presented, you can't meet it," he told Cleveland. "It will be all over before three o'clock." When Carlisle confirmed this, Cleveland abandoned the idea of a public offering, and asked, "What suggestions have you to make, Mr. Morgan?"[84]

Morgan suggested that the syndicate pay 3.5 million ounces of gold, at least half to come from Europe, in exchange for about $65 million in thirty-year 4 percent gold bonds, at 104½, and promised that what gold that went into the Treasury through this issue would not flow out again. This amounted to an agreement to temporarily rig the gold market. Furthermore, there was some question as to the legality of the proposed issue. But either Morgan or Carlisle dusted off an 1862 law, never repealed, that granted the Lincoln administration emergency powers to buy coin with U.S. bonds ("coin bonds") as an emergency measure in the national interest. Morgan added a proviso: should Congress agree within ten days to substitute the words "gold bonds" for "coin bonds" as the medium of redemption, the interest rate would be reduced to 3 percent. A contract was drawn up at once and signed at the Treasury. That afternoon Cleveland advised Congress of the deal, adding that the "gold bonds" provision could save the government $16 million on the issue price. Congress threw away the saving: the majority refused to tolerate the word "gold." (Perhaps the crafty Morgan had assumed this would be the case when he made that magnanimous offer.)[85]

The loan was a success, yielding $65,116,244 in gold for the Treasury in only two hours in London and twenty-two minutes in New York, bringing the reserve up above $107,550,000. The flow of gold to Europe was immediately halted, and Morgan and Belmont, through rapid arrangements with the Rothschilds and by obtaining pledges from important bankers, held the exchange rate at a point which prevented further exports till they had fulfilled their end of the bargain. The bottom line was that the syndicate kept faith with the government, justifying the bold action by Cleveland and Carlisle that they knew would earn them a blizzard of abuse.

That abuse was not long in coming. The syndicate disposed of the bonds at almost eight points over the agreed purchase price, and their price in the open market rose shortly to 119. This led to the belief that the government had been defrauded. The *New York World* of February 21, for one, charged the Morgan syndicate with pocketing profits in excess of $5 million, without any risk or service on its part; and that license to do so was "gratuitously given to the syndicate in a secret conference, and will be paid out of the public treasury."

It must be said in the syndicate's defense that if it had not been able to inspire confidence in its ability to keep the nation on the gold standard, the bonds could not have been sold at any price, and that it had every right to charge something for inspiring this confidence. Too, there were transaction expenses like maintenance of the exchange rate, plus the customary bankers' commission of 5 percent for placing so large a loan. Still, regardless of these allowances, the profits were indeed excessive. Questioned later by a Congressional investigating committee, Morgan refused to reveal the true amount. Convincing evidence at the time put the net profit at upward of $7 million.[86]

In Cleveland's defense—and he never denied Morgan's terms

were exorbitant—it must be stressed that he fought down to the wire against syndicating the loan; that he did his best to get moderate terms; and, above all, that he cannot be held answerable for Morgan's avarice. How desperate the nation's fiscal picture was at the end of January may not have been generally known, but the bankers knew it, big business knew it, and Cleveland knew it. As the gold was leaving the Treasury at a totally unacceptable pace, prolonged negotiations could not be seriously considered. Also, floating a public issue posed two fatal dangers: the Treasury's gold supply would have been gone even before any bids came in—and it is more than likely that no bids would have come in at all. No help was forthcoming from an obtuse Cleveland-hating Congress, and the nation's bankers were fed up with tossing their gold into a seemingly bottomless pit. There was, in short, a profound crisis in public finance, and extreme measures and great sacrifices were justified to save the public credit.

What Cleveland did was no more and no less than what any banker would have done in analogous circumstances in private business. But this did not keep his antagonists in the West—especially those in Congress whose antipathy to the very word "gold" had cost the government $16 million—from believing it was with Cleveland's tacit collusion that rapacious financiers had waited till they had the government at their mercy to apply the death lock.

One point lost amid the tempest of charge and countercharge: there was no longer any common ground upon which the silver and gold forces might meet in hopes for a round or two of calm reasoning. Bryan denounced the sale on the floor of the House (after reciting Shylock's speech from *The Merchant of Venice*). The *New York World* went a step further in this mode by declaring that the syndicate had been composed of "bloodsucking Jews and aliens." Populist rabble-rouser Mary Lease called the President a tool "of Jewish bankers and British gold." One of the major Farmers' Alliance house organs, taking a less ethnic approach, declared that "the great bunco game played in Washington by which the people have been defrauded of over $8 million, besides having another debt of $62 million saddled on their backs," should encourage the masses to join the Populist party.[87]

Most Americans were sure Cleveland and Carlisle had sold the nation's credit to the Morgans and Rothschilds, and then compounded the foul deed by pocketing a share of the profits. Cleveland, having taken the only proper course under the circumstances, could live with such ill-founded abuse. Nine years later (May 7, 1904), "Without shame and without repentance," he owned up to his "share of the guilt" in "the crime charged," adding that although Morgan and Belmont "and scores of other bankers who were accessories in those transactions may be steeped in destructive propensities, and may be constantly busy in sinful schemes, I shall always recall with satisfaction and self-congratulation my collusion with them at a time when our country sorely needed their aid."[88]

54

The Venezuelan Boundary Dispute

At a memorial meeting in New York on what would have been Grover Cleveland's seventy-fifth birthday, Dr. Joseph Bryant recalled he "was temperate in all things, unless unduly irritated by those who would annoy him persistently and selfishly—then appropriate and emphatic remarks were made."[89] Which is to say, as a rule Cleveland tolerated without complaint barbed denunciation, even egregious prevarication by his political enemies, but he blew up if he felt they had gone too far, especially in the context of what he presumed to be the best interests of the American people. His attack on Grady and the other Tammany senators over the fare bill in 1883, his assault on the tariff in 1887, his "perfidy and dishonor" letter when the Wilson repeal of the Sherman Silver Coinage Act did not meet his expectations—these are three instances that come most readily to mind. The only instance of such an explosion in his conduct of foreign relations was his 1895 message to Congress on the Venezuela Boundary Dispute, which brought the United States and Great Britain closer to war than at any time since 1812.

It came at a time when Cleveland was coping with an ailing economy and the onset of the so-called Western Revolt that would preoccupy him throughout his last year in office and cost him leadership of the Democratic party. Ironically, it marked the only time he enjoyed the support of even his most intractable critics in the Congress. There was an added irony: this was the first international crisis of the Cleveland years that called into play the Monroe Doctrine, the principle that the American continents were closed to colonizing by the European powers. Cleveland had steered clear of this traditional cornerstone of American foreign policy during his first administration, because he steered clear of involvement in Latin America. ("I knew it to be troublesome.")[90]

Most of America's major foreign disputes between the Civil War and Spanish-American War were with Great Britain, during this period the leading world power and the only major European nation with significant holdings in the Western Hemisphere. Troublesome as they were while ongoing, most, like the Canadian fisheries quarrel, were settled by arbitration, leaving the world's two greatest English-speaking nations in a state of mutual regard and high esteem.[91]

The genesis of the Venezuela dispute lay in what was to be the definitive boundary between that former Spanish colony and the contiguous colony of British Guiana (today Guyana), which the Netherlands ceded to Great Britain in 1814. Venezuela pressed insistently for a settlement that included access to the Orinoco River. The British stalled, partly because they doubted the stability of any Venezuelan government, partly because they hoped to keep the issue unsettled. Being infinitely the more powerful of the two, the British were prepared to wait until Venezuela became embroiled either with a neighboring state or in a civil war, or had a dictator who could be bought off; then they might obtain international recognition for the only boundary they deemed acceptable—the one drawn in 1843 by Sir Robert Schomburgk. Venezuela found this line totally unacceptable, as she found intolerable Great Britain's insistence that any other boundary she was prepared to discuss must lie west of the Schomburgk line. Exacerbating the stand-off, gold was discovered in the contested region. The controversy caused much concern in Washington over the years, with the United States taking a dim view of the British Empire having established itself in our own front yard.

In 1887, Cleveland proposed the United States as mediator in assisting the contesting parties to arbitrate a mutually satisfactory line. London refused the offer, as well as another in the following year. The problem was carried over to the Harrison administration, whose envoy made yet another offer, with the same results. Following his return in 1893, while dealing with pressing domestic issues, Cleveland directed his attention to the Venezuelan controversy. Ambassador Bayard was instructed to open discussions with the British. On January 23, 1895, he conveyed to Foreign Secretary Lord Kimberley the President's "strong and friendly desire" to see the boundary settled once and for all time. But Kimberley would not negotiate except on his government's terms, which is to say, consonant with its geographical determination of the disputed area.[92]

Meanwhile, the situation had become muddied by a potentially explosive rupture of relations between Nicaragua and England. A number of Britons, including a vice-consul, were arrested and expelled from Nicaragua, Lord Kimberley demanded reparations, and three British warships were dispatched to enforce the demands. On April 27, the demand having been refused, four hundred English marines seized the customs house at Corinto. Nicaragua protested to the United States as the region's protective Big Brother. When it became evident that the British had not overstepped the bounds of international law, given Nicaragua's provocation, Nicaragua had no choice but to pay the indemnity.

Still, the whole business left Cleveland further ill disposed toward Britain. During these days his desk was subjected to a good deal of presidential fist-banging. He viewed Britain's repeated refusal to accept arbitration in Venezuela as symptomatic of the willingness of the powerful nations to rob the weaker ones, such as the partitioning of Africa, Germany's greed over Samoa, even the United States' theft of Hawaii. (In that same year France was grabbing Madagascar, the British *uitlander* agitation in South Africa was entering a critical phase that would result in the Boer War, and Japan was quietly absorbing Korea.)

Realizing that our navy was no match for England's, and that British arrogance vis-à-vis Venezuela could never be checked by diplomatic language, Cleveland now asked Secretary of State Gresham to prepare a comprehensive memorandum on the Venezuela question for transmission to the British government that would force the issue short of armed conflict. Many an evening the two would retire to Woodley (the house outside Washington which the Clevelands leased as a private retreat) to discuss the situation. In the midst of the discussions, Gresham caught a cold that turned into acute pleurisy, followed by pneumonia and his death on May 28.

Gresham, so popular in political and diplomatic circles for his conciliatory nature and great personal warmth, had endeared himself to Cleveland more than any other cabinet member, as had Vilas in the first administration. Indicative of the depths of Cleveland's feelings toward Gresham, and his capacity to mourn the loss of any close friend, was what occurred when the President and entire cabinet accompanied the body to Chicago for burial. While en route, after sitting for hours deeply absorbed in thought, Cleveland asked one of the men to accompany him to the baggage car where the coffin lay, and then asked to be left alone. When he failed to return after an hour, two of the cabinet officers, fearing an accident had befallen him, went to the baggage car. There they found the President on his knees by the bier of his dead friend, his arms on the coffin, sobbing silently. He was helped to his feet and assisted back to his stateroom, where he remained in seclusion for the remainder of the journey.[93]

On June 10, Cleveland named Attorney General Richard Olney, who had been working on the Venezuela crisis during Gresham's illness, to succeed him. (Judson Harmon, a capable jurist and later governor of Ohio, was named Olney's successor.) Olney spent the rest of June working on the memorandum for the British Foreign Office. On July 2 he went to Cape Cod, where the President was summering at Gray Gables, left a draft of the text, and then went on to his own summer home at nearby Falmouth to await Cleveland's reaction. It came five days later, prefaced by some news of a personal nature: "About five hours ago our family was augmented by the addition of a strong plump loud voice little girl [their third child, who was named Marian]. Mother and daughter doing well—also the 'old man.' " As to the memorandum, he found it "the best thing I have ever read. . . . Of course I have some suggestions to make. I always have. Some of them are not of much account and some of them propose a little more softened verbiage here and there."[94]

After the "verbiage" was softened slightly, what Cleveland later referred to as "Olney's twenty-inch gun" was sent off to Bayard for presentation to the British government. Its demand that the British submit to arbitration was based on a broad construction of the Monroe Doctrine, which "has but a single purpose and object": that "no European power or combination of European powers shall forcibly deprive an American state of the right and power of self-government and of shaping for itself its own political fortunes and destinies." Threats against the territorial integrity of any American (i.e., Western

Hemisphere) state involved "the safety and welfare of the United States," whose interposition in the event of such a threat was justified on the grounds that these states, "by geographic proximity, by natural sympathy, by similarity of governmental constitutions, are friends and allies, commercially and politically, of the United States. To allow the subjugation of any of them by an European power is . . . to completely reverse that situation and signifies the loss of all the advantages incident to their natural relation to us."

Olney went on to insist that the United States was "practically sovereign" on the South American continent, "and its fiat is law upon the subjects to which it confines its interposition." The United States' "infinite resources combined with its isolated position render it master of the situation and practically invulnerable as against any or all the other powers." All the advantages of this dominance would be "at once imperiled if the principle be admitted that European powers may convert American states into colonies or provinces of their own."

Moving next from the general to the specific, Olney regarded Britain's course as effectively putting Venezuela "under virtual duress," since Britain had practically decided that the Latin nation could get none of the disputed territory by force because she was not strong enough; nor by treaty, because Britain would not acquiesce; nor by arbitration unless she was willing as a precondition to cede such territory contiguous to the Guiana colony as Britain might designate. It was an acknowledged principle of international law, Olney went on somewhat didactically, that a third nation could "justly interpose in a controversy" to prevent a result that could menace "its own integrity, tranquility, or welfare." As the concerned third nation thus "menaced," the United States must worry not only about Venezuela's interests but her own. In summation, he insinuated that while the United States had thus far been spared great "warlike establishments," with the European powers permanently encamped on American soil, "the ideal conditions we have thus far enjoyed cannot be expected to continue." Thus the United States was left with no option but to require "a definite decision" as to whether Great Britain "will consent or will decline to submit the Venezuela boundary question in its entirety to impartial arbitration."[95]

Just weeks before the note was sent, the year-old Liberal government fell to the Tories, bringing Lord Salisbury back to power. Bayard wrote Cleveland he was "anticipating a much more satisfactory" settlement of the dispute, and he believed it unnecessary to be confrontational with the British in Venezuela, which he looked upon with the same distrust he reserved for all unstable states; the Caracas government was "difficult to comprehend and may always be considered unreliable." The President was urged to "go slow."[96]

Olney had instructed Bayard to request a response from London before the President's Annual Message to Congress in December. By October, there was still no response, although the impatient Olney had twice inquired. Also by then a martial air of sorts had begun to pervade the country. Massachusetts's Senator Lodge insisted in *North American Review* that the integrity of the Monroe Doctrine be established "at once—peaceably if we can, forcibly if we must." The *Concord Monitor* ran an editorial by Lodge's New Hampshire colleague, William Chandler, under the heading "Our Coming War with England—A Prediction," in which such armed conflict was regarded as inevitable; if necessary, the United States should fire the first shot.[97] The text of the Olney note had not been made public; all these and other opinions were incited by leaks from the State Department.

Salisbury's delay was due neither to discourtesy nor a desire to stall, but to a miscellany of reasons, not the least of them being a misunderstanding as to when Congress was to receive the President's message. An overriding consideration, though, was a desire for sufficient time to fashion a strong argument of rebuttal. He feared that if Britain were to accept the concept of third-party arbitration the effect on its empire could be deleterious, since neighboring states worldwide might manufacture spurious boundary claims against Her Majesty's colonies. Also, Bayard had failed to impress upon Salisbury that Cleveland regarded the problem as an acute one, to be resolved expeditiously.

On December 7, while Cleveland was away from Washington duck-hunting, British envoy Sir Julian Pauncefote delivered Salisbury's response to Olney. Regarding the Monroe Doctrine, he insisted that Olney had "misapprehended" the meaning of America's historic policy regarding the Western Hemisphere as its unique sphere of influence and denied emphatically "that when a European power has a frontier difference with a South American community, the European power shall consent to refer that controversy to arbitration." Regarding the boundary dispute, he declared that London had made only the most conservative claims to the territory at issue; that Venezuela had for decades refused any reasonable settlement; and that he could never permit an insignificant little country to "drag her more unreasonable pretensions before an international tribunal." The bottom line: England would not budge.[98]

Olney, considering Salisbury's tone churlish and irritatingly didactic, drafted a special message to Congress, which Cleveland sat up all night rewriting when he returned to the White House a week later. What he sent to Congress was every bit as potent as Olney's "twenty-inch gun," no doubt because it retained so much of Olney's saber-rattling. It is one of Cleveland's shortest messages, one of his most truculent—and the only one to be received by a now-Anglophobic Congress as if relieved at finally getting its marching orders. Congress was asked to appropriate money for a commission to fix a definitive boundary, which it would be the duty of the United States to maintain in the face of any aggression by the British.

While suggesting an incipient call to arms, Cleveland was hoping to accomplish just the opposite. His reasoning: if the controversy was not resolved, and expeditiously so, England and Venezuela might resort to war, at which point the American Congress "would then take the bit in its teeth" and involve the United States in the conflict. Cleveland later said that his aim was "to bring the entire matter into his own hands," make England yield to arbitration, and put Congress in a position where it could not interfere ("my action, you see, has been in the interests of peace—permanent peace").[99]

One can find no fault with Cleveland's reasoning. Where one can find fault is in Cleveland's allowing himself to be influenced by the irascible Olney's fiery, often unmanageable temper, and the advice that ensued. As in the Pullman Strike, he let Olney take him farther than he should have—or perhaps even would have—gone, had he been more prudent. Cleveland's close advisers claimed it probable that he would have mitigated those belligerent passages of Olney's had he first consulted with other members of his cabinet. With the tunnel vision that so often informed important decisions and actions, Cleveland failed to foresee the message's effect on the nation.

The short-term consequences were disquieting, noticeably in the warlike enthusiasm and imperialist sentiment his words unleashed.

Congress quickly appropriated $100,000 for the requested boundary commission Great Britain had explicitly said she wanted no part of nor would recognize. Leading statesmen supported the formidable Henry Cabot Lodge's view that "[w]ar would be a good thing even if we get whipped, for it would rid us of English bank rule." Dana's *Sun* and Watterson's *Courier-Journal* joyously anticipated armed conflict with the nation whose torching of the White House in 1812 had yet to be avenged; the *Washington Post* said with a figurative smacking of the lips that the message was "the call to arms; the jingoes were right after all, and it is not to be the fashion henceforth to sneer at patriots and soldiers." Not unexpectedly, the Irish National Alliance weighed in with an offer of 100,000 men "to meet the British on the battlefield" (though no one was quite sure just precisely where such a battlefield was to be situated).[100]

Fortunately, the country was returned to its senses by a number of influential journals like Pulitzer's *World*, to which the message to Congress had been simply a ghastly *faux pas*, and Godkin's *Evening Post*, which agreed. A number of papers encompassing the political spectrum echoed the sentiments of the *Springfield Republican* that while it was all for adopting a rigid stance toward Great Britain, the President's assertion that the findings of the boundary commission must have behind it the armed support of the United States was unacceptable. A few papers, in condemning Cleveland, chalked it all up to his determination on a third term. The most unfortunate response came from Abram Hewitt, who opined to Lord Salisbury that the President must have been drunk when he sent the message to Congress.[101]

Cleveland refrained from making any public amplification of his intransigent attitude, believing that anything he might say would do nothing to dampen the war fever, and could well escalate it. He did, though, write a long letter to Bayard, in response to the latter's inability "to shake off a grave sense of apprehension in allowing the interests and welfare of our Country to be imperilled or complicated by such a government and people as those of Venezuela." Though they had, as Cleveland reminded his first Secretary of State, steered clear of the Monroe Doctrine during his first administration, he was nevertheless "entirely clear that the doctrine is not obsolete, and it should be defended and maintained for its value and importance *to our gov-*

ernment and welfare [emphasis in the original], and that its defense and maintenance involve its application when a state of facts arises requiring it."

Convinced that such a state of facts had indeed now arisen, Cleveland could "never be made to see why the extension of European systems, territory, and jurisdiction, on our continent may not be as effected as surely and as unwarrantable under the guise of boundary claims as by invasion or any other means." Since 1887, he further reminded Bayard, England had been slowly but steadily enlarging her boundary claims vis-à-vis Venezuela. He did not mean to imply "either that Great Britain's boundary claim is false, nor that the enlargement of her claims toward the center of Venezuela as now known, is unjustifiable beyond a doubt." But he did find "intensely disappointing" Britain's refusal to accept any examination of such claims by impartial arbiters.[102]

Cleveland went ahead with plans for the boundary commission, whose members he selected; and a commendable selection it was (perhaps because it was done without consulting Olney). The high caliber of all the members went a distance toward reassuring the American public, which, despite the chauvinism being spouted by so many men of prominence, did not want war any more than did the British.

Historians hypothesize that the situation was saved by England's involvement in South Africa and the threat of an Anglo-German clash there subsequent to the German Kaiser's gauche wire to President Paul Kruger of the Transvaal following the Jameson Raid, which in turn could have precipitated a general European war. In fact, London was just as anxious as Washington to resolve the boundary issue far short of armed conflict. On January 13, 1896, Bayard cabled Olney that it was the "earnest desire of both political parties here" that the Venezuela dispute "be promptly settled by friendly co-operation." It was suggested in London's highest diplomatic circles that Washington propose a conference with European nations having colonies in the "American Hemisphere" (i.e., Great Britain, France, Spain, and Holland) "to proclaim the Monroe Doctrine—that European Powers having interests in America, should not seem to extend their influence in that Hemisphere."[103]

Cleveland and Olney rejected the idea as tantamount to having judgment passed on the Monroe Doctrine, "and the doctrine requires no such 'judgment.' " They would deal with England in this matter only one-on-one. Salisbury assented, stating that the "mixture of the United States in this matter may conduce to results which will be satisfactory to us more rapidly than if the United States had not interfered."[104] Thus did the British concede the validity of the Monroe Doctrine. Cleveland was able to inform Congress that the boundary issue had "ceased to be a matter of difference between Great Britain and the United States." In February 1897, a month before Cleveland left the White House, a treaty between Great Britain and Venezuela submitting the whole controversy to arbitration was signed at Washington. Two years later, on October 3, 1899, the fifty-year dispute was ended when England's claim was substantially upheld, though Venezuela was awarded territory at two points within the Schomburgk line.

Undeniably, though Cleveland's contentious approach proved successful over the long run, he had risked involving the United States in a shooting war with England. But even had he given this the careful consideration it deserved, it would doubtless have been subsumed in his determination to bring about an immediate settlement of the issue totally consonant with his interpretation of the Monroe Doctrine and international justice. That's all he wanted. In Cleveland's own words, his handling of the crisis "established the Monroe Doctrine on lasting foundation before the eyes of the world; it has given us a better place in the respect and consideration of the people of all nations, and especially of Great Britain; it has again confirmed our confidence in the overwhelming relevance among our citizens of disinterested devotion to American honor; and last, but by no means least, it has taught us where to look in the ranks of our countrymen for the best protection."[105]

Additionally, public opinion here at home was awakened to the importance of the United States in world affairs and a willingness to consider a more active participation (something, ironically, that was to Cleveland inherently distasteful). But beyond doubt the greatest benefit from Cleveland's at times questionable handling of the Venezuela Boundary Dispute was that it cleared the air between the United States and Great Britain, presumably once and for all time.

55

The Democrats are driven into schism

When he first entered Congress in 1891, William Jennings Bryan said he hoped "the two wings of the Democratic party may flap together, but I believe the time has come when the Western wing shall have some say so in regard to the flapping."[106] By the time the nation geared up for the 1896 presidential election the western wing's flapping had driven the Democratic party into schism.

Since the previous spring, Cleveland had been striving to hold the party together. He accepted that most of the West was irretrievably lost. Still, he hoped to hold on to the South, the traditional Democratic stronghold. His hopes were well founded. The region had remained loyal against the Populist invasion of 1892. If it could be induced, even in part, to stand by the administration in 1896, Cleveland believed, the silverite frenzy that had crossed the Mississippi and metastasized eastward might yet be pushed back. It was more a hope than a belief. The South was desperately poor and thus readily susceptible to the allure of silverite agitation, especially among the agrarian class.

Toward the end of April, Cleveland initiated a systematic campaign to bring the region back into the hard-money camp. In a letter to Mississippi's governor, John Marshall Stone, he said it was incumbent upon those "who profess fealty" to the party to consider the effects of "this silver aberration" on party and country. If there were Democrats who thought they could "succeed upon a platform embodying" the doctrine of free and unlimited and independent coinage of silver, or were not prepared to labor against it, they should "look in the face the results that will follow the defeat, if not the disintegration, of the Democratic party." He had "never ceased to wonder" why the people of the region, "furnishing so largely as they do products which are exported for gold, should be willing to submit to the disadvantages and loss [incurred by] silver monometallism and to content themselves with a depreciated and fluctuating currency, while permitting others to reap a profit from the transmutation of the prices of their productions from silver to gold." He hoped southerners would "be permitted to see the pitfall which is directly before those who madly rush toward the phantom of light of free, unlimited, and independent silver coinage." Cleveland was "entirely certain" that the South could be "dislodged from their association with the West on the currency question." As he wrote Charles S. Fairchild, they had heard only one side of the issue; there was "plenty of proof at hand that they will respond properly if the other side is made plain." He called for a "campaign of education such as was waged for tariff reform" that would "produce quick and abundant results."[107]

As part of his campaign, Cleveland made sure that sound-money southern Democrats networked with northern brethren of like persuasion. Too, he had Treasury Secretary Carlisle tour the border states in May to explain before state party conventions the evils of the silverite philosophy. The market ratio of silver to gold now stood at 32:1, Carlisle explained. The free coinage at 16:1 demanded by the silverites would, he warned, halve the value of the dollar, with catastrophic results: all wages would be reduced, gold would be driven from circulation, and silver monometallism would bring on a contraction of, and then depreciation in, the currency. Twenty-one million Americans with funds in savings banks, insurance companies, and building and loan associations would wind up with fifty-cent dollars.

In late October, Cleveland, accompanied by Vice President Stevenson, Carlisle, and five other cabinet officers, received a cordial reception at the Cotton States Exposition in Atlanta. After reviewing a military parade, he spoke to fifty thousand people, avoiding the currency question—the people of Georgia were, after all, preponderantly pro-silver—and confining himself to denouncing all sectional and selfish interests in politics. In a series of conversations with party leaders, though, he addressed the issue head-on. Were the party to abandon advocacy of the gold standard, he warned, the Republicans would become sole champions of sound money, and would set in concrete their recent political gains. The Democrats had lost control of Congress to the Republicans in 1894. Must they lose the White House in 1896?

Overall, Cleveland's efforts to regain the South, while noble, were in vain. Most of the region's politicians were convinced the interests of their region would be best served by allying with the agrarian West instead of the creditor East. With the presidential election now less than a year away, a strong movement was begun throughout the

South and West aimed at electing soft money delegations to the national convention. Large silver conventions outside the South encouraged their brethren below the Mason-Dixon Line. In August, free-coinage Democrats met in Washington to establish an organization within the party strong enough to seize control of the 1896 convention. Among its leaders were a number of United States senators who denounced Cleveland and his "panic-breeding, corporation-credit currency" and appointed an executive committee to coordinate the fight. Thus was born the "Senatorial clique" that would dominate the coming conclave—in behalf of free-silver coinage.

Throughout the Midwest the fires of anti-Cleveland revolt spread rapidly beyond control, with the silverites well organized and financed, thanks to the mine-owning interests of the mountain states. Reprints of free-coinage speeches in Congress flooded the country; many publications—even books—were given away gratis. Bryan, who had left Congress in 1894 to run (unsuccessfully) for the Senate, spent 1895 lecturing across the West and South, where his appearance was hailed as if it were the Parousia, his every word reprinted in the *Omaha World-Herald* (of which he was editor) and disseminated nationwide as if it were incontestible theology. Educator David Franklin Houston, who heard Bryan speak at Fort Worth, "discovered that a prairie schooner could be driven through any part of his argument." It made no difference: "he was unrivalled in winning adherents."[108]

Though the Cleveland forces—now popularly known as the Gold Bugs—managed to fend off the silverites in a number of state Democratic conclaves, few were willing to wager that western agrarians would not control the convention. A sign of the times: in Nebraska, which was Bryan country, one foolhardy delegate moved that President Cleveland be endorsed, along with the 1892 campaign program. It took a full ten minutes to hustle the poor man safely out of the hall, calm down the delegates, and restore order.

When Congress met in December, Washington was swamped by a rumor that the President would seek reelection, in a last-ditch effort to stem the silver tide. The rumor was given credence by men who really should have known better. One disciple, saying Cleveland was the only logical nominee, rationalized that it would not really be a third term, but his second *consecutive* term. (While there was no constitutional constraint, the tradition of not seeking a third term derived from George Washington's refusal to do so. Now, of course, with the Twenty-second Amendment, no man can be elected more than twice, though he can serve a total of ten years if the unfinished term of the man he succeeds does not exceed two years. Cleveland, whose personal choices for the nomination were Carlisle first, then ex-governor Russell of Massachusetts, passed off the idea as ridiculous. The third-term talk, which he found tiresome, was soon forgotten for the moment, as the effect of the runaway silver movement now began to take its toll on the already battered American economy.

In the late summer of 1895 the Treasury's gold supply, which had been boosted by the Morgan bond issue, again began to decline as—again—large amounts of legal tender were presented for redemption in coin of that metal. On September 14, the reserve stood below the legal floor, at $97 million, and was falling at a rate of more than $1 million a day. The withdrawals fell off dramatically a month later after J. P. Morgan announced that his syndicate was accumulating gold in order to aid the government by increasing the reserve. They picked up again in November, with the withdrawal of $16 million, but in the following month the danger signals were flying. On that day over $4 million left the government vaults.

On December 20, accepting the inevitability of another bond issue for the singular purpose of increasing the gold reserve, the President appealed to Congress for enabling legislation. Predictably when it came to gold-raising bond issues, the silver Democrats were obstructionist, and the Republicans insisted that the real problem lay in the tariff. Their rather specious argument: higher duties would generate more revenue, and more revenue—more gold, less silver—was what the Treasury really needed to back up the currency and achieve fiscal stability. When it became evident that no legislation acceptable to either house would win approval by the other, and that whatever compromise the two might achieve would never win approval by Cleveland, the White House had no choice but to plan for yet another bond sale.

The climate for a new sale was less than favorable: Cleveland's belligerent message to Congress on Venezuela had adversely affected the market, raising call rates to 80 percent and forcing a number of brokerage houses to suspend trading. Under the circumstances, it was generally assumed that this fourth bond offering, like the third ("the Morgan"), would have to be handled by a syndicate through secret negotiation. In the vanguard of those pushing for such an arrangement was, of course, Morgan. He took steps at once to form a great international syndicate, to include other New York bankers in addition to German and Parisian houses, that would purchase for sale in America and Europe $100 million to $200 million in bonds on more or less the same terms as the previous offering. In return, it would furnish the Treasury an equivalent sum in gold coin, and, as before, take steps to prevent the export of gold abroad. But Cleveland and Carlisle, sensitive to the criticism the previous issue had generated, decided that this fourth offering, for $100 million, would be sold by public subscription. The sale was announced on January 6, 1896; when the bids were unsealed a month later the response was gratifying. Some $66 million went to 780 bidders who had made subscriptions at various rates the Treasury deemed most acceptable, with the balance going to Morgan and his syndicate at the same rate and terms.

The federal gold reserve, which had fallen to $44,500,000, spiked to a record high of $128,713,000. Once again Cleveland had prevailed over many obstacles and malicious denunciation, and the American people were the ultimate beneficiaries. As for the silverites, they were convinced that Cleveland had driven a golden nail into his political coffin, a conviction they were determined more than ever to impress upon the nation.

56

Detested within his own party

When the Democratic National Committee met to select the site for their nominating convention, the silver faction wanted St. Louis, the gold faction wanted New York; they compromised on Chicago. Days later a major convocation of silver delegates was held at Washington. The Senate was at the time giving final shape to a free-coinage bill that passed on February 1 by a vote of 48 to 41, with the Democrats accounting for 24 yeas and only 15 nays; two weeks later it went down in the House by a vote to nonconcur, with Democrats voting almost two to one—58 to 31—in favor of silver coinage. Here was another ominous sign for the administration's sound-money policy. Refusing to accept the loss of all the so-called silver states, the White House went on the offensive. In mid-April, Carlisle gave a speech at Chicago on free silver as it affected the workingman that failed to impress the soft-money faction. A few days later, the Missouri state nominating convention declared for silver, and in Nebraska, where the two factions held separate conventions, the silverites outnumbered the gold bugs.

Good news came for Cleveland out of Michigan, where the gold faction dictated the platform and locked up seventeen of the twenty-eight delegates to Chicago. The good news was attenuated a few weeks later when the Tennessee convention unexpectedly voted for silver, as did Illinois, which had come under the control of the pro-silver governor, Altgeld. From that point on, state conventions in the South and West gave the gold faction two defeats for every success east of the Mississippi. When Virginia instructed its twenty-four delegates to vote as a unit for free coinage at Chicago, Cleveland's name was greeted with hisses and catcalls. In Kentucky, the President and his Treasury Secretary were hooted at every mention of their names. By mid-June, North Dakota, Utah, Kansas, and California had fallen into the silver column. By month's end they were joined by Ohio, Texas, Georgia, and North Carolina. Even in New York, the epicenter of hard-money conviction, the convention at Saratoga voted a bimetal platform endorsing "gold and silver as the standard money of the country."

Though the silverites now had far more than a majority of the delegates to the national convention, they were not yet sure of two-thirds; this meant they could write the party platform, though it was uncertain they could name the candidate. Equally uncertain was whether the party could get through the Chicago convention without self-destructing. The rancor that had been building since the beginning of the year had to be lived through in order to be properly appreciated.

It started in January when South Carolina's "Pitchfork Ben" Tillman indicted Cleveland from the Senate floor, peppering his tirade with such epithets as "self-idolatrous," "besotted tyrant," and "arrogant and obstinate ruler." He served notice that "millions are on the march," and unless relief was at hand, small farmers and their sympathizers from all over the West and South would "come to Washington with rifles in their hands to regain the liberties stolen from them."[109] The hard-money eastern press dismissed Tillman as a "political ruffian" (*New York Mail and Express*) and a "filthy baboon" (*New York Times*). Tillman could not have cared less what they thought of him in the East. Behind him stood the nation's agrarians.

Cleveland's state of mind at this time, which seemed to seesaw between confidence and despair, is reflected in two letters to Don Dickinson. In the first, he offsets profound disgust with "the hatred and vindictiveness of ingrates and traitors who wear the stolen livery of Democracy" with his "supreme faith in the American people. While I believe them to be just now deluded, mistaken and wickedly duped, they will certainly return to sound principles and patriotic aspirations; and what I may suffer in the period of aberration is not important." A few weeks later, after expressing two things he was "longing for—the adjournment of Congress and the 4th day of March, 1897"—Cleveland told Dickinson that the present Congress was "a menace to the good of the country if not to its actual safety [and] every day develops more and more plainly the seeming desperation and wickedness of those in the Senate and House for whose conduct our party *will I suppose be held responsible.*" He was "positive" there was only one chance for future Democratic successes—"a perfectly and unequivocal sound money platform at Chicago." If this resulted in the party's defeat "or even a party division," he was nonetheless certain that "the seed will be saved from which I believe Democratic successes will grow in the future."[110]

Around the end of March, Cleveland, albeit unwittingly, played directly into enemy hands in—of all places—New York's Carnegie Hall, at a rally to benefit the home mission of the Presbyterian Church. Irritated beyond measure that the silver-mining states were putting their own selfish interests before those of the nation, he took note of the "lawlessness, the dram-shops and gambling-dens" that were to be found all over the nation's western frontier. "If unchecked and uncorrected," he warned, these conditions would "fix upon the new community, by their growth and expansion, a character and disposition which, while dangerous to peace and order in the early stages of settlement, develop into badly regulated municipalities, corrupt and unsafe Territories, and undesirable States." Presbyterian missionaries and their religious teachings, he insisted, were needed now more than ever in the trans-Mississippi, "where the process of forming new States is going on so rapidly, and where newcomers who are to be the citizens of new States are so rapidly gathering together."[111]

The storm of reaction his remarks generated in the West was hardly unexpected. The agrarians were apoplectic: this eastern-oriented hard-money President had the gall to suggest that home missions dedicated to bringing God's word to the jungle denizens of the world should direct their efforts to "civilizing" the "heroic Americans who were taming the West"! No one could convince those heroic Americans that they were not the victims of a mammoth machination by Wall Street and those other Clevelandian champions of the gold-standard. They fairly salivated at the prospect of the revenge they'd have "on the d——d East" when *they* took control of the White House.

Throughout the spring and into early summer, Cleveland was urged by his supporters to say something, anything, that might stem what was looming as the breakup of the Democratic party. "We feel that there is a great lack of leadership, political and national, for the sound money forces," wrote one in pleading that he address a letter to some prominent westerner or southerner on the folly of debasing the currency.[112] Cleveland yielded to the pressure with a statement to the country through the *New York Herald Tribune.* While not wishing to pose as his party's "dictator," he was "unable to refrain from making a last appeal in behalf of a party with so abundant an honorable legacy" in the "battle for the welfare of the American people." He refused to believe that when the time came for "deliberate action there will be engrafted upon our Democratic creed a demand for a free, unlimited, and independent coinage of silver." He knew in his heart that the Democratic party was "neither unpatriotic nor foolish"; that it realized such a course would "inflict a very great injury upon every interest of our country, which it had been the party's mission to advance," and would result "in lasting disaster" to the Democracy. Adoption by the Democratic party of a soft-money philosophy, he warned, would give the Republicans "an advantage, both in the present and future, which they do not deserve." Neither the convention, he urged, nor the party itself should submit to the will of the silver faction. "A cause worth fighting for is worth fighting to the end."

The message won unanimous endorsement by the hard-money

press, but opinion differed on its effectiveness. Most agreed the Gold Bugs must fight to the end; there was still hope the silverites could be brought to their senses. Others believed the free-coinage movement had become so powerful that not even divine intervention could halt it. Still others saw in the systematic abuse of Cleveland by western and southern Democrats evidence of their immunity to his pleas or his logic. One midwestern paper noted, "No President was ever so persistently and malignantly lied about as Grover Cleveland has been," and deplored that the "judgment of thousands of men has been warped by whispered stories that are too silly to discuss." As for Cleveland's reaction to all this abuse, he wrote one friend, "I am praying now that the prevalent infection may pass away, leaving life and hope of complete recovery. In the meantime, the brood of liars and fools must have their carnival."[113]

New York financier William Whitney, Cleveland's closest adviser on fiscal matters, determined to have a pro-gold instead of free-coinage plank written into the campaign platform, rushed to Chicago, where pre-convention strategy meetings were in progress. He was not a delegate, merely a loyal Democrat using his personal influence. While he sympathized "thoroughly with the feeling in the South that has caused the uprising and that will find expression in Chicago," he completely disagreed with "the principles which the uprising has brought forth and the issues being framed." William E. Russell, regarded by the eastern gold faction as Cleveland's successor, sounded a less encouraging note. Laboring alongside Whitney, he felt it was "of the utmost importance that the Democratic Party should take an absolutely sound position on the money question," though he had to "admit at present the chances seem against it."

But Russell's pessimism fell before a mini-wave of optimism out of St. Louis, where the Republican convention had opened on the 16th. That party's silver faction, whose numerical strength was nowhere near the figure it had been vaunting, primarily because Republicans were not all that well established in the South and West, had been routed by a platform plank calling for continuance of the gold standard that was written before the convention came to order. When the platform was adopted, the silverites bolted the convention en masse as the delegates screamed, "Go to Chicago! Go! Go!" To the *New York Times* this increased "immensely the probability of a like triumph for the gold standard at the Chicago convention"; to the *New York World,* "McKinley's triumph is Democracy's opportunity. Shall it be a campaign—or suicide?"

Meanwhile, the rumor that Cleveland might yet consider a third term continued apace. Cleveland realized that some disclaimer must be made, given the volume of letters coming in daily urging that he run. But he hesitated to speak out while the prospects of the party's sound-money wing appeared to be so increasingly murky. Better, he reasoned, to remain quiet for the time being, if by so doing he might inspire those who might otherwise become passive on the issue to work in support of his stance. When the hard-money faction carried the Michigan state convention, he believed the time was right to issue such a statement, but Don Dickinson talked him out of it.

This took no great effort on Dickinson's part. Feeling that the idea of seeking a third term was absurd, Cleveland was disinclined to dignify the gossip by even addressing it. Unfortunately, the harm had already been done. His failure to speak out earlier was a colossal tactical blunder, especially as he would not have considered running under any circumstances. But making this known while the states were holding their conventions would have strengthened the gold forces, given the intense hatred so many Democrats had for the President.

Cleveland may not have realized how detested he was within his own party, but he certainly realized he was not everybody's favorite. He took some comfort in Whitney's decision to lead the fight at Chicago for maintaining the gold standard. But he was never one to surrender to illusions of a promising nature. To be pleased is one thing, to face reality is something else. William Wilson believed Cleveland was "not specially hopeful of staying the lunacy of the convention." A remark he made to Wilson best expressed his state of mind at this point. They were discussing the accomplishments of the administration, and Wilson told the President that history would put his accomplishments in their true light. To this Cleveland answered only half-jokingly, "I am not concerning myself about what history will think, but contenting myself with the approval of a fellow named Cleveland whom I have found to be a pretty good sort of fellow." Shortly thereafter, having consigned to Whitney leadership of the fight at Chicago, he left for his summer home on Cape Cod.

57

Thrust aside

For the Gold Bugs, it began in a mood of modified confidence when a special three-car train chartered by Whitney departed New York for Chicago. Aboard were a number of party leaders who agreed to bury their mutual differences (for some, mutual hatreds) in a concerted effort to write a hard-money platform. As the train traveled west, picking up other leaders en route, hopes for beating back the silverites began to rise, influenced, no doubt, by the grand viands and potables Whitney had put aboard and the capacity of one and all to cheer each other up.

Those rising hopes began to subside when they reached Chicago, to find the streets adorned with crowds sporting silver badges and gaily waving silver banners. Not only the delegates and politicians but farmers, storekeepers, and spokesmen for various labor unions cluttered the hotels and restaurants. The Gold Bugs were unsure whether to weep or be ill. One told Whitney the silverites were "mad." Said another: "For the first time I can understand the French Revolution!"[114] Wherever William Russell, Cleveland's presumed successor, went trying to win over the opposition, he was told, "We'd like to vote for you, Governor, but not this year!" Few western and southern delegates mentioned Cleveland's name except to attack him as a President, as a Democrat, and as a man. At the New York delegation headquarters his portrait was mysteriously replaced by those of Tammany sachems Hill, Murphy, and Flower.

When the convention was called to order, the silver faction still lacked the two-thirds vote necessary to dictate the nomination. Next day, despite the violent objections of the gold faction, the committee on credentials guaranteed that necessary two-thirds by increasing the delegations from all the western territories and disqualifying a number of pro-gold delegates from east of the Mississippi. Amid a deafening cacophony and much flinging of newspapers, flags, and hats, a few fists, and an appreciable amount of spit, the newly accredited Nebraskan delegation, led by favorite son William Jennings Bryan, entered the hall.

When the platform was read to the convention, even many of the silverites were shocked by the vindictiveness of those planks aimed directly at Cleveland's policies, condemning the four bond issues ("trafficking with banking syndicates"), his use of injunctions during the Pullman Strike, and what they viewed as unwarranted federal interference in local affairs. Then came the currency debate. When Senator Hill of New York, who was to lead the debate for the gold faction, introduced a resolution commending Cleveland's presidency, the convention rejected it by a vote of 564 to 357. The President's old Tammany antagonist was barely able to suppress his glee: knowing this would be the outcome, he had introduced the resolution solely to humiliate him. One correspondent was moved to write, "Never before in American history has a President sunk so low as Cleveland has fallen. Never has a President been so held in contempt by the people. No one is interested enough to care what he does or says. Cleveland has been driven out of his party, and it was Hill who closed the door and double locked it with his resolution as Cleveland departed."[115]

A few men, led by Vilas, offered an admirable defense of the President and of the administration. Russell pleaded, in addition, against the destruction of the party. All to no avail. Next it was the turn of the silver men, led by Tillman. After castigating New York and the other eastern states for, as he saw it, living high off the hog at the South's expense, he said, in response to Vilas: "You ask us to endorse Cleveland's fidelity. In reply, I say he has been faithful unto death—the death of the Democratic party!"

Last to speak was the tall, dynamic, strikingly handsome Bryan. What was purportedly an extemporaneous address was in fact one he had crafted over the preceding months; he had even tried out parts of it on smaller audiences in pre-convention campaigning. Bryan has left a description of how the audience reacted when he gave what is enshrined in our history of political conventions as inarguably the best remembered of all keynote speeches:

"The crowd seemed to rise and sit down as one man. At the close of a sentence it would rise and shout, and when I began another sentence, the room was as still as a church. . . . The audience acted like a trained choir—in fact, I thought of a choir as I noted how instantaneously and in unison they responded to each point made." Unlike the other silverite speakers, Bryan refused to heap invective upon

Cleveland: "It is not a question of persons. It is a question of principle; and it is not with gladness that we find ourselves brought into conflict with those who are now arrayed upon the other side."

Declaiming with the characteristic deliberation, dignity, and eloquence that made him indisputably the greatest orator on the Chautauqua circuit, Bryan fired the twenty thousand delegates to rabid enthusiasm as he spoke of farms as the basis of the nation's prosperity, of the way in which "the common people" had been scorned and their entreaties mocked, and of the 1776 War of Independence and the contest under way for "popular independence." He trashed the gold standard on behalf of "the struggling masses." And he redefined the word "businessman" to include the wage earner, the farmer and miner, the country lawyer, and the local merchant—men whose interests, he insisted, had been so long neglected by the eastern plutocrats. Then came the words that gave the speech its name and its immortality:

> Having behind us the producing masses of the nation and the world, the laboring interests and the toilers everywhere, we will answer their demand for a gold standard by saying to them: "You shall not press down upon the brow of labor this crown of thorns—you shall not crucify mankind upon a cross of gold!"

The pandemonium these words evoked went on for thirty-five minutes, as Bryan stood accepting his ovation like the noblest of the Caesars. The Gold Bugs sat in sullen silence. When the platform came up for a vote calling for taking the nation off the gold standard it was adopted 628 to 301.

Thus was Grover Cleveland thrust aside as head of the party he twice led to victory, and its leadership thrust upon the Great Commoner.

During the nominating speeches that evening, the animosity toward the easterners was fairly palpable. By the time Bryan was nominated next morning, Whitney and the others were on their way home. (Nominated for second spot on the ticket was Arthur Sewall, a successful boat-builder but political nonentity from Maine. He had the good sense to play the moth to Bryan's flame.) When Bryan's nomination was announced, Otto Gresham, son of the late Secretary of State, heard George Graham Vest of Missouri, a leader of the "Senatorial Clique," chortle in a stage whisper, "Now we are even with old Cleveland!"[116]

We do not know old Cleveland's reaction on hearing the news, other than that he made himself unavailable to most callers, and answered few letters.

He could not have been too surprised.

Now facing the President and his partisans was the question of whether or not to support the convention's choice. Party loyalty precluded Cleveland's openly repudiating Bryan or, for that matter, supporting McKinley and the Republican party's gold platform. The Democratic press did not feel inhibited by any such loyalty. The *New York World* called Bryan the product of hysteria and the free-silver platform, while the *New York Evening Post*, which most reflected the extreme gold sentiment of Wall Street, described the convention as "a mob of repudiators" and Bryan as "the chief of blatherskites." But it remained for the *Richmond Times* to best assess what had happened at Chicago: "In a spasm of hysteria, the convention ran off and nominated a mere youth, who was scarcely known of, because he rattled off before it a studied piece of sophomoric rhodomontade that did not contain a single sound proposition, and abounded in nonsense and anarchy in equal proportions from beginning to end." In New York, William Randolph Hearst's *Journal* was the only major eastern paper to support Bryan. In New England the important Democratic papers bolted the party choice, as did those throughout the Midwest (where the Democrats were left without the support of a single paper) and even into the South, where the *Louisville Courier-Journal*, the *New Orleans Picayune*, and the *Charleston News and Courier* joined the *Richmond Times* in turning their editorial backs on what was popularly coming to be known as Bryanism.[117]

Before leaving Chicago a number of leading Gold Bugs issued a statement rejecting Bryan and his soft-money philosophy and calling for a new convention. Cleveland, who considered Bryan "a Populist without the remotest idea of true Democratic principles," wrote to a friend six days later, "Those who controlled the Convention displayed their hatred of me and wholly repudiated me. Those who at the Convention differed with them seem to have thought it wise to ignore me in all consultation, fearing probably that any connection with me would imperil success. I do not say they were not right. I only say that events have pushed me so much aside that I do not see how I can be useful in harmonizing or smoothing matters. I have an idea, quite fixed and definite, that for the present at least we should none of us say anything. . . . I am not fretting except about the future of the country and party, and the danger that the latter is to be compromised as an organization." To another he wrote the same day, along the same lines, "I am a good deal dazed politically, but my judgment is that it is best for the present to think much and *talk none.*"[118]

Cleveland decided to await the outcome of a conclave of Gold Democrat national committeemen called for Indianapolis on August 7. On July 20 he went to Boston to attend the funeral of Russell, who had died unexpectedly four days earlier. Adding poignancy to the fact that the leading Massachusetts Democrat was only thirty-nine, the hard-money faction could ill afford the loss of so eloquent a spokesman. Reporters attending the funeral noted that the President, though tanned by the Cape Cod sun, seemed weary and depressed. ("His face apparently was as full as ever, but there was a look of added age; the lines seemed harder and the gray mustache, for all its bristling, had less color than even a few months ago.")[119]

At Indianapolis the Gold Democrats, meeting as the National Democratic party, called for a convention to be held in that city September 2, though the driving forces behind it, led by Vilas and Dickinson, were at a loss who would be their standard-bearer. One delegate telegraphed Cleveland, "You will be nominated tomorrow unless you make definite refusal. We strongly urge that you communicate privately, to be used publicly if necessary. . . . Otherwise every indication is that you will be nominated by acclamation." Cleveland wired back, "My judgment and personal inclination are so unalterably opposed to your suggestion that I cannot for a moment entertain it."[120]

The nomination went to John Palmer of Illinois, a seventy-nine-year-old Union general who had helped establish the Republican party in that state and served as governor (1869–73) before becoming a Democrat and going on to serve in the United States Senate (1891–97). Seventy-three-year-old Simon Bolivar Buckner, a Confederate general who had edited the *Louisville Courier* before turning to politics and becoming governor of Kentucky (1887–91), was chosen for the second spot.

Here indeed was a curious ticket: two old men, a Confederate general and a Union one, both from doubtful states, and practically political abecedarians. But everyone accepted the ticket for what it was: a pair of heroic veterans willing to serve as sacrificial lambs in hopes of drawing enough votes away from Bryan to assure the election of McKinley. Cleveland was especially pleased that their platform lauded his administration and his patriotism and courage in the fight against free silver and protectionism, a fight they vowed to continue. But as for endorsing the ticket, he wrote Vilas, it was "a very delicate matter" since he still had "six months more of official life, during which time all I can do of public duty must be done in co-operation with those in another branch [i.e., Congress] whom perhaps I ought not to further irritate."

To Lamont, he wrote next day, employing one of his favorite adjectives, "I am perplexed concerning the course I should pursue. My inclination, of course, is to join the chorus of denunciation, but I am doubtful as to the wisdom of such action, in the light of a chance that it might do more harm than good." As President, he still must "attempt to co-operate" with an already contentious Congress "in the interest of needed legislation, and perhaps ought not to unnecessarily further . . . increase its hatred of me." He did, though, encourage his cabinet officers to support the new party, and did not "care how plainly you present the inference that I am in accord with your views."[121]

Cleveland, of course, played no active role in the campaign. He did come close to doing so, though, in October, when invited to address the sesquicentennial celebration of Princeton College, which had just become a university. (And to receive an honorary degree, which he declined for the same reason he had declined one from Harvard: only those who legitimately earned degrees should he awarded them.) Though he spoke on themes appropriate to the occasion—the duty of educated men, the responsibility of institutes of higher learning to the state, etc.—Cleveland slyly worked in a few passages germane to the campaign, then in its last weeks. For instance, he posited that it was as incumbent upon a nation as it was upon all citizens to be scrupulously honest and faithful to its obligations: "Neither the glitter of its power, nor the tinsel of its commercial prosperity, nor the gaudy show of its people's wealth, can conceal the cankering rust of national dishonesty, and cover the meanness of national bad faith." Then addressing the threat let loose by those who deal in the coin of social or political intolerance, he said, in words that won him great praise from the eastern Republican press as well as Democratic:

> When popular discontent and passion are stimulated by the art of designing partisans to a pitch perilously near to class hatred or sectional anger, I would have our universities and colleges sound the alarm in the name of American brotherhood and fraternal dependence. When the attempt is made to delude the people in the belief that their suffrage can change the operation of natural laws, I would have our universities and colleges proclaim that those laws are inexorable and far removed from political control. When a design is apparent to lure the people from their honest thoughts and to blind their eyes to the sad plight of national dishonor and bad faith, I would have Princeton University, panoplied in her patriotic traditions and glorious memories, and joined by all the other universities and colleges of our land, cry out against the infliction of this treacherous and fatal wound.[122]

The President and First Lady were then honored by the undergraduates with a gigantic parade that featured a number of large banners; one that both Clevelands enjoyed in particular read: "Grover, send your boys to Princeton." It is believed this reception influenced Cleveland's decision to settle at Princeton after retiring from office.

Cleveland may have kept out of the campaign, but he did have to contend with what to him was the rank treachery of high-ranking federal officeholders openly supporting Bryan. This, he wrote Vilas on September 5, left him "exceedingly angry and humiliated"; he was pondering the question of how to deal with "those who are behaving badly." One who behaved "badly" was his Interior Secretary, Hoke Smith. Though one of the few Georgia Democrats to uphold the gold standard, both in public speeches and through his newspaper the *Atlanta Journal,* Smith feared that to lead a revolt against his party in a Democratic state would raise the risk of Republican victory and, as so many Georgians dreaded, restore "Reconstruction-type Negro authority."

While he was "deeply distressed by the action of the Chicago convention, and by the situation it has produced," he wrote Cleveland,

and could never accept the party platform, he "must support the nominee," whom he detested; he had promised the people of Georgia, and the "local situation" obliged him to do so. Cleveland waited two weeks before replying ("I have delayed and hesitated because I could not satisfy myself as to what I should write") and then went on to rebuke him: "You say, 'While I shall not accept the platform, I must support the nominees of the Chicago Convention.' I cannot see how this is to be done. It seems to me like straining at a gnat and swallowing a camel."[123]

Cleveland then sent word that he would accept Smith's resignation. The other cabinet officers, in particular Wilson and Carlisle, urged him not to. Smith had done an excellent job at Interior, the administration had but a few months left, and accepting his resignation would create an unpleasant distraction in Democratic circles. But Cleveland was unyielding. When Smith tendered his resignation, it was accepted, albeit with genuine regret. It was believed that if Smith had gone to Gray Gables from the convention and explained his position, Cleveland might have understood and not have forced him from the cabinet. Perhaps. But only perhaps. Letting himself be persuaded to contravene potentially deleterious initial instincts was a quality Grover Cleveland steadfastly declined to cultivate. In the event, it is pleasant to report there was no ill feeling on the part of either man; when Cleveland invited Smith and his wife to attend the annual (and last) cabinet dinner at the White House, Smith accepted, and was made very welcome.

By mid-September the election result was a foregone conclusion. It was no secret that many who were most vociferous in supporting Bryan publicly were admitting in private that they could never vote for him. When Cleveland returned to the White House from Cape Cod in early October he was "looking thoroughly well and in excellent spirits, being fully convinced that there is no danger of Bryan's election."[124] He was elated by the extent of Bryan's rout: McKinley won by a plurality of 602,000 out of a total almost fourteen million votes cast, and in the South, Bryan's vote ran behind Cleveland's in 1892. Though the alternative Democratic ticket polled but an insignificant 135,000 votes, it had effectively pushed many more to McKinley. Another aftermath that pleased Cleveland: while the Bryan candidacy sought to set the poor and laboring classes against the nation's "plutocrats" and to arouse a degree of sectional passion not seen since Reconstruction, his defeat was accepted without so much as a hint of protest.

Amid their despair over McKinley's victory, which in fact owed more to Bryanism than to any other factor, the Democratic Gold Bugs rejoiced with their Republican counterparts that sound money had prevailed. There was further cause for rejoicing: the victory for sound money was Grover Cleveland's, rather than McKinley's.

Bryan summed up the cause of his defeat in one sentence: "I have borne the sins of Grover Cleveland." Not true. The sins Bryan had borne were the sins of fiscal heresy, and no blame for that heresy can be imputed to Grover Cleveland.

In appraising the election for the *Baltimore Evening News*, Dr. Fabian Franklin delivered an eloquent valedictory on Cleveland's eight years in the White House:

> When the history of the present time comes to be seriously written, the name of the hero of this campaign will be that of a man who was not a candidate, not a manager, not an orator; the fight which has just been won was made possible by the noble service of one steadfast and heroic citizen, and the victory which was achieved yesterday must be set down as the crowning achievement of his great record.
>
> It is impossible to overestimate the value of the service Grover Cleveland has done through his twelve years of unswerving fidelity to the cause of honest money. This is Cleveland's day, the vindication of his course, and the abundant reward of his steadfast adherence . . . to the principle of honor which he has held above self, above party, above expedience.

PART VIII

1897—1907

58

"My poor old battered name"

The interim between a presidential election and the transfer of power is discomfiting for the incumbent. If he has served the two terms allowed by the Constitution he is a lame duck; if he has served but one term and been defeated for reelection he is a dead duck. In either case, his leadership has become irrelevant. Of all our Presidents, only Grover Cleveland was both. In 1888 he was a defeated incumbent. Now he was an incumbent repudiated by his own party, which, in the bargain, had lost both houses of Congress and blamed him for that loss. Determined to avoid kinship with Bryanism, and convinced it was the party, not he, that had erred, Cleveland accepted what he termed a "splendid isolation" for the four months that remained of his administration.

He still had a band of devotees (what he termed "the true Democratic Party") who accepted his leadership, less out of absolute loyalty than out of an absolute certainty that history would vindicate him. Some of them, besides a few who were neither friends nor colleagues but simply admirers, wrote articles for important magazines recording and interpreting major events in Cleveland's presidency. "There are now three projects, in fact, to serve me up and help people to breast or dark meat, with or without stuffing," he responded when granting his friend Gilder sanction for just such a project. "I don't know in the shuffle what will become of me and my poor old battered name, but I think perhaps I ought to look after it a little. I shall probably avail myself of your kindness."[1]

First of the three projects was by Woodrow Wilson, whose well-balanced piece "Mr. Cleveland as President" ran in the March 1897 *Atlantic Monthly*. Gilder's was postponed for a number of reasons; when it was published in book form fourteen years later as *Grover Cleveland: A Record of Friendship*, what had begun as an essay had become a series of intimate, quite lovely sketches and personal recollections. The third project alluded to in Cleveland's letter, and one that he particularly appreciated, was Carl Schurz's splendid study of the second administration, published in the May 1897 *McClure's Magazine*.

Cleveland may have been turned out, rejected, cast aside as superfluous: call it what you will, he was still President of the United States until March 4, 1897, at high noon. And unlike some others over our history who chose to lie low and mark time, Cleveland discharged his office more like a man new to it than a man about to depart it. Two questions occupied most of his attention during this period. Ironically, both were in an area that never ranked high on Cleveland's list of priorities—international relations.

While abhorring a foreign policy of expansionism or intervention, Cleveland accepted that the United States could no longer remain isolated in world affairs. Ever since taking office in 1885 he had advocated international arbitration as the only sane alternative to discord, which could easily get out of control. His greatest ambition in this regard, an arbitration treaty with Great Britain, was negotiated even before resolution of the Venezuela Boundary Dispute. It pledged the two nations, for a five-year period, to submit to arbitration, consonant with the treaty's provisions and subject to its limitations, any and all questions and differences between them which they could not adjust by diplomatic negotiation.

Seeing the treaty as his valedictory, not only to lasting peace between the world's two great English-speaking nations but to the general cause of world peace, Cleveland sent it to the Senate for ratification on January 11. Reaction by the American press was enthusiastic, without regard to party. Bryan's *Omaha World-Herald* ecstatically (perhaps overly so) declared it to be "one of the grandest triumphs of humanity," "the supreme achievement of the nineteenth century."[2] The popular response was no less rhapsodic. Leaders from all walks of life mounted a massive propaganda campaign that culminated in a torrent of petitions to Congress from church groups, universities, chambers of commerce, even mass meetings, all urging ratification; many state legislatures passed resolutions to that effect.

Still, the treaty was defeated by a perfidious coterie of jingoists, Cleveland-haters, silverites who opposed England as the chief supporter of the gold standard, and a few under pressure from shipbuilding interests anxious to see a much larger American navy. But pride of place for reasons behind the defeat was assigned by Olney to the steady encroachment by the Senate on the executive and judicial branches in hopes of becoming the dominant power in the government, and its insistence that when it received a treaty for consideration "it must be either altogether defeated or so altered as to bear the unmistakable Senate stamp—and thus be the means both of humiliating the executive and of showing to the world the greatness of the Senate." Its defeat was "a calamity, not merely of national but of worldwide proportions."[3] Cleveland and Olney had obviously misjudged how the Senate might respond to public opinion. Still, their effort to get such an agreement was praiseworthy; and despite its failure, it further encouraged the growing harmony between the United States and Great Britain.

The second issue to disturb the closing months of Cleveland's public life—and the most consequential—was Cuba's struggle for independence from Spain. Cleveland's resistance to American intervention offers a stark contrast to McKinley's willingness to let a small band of egregious superpatriots, led by William Randolph Hearst, drag the United States into a war that was none of its business, simply to sell newspapers and wave the flag.

When the insurrection against Spanish rule broke out in February 1895, the last in a series that dated back to the collapse of Spain's New World empire earlier in the century, Cuba's population was some one and a half million, of whom some two-thirds were whites, the balance an admixture of mulattoes, Negroes, Indians, and half-white mestizos. Most were illiterate, poverty-stricken, and superstitious. The rebellion was openly led and fed by a Cuban junta in New York City, assisted by filibustering expeditions outfitted in the United States. Yeoman's service came from a coterie of American jingoism that saw Hearst's *Journal* and Pulitzer's *World* vying to outdo each other in malevolent sensationalism.

The rebels made sure the war raged in every part of the island, and in a most destructive fashion, in the belief that if they wreaked havoc with industries and resources and reduced Cuba to a barren ruin, Spain would willingly abandon it. The sugar crop fell by 80 percent as the other major cash crop, tobacco, fell by 90 percent. Losses to American investors and importers were damned in the United States, as was the ruthless behavior of Spanish officials and troops. Many Americans felt it incumbent upon the nation to support a New World colony of dedicated revolutionists in throwing off the yoke of an Old World monarchy, especially one so singularly repressive.

Moving promptly to define the American position, Cleveland proclaimed a neutrality that acknowledged the existence of a state of rebellion but did not recognize its legitimacy. Insisting that this neutrality be scrupulously enforced, he ordered the strict interdiction of filibusterers. Both he and Olney were convinced, as was the Madrid government, that without American assistance the uprising would be quashed within a month. (Though the U.S. Coast Guard was more effective than the Spanish in patrolling Cuban waters, fifteen of more than twoscore expeditions made it safely to the island.)

While disdaining war, Olney urged intervention in behalf of American citizens of Cuban birth or descent who were arrested in Cuba and claimed compensation for damage to American property. Making no secret of where his sympathies lay, he advised Cleveland that nine-tenths of the Cuban population supported the insurgents "in sympathy and feeling." Furthermore, the property class was to a man "disgusted with Spanish misrule, with a system which has burdened the Island with $300,000,000 of debt, whose impositions in the way of annual taxes just stop short of prohibiting all industrial enterprise, and which yet does not fulfill the primary functions of government by insuring safety to life and security to property." Illustrative of Spain's repressive methods, Olney mentioned "the short and effective way" the government had of dealing with noncombatant suspects: "A file of soldiers visits certain designated houses at night—the proscribed persons are carried off—but, partly for the torture of the thing, and partly because the noise of the firearms is to be avoided, they are not shot but chopped to pieces with the small axes that the Spaniards call *machetes*."

The Cuban revolution, he concluded, was "just in itself, commanding the sympathy, if not the open support, of the great bulk of the population," and was quite capable of establishing constitutional government. As things now stood, he was sure that within a few months Cuba would either drown in its own blood or be "in the market, for sale to the highest bidder," since Spain's chances of suppressing the rebellion were negligible. He concluded with the warning that American "politicians of all stripes, including Congressmen," were "setting their sails, or preparing to set them, so as to catch the popular breeze, which blew in the direction" of United States recognition of Cuban belligerency.[4]

The administration was now faced with pursuing a two-sided policy: convincing Spain to eliminate the causes of Cuban dissent, and thereby supporting recognition of the Cuban people's rights; and resisting the interventionist spirit now pervading Congress. In the spring of 1896, Cleveland had Olney send an *aide-mémoire* to Madrid urging concessions toward a peaceful settlement. Madrid replied that it was willing to make vague promises to the insurrectionists, but nothing more.

Congressional sympathy had from the beginning been generally with the Cubans. Now, in this presidential election year, given the popular dislike of Cleveland in the South and West, candidates of all parties were only too eager to solicit votes by causing trouble for the administration. In the Senate, which arrogated to itself the lead in provoking some altercation with Spain short of war, speeches abounded denouncing the Spanish "butcheries," while a glut of bills were introduced proposing appropriations for new battleships and fortifications, as were resolutions for an inquiry into the entire Cuban problem or even for "peaceful intervention" (never quite properly defined).

In April 1896, both houses of Congress passed resolutions recognizing the Cuban uprising and proposing that the President offer to serve as an interested third party in restoring peace to the island. Because there was no joint resolution, no presidential action was required. In a cabinet discussion, Olney suggested the President preclude any impetuous action on Congress's part by sending a commission to Cuba for a firsthand report on the conflict. The others did not consider the idea practical, and that was the end of it.

Soon there was talk in Congress of forcing the President to recognize Cuba diplomatically, which would have been tantamount to declaring war on Spain. Cautious as he was in his handling of Spanish relations, Cleveland became doubly cautious following the November election. Still, he was not about to simply stall so as to dump the problem in McKinley's lap. His sense of urgency in finding a peaceful solution, and as expeditiously as possible, was fueled by word that Spain had initiated a program whereby its policy of suppression became a policy of extermination. Thousands of peasants from the outlying districts, most of whom had shown sympathy for the rebellion though they had not taken active roles, were driven herdlike into fortified towns and confined in what were essentially urban corrals, where they were allowed to die from starvation and disease.

In his last Annual Message to Congress, Cleveland warned Spain to act humanely toward Cuba, pleaded that Congress give her a little more time to do so, and hinted at possible American intervention as a last resort. His words created more of a stir at home than abroad, further inflaming public opinion and encouraging Congress to hope it might force his hand. The Senate Foreign Relations Committee, not willing to wait for Madrid to decide the issue, took up a resolution offered by James Donald Cameron (R., Pa.) calling for recognition of Cuba's independence. This amounted to a demand that the United States go to war with Spain if she refused. When Olney registered his and Cleveland's opposition, he was assured that the committee was in complete accord with the President's handling of Cuban affairs and that the resolution would never come to the Senate floor. A day later, he was told the committee had decided to adopt Cameron's and all other resolutions on Cuban independence, and was asked to help with the phraseology!

Feeling outraged and betrayed, Olney issued a statement to the press in which he wished to correct "serious apprehensions both at home and abroad" about the Cameron resolution. The power to recognize any foreign government, he insisted, rested exclusively with the executive branch. The only thing the Cameron resolution would accomplish would be to inflame popular passions both at home and in Spain, imperil the lives and property of American citizens traveling abroad, and hamper the United States government in its conduct of foreign relations.[5]

Reaction in the Senate was positively rabid. One member (Republican) asserted that if Congress adopted a joint resolution requiring the President to recognize Cuban independence, and passed it over his anticipated veto, Cleveland must either execute the law or submit himself to impeachment. Another member (also Republican) furiously accused the President of "playing the role of Andrew Johnson" in order to intimidate Congress. But this was all so much grandstanding. Olney's statement had achieved its desired effect. With practically the entire press attacking the resolution, cooler heads prevailed, and it was put aside.

Though he had strictly enforced the neutrality laws and brought pressure on Spain to promise constitutional changes in Cuba, Cleveland still feared that war with Spain was imminent. He asked Frederic Coudert to go speak with the Spanish authorities in Havana. Coudert objected, on the grounds that within a few days there would be a new President and a new cabinet, "who would naturally wish to form their own policies and choose their own personnel in the face of the Cuban situation."[6] Cleveland said he believed McKinley would never embark upon an unnecessary war, and that if Coudert accepted the appointment, he himself would take up the matter with the incoming President. But Coudert backed off, pleading impaired health, and when McKinley entered office four days later the Cuban situation remained unresolved.

Cleveland and Olney in these months did much to damp the jingoism raging about them. Within two years McKinley was hailed for his role as a war President. From our own perspective, it would appear that the role Cleveland played in the Cuban revolt was the more creditable of the two.

59

Lame duck

Also during the closing months of his presidency Cleveland turned anew to the prosecution of the trusts under the Sherman Act of

1890. While Attorney General, presumably influenced by his own pro-corporate prejudices, Richard Olney had shown a distinct lack of initiative in this area. Government attorneys were allowed to go to trial with carelessly prepared, in some instances deplorably weak, cases so that major victories were reversed on appeal. Olney's successor as Attorney General, Judson Harmon, thought he could do better. When barely eight months in office, he told Congress of flaws in the Sherman Act and asked for corrective legislation.

Cleveland vigorously condemned the trusts and made of Harmon's request an outright demand in his last Annual Message to Congress. Meanwhile Harmon, encouraged by Cleveland, did his best within the limitations of the law as it then stood, bringing before the Supreme Court the case against the Trans-Missouri Freight Association, a dangerous railroad trust. Preparing his briefs and evidence with a fastidiousness never shown by Olney when Attorney General, Harmon personally argued the case against a group of the ablest attorneys in the land. As a result the Court, voting 5 to 4, reversed the decision of the lower courts, which had held the Sherman Act was not applicable in this instance. The ultimate significance of the victory was that it established the foundation for the successful program of trust-busting that illuminated the Theodore Roosevelt presidency. And thanks to the increased aggressiveness of his Department of Justice in pursuing similar cases and with similar results, Cleveland left office with a far more creditable record against the trusts than had seemed possible only a year before.

During his last week in office, Cleveland was obliged to take action upon a difficult question that resonates to this day: immigration restriction. As the number of incoming aliens climbed during the 1880s, mostly from southern and eastern Europe, a protest movement swept the nation—especially among descendants of earlier immigrants from western and northern Europe. In 1882, the number totaled 789,000; it declined in the next few years and then began to increase again, reaching 547,000 in 1888. The probability of an endless stream of more than half a million foreigners annually panicked the conservatives, who, conveniently ignoring their own immigrant ancestry, saw it as a threat to the basic character of the nation. They correlated the immigrants—mainly from Italy, Greece, Hungary,

Poland, and the Slavic nations—with anarchist agitation and labor disorders like the Haymarket Riot and Pullman Strike.

Demands for rigidly restricting immigration reverberated from lecture platforms, labor headquarters, and editorial offices, to the effect that the United States was getting the dregs of Europe (*Philadelphia Telegraph*, March 28, 1887); the moral fiber of the nation was being enfeebled by its absorption of the dregs of the Old World (*Chicago Times*, March 27, 1887); if there was not a stop, America would soon be dominated by foreign detectives and their offspring (*Milwaukee Journal*, March 27, 1887). Only a philosophy based on admitting carefully selected "desirables" was considered acceptable.

In 1896, the redoubtable Senator Lodge of Massachusetts introduced a bill that would deny entry to any immigrant over sixteen unable to read and write either English "or some other language." This would fall hard on those from southern and eastern European countries, where illiteracy was so extensive that, more often than not, those who could read and write were least inclined to emigrate. The bill, which passed the House by a large majority, and the Senate by 34 to 31, enjoyed general support of the public, especially among Protestants, as the source countries were predominantly Roman Catholic. Also supporting the bill were most leaders of unions representing unskilled workers, who feared the unskilled immigrants would be competitive, and social workers, who feared such problems as pauperism and social assimilation.

Signing the bill would have earned Cleveland more plaudits than any other legislation he signed over two presidencies, to judge by the encouragement he received from politically and philosophically diverse newspapers nationwide. But he refused to do so, explaining that he found it unnecessarily oppressive and uncharitable, and that the qualities of a prospective desirable citizen were not necessarily contingent upon one's ability to read and write. Besides, he saw no need to reverse existing immigration policy.

Lodge and his supporters on both sides of the aisle were outraged; his friend Theodore Roosevelt wrote, "I took a kind of grim satisfaction in Cleveland's winding up his career by this action, so that his last stroke was given to injure his country as much as he possibly could."[7] Inexplicably, given the passions aroused by the bill, public reaction was minimal. Perhaps it was tacitly agreed that further rebuking the

President two days before the expiration of his term was like flogging a dead horse.

Whether Cleveland took the right course in vetoing the Lodge bill is one of those historical milestones that can be debated endlessly. What cannot be debated is that he had the courage to take it.

On the day he left office, the *Atlanta Constitution* editorialized that "Grover Cleveland will go out under a greater burden of popular contempt than has ever been excited by a public man since the foundation of the government." On the previous day, the *Kansas City Times* had written: "The Democratic party which he has deceived, betrayed and humiliated, long ago stamped him as a political leper and cast him out as one unclean. The reproaches and contumely of the entire American people accompany him in his retirement." A Minnesota Populist, grandstanding for his constituency, told his state legislature the ludicrous story that Grover Cleveland was leaving the White House "with the ignominious distinction that he is the first President who ever accumulated millions during his term of office."[8] Cleveland took no public notice of the charges, but a hint of his inner feelings can be gleaned from an incident that occurred as he was completing arrangements for his final departure. He told his loyal major domo, Sinclair, to take down the official portrait by Eastman Johnson and put it in the attic. He saw no good reason why the White House should treasure his picture, and lacked enough vanity to want to see it left there.

Rarely if ever did Presidents of opposing political parties preside over the transfer of power with such cordial relations as did McKinley and Cleveland. On inauguration eve the two enjoyed a congenial dinner *à deux* (Frances and the children had already left for their new home). Next day, before they parted, Cleveland warned the new President of the danger of a war with Spain. But the subject uppermost in his mind, and on which he spoke most passionately, was the preservation of a sound currency. McKinley thanked him for all that he had done to smooth the way for the new administration, and said:

> "Now, Mr. Cleveland, isn't there something you would like me to do for you?"
>
> "No, Mr. President," replied Mr. Cleveland, "there is nothing

> that I want personally; but I beg you to remember that the time may come again when it will be necessary to have another union of the forces which supported honest money against this accursed heresy; and for this reason I ask you to use all your influence against such extreme action as would prevent such a union."[9]

McKinley assured Cleveland that he fully appreciated the necessity of avoiding the free-silver danger, and that he had in fact begun to act along that line in the composition of his cabinet. Cleveland thanked him and expressed the fervent hope that when McKinley's turn came to leave office, he would not have so many reasons to be glad. McKinley replied graciously that his [Cleveland's] place in history was assured.

Immediately after the inauguration, Cleveland left with three associates for two weeks of fishing and duck-shooting in North Carolina. Years later one of the three, noted military surgeon Leonard Wood, recalled Cleveland boarding ship:

> He was tired and worn from weeks of hard work and the strain of the long hard day, and as we were pulling off from the dock . . . he sat down with a sigh of relief, glad that it was all over.
>
> "I have had a long talk with President McKinley," he said. "He is an honest, sincere, and serious man. I feel that he is going to do his best to give the country a good administration. He impressed me as a man who will have the best interests of the people at heart."
>
> Then he stopped and added, with a sigh: "I envy him today only one thing, and that was the presence of his mother at his inauguration. I would have given anything in the world if my mother could have been at my inauguration."

Wood also recalled that for the entire voyage Cleveland would accept no special privileges. "If he found himself in a poor position for shooting, he would always insist on staying there, never permitting any of us to be displaced . . . nor would he allow anything to be done for him which would seem to give him an undue advantage." This included carrying his own gun: "On this expedition [Cleveland said] every fellow does his own carrying."

At trip's end, when Wood left him on the North Carolina platform to await his northbound train, the ex-President, as if suddenly realizing he was again a free man, waved a hand in fond farewell and called out gaily: "If you don't mind, just ask the conductor to roll me off at Princeton."[10]

Alan Nevins recounts a charming anecdote about the Clevelands' decision on where to retire, told him by a surviving member of their inner circle. It seems that one morning Frances, having scouted houses in New York City's suburban Westchester County, told her husband at breakfast, "I have had an inspiration about our future home." "So have I," he said. Simultaneously each asked the other, "What is it?" Simultaneously each replied, "Princeton!"[11] Since both were quite taken with Princeton as a result of their visit there two weeks before his election, and Cleveland had himself begun to make active inquiries just days after the election, the story is suspect.

Early in November, Cleveland wrote to Latin professor Andrew West that he was

> casting about for a resting place where we can settle with our three babies after the fourth of the next March. Somehow for the last few days the idea has entered our minds that we might be very comfortable and satisfied at Princeton. I think I would like to buy a house in which I may live and die . . . having plenty of room and a fair share, at least, of the conveniences of modern existence. . . . For my wife and children I want some ground about the house, a pleasant social life, a healthy and comfortable climate (especially in the winter), and good school advantages.[12]

Frances went to look over some places West suggested, and fell in love at first sight with a large colonial mansion of stucco-covered stone, surrounded by spacious grounds dotted with fine old trees on five woodland acres. The ex-President's first view of Westland, as they named the house to honor their new friend, came when the conductor "rolled him off at Princeton" amid a pouring rain on March 18, 1897—which just happened to be his sixtieth birthday.

60

The Princeton years

Cleveland believed himself the most unpopular man in America. Reviled by the Bryanite Democrats, who hated him for having, or so they believed, caused their defeat, disregarded by the Republicans, who were not yet ready to give him the credit he deserved for their success, Cleveland was a political Philip Nolan: a man without a party. But never one to dwell on the past, and convinced he would be vindicated in time, he put the election and its consequences out of mind and set about making a new life.

He yearned for a quiet retirement, far removed from public notice and its attendant discord. He felt a renewed attachment to his native state. And he found himself strongly drawn to the place where his father had once pursued his divinity studies. Princeton was a lovely village off the main railroad line where life was uncomplicated and leisurely. What saved it from succumbing to terminal provincialism was the cultural enrichment imparted by the university, then undergoing an active expansionist phase. Departments were being added and the student body enlarged without sacrificing established traditions. The Presbyterian ethos dating from the school's founding that was to Cleveland so compatible was still as pervasive as the ivied walls and hallowed halls. Greek-letter fraternities were proscribed, and athletics to an excessive degree were frowned upon. Conservatism was the Zeitgeist; liberalism was inadmissible. President Francis Patton, a former clergyman and professor of theology, believed that progress was best realized when it moved with the speed of a slug and the caution of a hare.

The faculty boasted men of academic distinction. With most, Cleveland shared a casual, friendly acquaintanceship. With a few he enjoyed a cordial intimacy—West, for instance, who resembled him in size and demeanor, and, like him, could be blunt and stubborn when he felt the occasion justified such behavior. The star attraction was Woodrow Wilson, Professor of Jurisprudence and Political Economy, who would succeed Patton five years thence. He and Cleveland, the only Democrats to occupy the White House between the Civil War and the First World War, shared a somewhat detached friendship best described as mutual respect rooted in a tacit compact not to intrude upon each other's space.

To an inquisitive reporter who greeted his arrival, Cleveland said, "I am enjoying the first holiday of my life. I have worked hard. Now I am entitled to rest. My mission in life has been accomplished." He set at once to supervise the proper arrangement of furniture in his office and cull from among the many crates of books he had shipped down from Washington those for which he saw no reason to create shelf space. Most were presentation copies of works on just about every conceivable subject, many sent along by foreign admirers ignorant of the fact that Cleveland's reading, like his speaking, was limited to the English language. The university librarian was invited to pick out any of the unwanted books he wanted. Cleveland's expansive mood should be obvious from his invitation when the librarian called. "Come in, and take what you want." Then, picking up a large volume, beautifully bound in red leather and inscribed in gold, he said, "This is a Bible in the language of Borneo. I seldom read it. Could the Library make use of that?"[13]

Five days later, with all the books properly shelved and the furniture arranged to his taste, Cleveland began summoning the faithful. On March 23 he began a series of letters to, among others, Gilder, Lamont, and L. Clarke Davis, inviting—actually, requesting—that they pay him, at the very least, an overnight visit, preferably longer. These and all subsequent invitations were expressed in the terms of intimacy Cleveland enjoyed with each, as in a note to West: "I have been here almost a week and have not seen you yet. How am I to get on in this way? Unless I see you within a brief period, I shall pull up stakes and clear out." To "Commodore" Benedict, who had already come for a day or two of cribbage (their favorite joint pastime), Cleveland wrote that he "discovered after you left yesterday that you had not taken with you a 'perfect wealth' of fine cigars which you brought. I don't think you can afford that on $2 winnings. If, however, you intended to leave them, I thank you most sincerely. If not, I will send them to you by express."[14]

Cleveland's relationship with Benedict was so close that from April to October every year—sailing season along the East Coast—the latter's yacht *Oneida* was at his disposal. (Benedict also insisted that the

Clevelands be his houseguests whenever they visited New York City.) Besides using the *Oneida* to go to Cape Cod for the summer, and for a number of cruises in the area, Cleveland and Benedict, often with one or two mutual friends, took two extended cruises yearly, including several to the South Carolina marshes, where Cleveland enjoyed duck-hunting, and once to Bermuda, one of the two times he left the continental United States. (The other was to the Bahamas on business attendant to his role as executor of his two deceased brothers' estate.)

Cleveland may have had to put up with the press while a public figure; as a private person he felt no such obligation. When a local reporter pleaded for an interview with the argument that "a vast number of people are interested in knowing what you do," he was told: "Well, we'll see how they get along without knowing." Just as he was determined to enjoy a privacy denied him all those years of high visibility, so was he determined to enjoy an informality he had not known since starting his climb to political eminence three decades earlier in Buffalo. Except on formal occasions, he affected a brown slouch hat, loose clothes of marked vintage, and wide, comfortable shoes. Not for Grover Cleveland the pose of an elder statesman. He preferred to be, as Andrew Jackson once said of Sam Houston, "A man made by God and not by a tailor."

Cleveland's presence was constantly solicited for charitable functions. Pleased to be remembered, he gave his time freely (though he did fuss to intimates about the constant intrusion upon the leisure he felt he had earned). Any decision to involve himself in a project was based not on the prominence of petitioner and cause, or lack of same, but on whether his involvement might do some tangible good. While he greeted and interacted heartily, and with surprising informality, with people he chose to see, with new acquaintances he practiced self-restraint to ward off undue familiarity. He was always conscious of the high office he had held, and wished others to share that consciousness.

Just as he never forgot the high office he had twice occupied, neither could Cleveland shed entirely the sadness he felt at having lost the love and confidence of the American people. This was obvious in some of his letters, especially those to former colleagues, and even slipped unbidden into his conversations like some intruder whose presence is not to be denied. Pulitzer Prize–winning playwright Jesse Lynch Williams, who lived for a time at Princeton and won Cleveland's friendship, came by with his dog one day to visit. Forbidden entrance to the house, the dog scouted around till he found another entrance, trotted into the drawing room where the two men were talking, and headed straight for his master to be petted. As Williams rose to remove him, Cleveland said, "No, let him stay. He at least likes me."[15]

It was expected that Cleveland would write his memoirs. For entreaties from friends that he get cracking on it, he had a stock response: he saw no reason to do so. "My official acts and public career are public property. There is nothing to say about them. What I did is done and history must judge of its value, not I. My private life has been so commonplace that there is nothing to write about." To West, who once interrupted a game of billiards to urge that he produce "at least a brief, dictated personal memorandum," Cleveland replied emphatically: "I'll tell you, I won't do it, and I'll tell you why. The moment I began, the newspapers would cry: 'There goes the old fool again.' "[16]

In 1905, three years before he died, Cleveland was offered $10,000 by *McClure's Magazine* for twelve articles. He offered to give a series of biographical interviews to a professional writer instead. *McClure's* turned the offer down, which is unfortunate. A skilled interviewer might have elicited information regarding Cleveland's public acts which, for one reason or another, he never put into his lectures or published articles. In describing the failed *McClure's* project, Cleveland told a friend, in one of his infrequent forays into sentiment:

> There is a circle of friends like you, who I hope will believe in me. I am happy in the conviction that they will continue in the faith whether an autobiography is written or not. I want my wife and children to love me now and hereafter to proudly honor my memory. They will have my autobiography written on their hearts where every day they may turn the pages and read it. In these days what else is there that is worth while to a man nearly sixty-eight years old?[17]

The older he got, the more emotional Cleveland became, especially when it came to children, his own or anyone else's. One St. Valentine's

Day his daughters Ruth and Esther told how they and their schoolmates had exchanged valentines. When one of the girls remarked how sad it was that a girl named Jean was the only child not to get one, Frances was surprised to see tears welling in her husband's eyes. Distressed at the thought of a disappointed little girl having been inadvertently overlooked, he immediately dispatched a messenger with a valentine "for Jean from Grover Cleveland." According to Frances, he could not bear to attend the Christmas-tree-lighting ceremony in the Princeton church they attended because the voices of the children singing Christmas carols always brought tears to his eyes.[18] (Old-timers recalled how while governor of New York, when walking to or from his residence to his office in the capitol building Cleveland would pause to greet every child in his path with a warm "Hello, little one!")

Life for Cleveland settled into a pleasant routine. He arose between seven and eight, and following breakfast and reading the newspapers, tended to his morning's mail, often strolling down to the village post office to collect it himself. He passed the days in reading, planning additions and changes to the new house, and, when the opportunity arose, fishing in the local ponds.[19] At some time during the afternoon, weather allowing, he took his wife for a drive, having indulged himself the luxury of a coach, coachman, and pair of horses (for which he built a stable on the property that also housed the children's ponies). When out-of-town visitors arrived, he was at the station to meet them. Dinner at Westland was formal, and there were invariably guests. Cleveland liked to entertain at home, and to enjoy a few evening hours with close male friends at the billiard table or cribbage board; he cared little for dining out, even less for concerts or lectures. He did, though, enjoy student sports, especially football, as did Frances, and seats for all games at Brokaw Field were put aside for them. (Many a game was halted momentarily by a tremendous uproar from the bleachers, the students feigning outrage; when alarmed strangers asked what was the matter, they were told, "Some guy got into Grover's seat.")

A reflection of Cleveland's identification with the Princeton community, and the swiftness with which students and faculty fairly overwhelmed him with cordiality and deference, no doubt influenced his decision to accept a degree of doctor of laws in June 1897. Perhaps in at last accepting an "unearned" degree after having declined so many, Cleveland felt he had "earned" it through active participation in university life.

Cleveland's formal connection with the university began two years later when a "Lectureship on Public Affairs" was endowed in his honor by wealthy alumnus Henry Stafford Little. In successive winters until 1904, he lectured in Alexander Hall before capacity audiences on themes taken from his own experiences in the White House. (Three—"Independence of the Executive," "The Government in the Chicago Strike," and "The Venezuelan Question"—were published in 1904 under the collective title *Presidential Problems.*) On Commencement Day he was always given the place of honor alongside the school president at the head of the academic procession. (In 1911–12, the imposing Cleveland Tower was erected by popular subscription as part of the graduate college building. Thus did Princeton honor his labors in behalf not only of the college but of the university as a whole, most notably as a fund-raiser.)

On October 15, 1901, Cleveland was made a trustee of the university, in which capacity he discharged his responsibilities faithfully, from chairing meetings and sitting in on examinations for doctoral candidates to traveling far afield to speak before Princeton alumni and raise endowments. He was known on more than one occasion to rebuke idlers among his thirty-one co-trustees with the remark "Every man must pull his full weight in the boat!" So much for telling West before coming to Princeton: "I want to be free from all sorts of social and other exactions that might interfere with the lazy rest I crave."[20]

As the university's leading trustee, Cleveland was asked to speak on two notable occasions, the memorial to William McKinley and Woodrow Wilson's installation as university president. Though he had quickly become disenchanted with McKinley the President, Cleveland never lost his respect for McKinley the man. It was with sincerity that he eulogized his slain successor as "a useful man who became distinguished, great, and useful because he had, and retained unimpaired, qualities of heart, which I fear university students sometimes feel like keeping in the background or abandoning."[21]

Wilson's installation was the occasion of Cleveland's most important academic address. After reviewing the university's historic obligations and defining its responsibilities, he said:

> We of Princeton are still willing to declare our belief that we are better able to determine than those who come to us for education what is their most advantageous course of instruction. We are not yet convinced that the time required for our ordinary term of study is too long, or that it unnecessarily and unprofitably retards the useful service expected of a genially educated man. If false educational notions should prevail, Princeton will bide her time till they are spent.[22]

It was Cleveland who made the motion before the board of trustees that granted Wilson wide latitude in reorganizing the university faculty. When Cleveland was made chairman of the trustees' standing committee on the graduate school, a dispute arose between the two over the school's organization and physical location. Cleveland sided with his friend West, by then dean of the school, partly from personal loyalty but mainly from distrust of Wilson's agenda for radical change. The controversy went on for the remainder of Cleveland's life. In the end, it was West's and his ideas that won out. Cleveland remained convinced that Wilson had shown bad faith on the whole question, while Wilson, for his part, remained convinced Cleveland had failed him in a sound cause. (Wilson was alleged by Olney to have said, "I am prepared to believe Cleveland was a better President of the United States than a trustee of Princeton.")[23]

On October 28, 1897, Frances gave birth to their fourth child and first son. Princeton students posted the following notice on the school bulletin board:

> Grover Cleveland, Jr. arrived today at twelve o'clock. Will enter Princeton with the class of 1919, and will play center rush on the championship football teams of '16,'17,'18, and '19.

In fact, Cleveland "named him Richard Folsom—my father's first name and my wife's father's last name. Some good friends thought we ought to call him Grover Jr., but so many people have been bothered by the name Grover, and it has been so knocked about, that I thought it ought to have a rest."[24]

61

"My beliefs and opinions are unsuited for the times"

Throughout Cleveland's first summer in retirement, politics were ignored, for the most part. Only occasionally did he break into the pleasures of life to launch a few darts in letters to close friends who had served with him in the trenches. "As far as I can see," he wrote to one, "the tendency at present is to enjoy being humbugged by the Administration, now in power and to forget or decry all that was done by the last one." To another he wrote a few days later, "The [Cleveland] Administration seems at present to be so little in the minds of the people and its achievements appear to be so nearly forgotten that I feel like apologizing to all the good and true men who cast in their lot with it." To a third, in a more rueful yet optimistic vein, he wrote: "I am such a political outcast these days that the role of looker-on seems quite a natural one and yet I feel that matters are brewing that may bring decent men into activity."[25]

Cleveland's pen became more active as the Republicans behaved, in his opinion, like "merchants of treachery." Having won the White House with the help of the low-tariff Gold Democrats, they promptly betrayed them by passing the Dingley Tariff Act, which outdid in protectionism the McKinley Act it superseded. Then the administration negotiated a treaty for the annexation of Hawaii, which to Cleveland so exemplified the imperialistic foreign policy that he both despised and feared. ("The mission of our nation is to build up and make a greater country out of what we have, instead of annexing islands . . . [O]ur interference in the revolution of 1893 was disgraceful. I would gladly, therefore, for the sake of our national honor and country's fair name, have repaired that wrong.")[26]

The sinking of the *Maine* on February 15, 1898, with the loss of two officers and 264 enlisted men, which many interpreted as a deliberate act of war on Spain's part, failed to alter Cleveland's opinion that "it would be an outrage to declare war." Though hardly a pacifist, he firmly adhered to the doctrine that nations should mind their own business. Asked by Hearst for permission to add his name to a long list of prominent men who endorsed the press lord's popular subscription for a memorial to those lost on the *Maine,* Cleveland, vehemently resenting the use being made by the press of the disaster, wired him: "I decline to allow my sorrow for those who died on the *Maine* to be perverted to an advertising scheme for the *New York Journal.*"

As war fever gripped the country, Cleveland continued to believe—though "hope" is probably closer to the mark—that a hands-off policy would prevail. "Notwithstanding warlike indications, I cannot rid myself of the belief that war will be averted," he wrote Olney. "There would be infinitely more credit and political capital in avoiding war when so imminent than to carry it on even well. And then there is Spain's condition and the reflection that may come to her that 'the game is not worth the candle.' " To Benedict he wrote ten days later, "I wish the President would stand fast and [follow] his own good sense and conscience; but I am afraid that he intends to defer and yield to Congress." In April, the envoys of six European nations at Washington expressed in a note to McKinley the hope that he would avoid war for humanity's sake. The President's cynical reply: should war come it would be a war for humanity's sake.[27]

Congress declared war April 25, 1898. While Cleveland's view remained constant, he told Benedict, "We, the people [must] stand by the action of our government." Still, he could not "avoid a feeling of shame and humiliation," he told Olney. It seemed to him "the same old story of good intentions and motives sacrificed to false considerations of complaisance and party harmony." McKinley he saw as "not a victim of ignorance, but of amiable weakness not unmixed with political ambition." Predicting that Teddy Roosevelt "will have his share of strut and sensation," Cleveland deplored that the United States, "having undertaken war in the interest of humanity and civilization," would find itself "in alliance and co-operation with Cuban insurgents—the most inhuman and barbarous cutthroats in the world." Moreover, he supposed "the outrages to which we shall then be privy, and the starvation and suffering abetted by our interference will be mildly called the 'incidents of the war.' " But he took consolation in "the hope, almost amounting to expectation," that Spain would be so weak and inefficient that the war would be short and the result no worse than "a depreciation of national standing before the world abroad, and at home, demoralization of our people's character, much demagogy and humbug, great additions to our public burdens, and the exposure of scandalous operations."[28]

Such cynical "results" were, of course, seen by Cleveland as acceptable alternatives to a drawn-out affair and its attendant bloodshed; his "hope" was realized with the cessation of hostilities a mere fourteen weeks after their inception. When McKinley instructed his peace commissioners in Paris that the United States must retain the Philippines, Cleveland wrote the following anti-imperialistic creed that was found in draft among his papers:

> We believe that the spirit of our free institutions, the true intent and meaning of the Constitution, and the interest and welfare of our people forbid either the absolute and permanent control of the Philippine Islands as colonies or dependencies, or their admission to the family of states [i.e., as a United States territory]; and we insist that a consistent adherence to the American idea of freedom and liberty, an honest and sincere belief that the consent of the governed is essential to just government, and a scrupulous and American regard for the obligations of good faith, demand that an occupation and control of these Islands shall only be for the purpose of leading their inhabitants to the establishment of their own government; that these inhabitants shall be at once reassured and pacified by an immediate declaration of such purpose; and that when with our friendly aid such purpose is accomplished, our control and occupation by force in the Isles shall cease—save only so far as they may be desired or be necessary for the maintenance of peace and order under the new government.

Cleveland intended this as a public statement. But he felt, given the climate of the times, that releasing it would have been no more effective than Hecate baying to the moon. "I am not the sort of man people want to hear in these days," he wrote his last Attorney General. "My beliefs and opinions are unsuited for the times. No word that I could speak would do the least good, and the announcement that I was to address my fellow countrymen on any subject whatever would be the signal for coarse abuse and ridicule."[29]

As the 1900 presidential campaign neared, with Bryan in full command of the Democratic party, Cleveland admitted to being "in a constant state of wonderment, when I am not in a state of nausea. Sometimes I feel like saying 'it's none of my business' but that's pretty hard for me to do, though it would be comfortable if I could settle down to that condition." He felt that "if it was only in tolerable condition," the Democratic party could easily take back the White House. But he feared it would "never be in winning condition until we have had a regular knock-down fight among ourselves, and succeeded in putting the organization in Democratic hands and reviving Democratic principles in our platform." There was, though, one thing "absolutely certain: If the plans of those now in charge of our party management are not interrupted, the dishes served up to us will be Bryan and the [1896] Chicago platform." To suppose that anything else might occur was "to ignore every indication in the political sky."[30]

The Bryan people hoped that Cleveland's anti-imperialism would lure him back to the party fold. Regardless of what they thought of him—which was precious little—there was no denying the following Cleveland enjoyed among men of great political influence, principally in the East, where McKinley's influence was also firmly entrenched. They were confident Cleveland would come around, now that so many of his loyalists decided they must support Bryan, reasoning, as did Olney, that "there can be no greater national calamity than the reelection of McKinley." J. Sterling Morton, the West's most intractable Bryan antagonist, reflected the feelings of many when he said: "It is a choice between evils, and I am going to shut my eyes, hold my nose, vote [for Bryan], go home, and disinfect myself."[31]

As usual, the Bryan people misread Cleveland. Replying to an invitation to address a dinner in New York intended to reconcile the splintered party which a bout of ill health prevented his attending, Cleveland felt that even though so many who had "struggled to maintain the true Democratic faith" may have been "forgiven by the apostles of the newly invented Democracy," he himself was as yet "beyond the pale of honorable condonation." Acknowledging that "among your guests of honor there will be those who lose no occasion, on the floor of Congress or elsewhere, to repudiate me as a Democrat, and to swell the volume of 'jeers' and 'laughter' that greet the mention of my name in that connection," he conceded that "perhaps they are justified; but if I have sinned against Democracy I am ignorant of my sin; and in any event, my love of country and party will not permit me to sue for forgiveness while being dragged behind the chariot of Bryanism."[32]

Cleveland's letters during this period were equally denunciatory of the incumbent administration. Not even the signing of the currency bill (March 14, 1900) which legalized the gold standard, fixed the federal gold reserve at $150 million, and authorized the Treasury Secretary to protect it by effective bond issues could restore his confidence in McKinley. (Militating in the bill's favor was the recent gold strike in Alaska, which made for considerably easier accessibility to that precious metal.) Cleveland felt rancorous that it had been left to the opposition to restore the gold standard while his own party was "in the hands of charlatans and put to the ignoble use of aiding personal ambition."

On July 4, 1900, the Democratic National Convention, meeting at Kansas City, renominated Bryan by acclamation (Adlai Stevenson, Cleveland's second Vice President, was chosen as his running mate). While making anti-imperialism the chief issue, the party reaffirmed the principles of the 1896 platform, including the free and unlimited coinage of silver and gold at the present legal ratio of 16:1. Such was Cleveland's disappointment, for weeks he ceased to discuss matters of public concern with even his closest friends and correspondents. He devoted his time at Gray Gables to fishing with neighbors and enjoying his wife and children, whom he "always counted upon to keep the blues at bay."

Still, every day's mail contained a large number of requests from loyalists, ranging from a request for political advice (e.g., whether or not to support Bryan) to demands that he aid the party which had three times bestowed upon him its highest honor. To Olney, he wrote nine days before the nominating convention, "The political situation is too much for me—that is, I cannot put it before me in any hope for satisfactory contemplation." Three weeks later, he addressed the issue at length: "Letters similar to yours come daily to me from all classes and conditions of men who still love the old faith, and who cannot plainly see the path of duty," he told Judson Harmon. "So with the arrival of every mail I have a season of cursing the animals who have burglarized and befouled the Democratic home." He found it "humiliating" that Democrats who were fighting the party's battles before Bryan was born "should be obliged to sue him for credentials; and as a condition for obtaining them forego all the political beliefs of former days." But, he insisted, "personal feelings should be sacrificed if by doing so the country can be saved from disaster." Suffice it to say, he could not see Bryanism saving the country from disaster.[33]

Cleveland advocated letting Bryan lead the party into self-destruction and thereby clear the way for the "rehabilitation" of the old Democracy. What was needed for "the safety of the country" was the defeat of Bryanism "and the sham Democratic organization gathered about him, and his and its disappearance in the darkness of accused Democracy's scorn and contempt." But this could not be achieved until new men were at the helm of the party—but only men who "now decline Bryanism because it is not Democracy, and Republicanism because it is in every way and at all times un-Democratic." As for him, he would "remain only an intensely anxious looker-on" and hope the day was "not far distant when sanity will succeed insanity and the Democratic masses will cry out for deliverance from Bryanism and a resurrection of true Democratic faith."[34]

Early in the fall of 1890, the *Baltimore Sun* requested ("strictly confidential, or as a matter for publication, as you may desire") the ex-President's opinion on the growing number of Gold Democrats coming out in support of Bryan as the only alternative to four more years of McKinleyism. Cleveland replied that for a number of years he had been

> abused and ridiculed by professed Democrats, because I have not hesitated to declare that Bryanism is not Democracy. I have had the consolation of seeing those who professed my belief run to cover, and of noting a more headlong Democratic rush after anti-Democratic vagaries. My opinions have not changed; why then should I speak when bedlam is at its height? Perhaps I am wrong in my opinions, at any rate I should say unwelcome things; and all to no purpose except to add to the volume of abuse, which, *undefended,* I have so long borne. . . .
>
> I suppose it is a case of being "damned if I do and damned if I don't"; but I have made up my mind that I am entitled to decline enlistment in the war between Bryanism and McKinleyism. This communication is strictly confidential. It is written because I cannot ignore your letter.[35]

Five days later he poured out his heart to his favorite correspondent, Bissell:

> The pending campaign has brought upon me much unhappiness. First there came numerous letters from apparently honest

> Democrats in every part of the country, asking my advice as to how they should vote. These have been largely succeeded by persuasions and demands from self-styled rock-ribbed Democrats, that I should public declare myself in favor of the ticket of the "party which has so greatly honored me"; and in many cases the insistence is made that a word from me would insure the success of the ticket. Through all this I have maintained silence, except to say that I have nothing to say. . . . I cannot write or speak favorably of Bryanism. I do not regard it as Democracy. . . .
>
> I have some idea that the party may before long be purged of Bryanism, and that the rank and file, surprised at their wanderings, and enraged at their false leaders, will be anxious to return to the old faith; and in their desire to reorganize under the old banners will welcome the counsel of those who have never yielded to disastrous heresy. . . . I cannot believe Bryanism will win.[36]

Attempts persisted to enroll Cleveland on Bryan's side, or at least create the impression to that effect. Six weeks before the election, John S. Green, a Kentucky Gold Democrat, sent him a copy of a letter Cleveland had written to a group of Chicago businessmen back in 1895 denouncing Bryan. "Are you still opposed to the Chicago platform," Green asked, "and do you advise our old friends to support Bryan and his present platform?" Cleveland's terse reply: "I have not changed my opinion as then expressed in the least."[37]

When Green gave the correspondence to the press, the Bryan organization said that the ex-President was referring to the currency issue alone, but this was no longer a vital issue; imperialism had taken its place, and Messrs. Bryan and Cleveland were in complete agreement on that issue. Cleveland let it go. By now he was so sick and tired of trying to dispel the impression being fostered by unscrupulous Democrats that he was zealously awaiting Bryan's occupation of the White House that he just gave up and awaited, like the rest of the country, the final outcome. When it came, McKinley fared better in the electoral college than four years before, carrying twenty-three of the forty-five states with a total of 271 votes to Bryan's 176. The popular vote was about the same as in 1896, with a spread of less than one million. (Cleveland wanted to assure his friends that his vote did not contribute to the Republican victory. On the other hand, voting for Bryan would have violated both his conscience and his personal wishes. Though he never discussed the matter, it is safe to assume he cast no vote in the 1900 election.) "It's a little comforting to see the end of Bryanism, in politics," Cleveland told an old loyalist, "but on the Democratic side I am constantly asking, 'What next?' "[38]

How ironic, given Cleveland's proximity and almost daily intercourse with the only Democrat fated to lead the nation during the coming three decades, that the possibility that what was "next" was Wilsonism never crossed his mind!

62

Public perception begins to change appreciably

Cleveland was still hated in the South and West, while in the East he was looked upon as a figure of the past. Thus his reason for turning down many invitations to write or speak in the first year of his retirement: the belief that he would be greeted with derision or abuse. When sent a copy of the compilation of his public papers, he could hardly have cared less: "[T]here will be but little need of unpacking them," he told Lamont, "as but a few people care for that sort of literature in these days." The belief that as a repudiated President he should remain in obscurity influenced his decision to decline President Joaquín Crespo's invitation to represent Venezuela on the boundary arbitration commission and Roosevelt's offer to serve as a permanent member on the Hague Permanent Court of Arbitration.[39]

As time went on, with more and more people realizing how right he'd been on such decisive and divisive issues as the tariff and the currency, the public perception of Cleveland began to change appreciably. Invitations to speak became not only more numerous but more importuning. Public appearances became more frequent as he accepted—with a tactfully concealed sense of vindication—the countless tributes that came pouring in. Especially those from the opposition, as in a letter he received from Roosevelt a few days after the 1900 election. McKinley's second Vice President wanted him to know that during the campaign he

> grew more and more to realize the very great service you had rendered to the whole country by what you did about free silver. . . . I think your letter on free silver prior to your second nomination was as bold a bit of honest wresting as I have ever seen in American public life. And more than anything else it put you in the position of doing for the American public in this matter of free silver what at the time no other man could have done. . . . I think now we have definitely won out on the free-silver business and therefore I think you are entitled to thanks and congratulations.[40]

Cleveland knew he could always take for granted the high regard in which he was held among reform groups and the eastern conservatives. Now joining their number were the legions of Tammany-influenced rank-and-file New Yorkers who had never stood in the front ranks of his admirers. Invited to lend his presence and moral authority at a mass meeting in New York City to protest the anti-Jewish czarist pogroms in Kishnev, Cleveland happened to step onto the stage while Mayor Seth Low was in the midst of his remarks. On spotting him, the audience broke into a deafening storm of applause. When Cleveland finished his own brief remarks, the applause was even more enthusiastic. At the close of the meeting, the crowd literally stormed the stage to pay homage to the man they now realized represented as did no other President since Lincoln the sense of compassion and strength of purpose that so many of the immigrants present felt best represented the American ideal.[41]

Soon, whisperings were heard in the land that Grover Cleveland was preparing to again take the field and lead the armies of Democracy to victory in 1904. "There appears to be," wrote Joseph Garretson of Cincinnati, "a strong and growing sentiment in the Middle Western States in favor of your nomination. The *Times-Star* has investigated this sentiment, and the general tenor of all our correspondents is along the line that you are the only logical candidate in the field." (In a letter to Henry Cabot Lodge, Theodore Roosevelt reported that a coterie of leading Republicans, led by J. P. Morgan and Mark Hanna, tried in May 1903 to draft Cleveland for a third term, on the grounds that they, Roosevelt-haters all, would switch parties to support Cleveland "with all their power.")[42]

To Cleveland, this was too much. He could not possibly believe "that a condition of sentiment exists that makes any expression from me on the subject of the least importance," he replied. For some bizarre reason that probably owed as much to wishful thinking as gross misinterpretation, no less an influential organ than the *New York Times* editorialized that the ex-President's letter "is taken as an assurance that at the proper time the reformer Buffalonian will enter the field." Other papers around the country took up the theme, expending forests of newsprint and rivers of ink, many insisting he would run again, and as many insisting he would not.

Cleveland issued a stinging reproof that he hoped would end the discussion once and for all: "Words have been put in my mouth which entirely misrepresent my position in politics," he told Elias Benedict. "I never said I had retired from active politics to act as the party's adviser. To be thus pictured as an old Brahmin seated in the background and aspiring to manage things my own way is alike distasteful to me and absolutely false as to my true position." In a follow-up letter to Benedict he elaborated in a more personal vein about attempts to resurrect his political career: "It would be foolish and insincere for me to disclaim the pleasure I derive from the kindly sentiments of my fellow-citizens which come to me from many quarters. It seems to me, however, that I have expressed myself with sufficient clearness to enable all who believe in my sincerity to understand how settled is my determination to spend the remainder of my private citizenship."[43]

Actually, he hadn't.

At the Jefferson Day Dinner on April 13, 1903, in New York City, little more than passing interest was evinced from the crowd of Tammany men when letters were read from Senator Hill, its erstwhile avatar who had taught them the most effective way to hate Cleveland, and the party's current leader, Bryan, hardly a Cleveland admirer. When the toastmaster next read a simple note of regret for nonattendance from Cleveland, whom he hailed as "the next President," the eight hundred sachems and braves leaped to their feet in an orgy of cheering. On getting reports of the occasion, Cleveland was as unmoved by their present admiration as he had been by their past abhorrence.[44]

Such was the case with yet another, infinitely more widespread group—the westerners—who, when Cleveland left the White House, celebrated with the gaiety and abandon usually reserved for dancing on the grave of one's most hated enemy. Two weeks after the Jefferson Day Dinner, he attended the opening of the Louisiana Purchase Exposition at St. Louis under pressure from friends, and from officials who insisted that as ex-President he join the incumbent President and other figures of national eminence. Wherever his train stopped along the line, waiting crowds greeted him with enthusiastic cheering and prolonged applause.

When Cleveland was introduced along with the other dignitaries at the opening-day ceremonies, he "so far overshadowed President Roosevelt in popular applause, when both stood on the same platform, as to make the latter feel aggrieved." Given that the platform was fairly inundated with the nation's foremost Republican politicians, including all the cabinet officers, Roosevelt "ought easily to have drawn out the most vociferous and continued applause." Yet when he sat down and Cleveland, the private citizen, arose,

> the crowd, on the platform, and out in front, so instantly and so vigorously applauded, and so wildly manifested delight, that the President's greetings a few minutes before seemed like a whisper compared with a long-continued peal of thunder. It was an unexpected, instantaneous, generous, unmistakable ovation. It indicated clearly the state of the public mind toward the ex-President. It was a revelation to the politicians. It was an eye-opener to the anti-Cleveland Democrats. It was a warning to the Roosevelt Republicans. It was plainly the voice of public sentiment, and it thrust Grover Cleveland to the front as the strongest man in American politics to-day.[45]

And what was Cleveland's own reaction to this "apology of the West"? The joy and sense of satisfaction would last for the remaining five years of his life, according to his wife: "From that moment, he was a different man."[46]

63

Cleveland's "True Democracy" again in the ascendancy

Cleveland's second son and last child, Francis Grover, was born at the family's Cape Cod summer home on July 18, 1903. Six months later, his joy at having sired a child at the age of sixty-six turned to ashes with the death of twelve-year-old Ruth, his firstborn. As his diary shows, her death was totally unforeseen:

> January 2, Ruth is a little sick with tonsillitis.
>
> January 3, Ruth is still sick, but better.
>
> January 6, Doctor said this morning Ruth had diphtheria [and] a trained nurse came at 5:25. . . . Dr. treated us all with antitoxin and reported that Ruth was getting on well. . . . At 2 o'clock in the night word came . . . that Ruth was not so well. Dr. Carnochan came at 2:30 and Dr. Wykoff at 3:30. We had been excluded from Ruth's room, but learned that dear Ruth died before Dr. Wykoff came, probably about 3 o'clock A.M., Jan. 7th.
>
> January 8 [in a trembling, almost illegible hand], We buried our daughter, Ruth, this morning.

Death was no more a stranger to Cleveland than it is to any man in his seventh decade, when he can expect to see dear friends die off as he comes to terms with his own mortality. Bayard had died in 1898 shortly after paying a farewell visit at Princeton; Endicott died two years later, as did William Wilson; in 1903, Cleveland was especially saddened by the death of Wilson Bissell, his oldest and closest friend. ("Bissell's death is another reminder . . . that the shafts are flying.") But these were men who had lived long and fulfilling lives. The death of his own child was to Cleveland almost unbearable; the depth of his grief is readily perceived in diary entries from this period, particularly the thoughts that haunted him despite his deep religious faith:

> January 10, I had a season of great trouble in keeping out of my mind the idea that Ruth was in the cold, cheerless grave instead of in the arms of her Saviour.

> January 11, It seems to me I mourn our darling Ruth's death more and more. So much of the time I can only think of her as dead, not joyfully living in Heaven.
>
> January 15, God has come to my help and I am able to adjust my thought to dear Ruth's death with as much comfort as selfish humanity will permit.

A few months later he was able to tell his sister, Mary, "We still miss dreadfully our dear Ruth; but I believe there has been given to both Frank and me such confident faith that it is well with her, and such a feeling that we are the only losers, as seems to be of very great comfort to us."[47]

A consequence of Ruth's death was the abandonment of Gray Gables; he and Frances could not bear returning to the scene of remembered summer joy without her. From 1904 on, the family summered in the hills of New Hampshire, where he ultimately bought a house near Tamworth, which he named Intermont, as it lay within range of Mounts Chocorua and Passaconaway. Cleveland loved the clear mountain air, and fishing in nearby Lakes Ossipee and Winnipesaukee. He also took warmly to the locals, who for their part took him to their collective heart. Still, a sense of wistfulness for all those summers spent at Gray Gables would impel him to steal away for a day or two of fishing on Buzzards Bay.

A number of Cleveland loyalists suggested he consider reentering politics as a way to divert his mind following Ruth's death. One, Nathan Straus, told him, "Nothing but time can heal such a wound as you have received; but a change of scene, an active life, the compelling of thoughts in other directions would naturally leave you less time to dwell upon your sorrow." Seeking to divert Cleveland's mind was not the sum of it. The eastern Democrats, anxious that the nomination not go again to Bryan, were unable to come up with an acceptable alternative. In a letter dated January 4, 1904, that he asked to be read to a Democratic party dinner in New York City, Cleveland said that "the skies are bright with the promise of victory, if Democrats stoutly reaffirm old principles which the times demand." Left unsaid was the obvious: that the party must come up with the right candidate.[48]

Of the many mentioned for the nomination, five stood out: Richard Olney, Senators George Gray of Delaware and Francis M.

Cockrell of Missouri, Chief Justice Alton Brooks Parker of the New York Court of Appeals, and newspaper magnate William Randolph Hearst. Cleveland's name was now added to the list by mostly conservative businessmen who were as put off by Roosevelt's progressivism as by Bryan's populism. Diplomat Henry White wrote Roosevelt from London that as a result of conversations with rich American tourists there, he was "struck by the fact that many of those who have affiliations with what I may describe as Wall Street, although not necessarily belonging to New York, say that they mean to vote for you 'unless Cleveland is nominated,' in which case they would without hesitation vote for him." Banker James Stillman told Tammany chief J. S. Cram: "If you will nominate Mr. Cleveland, I will personally see that there is a fund raised bigger than was raised at the time Mckinley was elected, and you know when he ran they had more money than they could use."[49] The *Brooklyn Eagle* and *New York Herald* were soon calling for a Cleveland draft.

While flattered at being mentioned for yet another go at the White House, Cleveland knew the idea was preposterous. He was approaching seventy, and his health was on a slow decline. Suffering from rheumatism, he was periodically unable to leave his bed for weeks at a time; his digestion had become increasingly troublesome. And apart from lacking the strength a presidency demanded, he was unalterable in his opposition to third terms in general, and for himself in particular, even though the terms were not successive. He tried to make his position as definite as possible in a letter to St. Clair McKelway, editor of the *Brooklyn Eagle,* when it turned from backing Parker to advocating Cleveland's candidacy. He could not "open my mind to the thought that in any circumstances or upon any consideration I would ever again become the nominee of my party for the Presidency." His determination not to do so was "unalterable and conclusive. This you at least ought to know from me. I should be glad if the *Eagle* was made the medium of its conveyance to the public."[50]

By early 1904, though, he saw the wisdom of allowing his name to be used to rally and unify the eastern Democrats against the Bryan wing. That this once rejected ex-President was again a force to be reckoned with was by now acknowledged by his most confirmed political foes. Parker's supporters, led by Cleveland's quondam nemesis Daniel Hill and New Jersey state Democratic boss James Smith, Jr., hoped to use Cleveland as a Judas goat; so long as he was a potential candidate, they reasoned, the Bryan and Hearst factions would concentrate much of their fire on him. In February 1904, Tammany boss Charles Murphy told Dan Lamont that Cleveland "would be elected without question" were he to accept the nomination. Obviously Murphy, an opportunistic Cleveland-basher from way back, was also playing the Judas goat game. When Lamont insisted that Cleveland was adamantly against even a draft, Murphy replied that if it couldn't be Cleveland, "then let's get the nearest to him that can be found." He asked that Lamont urge Cleveland to "do no further declining now," adding: "Let's have the benefit of his name to round up a Cleveland party, and all will agree on a Cleveland candidate." Lamont seconded the advice.

Cleveland told Lamont he saw the wisdom of Murphy's strategy and was willing to "do no further declining—up to the point that continued silence might be construed as indicating a departure from my expressed determination not to be a candidate, or until such silence will subject me to the accusation of misleading my good friends." Eighteen days later, convinced that "if there is to be an effort to get our party in any kind of promising shape there ought to be a movement in a hard-headed sensible way," Cleveland advised that Parker was "the best one to concentrate on." He had an excellent record as a jurist and was favored by a number of important eastern newspapers. In the meantime, Lamont was "to tell all who talk 'Cleveland' nonsense" that it was "a waste of time that might be profitably spent in other ways." He would not accept a nomination, period. He was "content" in his newfound status as the party's retired elder statesman. He wanted the party to succeed, "but I hope there will be no idea of playing any kind of trick on me."[51]

Though adamant about remaining on the sidelines, Cleveland was prepared—indeed, eager—to work toward a Roosevelt defeat. "There is one thing about our young President," he told Dan Lamont, "which I think cannot be denied. He has but little of the proprieties that belong to his high office or, for that matter, to its incumbent. . . . There never was a time I believe when the country would be a greater gainer than now, by the clearing out of an administration." Cleveland now asked William B. Hornblower, who had great influence among the Independents, to spread the word that while he personally preferred Olney or Gray, the best chance for "clearing out the administration" lay in nominating Judge Parker. "He is clean, decent, and conservative and ought on those grounds to inspire confidence in quarters where it is sadly needed, if our party is ever going to be a political power again." Above all, it was "immensely important" that the party's Cleveland wing "be as united on a decent candidate as circumstances will permit—to the end that the movement now threatened in the direction of insanity and indecency may be run over and killed 'beyond recognition.' "[52]

The convention met in St. Louis on July 6. More striking than Parker's nomination—easily effected despite Bryan's effort to stampede the convention to Cockrell, and Hearst's effort to purchase the nomination for himself—was Cleveland's spiritual presence, rather like that of a very welcome Banquo's Ghost. In his keynote speech, John Sharp Williams declared that "the gold standard established by the dogged persistency and indomitable will of Grover Cleveland in securing the repeal of the Republican [Sherman] silver-purchase law, is and is definitely to be the money standard of the country."

The party which had deserted Cleveland in 1896 and scorned and insulted him in 1900 "burst into applause which lasted so long that Williams had twice to take his seat before it subsided." Throughout the ensuing proceedings there were repeated calls of "three cheers for Grover Cleveland," all of which set off a resounding response. Bryan again tried to push his fight for free and unlimited silver coinage, but though he charmed the galleries with his eloquence, he failed to charm the delegates. This time in going before the country, the party was not about to hitch its wagon to a dead horse.[53]

Cleveland's "True Democracy" was again in the ascendancy. Never before had a political leader within a period of eight years lost control of his party only to see it return to his side with the acknowledgment that he had been right and it had been wrong. He was "very much pleased with the outcome of the Convention," he told Olney. "Bryan and Bryanism are eliminated as influential factors in Democratic councils, true Democracy has a leader, and its time-honored and approved principles again are set before the people of the land without apology or shamefacedness." He believed there was "a good chance to rid the country of Rooseveltism and its entire brood of dangers and humiliations."[54]

Though able to make only two speeches in Parker's behalf, in New York and New Jersey, Cleveland wrote a number of campaign articles for *Collier's, McClure's,* and *The Saturday Evening Post.* It didn't help the Democrats. Nothing could have. Roosevelt's rout of Parker was recorded with laconic brevity in Cleveland's diary for November 8, 1904: "Election day. Voted about 10 o'c. Began to receive returns abt. ½ past 7 I think. It took but a few reports to enable me to see that we the Democrats were dreadfully left. Went to bed a little after 10." Roosevelt won more than half the 13.5 million popular votes in a field of seven. In the electoral college, he carried thirty-two states (336 votes); Parker carried the thirteen states of the solid South (140 votes).

Such was the degree of Cleveland's disappointment, not till a month later was he willing to verbalize it. "The result of the election was so astounding, that I have hardly sufficiently recovered my composure to contemplate the reasons which led to it or the results likely to follow it." As an "intense and unalterable believer in the saving common sense of the American people," he could not yet believe that the Roosevelt landslide "should be taken to indicate the people's willingness to allow the principles and practices of Republicanism to be unalterably fixed in the affairs of our body politic." He did, however, find consolation in the belief that "the next swing of the pendulum of public sentiment will be quite to the Democratic side of the dial, and that, if Democracy is prepared to do its duty, when that time arrives, it will become again the beneficent agent of the people's salvation."[55]

Cleveland's prediction was, of course, fulfilled. But when that happened, he was four years in his grave.

64

One more opportunity to exercise his statesmanship

Cleveland watched somewhat apprehensively as Theodore Roosevelt imposed his unique brand of leadership upon the nation, anxious to give the Rough Rider every benefit of the doubt, but doubtful he could ever succumb to TR's sedulously cultivated charisma. What to Roosevelt was the methodology of presidential leadership was to Cleveland totally out of keeping with his notion of the dignity that should surround the office. Being slower of mind and thus mistaking

Roosevelt's rapidity for superficiality, Cleveland confounded his drama-laden popular appeal with the technique of a demagogue.

Temperamentally, each was the other's antipode. Where Roosevelt was mercurial, Cleveland was phlegmatic; where Roosevelt was quick to form friendships and create enmities, Cleveland approached people with near-glacial circumspection. Both did share courage and resourcefulness when confronted by danger, were loyal to Judeo-Christian values and American traditions when confronted by temptation, eschewed self-aggrandizement when it came to what was best for the people they had been fated to preside over as Chief Magistrate, and were men whose honesty and probity were beyond question.

Despite his reservations about the man, Cleveland was prepared to support Roosevelt when he acted in the nation's best interests. The chance to prove that came in May 1902, when the 145,000-member United Mine Workers of America struck the anthracite coal fields for fair wages and better working conditions. Throughout the summer the owners tried unsuccessfully to get the mines running again with scab labor. By August it was obvious that barring settlement, a coal famine must follow. On September 26, New York City schools were closed down in order to conserve the scant supply of coal, which by then had become prohibitive in price, and the threat of suffering and rioting loomed as the winter set in. The owners had a large stockpile, but deliberately withheld it from the market in hopes that public opinion would drive the miners into submission. This had the adverse effect of escalating public sympathy for the miners.

On October 3, Roosevelt convened a meeting of operators and union leaders, at which he hoped to play the peacemaker. UMW head John Mitchell was amenable to the President's naming an arbitration commission and vowed his men's compliance with its findings. But George F. Baer, speaking for the owners, refused to consider the idea, with a display of impudence that set the oft-caricatured Rooseveltian teeth on edge. When Baer demanded an end to the strike on the owners' terms, the meeting broke up on a note of mutual enmity between the two groups. "There was only one person there who bore himself like a gentleman," Roosevelt later said of the conference, "and it wasn't I!" (It was Mitchell.) Roosevelt was prepared to act as if the country had been attacked by a foreign power; but only as a last resort. Meanwhile, pressure was mounting that he follow the same "constitutional" course taken by Cleveland in the Chicago Pullman Strike—

that is, send in troops to preserve order and protect property. Doubtless he would have gone that route—with God only knows what consequences—had it not been for a letter from Cleveland.

While returning to Princeton from a brief nostalgic visit to Buzzards Bay, he read a newspaper account of the White House meeting, and was "so surprised and 'stirred up' by the position taken by the contestants" that he could not "refrain from making a suggestion." His suggestion: that the two sides cooperatively produce enough coal, for however long it took, to serve the needs of consumers, "leaving the parties to the quarrel, after such necessities are met, to take up the fight again where they left off 'without prejudice' if they desire." Cleveland believed that "when quarrelling parties are both in the wrong, and are assailed with blame so nearly universal, they will do strange things to save their faces."[56]

The plan was impractical; even, it must be said, rather naive. But that did not matter; what mattered was that the letter gave Roosevelt sorely needed moral support when it came to interfering in the strike with the use of federal troops. Since Cleveland still enjoyed great influence among many Democrats, it helped Roosevelt deflect Democratic criticism as he now arranged with the governor of Pennsylvania, at a prearranged signal, to request federal aid for the coal fields: U.S. troops would then move in to seize and operate the mines—thereby appeasing labor's rage at the owners' use of scabs—while a special commission investigated all aspects of the controversy and proposed mediation.

Roosevelt asked Cleveland to accept chairmanship of such a commission, which he did. Armed with his reply, Roosevelt had Secretary of War Elihu Root meet with J. Pierpont Morgan, the man best able to influence the mine operators. Impressed by the fact that the President could count on the support of the Cleveland Democrats, still a force to be reckoned with in eastern financial circles, Morgan pressured the operators to accept binding arbitration. Consistent with their chronic obtuseness, which at times spilled over into downright inanity, the operators spent days objecting to "such a dangerous radical" as ex-President Cleveland chairing the commission. When at last a mutually agreeable commission was empaneled, Roosevelt wrote apologetically to Cleveland his regret at having to give in to the operators' demand "in order to get the vitally necessary agreement between the operators and miners."[57]

In fact, Cleveland had never expressed willingness to serve on the arbitration commission—only on a commission to suggest avenues of arbitration. In other words, he was willing to help ascertain the facts of the dispute, but for some reason, which he never revealed, he was not willing to act as a judge over such matters as hours and wages. He distinctly told this to Roosevelt when the two met, after the strike was settled, at the dedication of the new Chamber of Commerce building in Washington. When in his 1904 presidential campaign Roosevelt made unauthorized use of Cleveland's letter and knowingly misrepresented his intentions, Cleveland was furious. He was "amazed at Mr. Roosevelt," Cleveland told a friend in commenting on the President's penchant for self-glorification; if necessary, at anyone's and everyone's expense. "There are some people in this country that need lessons in decency and good manners."[58]

Cleveland had one more opportunity to exercise his statesmanship for the nation's advantage, this time in the insurance industry. Three great companies—Equitable Life, Mutual Life, and New York Life—while supposedly operating solely in the interest of their policyholders, were in fact being operated in the interest of their top officers. Besides using the policyholders' money to speculate in stocks, underwrite dubious financial schemes in quest of large, preferably quick, profits, subsidize trust companies in which they held an interest, and make improper "loans" to friends and relatives, they paid themselves exorbitant salaries and met personal expenses, took graft in the construction of company-owned buildings, and purchased political clout (and immunity from prosecution) by donating company money to campaign funds and employing powerful politicians at inflated salaries. All this was carried out under a cloak of outward respectability, presumably supervised by boards of directors chosen for their ability, integrity, and honesty. The directors—who included such luminaries of finance as Edward H. Harrimann, James J. Hill, Henry C. Frick, Jacob H. Schiff, and August Belmont—were, for the most part, "corporate board dummies" who lent their name and prestige to the companies but were denied any knowledge of what was going on.[59]

Early in 1905, an internal dispute over management of the Equitable brought matters to a head—and knowledge of what was going on to the public. Goaded by Pulitzer's *World*, the New York State

Insurance Department launched an investigation. In June, the state legislature established the Armstrong Committee to launch an inquiry, with Charles Evans Hughes, future Chief Justice of the United States, as chief counsel. When a group of disreputable financiers sought control of the Equitable, largest and most tainted of the three companies, Thomas Fortune Ryan purchased the controlling block of stock and set out to effect a major reorganization. He knew this could succeed only if supervised by a triumvirate of trustees in whom he had enough confidence to place the administration of his majority stock. He wanted a man the public trusted fully, since with the majority stock went full control of Equitable. Who better to fit the bill, he decided, than Grover Cleveland.

When Ryan wrote asking him to head the trustee group as first among equals (the other two being New York Appellate Court Judge Morgan J. O'Brien and industrialist George Westinghouse), Cleveland accepted. Previously, Equitable's fifty-two directors had been elected by the stockholders. Ryan proposed to mutualize the company by letting the policyholders elect a majority, twenty-eight; the trustees would guide them in their selection, and themselves select the remaining twenty-four. During the intervening period between his appointment and first formal meeting with O'Brien and Westinghouse, Cleveland mastered the problems of the insurance industry in general, and of Equitable in particular, so that he could speak with knowledge and authority. Attorney Paul D. Cravath, who executed Ryan's deed of trust, recalls the following incident:

> At his request I had drafted a statement or paper of some kind, I forget just what it was, for which he was to become responsible. One afternoon I went to Princeton to submit it to him. He seemed to like it. I went to bed at a normal hour, say eleven o'clock. When I came down to early breakfast the next morning Mr. Cleveland greeted me with an entirely new paper which he had prepared after I had gone to bed. He must have stayed up most of the night. It is needless to say his paper was very much better than the draft which I had proposed.[60]

Assuring the policyholders that he and his two co-triumvirs would accept for the board of directors only men with proven experience in the field whose probity was above suspicion, Cleveland personally drew up the elaborate instructions that were sent out to every policyholder, accompanied by blank ballots and proxies; 94 percent of the respondents gave their proxies to the trustees—a token of absolute confidence in Cleveland and his associates.

The work of reorganization was done before year's end. Also by then, the Hughes investigation had aired the evils infesting the entire insurance industry and cleared the way for drastic reformative legislation. The humiliated industry leaders, distrusted more than ever by their policyholders, believed they might perhaps regain that trust through Cleveland. For serving as trustee he was paid $12,000. In December, he was offered an additional $12,000 yearly to referee any disputes that might arise between the companies concerning the allowance by their respective agents of rebates on their premium commissions. It was unlikely there would be too many such disputes, and as a convenience they could be submitted to him at Princeton by mail.

Eager to stamp out the abuse of this "vice that can have no place in well-conducted life insurance," Cleveland accepted, on the assumption that "those for whom you speak are seriously determined to prevent the vice referred to and will unreservedly second every effort directed to that end."[61] In February 1907, he was asked to head an umbrella protective organization, the Association of Presidents of Life Insurance Companies, whose main object was to resist regulatory legislation regarded by the industry as unnecessary or ill-advised. He hesitated to become what was tantamount to being the public's ombudsman for the entire life insurance business, but gave in at the group's importuning; thereafter, despite declining health, he made a number of effective statements and addresses on insurance affairs.

Though the most important reforms derived from Hughes's investigation (it led to his becoming governor of New York in 1908), the work Cleveland did for honest insurance was considerable in both its direct and indirect results. He not only performed a valuable service in helping reorganize the rich company which was at the center of the scandal, he helped promote an early return of public confidence in the entire industry.

65

"You know how dearly I love you"

To escape the penetrating dampness to which Princeton now fell victim, Cleveland spent his sixty-ninth birthday in Florida duck-hunting with friends. In his wake came a deluge of birthday letters and wires, some from intimate friends, some from mere acquaintances, many from admirers who knew him only by reputation. Richard Olney was only stating the obvious when he wrote that "on your 69th birthday you find yourself the object of higher and more general respect and esteem among your fellow countrymen than any other living American." One letter Cleveland especially enjoyed was from Mark Twain. Addressing him as "Honored Sir" and signing off "With profoundest respect," Twain wrote:

> Your patriotic virtues have won for you the homage of half the nation and the enmity of the other half. This places your character as a citizen upon a summit as high as Washington's. The verdict is unanimous and unassailable. The votes of both sides are necessary in cases like these, and the votes of the one side are quite as valuable as are the votes of the other. When the votes are all in a public man's favor the verdict is against him. It is sand, and history will wash it away. But the verdict for you is rock, and will stand.

Cleveland also appreciated hearing from Woodrow Wilson, who wrote both personally and on behalf of the Princeton faculty:

> I should think that a birthday would bring you very many gratifying thoughts, and I hope that you realize how specially strong the admiration and affection of those of us in Princeton who know you best have grown during the years when we have been privileged to be near you. It has been one of the best circumstances of my life that I have been closely associated with you in matters both large and small. It has given me strength and knowledge of affairs.

> But if I may judge by my own feeling, what a man specially wants to know on his birthday is how he stands, not in reputation or in power, but in the affection of those whose affections he cares for. The fine thing about the feeling for you yourself which I find in the mind of almost everyone I talk with, is that it is mixed with genuine affection. I often find this true even of persons who do not know you personally. How much more must it be true of those who are near you.

To his friend Richard Gilder, Cleveland wrote rather reflectively of being so deeply impressed by all the birthday felicitations that

> I have had many struggles between smiles and tears as I read the words of affection and praise that have met me at the gate of entrance to another year. Somehow I am wondering why all this should be, since I have left many things undone I ought to have done in the realm of friendship, and since in the work of public life and effort, God has never failed to clearly make known to me the path of duty. And still it is in human nature for one to hug the praise of his fellows and the affection of friends to his bosom as his earned possessions.[62]

With his health now in a state of irreversible decline, Cleveland limited his activities to Equitable, and to his responsibilities as the leading Princeton trustee. Though turning down numerous requests to speak before various organizations and functions, he did agree, at the urgent request of the Union League Club of Chicago, to deliver the 1907 Washington's Birthday address in that city under their auspices. The text was both a eulogy of the nation's father and a warning to those of his metaphorical children who trod false paths. Indicative of his failing health, Cleveland read from manuscript, without gesture or emotion, till he moved from praising Washington to denouncing the corruption, wastefulness, and duplicity of demagogues and castigating a preternatural fidelity to partisan interests. "If your observance of this day," he said in peroration, now forcefully and from memory,

> were intended to make more secure the immortal fame of Washington, or to add to the strength and beauty of his imper-

> ishable monument built upon a nation's affectionate remembrance, your purpose would be useless. Washington has no need of you. But in every moment from the time he drew his sword in the cause of American Independence to this hour, living or dead, the American people have needed him. It is not important now, nor will it be in all the coming years, to remind our countrymen that Washington has lived. . . . But it is important—and more important now than ever before—that they should clearly apprehend and adequately value the virtues and ideal of which he was the embodiment. . . . There should be no toleration of even the shade of a thought that what Washington did and said and wrote . . . has become in the least outworn, or that in these days of material advance and development they may be merely pleasantly recalled with a sort of affectionate veneration, and with a kind of indulgent and loftily courageous concession of the value of Washington's example and precepts. These constitute the richest of our [nation's] crown jewels.[63]

1907 marked ten years since Cleveland left the White House a despised President. Now that he had risen phoenixlike and become a national figure held in near-universal respect and admiration, his seventieth birthday was the occasion for an informal national celebration. For the first time in a half century the mayor of New York City ordered flags raised in honor of a private citizen. When his friend John Finley, at the time president of New York's City College, suggested the day be celebrated as "out-of-doors day," reporters from all the major dailies rushed down to Princeton for Cleveland's reaction to the idea. Receiving them most cordially—a sign in itself of how he had mellowed in his twilight years—Cleveland used the occasion to rhapsodize on the joys and benefits of the simple life. It was, in essence, his valedictory to the nation:

> I look with apprehension upon the mad rush of American life, which is certain to impair the mental and physical vigor necessary to every human being. The wholesome sentiments which spring from country life are being overwhelmed by the ambitions and tendencies that flow out from our great cities. Few have the hardihood to withstand the swirl and rush of city life, or to remain indifferent to the promises of sudden wealth and

the excitement of speculation in a metropolis, where immense fortunes are made and lost in a single day. . . .

We are proud of our cities, of course. But we must not allow them wholly to shape our ideals and our ambitions. Nothing that the wealth of a city can buy will atone for the loss of that American sturdiness and independence which the farm and the small town have so frequently produced. . . . In my experience I have found that impressions which a man receives who walks by the brookside or in the forest or by the seashore make him a better man and a better citizen. They lift him above the worries of business and reach him of a power greater than human power.[64]

To escape any fuss by friends and neighbors attendant upon the occasion, Cleveland observed the birthday with his own version of "out-of-doors day"—another voyage south on Benedict's *Oneida* for a little duck-hunting. As the trip was not announced, only one letter reached him on his natal day. No other could have given him more pleasure:

My Dearest:

I hate to have you away on your birthday, but I realize that it will save you some strain—for many people seem to be thinking of you at this time. We all send much much love, and all the deepest best wishes of our hearts—and my heart is full of gratitude for what the years of your life have meant to me. You know how dearly I love you. You do not mind my saying it over, any day, and you won't mind it on this especial day—so I repeat it and repeat it, and I ask God's blessing on you for all the days.

Your loving wife Frank[65]

Cleveland found awaiting him upon his return home hundreds of congratulatory letters and telegrams from men, women, even children from all walks of life. Unable to express his personal gratitude to all those who had remembered him, Cleveland had the following notice inserted in the *New York Times*:

It seems to be impossible for me to acknowledge, except through the press of the country, the generosity and kindly consideration of my countrymen, which have been made manifest

> by congratulatory messages and newspaper comment on the occasion of my seventieth birthday. These have deeply touched me, and in the book of grateful recollection they are written where every remaining day of my life I can turn a page and read them.[66]

One tribute he valued was an editorial in the *New York Sun*, his most adversarial newspaper during the public years, which concluded: "As President, Mr. Cleveland enforced the laws and did not truckle to organized violence or crouch before public clamor. The man who taught the Chicago labor lords that there was a Government at Washington . . . is sure of an honorable place in history and of the final approval of his countrymen."[67]

Cleveland was moved to tears on learning that three of his closest friends—Dean West, Richard Gilder, and John Finley—had marked his birthday by placing a bronze plaque in the room where he was born at Caldwell, New Jersey. He was again moved to tears when, a few days after his return, he received the formal congratulations of the Princeton student body, who came in procession to his house to present a loving cup to "our Grover."

66
Last words

Cleveland refused to abandon hope that the Democratic party would in time throw off the curse of Bryanism. While disappointed with where Roosevelt had taken the Republicans, he did admit that if Bryan should again be nominated by the party, he would vote for a Republican, provided they fielded a candidate acceptable to him. (Roosevelt, having promised to serve only one elected term, had by then removed himself from consideration and anointed William Howard Taft as his heir, a move for which he would never forgive himself.) Concerning political affairs, Cleveland told Benedict, "I feel like the farmer who started at the bottom of a hill with a wagon load of corn and discovered at the hilltop that every grain of his load had slid out under the tail-board. Though of a profane temperament, he stood mutely surveying his disaster until to a passing neighbor, who asked him why he didn't swear, he replied: 'Because, by God, I cannot do the subject justice.' "

In one of his last letters, three days before his seventy-first and last birthday, Cleveland felt confident of a future for the party without Bryanism: "In my last letter to you I expressed myself as seeing some light ahead for Democracy. I cannot help feeling at this time that the light is still brighter. It does seem to me that movements have been set in motion which, though not at the present time of large dimensions, promise final relief from the burden which has so long weighed us down." (The nomination went once more to Bryan.)[68] That same day, he sent the editor of the *New York World* his response to the question "What is the best principle and what is the best policy to give the Democratic party new life?":

> As a general proposition I might answer this question by saying that in my opinion this could be most surely brought about by a return to the genuine Democratic doctrine and a close adherence to the Democratic policies which in times past gave our party success and benefitted our people. To be more specific in my reply, I should say that more than ever just at this time the Democratic party should display honesty and sincere conservatism, a regard for constitutional limitations, and a determination not to be swept from our moorings by temporary clamor or spectacular exploitation.
>
> Our people need rest and peace and reassurance; and it will be quite in line with true Democracy and successful policy to impress upon our fellow-countrymen the fact that Democracy still stands for those things.

Cleveland spent the last six months of 1907 in "substantial confinement," as he described it to his sister Susan, devoting a great deal of time to reading.[69] Throughout his public life, he had read mainly to research what he was writing at any given time. The style of the writers of the *Federalist Papers,* in which he read abundantly, left him with both delight and a sense of inadequacy about his own efforts. ("How did they ever do it?") Only now in his last years did he turn to contemporary novels, strictly as a diversion.[70] His last official university function was on March 2, 1908, when he presided at a meeting of the board of trustees. On April 8 he chaired a conference on the graduate school at his home. Cleveland was by then in the throes of his final illness: heart and kidney disease, complicated by chronic gastroenteritis.

He never again appeared in public.

"We have tried not to have it known, but he has had another attack within the last few days," Frances wrote George Parker in April. "While not so serious in itself, it came so soon after the one preceding that he was not so strong as usual, and it has left him in much weaker condition."[71] In fact, it was very much "serious in itself." But Frances was keeping with her husband's wishes that his medical problems not become a matter of public conversation. Whenever word got out that he had suffered a setback, the press would be advised that the facts had been exaggerated, the former President was doing just fine. Following this latest attack, which was not only debilitating but painful, it was thought best that he recuperate at Lakewood, with its restorative sea breezes.

It was there, surrounded by his family, that Grover Cleveland celebrated his last birthday. As his condition deteriorated, he longed for Princeton. In the late spring, he was brought back to Westland in secrecy, strapped to a mattress spread across the back seat of a touring sedan. The faithful William Sinclair, who had served Cleveland so loyally from the Buffalo days through the White House years, came out of retirement to help nurse him.

In the last days, Cleveland's innate religiosity became manifest. He had his sister Susan send the worn hymn books that were used at family prayers in his boyhood; these he kept at his bedside in a small oak box which included, along with a few prized mementos, a printed copy of Whittier's spiritual poem "At Last," which he had always cherished and which he now recited to himself from time to time:

When on my day of life the night is falling,
        And, in the winds from unsunned spaces blown,
I hear far voices out of darkness calling
        My feet to paths unknown,
Thou, who hast made my home of life so pleasant,
        Leave not its tenant when its walls decay;
O Love Divine, O Helper ever present,
        Be Thou my strength and stay!

On June 2, the Clevelands celebrated their twenty-second wedding anniversary quietly with a few intimate friends; the children had been sent to the New Hampshire summer home with their maternal grandmother, having been led to believe their father was recovering from his prolonged indisposition and would be joining them there shortly to recuperate. Three weeks later, at two o'clock in the afternoon, Cleveland went into heart failure. His longtime friend and physician, Dr. Bryant, came rushing down from New York with a specialist, R. L. Lockwood. They, along with the family's local physician, J. M. Carnochan, could do little but join Frances in the deathwatch. Throughout the evening, Cleveland drifted in and out of consciousness. Early the following morning he lapsed into a coma; he died at 8:40 A.M.

Cleveland's death came as a shock to the nation, which believed his seclusion from the public was a combination of his known desire for privacy and an ephemeral illness associated with his advancing years. In a proclamation calling for thirty days of official mourning, to include lowering the flag to half-mast on the White House and all federal buildings, and for suitable military and naval honors to be rendered on the day of the funeral, President Roosevelt hailed his predecessor as a man who throughout his public career "showed signal powers as an administrator, coupled with entire devotion to the country's good, and a courage that quailed before no hostility when once he was convinced where his duty lay."[72]

The nation's press was, without exception, laudatory in its eulogies. So, too, the foreign press. In England, the *Daily Mail* said, "Cleveland will stand out in history as one who achieved his popularity by invariably placing the interests of the Nation above those of classes, however influential," while the *Morning Post* hailed him as "one of the great men of his time. He had Bismarck's strength and Bismarck's breadth of views and more than Bismarck's honesty." In the land of Bismarck, the *Berlin Neuesten Nachrichten* said that Cleveland "gained renown among partisans and adversaries as a stainless, high-principled patriot," while the *Berlin Tageblatt* called him "the personification of the modest, quiet, fearless, honorable American type, which latterly has been pushed into the background."

The family's request that the funeral be private was respected, to the extent that the official mourners—who included, in addition to family and close friends, the President and First Lady, Chief Justice Fuller, three governors, and most of the Roosevelt cabinet—numbered fewer than a hundred. At the widow's insistence, there was no music, no eulogy; only a few favorite Cleveland passages from Scripture were read. Dr. Henry Van Dyke, the eminent Princeton clergyman and educator, with whom Cleveland had shared a close friendship, concluded with lines which so befit the man the nation was pausing that day to honor: Wordsworth's "Happy Warrior,"

> Who, if he rise to station of command,
> Rises by open means; and there will stand
> On honorable terms, or else retire,
> And in himself possess his own desire;
> Who comprehends his trust, and to the same
> Keeps faithful with a singleness of aim . . .
> Whom neither shape of danger can dismay,
> Nor thought of tender happiness betray.

There then followed a prayer, and without pause or further ceremony, the procession formed and everyone, led by Cleveland's immediate survivors and President Roosevelt, accompanied the body of the dead Chief Executive to the nearby Princeton Cemetery. "It passed through streets hung with half-masted flags, many of them draped with bands of crepe, and between lines of silent men and women [nearly the entire Princeton population of five thousand] standing with reverently bowed heads."[73]

At the gravesite, next to where Ruth lay buried, just as the sun was sinking beyond the horizon Dr. Beach, minister of the church the Clevelands attended, read the simple Presbyterian committal service ("I am the resurrection and the life . . ."). Then, Frances and the children turned in the direction of their house, President Roosevelt led all the public officials in going about their business, and the little crowd began to disperse.

A few days later a simple headstone was placed over the grave:

GROVER CLEVELAND
Born Caldwell, N.J. March 18, 1837
Died Princeton, N.J. June 24, 1908

If words are needed at this point to sum up Grover Cleveland's accomplishments and give underpinning to the thesis of this biography that he remains America's most underrated President, we can do no better than to quote from the following *New York Times* editorial:

> By native endowment Mr. Cleveland possessed a just mind, a clear vision, manly courage, and a humble spirit. These qualities, chiefly, made him one of the wisest and greatest of our Presidents. He conceived it to be the duty of the President to administer the statute law within the organic law, to urge upon Congress new laws demanded by the interests of the people and none other. He conceived of his fellow-citizens as an adult, capable, self-governing body of men, not as blind folk to be guarded against pitfalls and posts, nor yet as children to be led by the hand and incessantly plied with parental counsel.
>
> In the office of President Mr. Cleveland felt that he was one of the American people whom the others had charged with the duty of looking out for their public business. That he did, but soberly, with little declamation. It was not essential to his happiness that the eyes of the people should be continually fixed upon him. Personal glory never allured [him]. His contentment in the modest performance of duty and his indifference to adulation and the splendor of power left him at all times free to follow the honest convictions of his trained mind. He never considered himself a ruler, only a servant. That "virtue of humility which has a calmness of spirit and a world of other blessings attending upon it" set its stamp upon his statesmanship and upon his public record. He professed no mastery over the views and acts of his countrymen. He was of them, with them. . . . the embodiment of the spirit of the American people, just, straightforward.

Thus we may eulogize a man of no towering intellect who seemed fated for a life of successful mediocrity but who was in fact blessed with a capacity to fit the needs of his generation with a completeness possessed by few of our leaders past and present; who restored honesty and objectivity to government; who taught the American people that in their handling of foreign affairs, as in their handling of domestic ones, conscience must always be the unique dominant consideration.

Grover Cleveland was a man whose character was rooted in a simple, unshakable piety complemented by an inflexible conviction that the universe is governed by a divine force which demands the equating of personal endeavor with the noblest eternal precepts;

—a man who faced a problem head-on by assaying every shred of evidence before arriving at what he believed to be the correct decision, and would not be shaken from that decision by any argument or entreaty, be it from friend or foe, even if doing so placed his political career in jeopardy;

—a man to whom the idea of commissioning polls and governing by consensus was as unacceptable as second-guessing himself;

—a man whose fearlessness rendered him as inherently incapable of abandoning a principle as of surrendering one to political expedience;

—above all, a man whose last mortal words, to his beloved Frank, will stand as the epitaph the ineluctable truth of which can never be denied:

"I have tried so hard to do right."

AFTERWORD

Frances, who declined a pension voted her by Congress, survived her husband by thirty-nine years, during which she served as trustee with a number of various charities and women's organizations. In 1913, she married Thomas Jax Preston (1862–1955), a successful New York businessman who retired at the age of forty and enrolled at Princeton, where he earned a doctorate in classical archaeology. She died suddenly in her sleep at the age of eighty-three, on October 29, 1947, while visiting her eldest son, Richard, an attorney in Baltimore.[1]

Not long before her death, at a White House luncheon given by President Truman, Frances Cleveland Preston, as she styled herself and wished to be known, was chatting with Truman's daughter Margaret about life in Washington when General Dwight Eisenhower, Margaret's luncheon partner, came by. She introduced him to the former First Lady, but he did not seem to realize who she was.

"And where did you live in Washington, ma'am?" Eisenhower asked, joining in the conversation.

Frances smiled demurely and said: "In the White House."[2]

APPENDIX I: CLEVELAND AND THE BLACKS

In the context of our own perspective, Grover Cleveland's attitude toward the black race comes off as considerably less than commendable. But in the context of his era it comes off as, while not singularly commendable, certainly understandable, even defensible. Democratic racial pronouncements in the post–Civil War period tended toward the negrophobic. Cleveland would have been expected to follow the party line. But he cannot, by any stretch of the imagination, be written off as a racist. It was simply not in his character. He was genuinely fond of some blacks, ranging from his servant William Sinclair to such prominent men as Frederick Douglass and Booker T. Washington, though he could not bring himself to socialize with blacks unless such socializing was a necessary concomitant of his official position. But then, this sort of thinking was par for the course among white politicians of the time and down to our own—in particular, southern politicians, and northern politicians who did not wish to alienate the southern voter.

Just as he believed that educating the Indians was the surest way to integrate them, Cleveland believed education of the blacks would lead "to the proper solution of the race question in the South." "If our colored boys are to exercise in their mature years the right of citizenship," he wrote to one prominent black educator, "they should be fitted to perform their duties intelligently and thoroughly."[1] After reading Booker T. Washington's famous Atlanta Exposition speech with "intense interest," Cleveland wrote him: "Your words cannot fail to delight and encourage all who wish well for the race. And if your colored fellow-citizens do not favor your utterances, gather new hope and form new determinations to gain every valuable advantage offered them by their citizenship, it will be strange indeed."[2]

While one of Cleveland's primary concerns was to effect reconciliation between North and South, he did not favor that reconciliation at the expense of the black people, believing as he did in their parity with the white man, as guaranteed by the Thirteenth, Fourteenth, and Fifteenth Amendments to the Constitution.[3] In his first Inaugural Address, in what was decidedly an act of courage for the times, Cleveland sought to reassure the anxious blacks, who feared that the election of the first Democratic President since the Civil War signaled a return to the thinking of James Buchanan: "In the administration of a government pledged to equal and exact justice to all men, there should be no pretext for anxiety touching the protection of the freedmen in their rights, or their security in the enjoyment of their privileges under the Constitution and its amendments." Among numerous prominent blacks expressing pleasure with these sentiments was Frederick Douglass, who said they were "all that any friend of liberty and justice could reasonably ask for the freedmen," adding that "no better words have dropped from the east portico of the Capitol since the inauguration days of Abraham Lincoln and Gen. Grant."[4]

Cleveland could at times be less than totally admirable politically in his thinking toward blacks. Though hardly unique in this regard among American Presidents whose record on racial equality does not quite jibe with the estimable record imputed to them by partisans, still he cannot escape reproof.[5] In a speech on October 31, 1891, reiterating the need to reunite all sections of the country, he urged the "avoidance of unnecessary irritation, and the abandonment of schemes which promise no better result than party supremacy through forced and unnatural suffrage." Here he was referring obliquely to an impending federal elections bill calling for strict supervision of voting procedures intended to aid blacks in the South. Labeled a "force bill" by its southern opponents, it was intended to enforce the Fifteenth Amendment. Cleveland's opposition to it, and his terming of black suffrage in this context as "unnatural," must be weighed against his belief, dating from his days as New York governor, in local home rule. In his second Inaugural Address, about all he could say regarding the blacks was to reaffirm the principle that "the equality before the law which [the Constitution] guarantees to every citizen should be . . . unimpaired by race or color. . . ."[6]

For a politician to accept the charge of social equality, or anything remotely suggesting it, during this period in American history was to commit political suicide. Southern whites not only denied blacks their constitutionally guaranteed rights, they became vindictive toward others who did, and the southern influence in Congress throughout this period cannot be overstated. There were any number of occasions when, whether as governor or President, or even out of office, Cleveland had to defend himself against such malevolence. As George Sinkler, a leading scholar on the racial attitudes of Lincoln and all succeeding nineteenth-century Presidents, observes, "Race prejudice and state and national Jim Crow rulings of the period seemed not to have entered Cleveland's thinking at this point."[7]

Within four years, they did.

Addressing a meeting of the Southern Educational Association in Boston in 1903, he delivered what was tantamount to his valedictory on the race question. It makes for curious, at times infuriating reading. As "a sincere friend of the Negro and a believer in the Booker Washington–Tuskegee" school of thought, he hoped that "the days of 'Uncle Tom's Cabin' are passed." But sadly, as he saw it, the Civil War Amendments had no more purged the blacks of their "racial and slavery bred imperfections than it changed the color of their skins." Even as freedmen, they retained "a grievous amount of ignorance [and] a sad amount of laziness and thriftlessness." Because of the "racial deficiencies" of the blacks, "our fellow-countrymen [i.e., the Caucasians] in the Southern and late slave-holding states . . . are entitled to our utmost consideration and sympathetic fellowship." Cleveland then went on to admit a willingness to trust the southern whites with the blacks, and a remarkable tolerance of southern racial folkways:

"I do not know how it may be with the other Northern friends of the Negro, but I have faith in the honor and sincerity of the respectable white people of the South in their relations with the Negro and his improvement and well being. [The southerners] do not believe in the social equality of the race, and they make no false pretense in regard to it. That this does not grow out of hatred for the Negro is very plain."[8]

Cleveland perceived "abundant sentiments and abundant behavior among Southern whites toward the Negro to make us doubt the justice of charging this denial of social equality to prejudice, as we understand the word." Like Abraham Lincoln, one of his paramount idols, Cleveland posited that the sensitivity of some whites to social intercourse with blacks was instinctive, as opposed to traditional. The implication was that instinctive feelings could not be properly labeled a prejudice. Too, he wanted it known how impressed he was that the South had "forgiven the blacks" for the "Saturnalia of Reconstruction Days" and the "spoliation of the white men of the South."[9]

What was the destiny of the black man in America? Cleveland asked rhetorically. He could not be certain. But whatever that destiny, "mental and manual education" of the Tuskegee variety would prepare blacks for the "responsibilities" incumbent upon their citizenship. He consigned to God the black man's fate and the white man's prejudice; and if it was "within the wise purposes of God, the hardened surface of no untoward sentiment of prejudice can prevent the bursting forth of the blade and plant of the Negro's appointed opportunity into the bright sunlight of a cloudless day."[10]

Cleveland foresaw a time—admittedly distant—when blacks, no longer ignorant (i.e., in terms of education), would realize fully their constitutionally mandated citizenship free of prejudice and discrimination. That prejudice, instinctive or otherwise, which made the average Caucasian wince at the idea of social equality Cleveland believed was best left to time.[11]

Of course, for the blacks there were too many *ifs* for this kind of reasoning. Notwithstanding constitutional guarantees, Cleveland seemed to be implying that the black man could anticipate equality with his white neighbor *if* he educated and otherwise improved himself; *if* he remained in America and was not expatriated (whether through force or by choice); and *if* the white man was prepared to concede that such equality was indeed his black neighbor's birthright.

Given the Zeitgeist of the American nation's post-Reconstruction, can it truly be denied that Grover Cleveland had stated the case dispassionately?

APPENDIX II: CLEVELAND AND THE CHINESE IMMIGRANTS

Cleveland's attitude toward any immigrant group was predicated solely on whether he believed its members were willing to accept American values and become a contributory factor in American society. He loathed nativists who sought to shut the door on the great tide from southern and eastern Europe hoping to become permanent and productive residents. He was also free from religious prejudice. The only group against which he can be accused of harboring any such prejudice was the Mormons. But here his intolerance was not based on religious principles but on religious practices. (It was for that reason he signed legislation on March 3, 1887, authorizing the federal government to seize and administer Mormon Church property until it formally vowed to abandon polygamy.) We already have seen that he tended to patronize blacks and Native Americans, though he did believe both groups were "assimilable," and, particularly with the Indians—the only authentically native Americans—he was adamant that their rights be guaranteed against rapacious white entrepreneurs and settlers.

But Cleveland's willingness that all races and creeds be permitted to assimilate did not extend to the Chinese.

The scarcity of workers, particularly on the railroads, following the discovery of gold in California in 1848 led to an influx of Chinese laborers, facilitated by the Burlingame Treaty of 1868. But as completion of the transcontinental railroad brought more white laborers to the West, competition from the Orientals for jobs led to armed confrontations. In 1877, for example, twenty-one Chinese were killed in a San Francisco riot. With agitation growing for modification of the Burlingame Treaty, Congress in 1879 enacted legislation that restricted Chinese immigration, but President Hayes vetoed it as a violation of the treaty. Three years later, by which time some 375,000 Chinese—over 90 percent of them male—were recorded as having entered the country, Congress passed the Exclusion Act, which suspended Chinese immigration for ten years. (Much of the figure represents multiple entries by the same individuals—that is, those who returned home for a visit or to find and bring back a bride—so that the peak Chinese population in the United States for the century has been estimated at about 125,000. Besides railroad construction, they were employed in manufacturing, agriculture, and, marginally, mining.)

Cleveland insisted the Chinese were as entitled as any immigrant group to federal protection. But he soon concluded that prejudice against them was so ingrained, and their and the Caucasians' backgrounds so disparate, as to preclude their absorption into American society. ("Our immigration laws were designed to invite assimilation and not to provide an arena for endless antagonism.")[1] He devised a twofold plan: protect those already here against racial and economic harassment, and negotiate a new treaty with the Chinese government restricting further immigration.

Historians claim Cleveland was motivated by partisan consideration: anti-Chinese prejudice on the West Coast, where the preponderance of the Chinese were located, was an explosive issue among the Caucasians and their legislative representatives and politicians. They conveniently overlook that he plowed ahead in protecting and assimilating the blacks in the South and Indians in the West despite political consideration. Still, it would be equally convenient for us to overlook the fact that Cleveland saw a successful resolution of the Chinese problem redounding to his political advantage, particularly in the West, where his political support was in short supply.

In 1887, Secretary of State Thomas Bayard began negotiations with the Chinese government. By the following spring, agreement seemed near. Chinese laborers would not be permitted to emigrate to the United States for twenty years; any Chinese immigrant presently in the United States who returned to China would be denied reentry; and the Chinese government would receive $276,619 with which to compensate Chinese residents in the United States who had suffered injury at the hands of private American citizens. While the Republican-controlled Senate stalled on confirming the treaty, the Chinese government, apparently having second thoughts, suggested a reduction of the twenty-year ban and a revision of the reentry clause.

With a presidential election approaching, it was imprudent for Cleveland either to extend the negotiations or conciliate the Chinese government. Without consulting Bayard, he called for legislation prohibiting reentry by Chinese laborers. It sailed easily through both houses and was ready for Cleveland's signature on October 1. "The experiment of blending the social habits and mutual race idiosyncrasies of the Chinese laboring classes with those of the great body of the people of the United States has been proved by the experience of twenty years . . . to be in every sense unwise, impolitic, and injurious to both nations," he told Congress at the time.[2]

During Cleveland's second administration the "Chinese question" was forced into the background by other, more urgent domestic and diplomatic problems. A treaty had by then been signed whereby the Chinese government agreed to the exclusion of Chinese laborers for ten years. The whole question of Chinese immigration remained frictional, and was low on the list of Cleveland's priorities. Still, it must be noted that he had to have harbored some belief in the inferiority of the Chinese, to judge by his reaction to the arrival at Washington of a member of the Chinese royal family while on a worldwide tour. Reluctant to entertain him officially, Cleveland suggested that "a more appropriate greeting" for "Esquire Li Hung Chang" might be "the firing off of a bunch of Chinese firecrackers."[3]

The remark was racist, if not by the prevailing standard of the times then certainly by today's. Grover Cleveland was no freer of prejudice of one nature or another than any other man ever to occupy the White House. While his demand that the Chinese laborers be protected in no way justifies an obvious bias, the fact remains that, like it or not, perhaps we should measure our leaders not by what they say but, rather, by what they do.

ACKNOWLEDGMENTS

I wish to thank my dear friends Marion Levien and Sherry Armstrong for their encouragement in the writing of this book, and to my brother and sister-in-law, Lowell and Adeline Burton, not only for their moral support but for their financial support as well. I am deeply indebted to Sharon Farrell, caretaker of the Grover Cleveland Birthplace in Caldwell, New Jersey, for her incalculable assistance in collecting the photographs used herein. Another in whose debt I am for his editorial expertise and love of biography is my editor-publisher, Truman "Mac" Talley at St. Martin's Press. Jill Sieracki, Mac's assistant, has been a great source of much appreciated assistance. But inarguable my greatest debt is to my agent, Sam Fleishman. If there were a few more agents like Sam, ours would be a better publishing world.

BIBLIOGRAPHY

Alexander, De Alva Stanwood. *The Political History of the State of New York.* 4 vols. Vol. 4. *Four Famous New Yorkers: The Political Careers of Cleveland, Platt, Hill, and Roosevelt.* New York: Henry Holt, 1923.

Andrist, Ralph K., ed. *The American Heritage History of the Confident Years.* New York: American Heritage, 1969.

Anthony, Carl Sperazza. *First Ladies: The Saga of the Presidents' Wives and Their Power, 1789–1961.* New York: Morrow, 1990.

Armitage, Charles H. *Grover Cleveland as Buffalo Knew Him.* Buffalo, NY.: Buffalo Evening News, 1926.

Beer, Thomas. *The Mauve Decade: American Life at the End of the Nineteenth Century.* New York: Knopf, 1926.

———. *Hanna.* New York: A. A. North, 1929.

Berg, Albert Ellery. *Addresses and State Papers of Grover Cleveland.* New York: Sun Dial Classics, 1909.

Boller, Paul, Jr. *Presidential Anecdotes.* New York: Oxford, 1981.

Boardman, Fon W., Jr. *America and the Gilded Age: 1876–1900.* New York: H. Z. Walck, 1972.

———. *Presidential Campaigns.* New York: Oxford, 1984.

———. *Presidential Wives.* New York: Oxford, 1988.

Branch, Taylor. *Parting the Waters.* New York: Simon & Schuster, 1990.

Brayman, Harold. *From Grover Cleveland to Gerald Ford . . . The President Speaks Off-the-Record.* Princeton, N.J.: Dow Jones Books, 1976.

Cashman, Sean Dennis. *America in the Gilded Age: From the Death of Lincoln to the Rise of Theodore Roosevelt.* New York: New York Univ. Press, 1984.

Chernow, Ron. *The House of Morgan.* New York: Atlantic Monthly, 1990.

Cleveland, Grover. *Presidential Problems.* 1904. Reprint. Freeport, N.Y.: Books for Libraries Press, 1971.

Cleveland, Horace Gillette. *The Genealogy of the Cleveland and Cleaveland Families.* Hartford, Ct.: privately printed, 1899.

Commager, Henry Steele. *Documents of American History.* New York: F. S. Crofts, 1938.

Crook, William H. *Memories of the White House.* Boston: Little, Brown, 1911.

Cross, Wilbur, and Ann Novotny. *White House Weddings.* New York: David McKay, 1967.

Dennis, Alfred Lewis Pinneo. *Adventures in American Diplomacy, 1896–1930.* New York: Dutton, 1928.

Dorsheimer, William. *Life and Public Services of Grover Cleveland.* Philadelphia: Hubbard Bros., 1888.

Foner, Philip Sheldon, ed. *The Life and Writings of Frederick Douglass.* 4 vols. New York: Citadel, 1964.

Foraker, J. B. *Notes of a Busy Life.* Cincinnati: Stewart & Kidd, 1916.

Ford, Henry Jones. *The Cleveland Era: A Chronicle of the New Order in Politics.* New Haven: Yale University Press, 1919.

Gilder, Richard Watson. *Grover Cleveland: A Record of Friendship.* New York: Century, 1910.

Goode, James M. *Capital Losses: A Cultural History of Washington's Destroyed Buildings.* Washington, D.C.: Smithsonian Institution Press, 1979.

Green, Constance. *Washington: A History of the Capital, 1800–1950.* Princeton, N.J.: Princeton University Press, 1976.

Hamilton, Gail. *James G. Blaine.* Norwich, Ct.: H. Bill, 1895.

Harvey, George. *Henry Clay Frick.* New York: privately printed, 1928.

Hicks, John D. *The American Nation: A History of the United States from 1865 to the Present.* Boston: Houghton Mifflin, 1971.

Hollingsworth, J. Rogers. *The Whirligig of Politics: The Democracy of Cleveland and Bryan.* Chicago: University of Chicago Press, 1963.

Hoover, Irwin Hood. *Forty-two Years in the White House.* Boston: Houghton-Mifflin, 1934.

Howe, M. A. DeWolfe. *Portrait of an Independent: Morfield Story, 1845–1929.* Boston and New York: Houghton Mifflin, 1932.

Hudson, William C. *Random Recollections of an Old Political Reporter.* New York: Cupples & Leon, 1911.

Hugins, Roland. *Grover Cleveland: A Study in Political Courage.* Washington, D.C.: Anchor-Lee, 1922.

James, Henry. *Richard Olney and His Public Service.* Boston and New York: Houghton Mifflin, 1923.

Johnson, Paul. *A History of the American People.* New York: HarperCollins, 1997.

Kuykendall, Ralph. *The Hawaiian Kingdom.* Vol. 3. *1874–1893, the Kalakaua Dynasty.* Honolulu: University of Hawaii Press, 1967.

La Follette, Robert Marion. *La Follette's Autobiography.* Madison, Wis.: La Follette, 1913.

Lodge, Henry Cabot, ed. *Selections from the Correspondence of Theodore Roosevelt and Henry Cabot Lodge, 1884–1918.* 2 Vols. New York: Scribner's, 1925.

Lorant, Stefan. *The Glorious Burden: The History of the Presidency and Presidential Elections from George Washington to James Earl Carter, Jr.* Lenox, Mass.: Authors Edition, 1968, 1976.

McElroy, Robert McNutt. *Grover Cleveland, the Man and the Statesman.* 2 vols. New York: Harper & Brothers, 1923.

Merrill, Horace Samuel. *Bourbon Leader: Grover Cleveland and the Democratic Party.* Boston: Little, Brown, 1957.

Miller, Nathan. *Theodore Roosevelt: A Life.* New York: Morrow, 1992.

Morgan, H. Wayne. *From Hayes to McKinley: National Party Politics, 1877–1896.* Syracuse, N.Y.: Syracuse University Press, 1969.

Morris, Edmund. *The Rise of Theodore Roosevelt.* New York: Coward, McCann & Geoghegan, 1979.

Nevins, Allan. *Grover Cleveland: A Study in Courage.* New York: Dodd, Mead, 1932.

———. *The Letters of Grover Cleveland, 1850–1908.* New York: Houghton Mifflin, 1933.

———, and Henry Steele Commager. *A Short History of the United States.* New York: Random House, 1942.

Nugent, Walter T. K. *From Centennial to World War: American Society, 1876–1917.* Indianapolis: Bobbs-Merrill, 1977.

Parker, George F. *Recollections of Grover Cleveland.* New York: Century, 1909.

———. *The Writings and Speeches of Grover Cleveland.* New York: Cassell, 1892.

Peck, Harry Thurston. *Twenty Years of the Republic, 1885–1905.* New York: Dodd, Mead, 1906.

Platt, Thomas C. *Autobiography.* New York: Dodge, 1910.

Porter, Kirk H. *National Party Platform.* New York: Putnam, 1924.

Richardson, James D., ed. *Messages and Papers of the Presidents.* 10 vols. Washington, D.C.: Government Printing Office, 1896–99. Vols. 8–9 contain the official executive documents issued by Cleveland as President.

Roseboom, Eugene H. *A History of Presidential Elections from George Washington to Richard M. Nixon.* New York: Macmillan, 1957.

Sahenkman, Richard. *Presidential Ambition.* New York: HarperCollins, 1999.

Schurz, Carl. *Sketches, Correspondence, and Political Papers.* New York: Putnam, 1913.

Seale, William. *The President's House, a History.* 2 vols. Washington, D.C.: White House Historical Association, 1986.

Simkin, Francis B. *Pitchfork Ben Tillman, South Carolinian.* Baton Rouge: Louisiana State University Press, 1944.

Sinkler, George. *The Racial Attitudes of American Presidents from Abraham Lincoln to Theodore Roosevelt.* New York: Doubleday, 1971.

Smith, Page. *The Rise of Industrial America—A People's History of the Post–Reconstruction Era.* Vol. 6. New York: McGraw-Hill, 1984.

Strouse, Jean. *Morgan: American Financier.* New York: Random House, 1999.

Truman, Margaret. *Souvenir: Margaret Truman's Own Story.* New York: McGraw-Hill, 1956.

Tugwell, Rexford. *Grover Cleveland.* New York: Macmillan, 1968.

Vexler, Robert I., ed. *Grover Cleveland, 1837–1908: Chronology, Documents, Bibliographical Aids.* Dobbs Ferry, N.Y.: Oceana Publications, 1968.

Villard, Henry. *Memoirs.* Boston and New York: Houghton Mifflin, 1904.

Welch, Deshler. *Stephen Grover Cleveland.* New York: J. W. Lovell, 1884.

Welch, Richard E., Jr. *The Presidencies of Grover Cleveland.* Lawrence: University Press of Kansas, 1988.

Williams, R. Hal. *Years of Decision: American Politics in the 1890s.* New York: John Wiley, 1978.

Woodward, C. Vann. *The Origins of the New South, 1877–1913.* Baton Rouge: Louisiana State University Press, 1951.

PUBLIC DOCUMENTS AND ARCHIVAL MATERIAL

The Public Papers of Grover Cleveland, Twenty-second President of the United States, March 4, 1885, to March 4, 1889. Washington: Government Printing Office, 1889.

The Public Papers of Grover Cleveland, Twenty-fourth President of the United States, March 4, 1893, to March 4, 1897. Washington: Government Printing Office, 1897. (Referred to in Notes as "Cleveland Papers.")

State Department Papers Relative to the Foreign Relations of the United States, 1895 (Washington: Government Printing Office, 1895).

United States Congress, Senate, 49th Congress, 1st Session; House Reports, 49th Cong., 2nd session.

Annual Reports, Department of Interior, 1885, 1886, 1887.

Annual Report, Secretary of the Treasury, 1885.

Democratic Campaign Book, 1886.

Congressional Record, 1885–89, 1893–97.

House Executive Documents, 53 Congress, 2 session, no. 47, Report of Commissioner to the Hawaiian Islands (the "Blount Report"); United States Senate Reports, 53 Congress, 2 session, no. 227 (the "Morgan Report"); United States House of Representatives Executive Documents, 53 Congress, 3 session, no. 1, part 1, Foreign Relations of the United States, 1894.

U.S. Department of Justice, Report, Attorney General, 1896, Library of Congress.

Thomas F. Bayard Papers, Library of Congress.

Abram Hewitt papers, Library of Congress.

Daniel Lamont Papers, Library of Congress.

Richard Olney Papers, Library of Congress.

Henry Watterson Papers, Library of Congress.

PERIODICALS

American Heritage

Appleton's Annual Cyclopedia

Atlantic Monthly

Arena

Century Magazine

Columbia Historical Society (1966–68), Records of

Commoner

Congressional Studies

Foreign Relations

Harper's Magazine

Journal of American History

Ladies' Home Journal

Life

McClure's Magazine

McPherson's Handbook

Mississippi Valley Historical Review

Nation

New England Quarterly

North American Review

North Missourian

Proceedings of the Massachusetts Historical Society

Public Opinion

Review of Books

Saturday Evening Post

Scribner's Magazine

South Atlantic Quarterly

Wisconsin State Journal

NEWSPAPERS

Albany Argus

Albany Evening Journal

Albany World

Atlanta Constitution

Boston Advertiser

Boston Globe

Boston Journal

Boston Post

Buffalo Commercial Advertiser

Buffalo Courier

Buffalo Evening Telegram

Buffalo Sunday Times

Charleston News and Courier

Chicago Record

Chicago Times

Chicago Tribune

Concord [New Hampshire] Monitor

Denver Republican

Indianapolis Sentinel

*Jackson (*Mich.*) Industrial News*

Kansas City Times

Louisville Courier-Journal

Millwakee Journal

New Orleans Picayune

New Orleans Times Democrat

New York Commercial Advertiser

New York Evening Post

New York Herald

New York Press

New York Sun

New York Times

New York Tribune

New York World

Omaha World-Herald

Philadelphia Public Ledger

Philadelphia Telegraph

Richmond Times

Springfield Republican

Utica Observer

Washington Post

NOTES

NOTE: If a reference work is listed in the bibliography, only the author's name will be given in the citation unless more than one work by an author is listed, in which case the citation will include an abbreviation of the title. All letters quoted in the text, unless otherwise noted, are from Allan Nevins, *The Letters of Grover Cleveland, 1850–1908.*

INTRODUCTION

1. "The U.S. Presidents," *Life,* Nov. 1, 1948, pp. 65–74.
2. Nevins, *Grover Cleveland,* p. 766; Tugwell, p. 139.
3. Robert F. Murray and Tim H. Blessing, "The Presidential Performance Study: A Progress Report," *Journal of American History* 70, No. 3 (December 1983), pp. 535–55.
4. Geoffrey Blodgett, "Political Leadership of Grover Cleveland," *South Atlantic Quarterly,* Summer 1983, p. 292.
5. Gilder, p. 35.
6. Parker, *Writing and Speeches,* p. 118 (July 13, 1887). Parker, a journalist, attached himself to Cleveland at the start of his second run for the White House. His books and articles are an invaluable primary source on Cleveland's life.

PART 1: 1837-1881

1. Parker, *Recollections,* p. 15.
2. Elizabeth Donnan, *New England Quarterly* 3, p. 271.
3. McElroy, I, p. 34.
4. Nevins, *Grover Cleveland,* pp. 57–58.
5. Armitage, p. 28.
6. Parker, *Writings and Speeches,* pp. 10–11.
7. Nevins, *Grover Cleveland,* pp. 18–19.
8. Parker, *Recollections,* p. 21.
9. Crosby, "Cleveland as a Teacher in the Institution for the Blind,"*McClure's Magazine,* March 1909, pp. 581–83.
10. Nevins, *Grover Cleveland,* p. 37.
11. Parker, *Recollections,* p. 30.
12. Dec. 24, 1863. The *Courier* became one of Cleveland's strongest boosters.
13. Parker, *Recollections,* p. 33.
14. Gilder memorandum, Cleveland Papers.
15. Gilder, p. 191.
16. *Buffalo Courier,* Oct. 2, Nov. 6, 1865.
17. During the campaign, the friendly opponents agreed to limit their daily beer consumption to four glasses. After a few summery evenings, they agreed that

such a ration was too skimpy, and from then on took to "anticipating" their future intake at each sitting. One evening, Bass said, "Grover! Do you realize we have by now 'anticipated' the whole campaign?" The next night, both jointly resolved the ration problem by ordering their brew in huge tankards they christened "glasses." George F. Parker, "Grover Cleveland's Career in Buffalo, 1855–1882," *Saturday Evening Post,* Aug. 28, 1920.

18. Nevins, *Grover Cleveland,* p. 70.
19. Dorsheimer, p. 35.
20. Parker, *Recollections,* pp. 37–41. See also Parker, "Cleveland as a Lawyer," *McClure's Magazine,* New York, 1909, Vol. 32.
21. Richard E. Welch, Jr., pp. 26–27.
22. Deshler Welch, p. 32.

PART II: 1881-1884

1. Armitage, pp. 86–87.
2. *Buffalo Commercial Advertiser,* Oct. 26, 1881.
3. Hudson, pp. 178–80.
4. *Buffalo Courier,* Jan. 1, 1882.
5. McElroy, I, p. 31.
6. Nevins, *Grover Cleveland,* p. 90.
7. *Buffalo Sunday Times,* June 23, 1882.
8. McElroy, I, p. 35.
9. Armitage, pp. 157–58.
10. McElroy, I, p. 39.
11. Apgar's entire letter reproduced in Parker, *Recollections,* pp. 49–50.
12. GC to Apgar, Aug. 31, 1882.
13. E. Jay Edwards, "The Personal Force of Cleveland," *McClure's Magazine,* November 1893, p. 493. See also Parker, *Recollections,* p. 341.
14. Parker, *Writings and Speeches,* pp. 533–34.
15. *Buffalo Courier,* Aug. 10, 1882.
16. Robert Lincoln O'Brien, "Grover Cleveland as Seen by His Stenographer, July, 1892–November, 1895," *Proceedings of the Massachusetts Historical Society,* 50 (October 1950–May 1953), p. 128.
17. McElroy, I, p. 49.
18. Parker, *Recollections,* p. 54.
19. Feb. 2, 1883, Cleveland Papers.
20. Dorsheimer, p. 137.
21. *Albany Evening Journal,* March 21, 1883.
22. Nevins, *Grover Cleveland,* p. 128.
23. *Albany Argus,* July 17, 1883; Nevins, *Grover Cleveland,* p. 128.
24. Parker, *Recollections,* pp. 60–61.
25. *Albany Argus,* March 5, 1883. See also Parker, *Writings and Speeches,* p. 438.
26. Gilder, p. 35.
27. *Albany Evening Journal,* March 2, 1883; *Albany Argus* and *New York World,* March 3, 1883.

28. Hudson, pp. 147–49. See also Miller, p. 18.
29. Parker, *Recollections,* pp. 250–51.
30. Nevins, *Grover Cleveland,* p. 125.
31. GC to Kelly, Oct. 20, 1883.
32. *New York Herald,* Nov. 23, 1883.
33. *New York World,* Oct. 28, 1883.
34. *New York Herald,* Nov. 23, 1883.
35. GC to Fairchild, March 17, 1884.
36. McElroy, I, p. 68.
37. Hudson, p. 154.
38. McElroy, I, pp. 71–72.
39. GC to Manning, June 30, 1884.
40. Hudson, p. 164.
41. Andrist, p. 10. See also Merrill, pp. 51–52.
42. Nevins, *Grover Cleveland,* p. 156.
43. Alexander, IV, p. 26.
44. Geoffrey Blodgett, "The Mind of the Boston Mugwump," *Mississippi Valley Historical Review* 48 (March 1962), p. 614.
45. Morgan, p. 136.
46. *Harper's Weekly,* July 5, 1884, p. 426.
47. *Boston Advertiser,* July 12, 1884. Cleveland was a favorite with reporters, even those from papers that disliked him, and in some cases hated him, and despite his own widely known negative opinion of the press in general and correspondents in particular. The only exceptions were political allies like William Hudson and William Dorsheimer and close personal friends like Richard Gilder and L. Clark Davis. For an amusing recounting of his dealings with the press, see Brayman.
48. *Wisconsin State Journal,* July 10, 1884.
49. *Albany World,* July 11, 1884.
50. Parker, *Writings and Speeches,* pp. 6–7.

PART III: 1884

1. See Shenkman, p. 50; Boller, *Presidential Campaigns,* pp. 149–53.
2. Porter, pp. 116–23, 132–36.
3. GC to D-Cady Herrick, July 26, 1891.
4. Berg, p. 58.
5. Quoted in Richard Welch, p. 33.
6. See *New York Sun,* Aug. 4, 10, 17, 1884.
7. GC to Daniel Lamont, Aug. 31, 1884.
8. Sinkler, p. 216*n.*
9. *Nation,* Feb. 26, 1885.
10. Marvin and Dorothy Rosenberg, "The Dirtiest Election," *American Heritage,* August 1962.
11. Ibid.
12. GC to Daniel Lockwood, July 31, 1884, Nevins, *Grover Cleveland,* p. 165.
13. GC to Charles W. Goodyear, July 31, 1884.

14. Welch, p. 36; see also Smith, VI, p. 459. The Senator was George Vest of Missouri.
15. Cleveland's nephew, Cleveland Bacon, to Allan Nevins, Dec. 15, 1931.
16. See Nevins, *Grover Cleveland,* pp. 164–66.
17. See Cleveland's correspondence on this issue in Nevins, *Letters,* pp. 37–45.
18. Howe, p. 151; Andrist, p. 207.
19. Hudson, p. 190.
20. See Rosenberg, op. cit.
21. Ibid.
22. See Schurz, IV, pp. 239–48.
23. GC to Lamont, Aug. 14, 1884, Lamont Papers, Library of Congress.
24. *New York Times,* Sept. 15, Oct. 7, 1884.
25. Schurz, op. cit.
26. GC to George F. Dege, Oct. 28, 1884. When this letter was made public, Joseph Pulitzer cited four good reasons for endorsing Cleveland's candidacy: "1. He is an honest man. 2. He is an honest man. 3. He is an honest man. 4. He is an honest man." *New York World,* Sept. 22, 1884.
27. GC to John Hall, Sept. 13, 1887.
28. *New York Tribune,* Oct. 28, 1884; *New York Times,* Nov. 2, 1884; *New York Herald,* Oct. 16, 1884.
29. Hudson, pp. 208–9.
30. Andrist, p. 212.
31. Merrill, p. 68.
32. *New York World,* Oct. 31, 1884.
33. Nevins, *Grover Cleveland,* p. 186.
34. See W. G. Rice and F. L. Stetson, "Was New York's Vote Stolen?" *North American Review,* January 1914.
35. GC to Bissell, Nov. 13, 1884. "the place I hate above all others": GC to W. F. Vilas, May 20, 1889.

PART IV: 1885-1888

1. McElroy, I, p. 100.
2. GC to Bissell, June 25, 1885.
3. McElroy, I, pp. 117–20.
4. La Follette, p. 52. The oath of office, administered by Chief Justice Morrison Remick Waite, was taken on the little Bible that had on its flyleaf the inscription "My son, Stephen Grover Cleveland, from his loving Mother." The clerk of the Supreme Court inscribed on the flyleaf: "Used to administer the oath of office to Grover Cleveland, President of the United States, on the fourth of March, 1885." Cleveland always kept the Bible on his bedroom bureau, except during his White House years, when it was kept in the upper left-hand drawer of the desk presented to him by Queen Victoria as a memento of Sir John Franklin's expedition to the Arctic.
5. For the complete text, see Vexler, pp. 36–37.
6. While Cleveland consistently consulted with the cabinet on major issues, as much cannot be said vis-à-vis his Vice President. Thomas Hendricks typified in Cleve-

land's mind the dedicated professional politician whose primary concern was patronage rather than efficiency in government. His death eight months into office led to the Presidential Succession Act of 1886, which provided that on the death of an incumbent the presidency would pass to the Vice President, or, were he to predecease the President, to the cabinet member in chronological order of the department's creation: State, Treasury, War, etc. This act was superseded by the Twenty-fifth Amendment to the Constitution (1967) after the American people got around to the realization that the presidency could conceivably devolve upon someone who had been selected, not elected. Little did they know there was a Ford in their future.

7. GC to George W. Curtis, Dec. 25, 1884.
8. Nevins, *Grover Cleveland,* p. 201. Most petitioners for top positions accepted the President's decisions reluctantly, and endured no more than the ephemeral pain of denial and rebuff. Not so a pair of Minnesota Democrats, who presented Cleveland with a rather extended shopping list of proposed appointments for some of their constituents. They came away with just a single appointment. When news of their less than spectacular success got back to Minnesota the two were burned in effigy, whereupon one gave up his place on the Democratic National Committee, while the other departed expeditiously for an extended tour of Europe. *New York Evening Post,* March 9, 10, 1885.
9. See *Foreign Relations,* 1885, 549 ff.; *Nation,* Jan. 21, 1886; *New York Evening Post,* April 16, 1885, and Jan. 2, 1886.
10. *New York Tribune,* Jan. 9, Feb. 13, 1885.
11. GC to George W. Curtis, Dec. 25, 1884.
12. Schurz to Cleveland, March 22, 1885, Cleveland Papers.
13. McElroy, I, pp. 130–31.
14. *New York World,* Sept. 10, 12, 1885.
15. GC to Joseph Keppler, founding editor of *Puck,* Dec. 12, 1885.
16. GC to Bissell, Dec. 12, 1885.
17. Shepard to Cleveland, Sept. 19, 1885, Cleveland Papers; GC to Shepard, Sept. 29, 1885, Nevins, *Letters,* p. 80; Shepard to Cleveland, Oct. 12, 1885, Cleveland Papers.
18. McElroy, I, p. 153.
19. GC to Alton V. Parker, Oct. 22, 1886.
20. July 14, 1886, Cleveland Papers.
21. GC to Benton, Nov. 16, 1886.
22. *The North Missourian,* Nov. 27, 1886.
23. Schurz to Cleveland, Dec. 3, 1886, Cleveland Papers.
24. See Cleveland, "The Independence of the Executive," in *Presidential Problems,* pp. 43–45.
25. United States Congress, Senate, 49th Congress, 1st Session, *Journal of the Executive Proceedings of the Senate,* XXV, 294.
26. *Boston Globe,* Jan. 28, 1886.
27. Quoted in McElroy, p. 179.
28. For complete text of the message, see Vexler, pp. 39–47.

29. See Louis Fisher, "Grover Cleveland Against the Senate," *Congressional Studies*, Winter 1979, pp. 11–25.
30. Vexler, pp. 39–47.
31. Parker, *Writings and Speeches*, pp. 42, 400–9, 413–15.
32. GC to the Rev. James Morrow of Philadelphia, March 20, 1888.
33. McElroy, I, p. 223.
34. GC to Sheridan, April (?)1885.
35. Annual Reports, Department of Interior, 1885, 1886, 1887. See also *Democratic Campaign Book*, 1886, pp. 108–12.
36. Annual Reports, Department of Interior, 1885, 1886.
37. Hewitt Papers. See also Nevins, *Grover Cleveland*, p. 202.
38. See Nevins, *Letters*, pp. 56–57. See also Parker, *Recollections*, p. 340.
39. Annual Report, Secretary of the Treasury, 1885, pp. 31–32.
40. *Congressional Record*, Jan. 18, 1886, vol. 17, pp. 708 ff.; April 3, 1886, vol. 17, p. 3101.
41. GC to Wilson Bissell, Dec. 27, 1885.
42. *New York Herald*, *New York World*, Jan. 5, 1886.
43. Ibid., Jan. 6, 1886.
44. GC to Samuel J. Randall, July 14, 1886.
45. GC to Manning, June 1, 1885.
46. Seale, I, p. 537.
47. Seale (I, p. 558) gives the chef's name as Cupplinger. Nevins in *Grover Cleveland* (p. 212) identifies him as Fortin. To Cleveland, he was simply "that man who cooks."
48. Grover Cleveland, "Woman's Mission and Woman's Clubs," *Ladies' Home Journal*, May 1905.
49. On Frances's feminist orientation and overall persona: Green, p. 67; on the dancing servants: Hoover, p. 15; "She is a superior person": Anthony, p. 258; "She'll do! She'll do!": Nevins, *Grover Cleveland*, p. 311.
50. Cross and Novotny, pp. 114, 117.
51. McElroy, I, p. 184.
52. GC to Mary Cleveland Hoyt, March 21, April 19, 1886.
53. Women and children made up a significant share of the workforce but received lower wages than adult male workers regardless of the job. More than a half million boys and girls between the ages of ten and fourteen were gainfully employed when Cleveland entered office, over half of them in the South.
54. Hicks, p. 109.
55. See McElroy, I, pp. 139–40.
56. *House Reports*, 49th Cong., 2nd session.
57. Nevins and Commager, p. 302.
58. Merrill, p. 89.
59. Crook, p. 179.
60. For the fashion-conscious: the bridal gown was "a poem in its pure simplicity, of thick ivory satin of the kind that stands alone." *Paris Morning News*, quoted in Cross and Novotny, p. 129.

61. GC to Daniel Lamont, June 3, 1886; GC to *New York Evening Post,* McElroy, I, p. 187; details of the honeymoon, Cross and Novotny, pp. 131–32.
62. GC to Dr. S. B. Ward, Aug. 8, 1886.
63. Boller, *Presidential Anecdotes,* p. 174.
64. Nevins, *Grover Cleveland,* p. 454.
65. Merrill, p. 91; see also Tugwell, pp. 146–47.
66. Hoover, pp. 12, 14.
67. Anthony, p. 260.
68. *New York Press,* July 10, 1892.
69. GC to Leo Oppenheim, April 15, 1893.
70. "I am ready now": McElroy, I, p. 379; "You know how dearly": Anthony, p. 262.
71. Vexler, p. 39.
72. Charles Dudley Warner, "Impressions of the South," *Harper's Magazine,* September 1885.
73. *New York Herald,* July 19, 1887.
74. W. F. Tillett, "The White Man of the New South," *Century Magazine,* March 1887.
75. *Charleston News and Courier,* April 30, May 1, 1886; *Kansas City Journal, New York Tribune,* May 1, 2, 1886.
76. See GC to W. H. Rogers, April 1, 1887.
77. Surprisingly, southern veterans did not organize until 1889, when they formed the Union of Confederate Veterans. It was never an effective political force like the GAR; its peak membership barely topped 50,000, and its life span was brief. Conversely, the GAR lasted until 1956, when it expired along with its last surviving member.
78. See W. H. Glasson, "Federal Military Pensions in the United States," *Century Magazine,* August 1885.
79. E. V. Smalley, "The United States Pension Office," *Century Magazine,* July 1884.
80. *Congressional Record,* July 30, 1886, vol. 17, p. 7765.
81. See Vexler, pp. 54–61.
82. *New York Tribune,* June 16, 17, 19, 1887; Foraker, p. 242. Foraker, who seemed to be concerned more with politics than with a spurious morality, was up for reelection that year and had his eye on the 1888 presidential nomination. Months later, at a centenary celebration in Philadelphia of the Constitution, Mrs. Cleveland failed to greet Foraker and his wife, an act which many assumed was because of his flagrant discourtesy to the President. Cleveland went out of his way to make it known that the alleged slight was, in fact, simply an innocent result of being caught up in the crush of people. Both Clevelands despised the Ohio politician—but would never have let that stand in the way of observing the social amenities.
83. *Philadelphia Times,* July 9, 1887.
84. *Petersburg* (Va.) *Index-Appeal,* June 20, 1887.
85. *Nation,* Sept. 1, 1887.
86. GC to David R. Fields, July 4, 1887. For full correspondence on this issue, see Nevins, *Letters,* pp. 143–46.
87. GC to E. W. Fosnot, Oct. 24, 1887. Two decades had to pass before a Republican President, Theodore Roosevelt, in concert with a Republican Congress, accom-

plished Cleveland's intention to end at long last the Civil War by restoring the Confederate battle standards. Legislation to that effect, echoing the very sentiments for which Cleveland had been so roundly damned, passed both houses unanimously in February 1905.

88. Nevins, *Grover Cleveland,* p. 339.
89. GC to William Endicott, Nov. 5, 1886, Cleveland Papers. It was on this occasion that Cleveland called news reporters "ghouls."
90. GC to Bissell, Sept. 2, 1887.
91. *New York Times,* Sept. 22, 1887.
92. Ibid., Oct. 2, 3, 4, 8, 10, 1887.
93. *New York Times,* Oct. 2, 1887. See also Boller, *Presidential Wives,* p. 169.
94. *New York Times,* Oct. 8, 1887.
95. Ibid., Oct. 19, 1887.
96. Ibid., Oct. 6, 7, 18, 1887.
97. *New York Herald,* June 17, 1886.
98. Richardson, VIII, p. 507. (Volumes 8 and 9 contain the official executive documents issued by Cleveland as President.)
99. *New York Evening Post,* Dec. 14, 1886.
100. Nevins, *Grover Cleveland,* p. 377; McElroy, I, p. 271.
101. For the entire text, see Vexler, pp. 63–70.
102. See McElroy, I, p. 271.
103. *Chicago Tribune,* Dec. 11, 12, 1887; *New York Herald,* Dec. 6, 1888.
104. Among the major New York City newspapers alone, the *Herald* ran four columns of interviews on December 9, and more through December 16, while the *World* on December 8–9 and the *Tribune* on December 8–12 devoted much space to interviews.
105. *Congressional Record,* April 17, 1888, vol. 18, pp. 3057 ff.
106. *New York Evening Post,* July 22, 1888.

PART V: 1888-1889

1. Emma Folsom made her home with the Clevelands until May of 1889, when she married Henry E. Perrine of Buffalo. She and Frances remained close, exchanging visits often, and she and Cleveland remained the warm friends they had been since the day she married his close friend Oscar.
2. McElroy, I, p. 286.
3. *Public Opinion,* May 28, 1887.
4. Blaine to Reid, May 17, 1887, Hamilton, pp. 604–6.
5. Blaine interview, *New York World,* Feb. 8, 1887.
6. Cashman, p. 238.
7. GC to James Shanahan, March 7, 1888.
8. McElroy, I, pp. 283–85.
9. GC to Bissell, June 17, 1888.
10. See *State Department, Foreign Relations,* 1887, pp. 425 ff.
11. *Congressional Record,* 50th Cong., 1st Sess., vol. 18, p. 2191.
12. *New York Herald,* April 9, 1887.

13. Parker, *Writings and Speeches,* pp. 505–6.
14. Andrew Kelly McClure, editor/publisher of the *Philadelphia Times,* reflected the view of Cleveland's supporters when he wrote with great urgency: "Now kick out Lord Sackville with your biggest boot of best leather, and you've got 'em. *Hesitation is death* [emphasis in the original]." See Lorant, p. 406.
15. The full details did not become public knowledge until more than forty years later, following a letter from Osgoodby's son, Charles A., to the Library of Congress, Feb. 13, 1931. See Nevins, *Grover Cleveland,* pp. 428–31, where the whole story was revealed for the first time.
16. *New York Herald,* Sept. 13, 1888.
17. Henry Watterson, reminiscing in the *Louisville Courier-Journal,* April 11, 1904.
18. Bissell to Cleveland, Sept. 29, 1888, Cleveland Papers. See also *New York Herald,* Aug. 10, 13, 14, 1888.
19. GC to Chauncey Black, Sept. 14, 1888.
20. GC to Dr. S. B. Ward, Nov. 6, 1888.
21. *Appleton's Annual Cyclopedia* gives the first figure; the second is from *McPherson's Handbook.*
22. McElroy, I, p. 307.
23. *New York Herald,* Nov. 15, 1888.
24. Nevins, *Grover Cleveland,* pp. 441–42.
25. Parker, *Writings and Speeches,* pp. 89–98.
26. All quotations in this section, unless otherwise indicated, are from State Department documents covering the period under discussion.
27. The words are Bayard's interpretation of the pact.
28. From the *Berliner Tageblatt,* Oct 23, 1887, from a dispatch in the *Sydney Morning Herald:* "These islands cannot . . . remain independent forever, and it is therefore to be urgently wished that Germany should not exhibit too much delicacy with respect to Samoa, but take it while it is to be had. . . . America would have no serious objections to such a course, for her motto is 'Trade, no dominion'; and England would joyfully give her assent, if she were permitted in payment therefore to lay her hands on the Tonga Islands."
29. Quoted in McElroy, I, pp. 259–60.
30. Nevins, *Grover Cleveland,* p. 446.
31. To Bissell: Apr. 13, 1889. To the Massachusetts Tariff Reform Association: Dec. 24, 1888.
32. Quoted in McElroy, I, pp. 300–301.
33. *New York Herald,* March 4, 1889.
34. Crook, p. 176.

PART VI: 1889-1893

1. GC to Vilas, April 19, 1889.
2. Gertrude Allen, a cousin, to Allan Nevins, Aug. 6, 1931, in Nevins, *Grover Cleveland,* p. 457.
3. *Buffalo Courier,* May 11–13, 1891. See also GC to Bissell, May 16, 1991.

4. McElroy, I, p. 311.
5. Privately, though, he was active behind the scenes in behalf of close friends, as when he worked for Wilson Bissell's election to the U.S. Senate from New York. Bissell had risen high in the Erie County Democracy, but his antipathy toward Tammany, which now just about controlled the state legislature, doomed his chances.
6. Sept. 26, 1889. From the papers of legal scholar and Cleveland admirer Jeremiah S. Black, quoted in Nevins, *Grover Cleveland,* p. 462.
7. GC to L. Clarke Davis, March 9, 1891. Davis, a summer neighbor of Cleveland's on Cape Cod, was editor of the *Philadelphia Public Ledger*; he was the husband of novelist Rebecca Harding Davis and father of famed author and foreign correspondent Richard Harding Davis.
8. Gilder memorandum; Cleveland Papers.
9. Parker, *Writings and Speeches,* p. 155.
10. *New York Evening Post,* Dec. 13, 1889.
11. Parker, *Recollections,* p. 128.
12. Ibid., pp. 246–47.
13. GC to Dan Lamont, Sept. 13, 1890.
14. Undated. Quoted in McElroy, I, pp. 313–14.
15. Parker, *Writings and Speeches,* pp. 253–55.
16. Ibid., pp. 263–71.
17. The Cleveland Papers are full of clippings on the rumors; on the presumed Republican plot to embarrass Cleveland, see news stories in the *New York Commercial Advertiser* and *Boston Post* of January and February 1891.
18. McElroy, I, p. 319.
19. Parker, *Writings and Speeches,* p. 374.
20. Quoted in McElroy, I, p. 320 (speaker unidentified).
21. Lamont to GC, July 27, 1891, Cleveland Papers.
22. GC to Gilder, July 3, 1891.
23. Letter to GC, March 9, 1890, Watterson Papers, Library of Congress. Watterson, for fifty years editor of the *Louisville Courier-Journal,* though a loyal Democrat was sharply critical of Cleveland's policies, but thought highly of him as a person until they fell out during Cleveland's second term. They were never reconciled.
24. *New York Tribune,* March 31, 1891.
25. See Villard, II, p. 362.
26. Lamar to Cleveland, April 3, 1892, Cleveland Papers.
27. *Louisville Courier-Journal,* Feb. 23, 1892.
28. Parker, *Writings and Speeches,* p. 361.
29. GC to Lamar, May 1, 1892.
30. New York Republican boss Thomas Platt is believed to have led other disaffected party leaders in a pre-convention dump-Harrison movement, with Blaine the intended beneficiary. Blaine had unexpectedly resigned as Secretary of State just three days before, claiming poor health. Others claimed, and rather more convincingly, that it was because of Blaine's poor relations with the President—per-

haps even more so with the First Lady. But by the time the convention came to order, Harrison's men had the nomination locked up.

Platt, Roscoe Conkling's successor as leader of the Stalwarts, was the quintessential ruthless, unprincipled party boss. Years later he recalled how "Harrison's renomination caused a chattering of the teeth among the warm-blooded Republicans of the East. When there was added to it the choice of Whitelaw Reid, a persistent assailant of the New York organization, many of the New York delegates, including myself, wrapped ourselves in overcoats and earmuffs, hurried from the convention hall, and took the first train to New York!" Platt, pp. 246–47.

31. GC to Wilson Bissell, Aug. 10, 1892.
32. For complete text of the letter, see McElroy, I, p. 350.
33. GC to Wilson Bissell, Sept. 4, 1892.
34. McElroy, I, pp. 352–54.
35. *Harper's Weekly,* July 16, 1892.
36. Harvey, pp. 118 ff.
37. *Public Opinion,* July 30, 1892.
38. Harvey, p. 148.
39. GC to Richard Gilder, Sept. 18, 1889; Bryant to Daniel Lamont, July 7, 1891, Cleveland Papers.
40. This undated letter came to public attention only when it was published more than fifteen years later (July 1, 1908) in the *Utica Observer.*
41. *New York Evening Post,* Oct. 24, 1892.
42. Both candidates were invited to help lay the cornerstone for the 1893 Chicago Columbian Exposition. When Harrison refused at the last minute because of his wife's condition, Cleveland also declined as a courtesy.
43. Cleveland, with a popular vote of 46 percent (5,556,918), won the majority of electoral votes in twenty-three states (Alabama, Arkansas, California, Connecticut, Delaware, Florida, Georgia, Illinois, Indiana, Kentucky, Louisiana, Maryland, Mississippi, Missouri, New Jersey, New York, North and South Carolina, Tennessee, Texas, Virginia, West Virginia, and Wisconsin). Harrison, with 43 percent of the popular vote (5,176,108), won the majority in sixteen (Iowa, Maine, Massachusetts, Michigan, Minnesota, Montana, Nebraska, New Hampshire, Ohio, Oregon, Pennsylvania, Rhode Island, South Dakota, Vermont, Washington, and Wyoming). Weaver, the Populist candidate, with 9 percent of the popular vote (1,041,028), won the majority of electoral votes in Colorado, Idaho, Kansas, and Nevada. North Dakota's three electoral votes were divided evenly among the three candidates, so that none of them carried the state.
44. Woodrow Wilson, "Mr. Cleveland's Cabinet," *Review of Books,* April 1893, p. 289.
45. Idaho Senator William Boyd Allison, *New York Evening Post,* June 24, 1908.

PART VII: 1893–1896

1. *New York Times,* March 5, 1893.
2. Vexler, pp. 78–82. According to McElroy (II, p. 8), when the pastor of the New York church Cleveland frequently attended was shown a draft, he said, "I like it immensely and its conclusion ["a Supreme Being who rules the affairs of men"]

best of all." He never forgot "the way this strong man then paced up and down the floor, and returned and returned, with these words, 'I suppose at times you will not approve many things I do, but I want you to know that I am trying to do what is right. I have a hungry party behind me, and they say I am not grateful. Sometimes the pressure is almost overwhelming, and a President cannot always get at the exact truth, but I want you to know, and all my friends to know, that I am trying to do what is right—I am trying to do what is right.' "

3. *New York Times*, March 5, 1893.
4. Elden E. Billings, "Social and Economic Life in Washington in the 1890s," *Records of the Columbia Historical Society*, 1966–1968, p. 173.
5. For an insightful analysis of Cleveland in this context, see Hollingsworth, Chapter 1, "The Cuckoos Create a Storm."
6. The term "conservative," which first came into popular usage during this period, had a philosophical as distinct from political connotation. It indicated a desire by many to differentiate themselves from what they considered to be radical movements here at home as well as in Europe, whence came most of the nation's immigrants. Conservatives of both major parties supported the Hamiltonian idea of limited democracy, subscribing to the thesis that authority and rule were best entrusted to the "better elements." Such a view, as paternalistic as it was elitist, embraced, at least among Cleveland Democrats, a sincere desire to improve the lot of those ranging from the lower down to the lowest rungs on the socioeconomic scale. It is in this context, and not by today's understanding of the term, that the term "conservative" is used here.
7. GC to L. Clarke Davis, Jan. 25, 1893.
8. Olney was as known for his ungovernable temper as for his probity. When, for example, his favorite daughter married a young dentist who failed to win his approval, Olney, in a fit of anger, threw her out of his house and severed their relationship.
9. Bayard Papers, Library of Congress.
10. Unless otherwise indicated, all quotations are from *State Department, Dispatches, Hawaii* (a 34-volume series, covering the years 1843–1900, consisting of the original letters from the United States diplomatic envoy at Honolulu to the Secretary of State, together with enclosures); House Executive Documents, 53 Congress, 2 session, no. 47. Report of Commissioner to the Hawaiian Islands (the "Blount Report"); United States Senate Reports, 53 Congress, 2 session, no. 227 (the "Morgan Report"); United States House of Representatives Executive Documents, 53 Congress, 3 sessions, no. 1, part 1: Foreign Relations of the United States, 1894, Appendix II, "Affairs in Hawaii" (a volume of 1,437 pages comprising various Senate and House documents, with some duplications, dealing with Hawaii).
11. Blount's findings were backed by Charles Nordhoff, a veteran Washington correspondent sent to Honolulu by the *New York Herald* to investigate independently. See articles in the *Herald*, April and May 1893.
12. Vexler, pp. 88–100.
13. Villard to GC, II, pp. 363–64. See also Cleveland Papers, January–March 1893, for letters to GC from financiers Andrew Carnegie, Augustus Belmont, et al.

14. Carnegie to GC, Apr. 22, 1893, Cleveland Papers.
15. Economist John Kenneth Galbraith, noting that the nineteenth century underwent a new economic crisis every ten to twenty years (1819, 1837, 1857, 1873, 1884, and 1893), comments that the intervals between these economic crises corresponded "roughly with the time it took people to forget the last disaster." John Kenneth Galbraith, *Money* (Boston: Houghton Mifflin, 1975).
16. Cashman, p. 242.
17. Peck, *Twenty Years*, p. 511.
18. "Sown the wind": *Springfield Republican*, April 29, 1893. See also *Harper's Weekly*, July 29, 1893.
19. See *Denver Republican*, July 1, 1893; *Atlanta Constitution*, July 3, 1893.
20. Cleveland Papers.
21. *Saturday Evening Post*, Sept. 22, 1917. Unless otherwise indicated, all quotations are from the Keen article.
22. Dr. Erdmann in private conversation with Allan Nevins, Nov. 14, 16, 1931, Nevins, *Grover Cleveland*, p. 530.
23. McElroy, II, pp. 30–31.
24. See *New York Times*, Sept. 1, 1893. Dr. Bryant sent Hasbrouck his $250 fee by messenger; he never spoke to or corresponded with him again.
25. *Philadelphia Public Ledger*, Aug. 31, 1893.
26. Vexler, pp. 83–87.
27. GC to Dickinson, Oct. 9, 1893; GC to Gilder, and to Davis, both undated, Cleveland Papers.
28. *Washington Post*, Oct. 22, 1893. The letter was composed by Cleveland's former campaign manager Arthur Pue Gorman, who consistently favored compromise with the silverites, for which Cleveland never forgave him.
29. Cleveland Papers.
30. Robert Lincoln O'Brien (Cleveland's stenographer), Nevins interview Nov. 8, 1930, Nevins, *Grover Cleveland*, p. 563.
31. McElroy, II, pp. 107–8.
32. Carnegie in a letter to the *New York Tribune*, Jan. 3, 1894.
33. See *Public Opinion*, Nov. 30, 1893.
34. *Congressional Record*, Jan. 9, 1894, vol. 26, pt. 9 (Appendix), p. 201.
35. Morgan, p. 462.
36. A 3 percent war tax imposed in 1861 on incomes over $800, with succeeding increases, expired in 1872. Hill opposed any such taxes in time of peace; besides, he argued, the proposed amendment was sectional and unjust in its provisions, as it exacted more in the East than in any other sections of the country. The income tax clause effected by the tariff reform bill was subsequently declared unconstitutional. Income tax did not become a fact of American life until 1913 with passage of the Sixteenth Amendment.
37. GC to L. Clark Davis, Feb. 25, 1894.
38. Hornblower Memorandum, Cleveland Papers.
39. See *New York Times*, Jan. 23, 24, 25, 26, 1894. The paper's scathing opinion of Hill was such that in what was synonymous with a front-page editorial mas-

querading as a news story, it observed that if he were President "there is no doubt among the senators as to what he would do with the Supreme Court vacancy. He would fill it at once with the discredited Maynard, twice rejected at the polls by the discriminating and resentful voters of the State of New York."

40. Nevins, *Grover Cleveland,* pp. 571–72. White followed no clear philosophy, often veering between the liberal and conservative positions in the more than seven hundred decisions he wrote, though not a centrist as the term has come into fashion. He was raised to Chief Justice by Taft in 1910, the only Associate Justice ever to be put on the Court by the President of one party and elevated to the highest position by the President of another.
41. GC to Hill, Nov. 18, 1895.
42. McElroy, II, pp. 111–12.
43. GC to Wilson, July 2, 1894.
44. *Congressional Record,* July 23, 1894, vol. 26, pt. 7, pp. 7115 ff.
45. For summary of national reaction, see *Public Opinion,* Aug. 28, Sept. 6, 1894.
46. GC to T. C. Catchings, Aug. 27, 1894, McElroy, II, pp. 116–19.
47. Beer, *The Mauve Decade,* p. 133.
48. Smith, VI, p. 524.
49. *United States Strike Commission Report,* Senate Executive Document 7, 53rd Congress, 3rd Session, xxxiii–xxxv. See also *Public Opinion,* Sept. 6, 1894.
50. *United States Strike Commission Report,* xxxiii–xxxv.
51. Cleveland, "The Government in the Chicago Strike of 1894," in *Presidential Problems,* p. 87.
52. Quoted in McElroy, II, pp. 144–45.
53. Smith, p. 522.
54. Welch, p. 143.
55. *New York Times, New York Tribune,* July 2, 1894. Clarence Darrow resigned his legal position with one of the major railroads to support the strike; other prominent Chicagoans who supported the strikers included social reformers Jane Addams and Bertha Palmer.
56. *New York Times,* July 2, 1894.
57. *Strike Commission Report,* xxxiii–xxxv.
58. Ibid., p. 149.
59. Ibid.
60. Ibid., p. 344.
61. U.S. Dept. of Justice Report, Attorney General, 1896, Appendix, pp. 65–66.
62. *Washington Post,* July 5, 1894.
63. For the complete Alteld-Cleveland exchange, see Nevins, *Letters,* pp. 357–62. As printed in the *Chicago Times,* the Cleveland telegram ended at the point indicated in the text above. An autograph copy found among the Lamont papers adds the following postscript, which clearly shows how far Cleveland was from siding with management: "whatever arrangement is made by the [Pullman] Company with its employees must positively be made without relying upon the Government for any guarantee whatever. The Military power of the Government refuses to be drawn into any relation with the details of railroad management." McElroy, II, 157.

64. Miles also learned, but did not give his source, of "a general secret meeting today of Debs and the representatives of labor unions considering the advisability of a general strike of all labor unions. About one hundred men were present at the meeting. The result is not yet known." Cleveland, "The Government in the Ohio Strike of 1894," in *Presidential Problems,* pp. 104–5.
65. Ibid., pp. 106–7.
66. McElroy, II, p. 166. Cleveland does not mention this second proclamation in his own account of the strike.
67. *New York Times,* July 13, 1894.
68. Quoted in McElroy, II, pp. 170–72.
69. Gilder, pp. 148–52. Cleveland was reiterating a sentiment he had expressed to Gilder in the previous year when, after complaining of his "many perplexities and troubles," and of how this term of the presidency had cost him "so much health and vigor" that he "sometimes doubted if [he] could carry the burden to the end," he insisted: "My determination is to live and I believe God has put the belief in my mind that I can still be of use to my country." "The note of disappointment and despondency in some of the letters above was by no means constant," Gilder wrote by way of comment. "I have never seen such care in a human face as I have seen in his at times of harassing and overwhelming pressure. But President Cleveland had the strong man's love of action; and the most perplexing situations often led him to his most pronounced and successful decisions—decisions which now and again brought to him lasting satisfaction and wide-spread acclaim. His fishing and hunting excursions, while entered upon with appetite, were also considered by him a duty; for it was only on these little vacations that he was able to obtain the exercise, and release from mental strain, that kept him alive, and made him capable of the application which was a habit as well as a matter of public conscience with him. I have heard him say that while on the water he could cast his public cares aside, but they would come crushing down upon him the moment he put his foot on dry land" (pp. 157–58).
70. The nation's outdated banking system, devised before the Civil War for a decentralized agricultural society, was horribly antiquated, given that the postwar era saw the United States become, to all intents and purposes, an industrialized society. Between 1836, when Andrew Jackson terminated the second and last National Bank, and 1913, with establishment of the Federal Reserve, there was no central institution for regulating the nation's money supply and credit, no official lending institution to which the government might turn as a last resort, and no federal recourse during periods of grievous fiscal turmoil.
71. Gilder, p. 127.
72. Cleveland, "The Bond Issues," in *Presidential Problems,* p. 140.
73. William Elroy Curtis, *Chicago Record,* March 27, 1894.
74. Sam Small to Allan Nevins, May 23, 1931, in Nevins, *Grover Cleveland,* pp. 602–3. After leaving the White House that night, Crisp told Small, "Well, I'm a dead duck in the pit." The allusion here was to the fear that Crisp, himself a free-silver advocate, would be condemned as a traitor by his fellow silverites in Congress. Whether supporting Cleveland ruined his career is moot. He died two years later.

75. Peck, *Twenty Years,* p. 459; Hollingsworth, pp. 26–27; Simkin, p. 315. Tillman, who won the election and remained in the Senate until his death twenty-four years later, hated Theodore Roosevelt as much as he hated Cleveland. Both Presidents enjoyed some measure of satisfaction when, through Roosevelt's efforts, Tillman was exposed as an influence peddler in land purchases and his once inordinate power in South Carolina declined appreciably.
76. *Atlanta Constitution,* July 5, Aug. 28, 1895. See also Hollingsworth, p. 27; C. Vann Woodward, p. 273.
77. Nevins, *Grover Cleveland,* p. 654.
78. Within a generation, a number of nations, including Great Britain, would go off the gold standard without raising a ripple. But the United States' position at this point in time was isolated and uniquely difficult. Were it to go off the gold standard, the financial world would have been hit with yet another panic, resulting in yet more bankruptcies and near-total industrial paralysis.
79. Richardson, VIII, pp. 768–88.
80. Straus to GC, Jan. 24, 1895, Cleveland Papers.
81. Cleveland, "The Bond Issues," in *Presidential Problems,* pp. 144–46.
82. See *Public Opinion,* Feb. 7, 1895, for press summaries.
83. Bonds Sales Investigation, Senate Exec. Docs. No. 5, 54th Cong. 2nd sess.
84. Chernow, p. 75.
85. Recalling these events nine years later for *The Saturday Evening Post* (May 7, 1904), Cleveland dated his first meeting with Morgan three days later than it actually took place, so that it seemed he had negotiated with the bankers only after Congress rejected the public bond issue on February 7, 1895. In fact, sensing how the vote would go, he had carefully worked out terms for the private loan before Congress acted. The article was reprinted as "The Bond Issues" in his book *Presidential Problems.*
86. See *Public Opinion,* Oct. 23, 1895, and Senate Exec. Doc. No. 187, p. 297.
87. *Jackson* (Mich.) *Industrial News,* March 9, 1895.
88. Cleveland, "The Bond Issues," in *Presidential Problems,* p. 170.
89. Quoted in Nevins, *Grover Cleveland,* p. 629.
90. GC to Thomas F. Bayard, Dec. 29, 1895, Bayard Papers.
91. The Venezuela problem was not our first disagreement with Great Britain south of the American border. The first had come a decade earlier, over Nicaragua. For years the State Department proposed a canal across that isthmus, but a necessary prerequisite was abrogation of the 1850 Clayton-Bulwer Treaty that gave Britain the same degree of control as the United States over any isthmian canal constructed in Central America. Toward the end of the Arthur administration a treaty was negotiated with Nicaragua providing that any canal built by the Americans across that territory would be jointly owned by the two nations, and binding the United States to guarantee Nicaragua's independence. Ratification was still pending when Cleveland entered the White House. One of his first acts was to recall it from the Senate. It was never resubmitted.
92. State Department Archives, Dispatch No. 404, April 5, 1895.
93. McElroy, II, pp. 179–80.

94. GC to Olney, July 7, 1895, cited in McElroy, II, p. 181.
95. For complete text of the dispatch, see State Department Papers Relative to the Foreign Relations of the United States, 1895, I, 545–62. Speaking at Princeton seven years before his death, Cleveland declared: "In no event will the American principle [i.e., the Monroe Doctrine] ever be better defined, better defended, or more bravely asserted than was done by Mr. Olney in this dispatch." McElroy, II, pp. 181–82.
96. Bayard to GC, July 18, 1895, Cleveland Papers.
97. See *Public Opinion,* Nov. 21, 1895.
98. For complete text of Salisbury's reply, see State Department Papers Relating to the Foreign Relations of the United States, *1895,* I, 545–62, pp. 563–76.
99. For complete text, see Vexler, pp. 111–14. Olney was convinced that only a severe metaphorical rap across Salisbury's knuckles would arrest his attention. He later apologized for his admittedly audacious language by saying that "in English eyes the United States was then so completely a negligible quantity that it was believed only words the equivalent of blows would be really effective." A. B. Farquhar, "Recollections of Grover Cleveland," *Harper's Weekly,* July 21, 1908.
100. *Public Opinion,* Jan. 2, 1896.
101. Abram Hewitt Papers.
102. GC to Bayard, Dec. 29, 1895, Thomas F. Bayard Papers.
103. Richard Olney Papers.
104. Dennis, pp. 40, 41.
105. Cleveland, "The Venezuelan Boundary Controversy," in *Presidential Problems,* pp. 280–81.
106. Roseboom, p. 307.
107. GC to Stone, April 26, 1895; GC to Fairchild, Feb. 16, 1895.
108. *Arena,* November 1895. Houston would serve as, successively, Woodrow Wilson's Secretary of Agriculture and Secretary of the Treasury. Bryan would be Wilson's first Secretary of State.
109. *Congressional Record,* Jan. 29, 1895.
110. GC to Dickinson, Feb. 18, March 5, 1886, cited in McElroy, II, pp. 213–15.
111. *Public Opinion,* March 26, 1895.
112. J. C. Hendrix, Chairman of the New York State Chamber of Commerce Committee on Financial Legislation, to GC, June 3, 1896, Cleveland Papers.
113. "Adoption by the Democratic Party . . .": *Indianapolis Sentinel,* June 17, 1896; "I am praying now. . . ." GC to L. Clarke Davis, May 14, 1896.
114. Nevins, *Grover Cleveland,* p. 700.
115. Quoted in McElroy, II, pp. 224–25.
116. Bryan recollection quoted in Roseboom, p. 309; Gresham recollection in a memorandum to Nevins, Nevins, *Grover Cleveland,* p. 703.
117. *New York Post, New York Evening World,* July 10, 1896; *Richmond Times,* July 17, 1896; Hollingsworth, 70.
118. GC to Dan Lamont, GC to Hoke Smith, July 15, 1896. The Lamont letter was headed "Confidential." Cleveland's remark about Bryan is in Parker, *Recollections,* p. 272.

119. *Boston Journal,* July 21, 1896.
120. Nevins, *Letters,* pp. 455–56.
121. GC to Vilas, Sept. 5, 1896; GC to Lamont, Sept. 6, 1896.
122. *Public Opinion,* Oct. 29, 1896.
123. For the Cleveland–Smith exchange, see Nevins, *Letters,* pp. 451–53.
124. William Wilson Diary, Oct. 2, 1896. For a good overview of the campaign, see Hollingsworth, pp. 84–107.

PART VIII: 1897-1907

1. GC to Richard Gilder, Nov. 20, 1896.
2. See *Public Opinion,* Jan. 21, 1897.
3. Richard Olney Papers, Library of Congress.
4. Olney to GC, Sept. 25, 1895, Richard Olney Papers. Cleveland, and possibly Olney, believed Spain might be induced to sell Cuba for $100 million, judging from a letter later found among his private papers. Written from London by one H. Plasson to Senator Call of Florida, it declared that in 1872 a group of London bankers had raised £20 million with which to purchase Cuba's independence, with the provision that she assume responsibility of the debt, and that an agent had been sent to Madrid to present, and it was hoped to consummate, the deal. Plasson was cabled to join the agent, but two days before he reached Madrid the Spanish cabinet fell, thus ending negotiations.
5. See *Public Opinion,* Dec. 24, 1896.
6. McElroy, II, pp. 251.
7. See Henry Cabot Lodge, ed., *Selections from the Correspondence of Theodore Roosevelt and Henry Cabot Lodge, 1884–1918,* 2 vols. (New York: Scribner's, 1925).
8. Lamont issued the following statement: "The retiring President has property amounting all told to $300,000 or $350,000 acquired from salary during two terms, fees received during the period of New York law practice, and about $100,000 of profits from the purchase of real estate just outside Washington." McElroy, II, 253. It should be noted that Cleveland's secure financial position also owed much to his friend Elias ("Commodore") Benedict's wise investment counseling. Though he did not live penuriously by any means, Cleveland brought to fiscal matters the same conservatism that informed his politics. He was determined to "make everything snug" for the young family he knew he must leave behind. Less out of a need for money than a need to avoid idleness, which he found intolerable, Cleveland wrote over the next few years, for handsome fees, a number of articles to many of the leading periodicals, ranging from philosophical disquisitions of a political nature to pieces bearing such titles as "The Serene Duck Hunter" and "The Mission of Fishing and Fishermen."
9. Cleveland Papers.
10. Wood shared the reminiscences at a memorial service on March 18, 1919, what would have been Cleveland's eighty-second birthday.
11. Nevins, *Grover Cleveland,* p. 726.
12. GC to West, Nov. 8, 1896.
13. McElroy, II, pp. 256–57.

14. GC to West, March 23, 1897; GC to Elias, Apr. 2, 1897.
15. McElroy, II, p. 259.
16. Ibid.
17. Nevins, *Grover Cleveland,* pp. 738–39.
18. Ibid., p. 260.
19. One of Cleveland's first structural changes at Westland was the addition of a wing containing a billiard room downstairs and extra bedrooms upstairs. Shortly thereafter he purchased a small farm about three miles from Princeton, to serve as a convenient stopping place when he was out in pursuit of his sports of choice, shooting quail and rabbits on the surrounding fields and fishing on nearby Millstone River. The farm later became an embarrassment when the young man to whom he leased it opened a mini-agricultural school there and tried to give the misleading impression that it was being run under the ex-President's patronage.
20. GC to West, March 23, 1897.
21. Andrew F. West, "Grover Cleveland: A Princeton Memory," *Century Magazine* 77, No. 3 (January 1909).
22. *New York Times, New York Tribune,* Oct. 26, 1902.
23. Nevins, *Grover Cleveland,* pp. 733–35. Wilson's authorized biographer believes Cleveland's poor health contributed to his being ill-informed on Wilson's side of the graduate school dispute. See Ray S. Baker, *Woodrow Wilson, Life and Letters,* II, pp. 222 ff. Olney repeated the remark to Cleveland's former confidential secretary, Robert L. O'Brien. Richard Olney Papers, Library of Congress.
24. Quoted in McElroy, II, pp. 268–69.
25. GC to Dan Lamont, Aug. 1, 1897; GC to Judson Harmon, Aug. 3, 1897; GC to Don Dickinson, Oct. 31, 1897.
26. "Statement to the Associated Press," Jan. 24, 1898. The treaty was effected by joint resolution in July 1898.
27. GC to Hearst (telegram), Feb. 28, 1898; GC to Olney, March 27, 1898; GC to Benedict, April 6, 1898.
28. GC to Richard Olney, April 28, 1898; GC to Elias Benedict, April 28, 1898; quoted in McElroy, II, pp. 273–74.
29. GC to Judson Harmon, April 17, 1899.
30. GC to Richard Olney, March 19, 1899.
31. Quoted in Nevins, *Grover Cleveland,* pp. 746–47.
32. GC to Edward M. Shepard, Feb. 7, 1900.
33. GC to Richard Olney, June 25, 1900; GC to Judson Harmon, July 17, 1900.
34. GC to Don Dickinson, Oct. 12, 1890.
35. GC to A. S. Abell (the *Sun* publisher), Sept. 11, 1890.
36. GC to Wilson Bissell, Sept. 16, 1900.
37. McElroy, II, pp. 295.
38. GC to Don Dickinson, April 27, 1901.
39. GC to Lamont, Aug. 1, 1897; GC to Crespo, May 20, 1897; Cleveland re World Court: letter to Wilson Bissell, Sept. 16, 1900.
40. Roosevelt to GC, Nov. 22, 1900.
41. McElroy, II, p. 314.

42. Lodge, II, p. 17.
43. Joseph Garretson to GC, McElroy, II, pp. 315–16; GC to Garretson, Feb. 6, 1903; GC to Benedict, Jan. 18, March 29, 1903.
44. McElroy, II, p. 316.
45. From an editorial in an unidentified Electra, Texas, newspaper that was sent to Cleveland by an admirer, Cleveland Papers.
46. FFC to Robert McElroy, in McElroy, II, p. 320.
47. Cleveland Diary, Cleveland Papers; GC to Mary Hoyt, April 27, 1904, Nevins, *Grover Cleveland*, p. 741.
48. Cleveland Papers.
49. McElroy, II, p. 329. See also Nevins, *Grover Cleveland*, p. 754.
50. GC to McKelway, long one of his strongest boosters, Nov. 25, 1903. The editorial had run two days previously.
51. Lamont to GC, Feb. 10, 1904; GC to Lamont, Feb. 10, 28, 1904.
52. GC to Lamont, March 11, 1904; GC to Hornblower, March 23, 1904.
53. See McElroy, II, p. 335.
54. GC to Olney, July 19, 1904.
55. GC to A. B. Farquhar, Dec. 12, 1904.
56. GC to Roosevelt, Oct. 4, 1902.
57. Roosevelt to GC, Oct. 16, 1902, Cleveland Papers.
58. McElroy, II, pp. 374–75.
59. *Report of Joint Legislative Committee of the State of New York to Investigate Life Insurance, 1906*, cited in McElroy, II, pp. 355–56.
60. McElroy, II, p. 357.
61. GC to Paul Morton, Dec. 19, 1905.
62. Olney to GC, Cleveland Papers. Twain dated his letter March 6, 1906, but added the postscript "(as of date March 18, 1906)." Wilson to GC, March 5, 1906; GC to Gilder, March 18, 1906.
63. Cleveland Papers.
64. Ibid.
65. FFC to GC, March 15, 1907, Cleveland Papers.
66. *New York Times*, March 25, 1907.
67. *New York Sun*, March 18, 1907. In forwarding the editorial to Cleveland, its writer, Edwin Packard, added: "If Mr. Dana were living, I think that even he would make amends."
68. GC to Elias Benedict, Aug. 17, 1907; GC to E. Prentiss Bailey, March 14, 1908.
69. GC to Mrs. E. L. Yeomans, Dec. 23, 1907.
70. Andrew F. West, "Grover Cleveland: A Princeton Memory," *Century Magazine* 77, No. 3 (January 1909).
71. Quoted in McElroy, II, p. 384.
72. *New York Times*, June 25, 1908.
73. Ibid., June 27, 1908.

AFTERWORD

1. Richard had at one time been mentioned as a Democratic vice presidential candidate, but disillusionment with the New Deal and opposition to Franklin D. Roosevelt's 1936 reelection ended his political career.
2. Margaret Truman, *Souvenir: Margaret Truman's Own Story* (New York: McGraw-Hill, 1956), p. 172.

APPENDIX I: CLEVELAND AND THE BLACKS

1. GC to I. T. Montgomery, Jan. 24, 1891, Parker, *Writings and Speeches*, pp. 344–45.
2. GC to Washington, Oct. 9, 1895.
3. Because these three so-called Civil War Amendments were so constricting in their interpretation, Presidents of this period cannot be entirely faulted for failing to enforce them, especially when the Supreme Court ruled in a number of cases that the Fourteenth Amendment interpreted the rights of persons as citizens of the United States and not of the individual states, and therefore certain rights could be redressed only under state law. Commager, *Documents*, pp. 71, 86.
4. Parker, *Writings and Speeches*, p. 37; Foner, IV, p. 30. According to Philip Sheldon Foner, Douglass's best biographer, the great black leader "praised the President for his invitations to State dinners and other public functions at the White House, something neither Garfield nor Arthur had the courage to do." Douglass is quoted as saying: "I know manliness wherever I find it; and I have found it in President Cleveland. . . . Whatever else he may be, he is not a snob and he is not a coward." Douglass was Recorder of Deeds for the District of Columbia—a post mainly reserved for blacks—when Cleveland succeeded Arthur, and was kept on at Douglass's request until he resigned a year later of his own violation. When Cleveland nominated another black man, a New Yorker, to succeed Douglass, the Senate held up confirmation, insisting the post go only to a resident of Washington. Replied Cleveland, "Confessing a desire to cooperate in tendering to our colored fellow-citizens just recognition and the utmost good faith, [I] again submit this nomination to the Senate for confirmation." He won the point. Foner, IV, pp. 19–20.
5. Readers who question this idea would do well to compare the documentary evidence of John F. Kennedy's attitude toward the blacks when he assumed the presidency with quasi-hagiographic attitude ascribed to him by his most obdurate apologists. See Taylor Branch, *Parting the Waters.*
6. Parker, *Writing and Speeches*, p. 319. See Cleveland's letter to Thomas C. E. Ecclesine on the gubernatorial nomination, Oct. 7, 1882, Cleveland Papers; see also Vexler, p. 80.
7. Sinkler, pp. 228–29.
8. Ibid.
9. Ibid.
10. Ibid.
11. For the complete text of the Boston Speech, see Berg, pp. 423–25.

APPENDIX II: CLEVELAND AND THE CHINESE IMMIGRANTS

1. GC to Thomas Bayard, Dec. 18, 1887, Bayard Papers.
2. Cleveland Papers.
3. GC to Richard Olney, July 4, 1896, Olney Papers.

INDEX

INDEX